Peace, war and party politics

MANCHESTER 1824
Manchester University Press

Peace, war and party politics

The Conservatives and Europe
1846–59

Geoffrey Hicks

Manchester University Press
Manchester and New York
distributed exclusively in the USA by Palgrave

Copyright © Geoffrey Hicks 2007

The right of Geoffrey Hicks to be identified as the author of this work has been asserted by him in accordance with the Copyright, Designs and Patents Act 1988.

Published by Manchester University Press
Oxford Road, Manchester M13 9NR, UK
and Room 400, 175 Fifth Avenue, New York, NY 10010, USA
www.manchesteruniversitypress.co.uk

Distributed exclusively in the USA by
Palgrave, 175 Fifth Avenue, New York,
NY 10010, USA

Distributed exclusively in Canada by
UBC Press, University of British Columbia, 2029 West Mall,
Vancouver, BC, Canada V6T 1Z2

British Library Cataloguing-in-Publication Data
A catalogue record for this book is available from the British Library
Library of Congress Cataloging-in-Publication Data applied for

ISBN 978 0 7190 7595 7 *hardback*

First published 2007

16 15 14 13 12 11 10 09 08 07   10 9 8 7 6 5 4 3 2 1

Typeset
by Action Publishing Technology Ltd, Gloucester
Printed in Great Britain
by The Cromwell Press Ltd, Trowbridge

To my parents and Colin

and to Duncan and James

Contents

Preface	*page* ix
1 Introduction	1
2 Conservative perspectives	25
3 Prelude to power, 1850–52	38
4 1852: foreign affairs, domestic problems	67
5 *Entente cordiale*	116
6 From peace to war: opposing Aberdeen, 1852–55	139
7 From war to peace: opposing Palmerston, 1855–58	157
8 Disraelian undertones, 1858	186
9 The Italian question	205
10 European war, Conservative struggle	217
11 The politics of Conservative foreign policy	245
Bibliography	250
Index	261

husband/boyfriend, like going to concerts, eating Japanese food (or that big juicy steak!), or applying for that position as a fashion designer. Eventually, you can live on your own again and feel happy. You may not even think about the terrible relationship anymore. Each day, think positive thoughts and never forget to smile. Also, hope that your ex-partner realizes the consequences of his behavior, but don't worry too much about what he may or may not have learned. Leaving a relationship is heart-breaking, but this can be the last and best thing you can do to initiate change and healing in the man that you once shared your life with.

Preface

In producing a book out of a Ph.D thesis, one inevitably accumulates a long list of debts. I thank, first, those who have kindly permitted me to use primary material: the Trustees of the Broadlands Archives; the Earl of Clarendon; the Hon. Auriol Pakington; the Marquess of Salisbury; the British Library; the National Archives; Hampshire Record Office; Norfolk Record Office; Somerset Record Office; and West Sussex Record Office. The papers passed to the nation by the Earl of Derby and held at Liverpool Record Office have been a particularly valuable resource. The Earl and Countess were very welcoming hosts at the conference we held at Knowsley Hall in March 2004, encouraging us all in our research. I thank also the *International History Review*'s editor and staff, who have kindly permitted me to reproduce (in chapter 3) material which first appeared as an article in September 2004. I am indebted to the archivists and staff at all the record offices and libraries I have used over the last six years. Manchester University Press has been an understanding publisher, and I am immensely grateful for the help and efficiency of the Press's editor and staff in a frenetic year. I thank the anonymous referees of this book, who made suggestions which I think have greatly improved it. Much of the original research was funded by a grant from the Arts and Humanities Research Council.

    A number of individuals deserve my particular thanks. My research has benefited greatly from the kind comments and support of my PhD examiners, Angus Hawkins and Anthony Howe, and of John Vincent, whom we have been privileged to have with us at UEA as a visiting professor. He has shared with us his considerable knowledge of nineteenth-century history; and without his work on the Derby diaries, those of us examining Victorian politics would be much the poorer. At an early stage in the research, Carole Rawcliffe offered me advice which I have found consistently useful. Over a number of years, the friendship and support of Larry Butler, Stephen Church, Christopher

Harper-Bill and Thomas Otte have been invaluable. My fellow-researchers and friends Lloyd Mitchell, Bendor Grosvenor and Catherine Armstrong have regularly taken time out from their own research to comment on mine. Sally Ives and Sue Holland have put the past in perspective and made the present much more entertaining. Richard Avis and Michael Fake allowed me once again to call on their friendship, making a range of helpful suggestions about the original thesis. None of this work, however, would have been possible without the support and encouragement, over many years, of my supervisor, colleague and friend John Charmley. His knowledge and advice have, time and again, been indispensable. I have done my best to put all the comments and suggestions I have received to good use, but for whatever errors that remain the responsibility is, of course, mine alone.

This book is dedicated to those without whom much would have been impossible. My parents' support has been unstinting, and they have patiently tolerated my use of their home as a base for archive visits, while my brother has assisted with many a technical glitch. Finally, I express my thanks to James Jarrett and Duncan Kent, and I hope these words will go a small way towards doing so.

GH
August 2006

1

Introduction

To examine the role of the mid-Victorian Conservative Party in foreign policy is to leave oneself in splendid isolation. With a very few exceptions, there has been little historiographical interest in the Conservatives between 1846, when Sir Robert Peel's administration collapsed in turmoil over the repeal of the Corn Laws, and 1874, when Disraeli returned the party to majority government. There has been even less interest in the Conservatives' part in the politics of foreign policy.

The 'politics of foreign policy' constitutes a helpful shorthand description for three different – but fundamentally interlinked – aspects of diplomatic and political history: the ministerial direction of foreign policy; intra-party debate about foreign policy; and the place of foreign policy in wider political debate. 'Foreign policy' itself requires a little definition. This study examines Britain as a European power, its primary role until at least the late 1860s. Britain's colonial empire and the Anglo-American relationship are not explored here in detail; such subjects merit separate analysis, which they have to some degree received elsewhere.

Nineteenth-century foreign policy was for many years unfashionable as a research topic. While it has undergone something of a renaissance since the late 1990s, most historians have continued to focus on the role of one man: Viscount Palmerston. This is understandable. He was Foreign Secretary in Lord Grey's Whig administration from 1830 to 1834, under Viscount Melbourne from 1835 to 1841, and under Lord John Russell from 1846 to 1851. He was Home Secretary in the Earl of Aberdeen's coalition from December 1852 until January 1855. During his period at the Home Office he closely followed, and involved himself in, foreign affairs, though the Earl of Clarendon was Foreign Secretary from February 1853. As Prime Minister from February 1855, Palmerston oversaw Clarendon's policy until the Government fell from power in February 1858. He took a similarly close interest when he headed the first 'Liberal' Government, from 1859 until his death in 1865, although Russell occupied the Foreign Office.

Palmerston's immense significance between 1830 and 1865 is thus indisputable. Over the last century and a half he has attracted many biographers.[1] Whig and Liberal history has likewise had many chroniclers. Important new analyses of Whig foreign policy and its place in popular politics appeared in 2002 and 2003.[2] As the author of one of those studies reminds us, however, chronological coverage of the period has by no means been uniform.[3] When one turns to the early 1850s, for example, even the ubiquitous Palmerston has received less attention.

Historians examining the Conservative Party, even those studying foreign policy, have consistently turned to Benjamin Disraeli, thrice Chancellor of the Exchequer (1852, 1858–59 and 1866–68) and twice Prime Minister (1868 and 1874–80). Yet the Conservative Party was led from 1846 until 1868 by its longest-serving leader, Edward Smith Stanley, fourteenth Earl of Derby (known as Lord Stanley until his father's death in June 1851). As E. D. Steele has observed, Disraeli 'was no more than Derby's lieutenant in the Commons; his authority derived entirely from his position as such'.[4]

Despite serving three times as Prime Minister, from February to December 1852, from February 1858 to June 1859 and from June 1866 to February 1868, Derby has largely been neglected by historians. The notable exception is Angus Hawkins, though his important re-assessments of Derby have not focused upon foreign affairs.[5] Derby's part in foreign policy has never been analysed in depth. This study embarks on that task.

Similarly little attention has been paid to the role and policies of James Howard Harris, third Earl of Malmesbury, Derby's Foreign Secretary in 1852 and 1858–59. This is despite Malmesbury's unique position as the closest friend, in British politics, of both Derby and Louis Napoleon Bonaparte. The foreign policy of the 1852 Government has never been examined in published research. While the 1858–59 Government has received a little more attention, the last monograph to devote any significant space to its policies was published in the early 1960s.[6] Those governments had to respond to important international developments. The French Second Empire was proclaimed in December 1852. In April 1859, the first of the wars of Italian unification broke out between Austria and Piedmont-Sardinia (rapidly joined by France). These were only two among an array of problems that had to be addressed.

The Conservative Party's response to, and analysis of, foreign policy in opposition has also been neglected. Conservative criticism of foreign policy before 1852, and between 1852 and 1858, has generally been ignored or has received references so brief as to render them all but irrelevant. More often than not, when the party's work in opposition has attracted attention historians have focused on Disraeli. Contemporary opposition to Palmerston has usually been examined in the context either of Cobdenite radical criticism or of the contribution made by Peelites such as Aberdeen or William Gladstone.[7]

There is, therefore, a significant gap in the historiography of British foreign policy and domestic politics in the mid-Victorian period. As far as foreign policy is concerned, the Conservatives' assumptions, experiences, prejudices and policies constitute, for the most part, *terra incognita*.

Historiographical context

There are a number of historiographical problems facing any historian of this period and topic. The Conservative politicians of the mid-Victorian era left virtually no memoirs: in an age when politicians did not routinely publish their autobiographies, only some unusual situation would be likely to force their hands; even had they the desire, few senior politicians were likely to have much incentive to publish, as the publication of one's private papers was considered somewhat unseemly.[8] Money from book sales had little attraction for most wealthy aristocrats. In any case, the longevity of Victorian political careers often meant there was little opportunity for reflection: many died in office or soon after leaving it. Derby, for example, was dead within months of retirement. So was Disraeli, who – despite his literary pretensions and experience – had earlier been too busy or too ill to write his memoirs. He left only some unpublished, unfinished 'Reminiscences'.[9]

Fortunately for the historian, Malmesbury was an exception. He had the experience: in the 1840s, he had edited and published the papers of his grandfather, a noted diplomat.[10] More importantly, he needed the money: in old age he acquired a new and financially demanding wife.[11] Writing was an easy and obvious way for him to get cash quickly. His two-volume *Memoirs of an Ex-Minister*, published in 1884, became the first significant publication to consider the work of the Conservative governments of the 1850s.[12] It purported to have been drawn from his daily notes of events, and was published in diary form. But it was the only memoir published by a member of the mid-Victorian Conservative cabinets, and has been utilised by historians primarily as a source of illustrative quotation.

The Conservatives of the mid-nineteenth century have received little attention from biographers. For many politicians' careers, the Victorian and Edwardian 'tombstone' biographies are a useful starting-point and an invaluable source of primary material. In the late nineteenth and early twentieth centuries, volumes appeared detailing various political lives, but Conservative subjects were rarely among them. Of the 1852 and 1858–59 Derby cabinets, very few attracted early biographies. Some – like Derby – had offspring who took no particular interest in commissioning a 'life' of their fathers, while others – like Malmesbury – had no direct heirs to concern themselves with their public reputations. Although two single-volume accounts of Derby's life appeared, their authors had no access to valuable primary material.[13]

In the years since, with one notable exception, the mid-century Conservatives have largely been ignored. Disraeli, of course, has fascinated biographers. Initially, as Miles Taylor has suggested, this may have been 'because he was a cosmopolitan romantic, who seemed free of the prejudice and hypocrisy associated with his age'.[14] But Disraeli continues to stand out among nineteenth-century politicians; his life and career (literary and political) offer tempting opportunities for exploring wider Victorian culture and mores. His colleagues have fared less well, perhaps because their appeal as subjects is not as obviously broad. No biography of Malmesbury or full account of his foreign policy has ever been published. The life of the fifteenth Earl of Derby, twice Foreign Secretary, has been left similarly unchronicled. Hawkins's account of the fourteenth earl's life and career is only the second in over a century. W. D. Jones produced the first scholarly biography in 1956, but had no access to the Derby papers. Even when they became available, for a period they could be viewed only by leave of the late Lord Blake, who was working on a biography that was abandoned.[15]

Academic fashion has played its part in marginalising certain types of political history. The dearth of biographical material is not unique to the mid-Victorian period, nor does it apply only to those whose papers were difficult to access. Peel and Aberdeen have each been the subject of one significant modern biography, but no more, while the third Marquess of Salisbury – Disraeli's successor –began to attract renewed attention only in the last years of the twentieth century. From the mid-1960s, many historians turned away from conventional political and diplomatic history. Nineteenth-century aristocratic politicians, Conservative or otherwise, became a minority interest. For many academics, consciously rejecting a perceived 'history from above', cabinets and governments were simply froth on the waves borne by stronger tides.

From the early 1980s, however, political history started to attract significant attention again. This, as Michael Bentley has discussed, in part reflected dramatic changes in contemporary British politics and a new focus on political leadership.[16] But research has not been universal in its coverage; the Conservatives of the mid-nineteenth century have appeared only intermittently, with most new work examining liberalism and radicalism.[17] Meanwhile, those who wanted to study foreign policy in the last third of the twentieth century explored newly available archives. With a rich vein of primary source material to quarry, they wrote about appeasement, the Second World War and the Cold War. Only a few, such as A. J. P. Taylor and Kenneth Bourne, persisted with nineteenth-century foreign policy.

Nevertheless, the history of Conservative politics and foreign policy has by no means been dormant. In the historiography that has developed, the literature on Conservatism is overwhelmingly centred on Disraeli; foreign policy is dominated by Palmerston.

The focus on Disraeli started early. When Malmesbury's memoirs appeared, his comments about Disraeli were, to reviewers, of as much interest as, if not more than, material about the author and Derby.[18] This is unsurprising: Disraeli had been dead only three years, and was already attaining iconic status. But it was the beginning of a pattern that has largely been sustained to the present day.

Unlike his colleagues, Disraeli was fortunate not only in having biographers, but having extremely good ones. W. F. Monypenny and G. E. Buckle's multi-volume *Life of Benjamin Disraeli* was scholarly, comprehensive in its coverage, and incorporated extensive primary source material.[19] Volumes 3 (1914) and 4 (1916), the latter written by Buckle alone, dealt with the period examined by this study. Monypenny and Buckle's broadly sympathetic (but not uncritical) analysis of Disraeli's career set the scholarly agenda. In a number of ways, the parameters of subsequent discussion have been affected by what they wrote. Volume 4, for example, commented in great detail on one of Disraeli's interventions in foreign policy during the 1858–59 administration.[20] In this and other areas, it is a tribute to Monypenny and Buckle's work that their influence is still felt.

As far as foreign policy is concerned, the *Life of Benjamin Disraeli* has generated three historiographical trends: a tendency to emphasise the centrality of Disraeli; a corresponding marginalisation of Derby and Malmesbury; and the development of an accepted wisdom that, in

1859, a shrewd Disraeli perceived the inadequacy of Malmesbury's foreign policy, though his own imaginative solutions were rebuffed. Meanwhile, issues on which Monypenny and Buckle did not focus tend not to be examined in detail by others (e.g. the furore that blew up around Disraeli's controversial Slough speech in 1858). Their implicit judgements about the significance of episodes and policies have often been allowed to stand.

In the years after the First World War, neither political nor diplomatic historians displayed great interest in mid-Victorian Conservatism. As Britain sought peace and conciliation at home and abroad, academics examined the liberal centre-ground of British politics. For those working in this area, the period between the repeal of the Corn Laws and the 1867 Reform Act was a phase in the development of liberalism: the age of Palmerston. The Conservatives, where they were mentioned at all, were brief interruptions in Britain's affair with Palmerston's brand of conservative, patriotic Whiggery. G. M. Young's elegant study noted that 'overseas' was 'from 1850 onwards the focus of interest' in Victorian Britain.[21] But, in overseas affairs, his own focus was Palmerston. The Conservative Party was of interest only for presiding over occasional interregna in the Palmerstonian reign.

Woodward's volume of the inter-war *Oxford History* of Britain did discuss Conservative foreign policy, but similarly in a Palmerstonian context.[22] Drawing on Malmesbury's memoirs, he observed that, in 1852, the Foreign Secretary – 'not a clever man' – took Palmerston's advice and 'kept on good terms with France'.[23] When the volume was published, in 1938, that advice may have seemed all the more significant. Historiographically, it has become another item of accepted wisdom that Malmesbury (particularly in 1852) was a pupil of Palmerston.[24] Woodward thought that the Conservatives 'inclined towards Austria' during the Italian crisis of 1859, but did not discuss their diplomacy in detail.[25] Another chronicler of the Victorian era, Halévy, left his study sadly unfinished.[26] But McCallum's concluding essay observed of Malmesbury, in a similar vein to Woodward, that 'Palmerston was most willing to be his mentor'.[27]

In the post-war era, with a resurgence of interest in the Victorian period, both the Conservatives and their views on foreign affairs attracted a little more attention. Algernon Cecil, in his series of essays about Victorian prime ministers, considered foreign policy in his piece on Derby.[28] Malmesbury made an undistinguished appearance in Cecil's description of Napoleon, whom Malmesbury 'with indecorous haste saluted in glowing terms' when the French Second Empire was proclaimed.[29] The first close analyses of Conservative diplomacy appeared with the mid-Victorian centenary, at the same time that (coincidentally or not) the British political pendulum swung towards a Conservative Party firmly focused on foreign policy. W. G. Beasley discussed Malmesbury's 1858 Circular.[30] De Groot explored the controversial case of Mather, a young Englishman abused by Austrian soldiers in Tuscany in 1852, and concurred with contemporary criticism.[31]

A. J. P. Taylor assessed Conservative foreign policy in his masterpiece *The Struggle for Mastery in Europe*, and was similarly critical.[32] He noted that in 1852 the 'timid and inexperienced' Malmesbury accepted a Russian offer of support in the event of a Bonapartist irruption into Belgium; this was one of many reasons why the Russians misunderstood 'the spirit of British policy' in the early 1850s.[33] He paid Derby's administration the distinctly back-handed compliment that 'even a tory government, even Malmesbury, saw the folly of demanding guarantees' of Napoleon's peaceful intentions when he proclaimed the French Second Empire.[34] He also alleged that in 1859 the Conservatives 'secretly favoured' alliance with Prussia, in support of Austrian rule in Italy.[35] He concluded that the Conservatives 'had nothing to offer' during the crisis 'except moral disapproval'.[36] The resonance cannot have been lost on a generation that readily recalled Chamberlain.

But Disraeli remained centre-stage, if sometimes by default. G. B. Henderson's research had revealed details about Disraeli's secretary Ralph Earle,[37] which helped keep the spotlight on the Chancellor.[38] Although Harry Hearder's 1954 thesis analysed Malmesbury's diplomacy in 1858–59, and began to question the wisdom of Disraeli's interventions, unfortunately it was never published, limiting its impact.[39] And while Jones assessed Derby's career, no one followed him. He briefly noted foreign policy developments, putting a new gloss on 1859 by concluding that 'Derby was only mildly pro-Austrian, but he had an isolationist's disgust with the troubles of other nations'.[40]

Hearder's research influenced Beales's 1961 examination of British foreign policy in 1859–60, which dwelt for rather longer on Malmesbury and pointed out the 'excessively optimistic' nature of Disraeli's foreign policy proposals when he intervened in 1859.[41] Beales, however, like Hearder, could not draw on the Derby or Malmesbury papers. As a result, Disraeli's intervention in foreign policy could not be seen fully in context, and Beales went out of his way to demonstrate Disraeli's perceptiveness. W. L. Burn's *Age of Equipoise* appeared in 1964 – in an age familiar with party political equipoise – and attempted to give a unity to a confusing period, but foreign policy was left out; it remains an interesting question where, or whether, it fits.[42]

In 1966, Robert Blake produced his single-volume *Disraeli*, a work every bit as impressive as Monypenny and Buckle's.[43] Blake analysed certain foreign policy issues in detail, but he was not, of course, writing an account of diplomacy. Perhaps inevitably, his work perpetuated the Disraeli-centred presentation of foreign policy, though his portrayal of Disraeli's role was not uncritical. Malmesbury was a bit-player and Derby was of secondary interest, though his primary significance was acknowledged.

From the late 1960s until the 1980s, new research illuminated liberalism, but rarely focused on the Conservatives. Vincent's seminal analysis was, necessarily, concerned with the Conservatives' opponents.[44] And it was the liberals who attracted the biographers. The same year that Vincent's book was published, Southgate's biography of Palmerston appeared, followed by Ridley's, and Prest's *Lord John Russell* was published in 1972.[45] Conservative statesmen did not receive the same treatment, and as historians moved away from high politics, even Disraeli went through a leaner period.

Foreign policy tended not to attract the attention of those who did examine Conservative politics. J. T. Ward's analysis of Derby and Disraeli did not touch on it.[46] Robert Stewart dwelt on Derby in some detail, both in his study of protection and his history of the Conservatives.[47] He produced important new research about party organisation, but understandably there was limited room for foreign policy.[48] Bentley also explored the Conservative role in his broader study of politics.[49] He quickly dismissed the 1852 Government.[50] As far as the second Government was concerned, he suggested that, although Italy was not a 'rallying issue' in the 1859 election, it 'helped distract attention from reform'.[51]

There has been no consensus on the Italian crisis of 1859. Bourne, whose survey of Victorian foreign policy remains the only extensive one available, took the opposite view to Taylor's. He described the Conservatives in 1859 as 'not much less sympathetic' to Italian nationalism than their opponents.[52] He was sceptical, however, about whether Malmesbury's proposals for reform in Italy in early 1859 could ever have satisfied Austria; what was more, after war broke out, 'Malmesbury could only flounder'.[53] Paul Hayes, in his 1975 analysis of foreign policy, reached a similar verdict.[54] He observed that, in 1859, 'Disraeli believed, correctly, that the Foreign Secretary did not really understand Louis Napoleon's policies'.[55] He thought that positive reasons for Malmesbury's initial appointment at the FO were 'difficult to find'.[56] He noted, in the well-established trend, that Malmesbury drew on the advice of Wellington and Palmerston in 1852, 'though not with complete success'.[57]

There were significant archival developments in this period. In 1978, John Vincent published the first of the newly discovered diaries of the fifteenth Earl of Derby, which would yield invaluable data about both the Conservative Party and foreign policy.[58] Shortly afterwards, Malmesbury's papers became available. W. E. Major's 1980 thesis drew on these; his was the first – and, thus far, the only – detailed examination of Malmesbury's whole career.[59] While his discussion was necessarily curtailed by the constraints of space in a thesis examining a long career, he discussed a range of policies with which Malmesbury was involved. His chapter on 1852 remains the only analysis of that Government's foreign policy.

As the 1980s progressed, historians continued to utilise the newly available archives, and the mid-Victorian Conservative Party took on a more distinctive shape. McCracken's dissertation on the three Conservative minority governments incorporated an examination of the Malmesbury–Disraeli relationship.[60] Derby's career was a central part of the innovative work carried out by Gurowich in his thesis.[61] Hawkins's 1987 analysis of politics in the 1850s was significant, and was the first monograph to devote considerable space to Derby's second administration.[62] It demonstrated the coherence of the Conservative Party in the late 1850s, and explored its role in detail. Derby was no longer secondary to Disraeli. Though his was not a diplomatic history, Hawkins discussed Disraeli's intervention in January 1859 and placed foreign affairs firmly in the context of contemporary political debate. In his assessment of the Disraelian intervention, Hawkins concurred with the general verdict that Malmesbury and Derby were diplomatically shortsighted.[63]

The 1990s saw the publication of important new analyses of liberalism and radicalism. Biagini, Howe, Mandler, Parry and Taylor have re-evaluated the political, cultural and economic nature of the liberal polity.[64] The 1968–94 publication of the Gladstone diaries helped fuel interest in the growth of Victorian liberalism, and we now have a much more sophisticated picture of Gladstone himself.[65]

Aside from Disraeli, however, the Conservative politicians to have attracted attention are largely those of the post-1867 era. E. H. H. Green and Martin Pugh have illuminated grassroots Conservatism, connecting high politics with the party at ground level.[66] Salisbury's career has been the focus of three new studies.[67] John Charmley has explored the nature of Conservative foreign policy after 1874.[68] He speculated about a strand of Conservative thought that he defined as the 'Country Party tradition', which might have had earlier roots.[69] Those acting in that tradition, he suggested, from the fifteenth Earl of Derby in the 1870s to Neville Chamberlain in the 1930s, were committed to a non-interventionist, 'strong navy' policy. The antithesis of this policy was the kind of neo-Palmerstonian interventionism, based on 'prestige', that was embraced by Disraeli in the late 1870s and by Churchill in the twentieth century.

The mid-Victorian Conservatives are ripe for re-assessment, as Anna Gambles demonstrated when she built on Stewart's earlier work and examined economic discourse prior to 1852, revealing the painful learning curve through which the party went as it tried, and failed, to preserve protection.[70] In the field of foreign policy, however, it has been the Conservatives' opponents who have been the subject of new analysis. E. D. Steele and David Brown have begun to redefine the parameters of debate about foreign policy.

Steele took Palmerston as the focus of his study of liberalism. He explored the way in which Palmerston and his party functioned and interacted throughout the period 1855–65. As has become the pattern in discussions about liberalism, he drew on both domestic and foreign policy. Uniquely, he also examined the Conservatives in some detail, including their views and approach to foreign policy. He suggested that the 'first principle' of Conservative policy 'was to keep Britain from being too closely involved in the affairs of the Continent', though 'Tory spokesmen did not think isolationism either feasible or desirable'.[71] Desiring 'a stable Europe after the Crimean war', they regarded Palmerstonian policy as 'too personal and incautious, if not worse'.[72] Steele criticised Malmesbury, post-1856, for relying too much on 'Bonapartism's liberal side'.[73] His analysis of Conservative foreign policy skated over Derby and did not examine the pre-Crimean period, but his conclusions represent a significant historiographical departure.

Brown has built on Steele's analysis of Palmerston, examining his political role in the late 1840s and early 1850s, and asking new questions about its popular base. He incorporated analysis of Palmerston's manipulation of public opinion within a broader study of liberal high politics and foreign policy. In his account, Conservative opinion and policy is principally represented by Disraeli. Malmesbury's 1852 overture to the Papacy was unfortunately just beyond the chronological scope of Matsumoto-Best's study of Anglo-Italian relations, which also located foreign policy firmly in the context of popular politics.

The man responsible for Conservative foreign policy in the 1850s has received relatively little attention. Malmesbury was not one of those Foreign Secretaries examined in either the collection of biographical essays edited by Keith Wilson in 1987 or in that edited by Thomas Otte in 2002.[74] In both cases, discussions of Palmerston's role represented the mid-Victorian period. Wilson, however, observed in his Introduction that during the nineteenth century 'there was no consensus as to what British foreign policy should be', and that the 1858–59 Derby Government 'followed a quite different policy towards Austria and Italian affairs from that of its predecessor'.[75] That policy has subsequently been explored in detail by Nick Carter. His discussion of Anglo-Italian relations, in his thesis and a series of articles, incorporates a highly critical analysis of Malmesbury's management of foreign affairs in 1859.[76]

But the careers and policies of Derby and Malmesbury are still overshadowed by Disraeli, and the rich literature examining his role has helped reveal the potential for more work on his colleagues. In 1984, Ghosh produced a new analysis of Disraelian finance, and commented on its relationship with Disraeli's principles in foreign policy.[77] Smith, Vincent and Feuchtwanger have examined Disraeli's principles, philosophy and domestic policy.[78] The invaluable University of Toronto project to publish all Disraeli's letters has also provided much material about the broader party. In 1997, Ann Pottinger Saab focused on Disraeli and his newspaper the *Press* during the Crimean War, linking his political ideas with his Jewish background.[79] More recently, Jonathan Parry has discussed 'Disraeli's foreign policy' in the 1850s and 1860s,[80] and he focused on Disraeli when discussing the 1858–59 administration in his subsequent article about Napoleon III.[81] As Hawkins's work has demonstrated, however, adding more detail about Derby and his colleagues to analyses of Disraeli's role provides us with a fuller picture of mid-Victorian Conservatism, and this is as much the case in the foreign policy sphere.

The politics of Conservative foreign policy

This study assumes that it is possible to follow the progress of a clearly identifiable Conservative Party, made up of politicians who generally followed Derby's leadership (most of whom had supported protectionism in the late 1840s). Despite a confusing range of party names and descriptions, it accepts, as Hawkins and Gurowich have postulated, that the Conservatives had a coherent identity. Indeed, it offers further evidence as to the nature of that identity. The core of leading politicians with which this study is mainly concerned, though their allegiance and adherents were frequently the subject of speculation, consistently represented something distinct from Whigs, liberals and radicals. They were their clear opponents and alternatives, as was demonstrated in 1851, 1852, 1855 and 1858, when the Queen turned first to them to provide a government after the defeats of Russell, Aberdeen and Palmerston.

As Gurowich has shown, the parliamentary party was loyal to Derby throughout the period of his leadership.[82] The allegiance of backbenchers discussed in this study has been defined by their support for the established Conservative leadership in key parliamentary divisions, and/or contemporary reference works. In chapters 2 and 3, the term 'Protectionist' has also been used to refer to Derbyite Conservatives, both because it was a contemporary description and because this study consciously links their views on foreign and economic policy. Peelites, though many still called themselves Conservatives after 1846, increasingly personified a separate strand of opinion. They are here referred to separately.

The study takes as its focus the years between 1846 and 1859. The period is bounded by the great Conservative schism that followed Peel's abandonment of protectionism and the collapse of Derby's second Government in June 1859. During this period, there was a consistency of personnel, ideas and problems that provides a useful framework for discussion. The great themes of British politics and foreign affairs remained, broadly speaking, the same.

At home, once the dust had settled after 1846, Derby adopted what Hawkins has defined as a strategy of 'masterly inactivity'.[83] He and his party waited for the cracks to appear in the fragile alliance of Whigs, Peelites and radicals that kept them out of power. These non-Conservative forces shared some principles and differed greatly on others. But when they were united, as they were for most of the period, it was difficult for the Conservatives to make inroads, despite increasing their share of parliamentary seats in the elections called by Derby in 1852 and 1859. Throughout the period, the Conservative Party identified, broadly speaking, two threats posed by Whig–Peelite government: domestic innovation and radicalism, fostered principally by Russell and the Peelites; and what it perceived as an aggressively 'liberal' foreign policy, usually directed or inspired by Palmerston.

Palmerston and Palmerstonian ideas occupy a place at the heart of this study. Debate about foreign policy throughout the period was defined and dominated by Palmerston. His leadership, policies, influence and diplomatic style were consistently of central importance. He was the point around which politics, and particularly foreign affairs, revolved. Paradoxically, it looked quite possible, on more than one occasion, that Palmerston would join with the Conservatives. His distinctly conservative stance on domestic policy, particularly his opposition to reform, would have made him a natural bedfellow; and the party would probably have reaped electoral benefits. In foreign policy, however, the Conservatives defined themselves as both un-Palmerstonian and anti-Palmerstonian.

Their touchstone was the Vienna settlement, which had formally established the boundaries of post-Napoleonic Europe in the treaties of 1814–15. As far as the Conservatives were concerned, it had provided peace and stability for over thirty years, and they were much less ready to contemplate altering it than were their opponents. Derby and his foreign secretaries sought to utilise what a previous age would have called the 'Concert' of Europe: the loose system of international co-operation that had been developed to protect the settlement. When Castlereagh had been Foreign Secretary, there were regular congresses of the five great powers: Britain, Austria, France, Prussia and Russia. This system was not reconstituted, although the 1850s had their share of European conferences. Nevertheless, the principle of co-operation lay at the heart of Conservative policy-making. Through collaboration with other powers, Derby and Malmesbury (and Stanley in 1866–68) did their best to maintain the existing political boundaries of Europe. Like another of their predecessors, Aberdeen, they attempted to mend fences that Palmerston had torn down with his often deliberately indelicate approach to diplomacy.

The Conservatives opposed three elements of Whig foreign policy: what they perceived as the application of liberal and radical principles; Palmerston's and Russell's apparent encouragement of nationalism; and interference in the affairs of other nations. The preservation of the 1815 settlement was of more significance to the Conservatives than the extent of personal liberty in, or the politics of, any given power. Derby and Malmesbury were profoundly uninterested in applying liberal values to foreign policy. Derby explained in 1858 that, 'with regard to foreign countries, the peculiar form of Government which best suits the people is, if not a matter of indifference to us, at all events one into which we have no cause or right to inquire'.[84] The Conservatives duly pursued *rapprochement* with authoritarian Austria, collaborated with autocratic Russia, wholeheartedly welcomed Louis Napoleon's *coups* in 1851 and 1852, and sought the re-establishment of relations with the tyrannical King of Naples.

Steele suggested that Malmesbury, in particular, had 'a coherent, distinctively Tory standpoint on nationality'.[85] This was certainly the case, but it went beyond nationality. In international affairs, the Conservatives exhibited a streak of Burkean scepticism. Observing revolutionary France in 1790, Burke had scornfully noted that 'The effects of the incapacity shewn by the popular leaders ... are to be covered with the "all-atoning name" of liberty'.[86] In 1859, Malmesbury and Derby similarly wondered about the price of freedom, to which their liberal opponents seemed to attach great significance. Italy might end up free from outside interference (though that seemed an improbable outcome), but the Conservatives were unconvinced that it would necessarily be beneficial to the balance of power. These were genuine and profound differences about the impact of change in Europe.

The politics of foreign policy were inextricably linked with domestic considerations. Practical limitations were imposed on foreign-policy-makers by electoral and economic realities. Until the collapse of Derby's first Government, protectionism was hanging over the Conservatives and all their stratagems. By 1852, the parliamentary leadership had reached the conclusion that 'the issue of protection was imposing intractable electoral limits on the fortunes of the Conservative party'.[87] But until protection was definitively laid to rest, after Disraeli's budget failed in December 1852, its death throes had a significant impact. If Disraeli was to deliver the economic changes he did propose, every vote would be needed. The Foreign Secretary pursued *rapprochement* with Rome in the hope of political fruits in Ireland that would strengthen the Government's domestic support.

Meanwhile, the last thing Derby needed was a politically or economically expensive row with the new empire in France. Domestic circumstances thus offered a further incentive for Malmesbury to pursue the Anglo-French *entente* he temperamentally favoured, just as domestic considerations would reinforce the necessity for a conciliatory foreign policy in 1859. After protection was abandoned, the Conservatives lacked a grand cause; but, throughout the 1850s, foreign affairs provided the most powerful ammunition in domestic debate.

The search for the holy grail of majority government constantly affected Conservative calculations. After the 1846 schism had left the Derbyite Conservatives in the political wilderness, a Commons majority eluded them for twenty-eight years. Disraeli's victory in 1874 goes a long way to explaining his canonisation by the party that for most of his career regarded him merely as a necessary evil. Electoral considerations gave an extra impetus to certain policies. But to win and sustain a majority, the party also needed credibility. If the Conservatives were to secure credibility they had to be careful managers of foreign policy when they were in power. The popular basis of liberalism, in alliance with Peelite Conservatism, was such that Palmerston could slip up over Don Pacifico in 1850 and Schleswig Holstein in 1863–64, and survive; he could be censured over China in 1857 and still succeed at the ballot box. The Conservatives could not afford to take any risks. The minority status of their governments made them vulnerable and left them with little room for manoeuvre. The disproportionate criticism levelled at them during 1852 indicated the dangers they would face if their opponents spotted any opportunity, however small, while they had little flexibility in 1859 when facing a major international crisis.

And international crises were not infrequent. Overseas, the period was an eventful one. While the late 1840s were dominated by revolution within continental countries, the 1850s saw a revolution in the wider balance of power. The Crimean War, from 1854 to 1856, turned Russia from a conservative power into one seeking a revision of the international order, and above all a reversal of the restrictions imposed by the Treaty of Paris.[88] For Britain, however, the principal foreign policy consideration for most of the period was closer to home: Bonapartist France.

Louis Napoleon Bonaparte first obtained the presidency of the French Second Republic in December 1848, solidified his power in a *coup d'état* in December 1851, and made himself Emperor Napoleon III in December 1852. He was a particular concern for the Conservatives, who were, by chance, twice in power at crucial moments in his career. Bonaparte sought to disrupt the continental equilibrium, albeit shaky, that had persisted since the end of the Napoleonic Wars. He was at the root of most of the foreign-policy problems that required a Conservative response, in government and opposition.

Like most mid-Victorian British politicians, the Conservatives had a curious relationship with France: at once it provided Britain's most immediate threat and a significant ally. It was a threat because of its close geographical location and its political instability; but it had been an ally of sorts, as a broadly 'liberal' Western power, ever since 1830. Britain's only major war between 1815 and 1914 was, after all, fought alongside France, not against it. But governments of all hues had to respond to the danger represented by France, and in 1852, 1858 and 1859 the Conservatives faced domestic war scares. Indeed, political rows about the response to an apparent French threat brought the party to power in both 1852 and 1858. Yet the party leadership was notably pro-French: Malmesbury had been an adolescent friend of

Napoleon, and exploited his own personal *entente* in government and opposition.

This study is predominantly an analysis of high politics and the role of key individual politicians, and it is unapologetically so. As Bentley has noted, there is a 'persistent prejudice that historians who write about major political personalities and their thought-world suffer from some sort of simple-mindedness or theoretical *naïveté*'.[89] That prejudice needs resisting. This study deals with the mid-Victorian political world as it is revealed by the available evidence, not with modern democratic and cultural values superimposed on it. In this period, though a range of influences affected decision-making, a few individuals directed British foreign policy and led debate about it. They were patrician and aristocratic, and they did their best to guard their privileges. Derby even doubted the wisdom of consulting his Cabinet about foreign affairs. It might be interesting to discover what Britain's un-enfranchised masses thought about the subject, but it would tell us very little about the construction of policy.

Perhaps no other period of the nineteenth century demonstrates quite so strikingly the extent to which a small number of leading figures dominated party politics. In the 1850s, more governments (six) held office than in any other single decade of that century or the next, yet there was a remarkable lack of variety in senior personnel. A few leaders formed a nucleus around which parties ebbed and flowed. In the records of almost every major parliamentary debate, the names of the same leading politicians appear, time and again; they are mirrored in each successive list of ministers.

On the non-Conservative side, governments were dominated by Palmerston and Russell. A few senior Peelites, such as Aberdeen (before he fell in 1855) and Gladstone, wielded influence disproportionate to their numerical strength. They had necessarily to be considered in any political calculation made by either the Whigs or the Conservatives. Among the liberal and Peelite factions, others in the next tier – men like Clarendon, Earl Granville, the Duke of Newcastle and Sidney Herbert – regularly shuffled senior portfolios between them.

After the split over the Corn Laws, the Conservative Party had fewer men of ability from whom to choose. At the top, it was even more dominated by a few individuals; most prominent among them Derby, Disraeli, the much-overlooked Malmesbury, and Derby's son, Stanley. They have left rich archives. This study is centred on these men and their senior colleagues, their ideas and policies, and the relationships between them. But it is not exclusively concerned with them.

Consideration has also been given to backbench MPs, to the contributions by the Conservative-supporting press (such as it was) and political associates. It also draws extensively on the papers of opposition figures, and incorporates material generated by others whose work impacted on foreign policy, most notably the court and the diplomatic corps.

For the most part, however, foreign policy was monopolised by certain leading individuals; much more so than was the case with other policy areas. This was partly because of the nature of diplomacy. In government, whichever party was in power, immense influence was wielded by the Foreign Secretary, through whom all important (and much minor) business passed. Diplomats in this period had little control over the direction of policy; the only exceptions were those representatives who had built up significant personal relationships with foreign governments, such as Stratford Canning in Constantinople and Lord Cowley in Paris.

The extent of the Foreign Secretary's power depended, of course, on the degree to which the Prime Minister and/or the Cabinet exercised control over him. The Conservative Cabinets of 1852 and 1858–9 (with the important exception of Disraeli in the latter administration) seem to have taken very little interest in foreign policy. This may have been because of the particularly close and effective relationship between Derby and Malmesbury; they had one of the warmest political partnerships of the nineteenth century. In government and opposition, however, there were few Conservatives who displayed much interest in foreign affairs. If the surviving papers are an accurate guide, there was not, except at times of acute crisis, a huge body of Conservative opinion which concerned itself with overseas policy.

Insofar as the evidence demonstrates that public opinion impacted on decision-making and political strategies, this study notes its influence. But there are significant methodological problems with incorporating public opinion in analyses of foreign policy. Whose opinions mattered, and how do we interpret them? Paul Kennedy has noted that the press was regarded as 'the chief indicator' of nineteenth-century public opinion.[90] While the press certainly includes useful *examples* of opinion, however, its wider significance – in terms of the proportion of opinion represented or its influence – is often guesswork.

Similar hazards await the historian examining public opinion via election results and even parliamentary votes. For example, the Commons rejected Palmerston in 1857 after the bombardment of Canton, but the electorate voted for him. That might tell us something about public opinion with regard to foreign policy, or it might tell us nothing. In 1859, MPs rejected Derby's Government, but who can say, with any degree of certainty, what part foreign policy played? Malmesbury believed that the diplomatic correspondence relating to the Franco-Austrian War would have tipped the popular scales in favour of Derby's Government, if Disraeli had published it before the critical debate on 10 June.[91] But, of course, it is impossible to be certain whether foreign policy motivated MPs to vote one way or another. Malmesbury's bitterness indicates the state of his relationship with Disraeli; no greater claim can be made for it. In a study of this kind, public opinion only becomes significant when the interface between politicians and public opinion can clearly be identified, and the interaction was meaningful enough to have impacted upon policy.

The lack of research about those who unquestionably did influence foreign affairs reinforces the importance of studying the Conservative leadership in some detail. The dynamics of the Conservative leadership lie at the heart of this study. One of its principal claims is that, in the foreign policy arena, the relationships between the party leaders have been misunderstood. It explores the way in which Derby closely followed and controlled policy, and the way in which he worked with Malmesbury in pursuit of their objectives. Thus, the handling of Anglo-Italian relations in 1859 is examined principally as an episode in political, not diplomatic, history. The Italian crisis requires new analysis because of its significance for the dynamics of Conservative politics, as well as what it tells us about Conservative conceptions of foreign policy.

In discussing almost any other government, it would be stating the obvious to say that the Prime Minister played a crucial role in foreign policy. But Derby has rarely been accorded the analysis he merits; both his role and that of Malmesbury have been under-rated. For the most part, this is because they have been overshadowed by Disraeli. It seems very likely that the principal reason why Disraeli in the 1850s and 1860s has received attention is not because of his activities in those decades (at least, not prior to 1867). Rather, the attractiveness for historians and biographers of the successes and excitements of 1867–81 has led them to his earlier career to analyse the development of his ideas and contextualise his later activities.

Yet Disraeli was largely irrelevant in foreign policy, except, as in 1858–59, when he caused problems for those who were in charge of it. To understand Disraeli's place in the formation of foreign policy in the Conservative governments of the 1850s it is necessary to set aside the familiar images that dominate the historiography: the indispensable minister who adroitly championed the 1867 Reform Act; the orator who triumphantly delivered victory in 1874; the Prime Minister who developed his own bold foreign policy; the player to the jingoistic imperial gallery; the adventurer driving his Foreign Secretary to resignation. As one of Malmesbury's reviewers put it: 'We have to forget... Lord Beaconsfield'.[92]

Instead we need to focus on the Conservative leadership a quarter of a century before that title was awarded. The leadership included a rhetorically brilliant, but inexperienced and somewhat precarious Chancellor of the Exchequer. His determination to gain and maintain power produced persistent tensions in his relationship with the more cautious Malmesbury, who was almost invariably backed by Derby. In the corrosive disagreement between Derby's two chief lieutenants can be discerned very different analyses of foreign policy; when Disraeli was Prime Minister, similar problems would emerge.

This study stops in 1859; thereafter, the international and domestic context changed rapidly. By the time the Conservatives returned to power in 1866, the political map of the Continent was unrecognisable from that of the 1850s. The unification of Italy, though it awaited its conclusion, had already altered the dynamics of great power politics. More significantly, Bismarck's Prussia had replaced France as the greatest threat to European peace, and was well on the way to unifying Germany after the defeat of Denmark and Austria.

Domestic politics also took a different shape after 1859. First, between 1860 and 1865, the Conservative leadership saw little reason to challenge the domestic conservatism of Palmerston, whose foreign policy was increasingly constrained by practical and political difficulties. After 1865, Palmerston's death and Gladstone's consequent ascendancy accelerated the polarisation of politics. The Conservatives' Reform Act in 1867 increased the pace of change. By 1870, the world looked very different: Bismarck had changed Europe; Gladstone was changing the Liberal Party; the Reform Act had changed the electorate. Derby had finally ceded control of the Conservative Party to Disraeli in 1868. Conservative foreign policy would remain under Derbyite control, but only until 1878 when Stanley (after 1869, the fifteenth Earl of Derby) fell out with Disraeli and resigned. The 1860s are, unquestionably, in as much need of new analysis as the 1850s, but the story of the 1860s is a rather different one.

Some decades ago, George Kitson Clark considered the nature of mid-Victorian Conservatism: 'in most matters', he observed, 'it would not be easy to see what, save the personal leadership of Derby and Disraeli, separated the Conservative party from Lord Palmerston and those who thought like him'.[93] He raised a question all too rarely addressed. Though his subject was not diplomacy, Kitson Clark's words still have a resonance for the student of foreign policy. They represent an important challenge; this study aims to take it up.

Notes

1 See, e.g., Lord Dalling, *The Life of Viscount Palmerston*, 3 vols (1871–74); Marquis of Lorne, *Viscount Palmerston K.G.* (London, 1892); Philip Guedalla, *Palmerston* (London, 1926); H. C. F. Bell, *Lord Palmerston*, 2 vols (London, 1936); W. B. Pemberton, *Lord Palmerston* (London, 1954); Donald Southgate, *'The Most English Minister': The Policies and Politics of Palmerston* (London, 1966); Kenneth Bourne, *Palmerston: The Early Years, 1784–1841* (London, 1982); Muriel Chamberlain, *Lord Palmerston* (Cardiff, 1987); James Chambers, *Palmerston: 'The People's Darling'* (London, 2004).
2 David Brown, *Palmerston and the Politics of Foreign Policy, 1846–55* (Manchester, 2002); Saho Matsumoto-Best, *Britain and the Papacy in the Age of Revolution, 1846–1851* (Woodbridge, 2003).
3 Brown, *Politics of Foreign Policy*, p. 2.
4 E. D. Steele, *Palmerston and Liberalism, 1855–1865* (London, 1991), p. 137.
5 Angus Hawkins is preparing a biography of Derby. He has also written several articles on his subject: 'Lord Derby and Victorian Conservatism: A Reappraisal', *Parliamentary History* (hereafter *PH*), 6 (1987), pp. 280–301; 'Lord Derby', in R. W. Davis (ed.), *Lords of Parliament: Studies 1714–1914* (Stanford, CA, 1995), pp. 134–62; '"A Host in Himself": Lord Derby and Aristocratic Leadership', *PH*, 22 (2003), pp. 75–90.
6 Derek Beales, *England and Italy, 1859–60* (London, 1961).
7 See, e.g., A. J. P. Taylor, *The Troublemakers: Dissent Over Foreign Policy, 1792–1939* (London, 1957), pp. 53, 56–7; Muriel Chamberlain, *'Pax Britannica'? British Foreign Policy, 1789–1914* (Harlow, 1988), pp. 98–9; Brown, *Politics of Foreign Policy*, pp. 101–18.
8 For example, the fifteenth Earl of Derby doubted whether 'it is altogether delicate to publish gossip about living friends and acquaintances': *The Diaries of Edward Henry Stanley, 15th Earl of Derby (1826–93), between 1878 and 1893*, ed. John Vincent (Oxford, 2003), 2 October 1884, p. 845.
9 Subsequently edited and published as *Disraeli's Reminiscences*, ed. Helen M. Swartz and Marvin Swartz (London, 1975).
10 James Harris, *Diaries and Correspondence of James Harris, First Earl of Malmesbury*, ed. Earl of Malmesbury, 4 vols (London, 1844).
11 According to the fifteenth Earl of Derby, *Diaries of Edward Henry Stanley*, 2 October 1884, p. 845.
12 Earl of Malmesbury, *Memoirs of An Ex-Minister: An Autobiography*, 2 vols (London, 1884).

13 T. E. Kebbel, *The Earl of Derby* (London, 1890); George Saintsbury, *The Earl of Derby* (London, 1892).
14 Miles Taylor and Michael Wolff (eds), *The Victorians Since 1901: Histories, Representations and Revisions* (Manchester, 2004), p. 4.
15 W. D. Jones, *Lord Derby and Victorian Conservatism* (Oxford, 1956).
16 Michael Bentley, 'Victorian Prime Ministers: Changing Patterns of Commemoration', in Taylor and Wolff (eds), *The Victorians Since 1901*, p. 54.
17 See below, p. 9.
18 See, e.g., Anon., review of 'Lord Malmesbury's Memoirs', *Macmillan's Magazine*, 51 (November 1884).
19 W. F. Monypenny and G. E. Buckle, *The Life of Benjamin Disraeli, Earl of Beaconsfield*, 6 vols (London, 1910–20) (hereafter, *Disraeli*).
20 *Ibid.*, vol. 4, pp. 214–31.
21 G. M. Young, *Victorian England: Portrait of an Age* (London, 1936), 1960 edition, p. 81.
22 E. L. Woodward, *The Age of Reform 1815–1870* (Oxford, 1938).
23 *Ibid.*, pp. 240–1.
24 See, e.g., Brown, *Politics of Foreign Policy*, p. 138; an exaggerated version of this accepted wisdom is to be found in Chambers, *Palmerston*, pp. 344–5.
25 Woodward, *Age of Reform*, p. 289.
26 Elie Halevy, *Victorian Years: 1841–1895* (London, 1946).
27 *Ibid.*, 1962 edition, p. 325.
28 Algernon Cecil, *Queen Victoria and Her Prime Ministers* (London, 1953).
29 *Ibid.*, p. 153.
30 W. G. Beasley, 'Lord Malmesbury's Foreign Office Circular of 8 March, 1858', *Bulletin of the Institute of Historical Research* (hereafter *BIHR*), 22 (1950), pp. 225–8.
31 E. De Groot, 'The Florentine Tragedy of Mr. Mather of South Shields', *Durham University Journal* (hereafter *DUJ*), 44 (1952), pp. 95–106.
32 A. J. P. Taylor, *The Struggle for Mastery in Europe, 1848–1918* (London, 1954).
33 *Ibid.*, p. 47.
34 *Ibid.*, p. 48.
35 *Ibid.*, p. 108.
36 *Ibid.*
37 G. B. Henderson, 'Ralph Anstruther Earle', *English Historical Review* (hereafter *EHR*), 58 (1943), pp. 172–89; G. B. Henderson, *Crimean War Diplomacy and other Historical Essays* (Glasgow, 1947).
38 Throughout this study, 'Chancellor' is used in the modern sense, signifying the Chancellor of the Exchequer, rather than the *Lord* Chancellor, as was the nineteenth-century custom.
39 H. Hearder, 'The Foreign Policy of Lord Malmesbury, 1858–9' (Ph.D thesis, University of London, 1954).

40 Jones, *Derby*, p. 253.
41 Beales, *England and Italy*, p. 49.
42 W. L. Burn, *The Age of Equipoise: A Study of the Mid-Victorian Generation* (London, 1964).
43 Robert Blake, *Disraeli* (London, 1966).
44 John Vincent, *The Formation of the British Liberal Party* (London, 1966).
45 Southgate, 'The Most English Minister'; Jasper Ridley, *Lord Palmerston* (London, 1970); John Prest, *Lord John Russell* (London, 1972).
46 J. T. Ward, 'Derby and Disraeli', in D. Southgate (ed.), *The Conservative Leadership 1832–1932* (London, 1974).
47 Robert Stewart, *The Politics of Protection: Lord Derby and the Protectionist Party, 1841–1852* (Cambridge, 1971); *The Foundation of the Conservative Party 1830–1867* (London, 1978).
48 During his discussion of the 1858–59 Government: *ibid.*, p. 321.
49 Michael Bentley, *Politics Without Democracy 1815–1914* (London, 1984).
50 *Ibid.*, 1996 edition, p. 95.
51 *Ibid.*, p. 114.
52 Kenneth Bourne, *The Foreign Policy of Victorian England 1830–1902* (London, 1970), p. 99.
53 *Ibid.*, p. 100.
54 Paul Hayes, *Modern British Foreign Policy: The Nineteenth Century 1814–80* (London, 1975).
55 *Ibid.*
56 *Ibid.*, p. 113.
57 *Ibid.*, pp. 113–14.
58 *Disraeli, Derby and the Conservative Party: Journals and Memoirs of Edward Henry, Lord Stanley, 1849–1869*, ed. John Vincent (Hassocks, 1978) (hereafter *DDCP*).
59 W. E. Major, 'The Public Life of the Third Earl of Malmesbury' (Ph.D dissertation, University of Georgia, 1980).
60 D. E. McCracken, 'The Conservatives in Power': The Minority Governments of 1852, 1858–9 and 1866–8' (Ph.D thesis, University of Virginia, 1981).
61 P. M. Gurowich, 'Party and Independence in the Early- and Mid-Victorian House of Commons: Aspects of Political Theory and Practice, 1832–68, Considered with Special Reference to the Period 1852–68' (Ph.D thesis, Cambridge University, 1987).
62 Angus Hawkins, *Parliament, Party and the Art of Politics in Britain, 1855–59* (Stanford, CA, 1987).
63 *Ibid.*, p. 195.
64 See, among others, Eugenio F. Biagini, *Liberty, Retrenchment and Reform: Popular Liberalism in the Age of Gladstone, 1860–1880* (Cambridge, 1992); Anthony Howe, *Free Trade and Liberal England, 1846–1946* (Oxford, 1997); Peter Mandler, *Aristocratic Government in*

the Age of Reform: Whigs and Liberals, 1830–1852 (Oxford, 1990); Jonathan Parry, *The Rise and Fall of Liberal Government in Victorian Britain* (New Haven, CT, 1993); Miles Taylor, *The Decline of British Radicalism, 1847–1860* (Oxford, 1995).

65 See, e.g., H. C. G. Matthew, *Gladstone* (Oxford, 1986); Roy Jenkins, *Gladstone* (London, 1995); Travis L. Crosby, *The Two Mr Gladstones: A Study in Psychology and History* (London, 1997); Peter J. Jagger (ed.), *Gladstone* (London, 1998); Peter Francis (ed.), *The Gladstone Umbrella* (Hawarden, 2001); D. W. Bebbington, *The Mind of Gladstone: Religion, Homer and Politics* (Oxford, 2004).

66 See, e.g., Martin Pugh, *The Tories and the People, 1880–1935* (Oxford, 1985); E. H. H. Green, *The Crisis of Conservatism: The Politics, Economics and Ideology of the Conservative Party, 1880–1914* (London, 1995).

67 Andrew Roberts, *Salisbury: Victorian Titan* (London, 1999); David Steele, *Lord Salisbury: A Political Biography* (London, 1999); Michael Bentley, *Lord Salisbury's World: Conservative Environments in Late-Victorian Britain* (Cambridge, 2001).

68 John Charmley, *Splendid Isolation? Britain and the Balance of Power 1874–1914* (London, 1999), pp. 397–401.

69 *Ibid.*, p. 400.

70 Anna Gambles, *Protection and Politics: Conservative Economic Discourse 1815–1852* (Woodbridge, 1999).

71 Steele, *Palmerston and Liberalism*, p. 150.

72 *Ibid.*, p. 146.

73 *Ibid.*

74 Keith M. Wilson (ed.), *British Foreign Secretaries and Foreign Policy: From Crimean War to First World War* (Beckenham, 1987); T. G. Otte (ed.), *The Makers of British Foreign Policy from Pitt to Thatcher* (Basingstoke, 2002).

75 Wilson (ed.), *British Foreign Secretaries*, p. 18.

76 Nick Carter, 'Sir James Hudson, British Diplomacy and the Italian Question, February 1858 to June 1861' (Ph.D thesis, University of Wales, Cardiff, 1994); 'England and the Building of the Italian Nation, 1848–61', in Paul Cooke, David Sadler and Nicholas Zurbrugg (eds), *Locating Identity: Essays on Nation, Community and the Self* (De Montfort University, Leicester, 1996); 'Hudson, Malmesbury and Cavour: British Diplomacy and the Italian Question, February 1858 to June 1859', *Historical Journal* (hereafter *HJ*), 40 (1997); 'Administering the Constitutional Pill: Britain, Italy and the Italian Policy of Lord Malmesbury', in Robert Stradling, Scott Newton and David Bates (eds), *Conflict and Coexistence: Nationalism and Democracy in Modern Europe: Essays in honour of Harry Hearder* (Cardiff, 1997).

77 P. R. Ghosh, 'Disraelian Conservatism: A Financial Approach', *EHR*, 99 (1984), pp. 268–96.

78 See, e.g., Paul Smith, 'Disraeli's Politics', *Transactions of the Royal*

Historical Society (hereafter *TRHS*), Fifth Series, 37 (1987), pp. 65–85; John Vincent, *Disraeli* (London, 1990); Paul Smith, *Disraeli* (London, 1996); Edgar Feuchtwanger, *Disraeli* (London, 2000).

79 Ann Pottinger Saab, 'Foreign Affairs and New Tories: Disraeli, the *Press*, and the Crimean War', *International History Review* (hereafter *IHR*), 19 (1997), pp. 286–311.
80 J. P. Parry, 'Disraeli and England', *HJ*, 43 (2000), p. 720.
81 J. P. Parry, 'The Impact of Napoleon III on British Politics, 1851–1880', *TRHS*, Sixth Series, 11 (2001).
82 Gurowich, 'Party and Independence', p. 261.
83 Hawkins, *Parliament, Party*, p. 7.
84 Lords, 1 March 1858, *Hansard's Parliamentary Debates*, Third Series (hereafter *Hansard*), 149, col. 29.
85 Steele, *Palmerston and Liberalism*, p. 148.
86 Edmund Burke, *Reflections on the Revolution in France* (1790), 1968 edition, p. 373.
87 Gambles, *Protection and Politics*, p. 232.
88 Britain and France were formally at war with Russia from March 1854, although Turkey had been fighting Russia since October 1853.
89 Bentley, *Lord Salisbury's World*, p. 3.
90 Paul Kennedy, *The Realities Behind Diplomacy: Background Influences on British External Policy, 1865–1980* (London, 1981), p. 51.
91 Malmesbury, *Memoirs*, 2, pp. 188–9.
92 Anon., review of 'Lord Malmesbury's Memoirs', p. 8.
93 G. Kitson Clark, *The Making of Victorian England* (London, 1962), 1965 edition, p. 208.

2

Conservative perspectives

Tho' nobody talks of foreign affairs, I hear, among the initiated, that there are odd whispers, & the general state of things is anything but satisfactory. (Disraeli to Lady Londonderry, 30 December 1849)

On the formation of the fourteenth Earl of Derby's first Government, in February 1852, Lord Aberdeen – the previous Conservative Foreign Secretary – observed that British politicians had been 'so much occupied of late, with domestic affairs, that European questions have received little attention'.[1] Given the European upheavals of late 1851, this was not a terribly accurate assessment of the immediate past, but to some extent it was true of the years before. After the dramatic Conservative split over the repeal of the Corn Laws in 1846, party politics had been dominated by domestic questions. Despite the convulsions of continental revolution in 1848–49, the recurrent themes of political debate were provided by matters closer to home. A great deal of political energy was generated by the Russell Government's continued pursuit of free trade and by periodic bursts of anti-popery. Both Protectionist and Peelite Conservatives were focused on the consequences of a party schism that few imagined would be permanent. When foreign policy did attract attention, it was therefore inseparable from domestic considerations, as would be the case throughout the mid-Victorian period.

It had swiftly become clear in 1846 that the only credible candidate for the leadership of the Protectionist Conservatives was their most experienced spokesman, Edward Stanley – the heir to the earldom of Derby – who sat in the Lords as Stanley of Bickerstaffe. A former Whig, he had served in Grey's Cabinet before transferring his allegiance to the Conservatives, later serving for four years in Peel's Cabinet. It was a less straightforward matter to resolve the question of the party leadership in the Commons after the resignation of Lord George Bentinck in December 1847. Disraeli's rhetorical destruction of Peel had made him a formidable reputation, but also many Conservative enemies; the leadership passed formally to him only in 1849, and initially as one of a nominal triumvirate.

From 1846, with the Peelites propping up Russell's Whig administration, the Protectionist Party became the most numerous force regularly opposing the Government; Stanley became, *de facto*, leader of the opposition. Throughout the period from 1846 until 1852, Stanley's preoccupations were twofold. Firstly, he sought to maintain the party that had been spawned by the schism as a coherent organisation, and to provide it with parliamentary opportunities. Such opportunities were essential if the country was to have an effective parliamentary opposition (a duty taken very seriously by Stanley), and if the damaged morale of his own troops was to be boosted. Secondly, he sought to foster the conditions for Conservative reunion, even if that was only likely in the medium term. Foreign policy had a part to play in the pursuit of both objectives.

Stanley was bleakly realistic about the chances of establishing any viable alternative government all the time the Conservatives remained divided, and given the more extreme views of some of the country gentlemen into whose company he was forced.[2] In June 1847, when John Wilson Croker of the Conservative *Quarterly Review* enquired of Stanley what line he should take, the Protectionist leader was pessimistic: 'Not only is there no subject at this moment prominently occupying the public mind, but there seems to be a general confusion of parties, persons, & principles'.[3] He bemoaned the fact that he found himself 'in the position of watching, rather than opposing a govt. which I cannot trust, yet aware that on some points on which they are most likely to be attacked by those with whom I am acting ... I am unable to go the lengths of my supporters'.[4]

The difficulties of providing effective opposition could not be quickly overcome. Over a year later, praising a speech by Disraeli, Stanley noted that only one section left him uneasy: his lieutenant had 'reproached the Government with continuing to hold office'.[5] Stanley was bemused: 'as nobody else seems ready to take it, I do not see how they can well help themselves, though it is melancholy to see so weak a Govt. able to hold their places merely for want of a combined Opposition'.[6] In the wake of confusion over the leadership of the party in the Commons, by the end of 1848 he was even contemplating 'the increasing danger of its crumbling to pieces'.[7] He could only hope to maintain a Protectionist profile in Parliament by concentrating the party's limited firepower on issues of particular significance, and trying to generate debate on questions that might unite the two Conservative factions.

Throughout the mid-Victorian era, foreign policy had an important part to play in Conservative strategy. It was, for most of the period, directly or indirectly the responsibility of Palmerston, who conducted policy in an increasingly controversial manner. It was thus often an ideal target for opposition assaults. Debate about foreign affairs centred around Palmerston's policies and rhetoric, and would do so almost uninterruptedly until his death. Between 1846 and 1852, his policies provided regular opportunities for opponents of various political hues. In December 1848, when the Duke of Newcastle requested Stanley's assistance in obtaining a position for his son through the Foreign Office (FO), the Protectionist leader's response was instructive. He politely refused, noting that 'if there is one Member of the Govt. rather than another, to whom I ought not to place myself under obligation, it is L[or]d Palmerston, whose policy I have so often had occasion to attack, & who seems determined that I should not want an opportunity for doing so again as soon as Parliament meets'.[8] The Protectionists perceived the value of an opponent who was frequently presenting them with parliamentary ammunition.

Palmerston's foreign policy was significant for another reason: because of its apparently liberal characteristics, it also provided opportunities for potential Conservative reunion. It was by no means always clear that Palmerston was irrevocably wedded to the Whigs; nevertheless, it was his foreign policy that produced some of the clearest party divisions on the pre-1846 model. It is a commonplace that governments use foreign policy to unite their supporters and to distract attention from disagreements over contentious domestic issues; the same is true, *mutatis mutandis*, of the Protectionist opposition. As Stanley reminded another of his Commons lieutenants, the Marquess of Granby, in January 1849, his constant concern and refrain was that the Peelites 'should be dealt with as tenderly as possible, and, if at all practicable, induced to rejoin us'.[9] Foreign policy offered a promising road back to Conservative harmony.

As time would demonstrate, nothing was more likely to unite Conservatives than an attack on the liberal assumptions apparently underlying Palmerston's conduct. Foreign policy was also untainted by the disputes over economic questions that otherwise divided the Protectionists from the Peelites. The attacks on Palmerston did not produce an immediate success, but in 1850 the tactic would deliver a significant blow to the Government in the Lords. While the hope of Conservative reunion would diminish with the passing years, foreign policy would continue to provide opportunities for the Conservatives to unite the disparate elements in opposition politics. Time and again, it would prove the most fruitful area to exploit. But foreign policy was not merely a debating tool. It also had a utility because it produced genuine divisions between the Conservatives and their leading opponents. These divisions have been obscured by a historiography that has either overlooked the Conservative contribution or assumed a foreign policy consensus among the major parties, with serious dissent provided by the radicals.

That is not to say that all in the Conservative leadership during this period were regularly devoting time to the subject. Disraeli did not exaggerate much when he noted in December 1849 that 'nobody talks of foreign affairs'.[10] During this period, his own involvement in debate about foreign affairs was limited. His correspondence on the question was minimal. For example, his surviving letters from 1847 (published in the invaluable and comprehensive *Disraeli Letters*) yield barely a word about foreign policy. While the revolutionary period provoked more Disraelian comment, it consisted largely of brief, semi-romantic reflection; more the notes of a novelist than a coherent analysis of policy. On 1 May 1848, for example, in the wake of revolution, he asked Lady Londonderry if she had 'yet recovered the great catastrophe? Its cause is inexplicable, its consequences an alarming mystery. No judgement & no imagination can fathom its probable results'.[11] To the same correspondent, the following year, he admitted: 'I know nothing of foreign affairs, & never read the rival bulletins in the newspapers'.[12]

After the revolutions of 1848, Disraeli did take the opportunity to dabble in the politics of the exiled conservative statesmen, notably through meetings with Guizot and Metternich. He even asked Metternich's advice about British politics, a request which, ironically – as Muriel Chamberlain has described – was passed on to the Peelite Aberdeen for comment before Metternich replied.[13] Disraeli's contacts with the exiles may, in the short term, have influenced some of his parliamentary contributions; they certainly provided him with a new supply of the gossip in which he loved to indulge.[14] It must be doubted whether those contacts had any greater significance.

It is far from a straightforward exercise to analyse Disraeli's position on foreign policy in the 1840s and early 1850s, not least because – as Brown has recounted – he also conducted a strange political flirtation with the Foreign Secretary.[15] John Vincent has described the curious way in which, in 1845, Disraeli had acted as Palmerston's secret envoy in Paris.[16] The spirit of this cross-party relationship, though probably not its more controversial substance, survived into the late 1840s and early 1850s. In January 1849, Stanley heard a 'story' about Disraeli's 'coquetting with Palmerston', and grimly observed that if there was any substantive proof of 'overtures, direct or indirect', then Disraeli was 'not fit' for the Commons leadership.[17] No such proof landed on Stanley's desk, but there is no question that Disraeli was, for some time, deliberately restrained in his criticism of Palmerston.[18] It seems probable that Disraeli saw little point in antagonising him, given their good personal relations, Palmerston's popularity and the potential for a future Palmerstonian union with the Protectionists. Whatever the reason, Brown has suggested that, as a result of Disraeli's ambivalence, Palmerston's foreign policy 'tended to find a favourable reception across the floor of the House of Commons'.[19] This would be particularly noticeable in Disraeli's contribution to the Don Pacifico debate in 1850. As a body, however, the Protectionists were by no means necessarily well-disposed to Palmerston.

One of Disraeli's colleagues (and a rather closer ally of Stanley) certainly had little time for Palmerston's policies. Though he too has been overlooked by a historiography focused on the more colourful Commons leader, Malmesbury had a long-term interest in foreign policy. He had acted as Protectionist Whip in the Lords since 1846, and was being considered in hypothetical Conservative Cabinets by the early 1850s.[20] Given that it was assumed that some Peelite Conservatives might ultimately join with the Protectionists in government, he was some way down the pecking order. In foreign policy terms, however, Malmesbury had a significance which marked him out from his colleagues. He had been a friend of Louis Napoleon Bonaparte since 1829, when the 22-year-old English aristocrat (then Lord Fitzharris) had been undertaking the nineteenth-century equivalent of the 'grand tour'.

While travelling, Malmesbury had made a number of interesting acquaintances. In Rome, he made 'great friends' with Byron's bereft lover, the young and beautiful Countess Guiccioli.[21] According to the fifteenth Earl of Derby's later recollection, Malmesbury throughout his life 'courted women, respectable and disrespectable: succeeded in the pursuit: and was somewhat promiscuous in his love affairs'.[22] His success with the Countess led him to what would become an even more significant relationship, if of a rather different kind. Through her he had met Hortense, the former Queen of Holland, and her son Louis Napoleon, a few months Malmesbury's junior. Malmesbury kept in regular touch with the young Bonaparte, even visiting him during his imprisonment by King Louis Philippe's regime. Malmesbury maintained this contact throughout the Conservatives' years in opposition.

Malmesbury had a broader interest in foreign affairs. In 1837, he had publicly demonstrated that interest, and his opposition to Palmerston, by publishing a pamphlet attacking Whig policy in Spain.[23] The Whigs had been actively supporting the constitutionalist regimes of the two young Queens of Portugal and Spain.[24] Palmerston had co-ordinated both political and material assistance in the struggle against the absolutist pretenders Dom Miguel in Portugal and Don Carlos in Spain. Malmesbury had been stung into publishing by Lord Carnarvon's pamphlet, in which he had supported Whig policy and called for more British action against the Carlists in Spain. Malmesbury had condemned the 'deep immorality of England's active interference in this struggle'.[25] In his view, whatever the injustices of Spain's internal politics, 'this question *regards Spain and not England*'.[26] Such remarks foreshadowed his stance as Foreign Secretary, as well as aligning him firmly with the non-interventionist wing of British politics, a position from which he never wavered.

In 1847, Protectionist condemnation of another Palmerstonian intervention in Iberian affairs demonstrated the way in which foreign policy could provide opportunities to attack the Government. In the midst of civil disorder in Portugal, Palmerston's mediation – in order to support Queen Maria and provide stability –presented the Protectionists with a chance. In June 1847, in both the Commons and the Lords, they assaulted Palmerston's policy.[27] Given the imminence of the first general election since the repeal of the Corn Laws, Stanley recognised the importance of meeting the party's desire 'to bring forward an important motion'.[28] Palmerston's area of responsibility provided the opportunity, as it frequently would over the next decade; it did so again when British dabbling in Spanish affairs in 1848 prompted the expulsion of Britain's representative in Madrid. While the party mounted a sustained assault in the Commons over the question of Portugal, however, Stanley was infuriated by the lack of support from his colleagues in the upper house.[29] No matter how useful the opportunity, it demonstrated the profound difficulty in motivating the Protectionists to speak, particularly on a subject outside their normal area of expertise. On the Peelite side, Aberdeen was 'well pleased to have been absent'.[30] Though he shared Stanley's views about the danger of foreign entanglements, he viewed the partisan debate with distaste.

British interventions in the Iberian peninsula were not much more than sideshows compared with the continental upheavals of 1848. Revolution in France was followed by disorder in the Austrian-dominated Italian and German states, and across the Continent. Nationalists, republicans and opportunists – chief among whom was

Charles Albert of Piedmont–Sardinia – took advantage of the disorder to advance their own causes. One important consequence of the 1848 revolutions was that, for conservatives, they emphasised common concerns. Aberdeen, for example, had for some time feared the 'rapid progress of the democratick [sic] spirit throughout Europe'; Stanley shared that fear, viewing the danger of the 'Republican spirit abroad in this country' as sufficient reason to withhold recognition from the French Second Republic.[31] Foreign affairs threw domestic questions into sharp relief. In the period immediately after 1848, the Conservatives increasingly saw British politics in a broader continental context.

While a Protectionist reunion with Peel himself was out of the question, the more amenable Aberdeen was a different matter, and, given his seniority among the Peelites, he was potentially a valuable ally. The late 1840s and early 1850s saw a thawing of the Protectionist relationship with Aberdeen, in which foreign policy played no small part. He was outraged by what he regarded as Palmerston's tacit approval of 'injustice and spoliation' in Italy.[32] Radicals in Britain had initially been jubilant at concessions by the hated King of Naples and Sicily, the overthrow of papal government in Rome and Piedmont's advancement at the expense of Austria. Palmerston did little to hide his sympathies with the Italians, particularly in Sicily and Piedmont, and he and the British Court became embroiled in an increasingly acrimonious dispute about policy.[33] For the most part, however, until a foolish slip over the supply of armaments to Sicilian rebels, he avoided presenting his parliamentary enemies with many opportunities for direct attack. But in early 1849, Conservatives were able to launch two separate debates, on Sicily and on Italian affairs in general. In sharp contrast to his lofty disdain over Portugal in 1847, Aberdeen supported Stanley by speaking up in the debate about Sicily in March 1849.[34] Three weeks later, Stanley duly returned the favour during the debate in which Aberdeen led the attack on Palmerston.[35] Foreign policy was increasingly the focus for Conservative efforts.

The revolution in France gave a new significance to Malmesbury's relationship with his old friend 'Louis'. At the end of 1848, Bonaparte was elected as President of the Second Republic, and Malmesbury seems thereafter to have acted as an unofficial Conservative envoy to the regime. The significance of this relationship would take some time to manifest itself even to Stanley. For the historian seeking to contextualise Conservative foreign policy, however, Malmesbury's communications with Louis Napoleon and his early thoughts on Anglo-French relations are significant.

Malmesbury's *Memoirs* records visits to France in 1849 and 1850.[36] On both occasions, apparently, he discussed European affairs with Louis Napoleon. As Malmesbury recorded for Stanley's benefit, probably on the 1850 visit, in 'a long talk together', the French President discussed 'the probable foreign policy of England towards France if *you* [Stanley] came into office, an event which he seemed to consider sooner or later inevitable'.[37] Malmesbury outlined to the French leader what he considered to be the Conservative view of Anglo-French relations. Though two months later Stanley would still list Aberdeen as his first choice for Foreign Secretary, and it would be two years before Malmesbury's name would appear instead, such a note from a significant Conservative is an important record.[38]

In contrast, a few months earlier Disraeli had all but dismissed France, which he looked on 'as quite exhausted: insolvent in purse & soul: no republic can restore it, for there is no plunder left to support a Republic'.[39] With his usual hyperbole, he had even lamented: 'France is finished. What a mournful fate to be born in the decline & fall of g[rea]t countries'.[40] Disraeli's views tell us little about France and much about his tendency to over-dramatise. France was, of course, very far from 'finished'. Louis Napoleon, as Malmesbury recognised and reported, had grand plans for his country; if the Conservatives were serious about forming a future government with a sustainable foreign policy, they needed to understand him and engage with him.

The conversation Malmesbury recorded for Stanley ranged across the President's and his own views on foreign affairs. In discussion with Louis Napoleon, Malmesbury had dwelt on the primary importance Stanley attached to Anglo-French relations: 'nobody more than yourself', he had suggested, 'valued the continued friendship of France'.[41] He stressed that the Conservatives were neutral in French domestic and constitutional questions: 'you [Stanley] and your Party ... thought it entirely a *French* question about which we never could meddle, & ... he [Louis Napoleon] might be sure that it never would enter your head to thwart any of his domestic or dynastical policy'.[42] Louis Napoleon had apparently believed, until Malmesbury disabused him, that '*you* & *Aberdeen* would pick a quarrel with him'.[43] Malmesbury assured the French leader that 'you had expressed to me your approbation of the good sense & courage he [Bonaparte] had shewn in his very difficult position'.[44]

The President had then outlined his view of the Vienna settlement. He had thought it was 'most important to modify' the 1815 treaties and '*reconstruct* the European System *before* a war takes place, & this should be done by a European Congress'.[45] He reportedly declared that 'France and England could *remodel* everything'.[46] He asked Malmesbury which side England would take if an anticipated Austro-Prussian war broke out. Malmesbury's prophetic response was that his 'private opinion' was 'that England would not care a d—n about it, until the interference of others might force her to execute the contracts of 1815'.[47] As far as any new Congress was concerned, his non-committal reply was that he thought England would not object 'if any good might be produced'.[48] In Malmesbury's opinion, the President 'leans to join Prussia versus Austria', and he claimed that if victorious in such a scenario Prussia would 'give up some Rhenish ground to France as the price of her services, & compensate herself with some German rubbishy states [sic]'.[49] He also noted the President's new antipathy to Russia, which was 'remarkable, because he used to be *very Russian*'.[50]

This letter was one to which Malmesbury clearly attached some importance. In January 1852, he recalled Derby's attention to it. With studied modesty, he reminded the Conservative leader: 'I do not suppose you have kept a long letter I remember writing to you from Paris 2 or 3 years ago with an acc[oun]t of the President's views on foreign policy. If you have by chance done so it would give some idea of his probable movements'.[51] It seems extremely likely that this was the letter to which he referred. The views expressed in it offer some insights into the development of Conservative policy.

Preparing and nurturing a Protectionist–Bonapartist (and therefore Anglo-French) *entente* was a significant part of Malmesbury's strategy from this early point. Malmesbury's visits to France in 1849 and 1850 were personal ones and (so far as we know) not missions on behalf of Stanley. A link with France, however, was being forged and maintained by a senior Conservative regarded by Louis Napoleon as a credible spokesman for the party leader. Malmesbury had made the important point to Louis Napoleon that Stanley was pro-French and not opposed to the President. This was significant in itself for a party seriously planning for government; it has echoes today in the links built up by British opposition parties with American administrations.

This was, however, a very personal version of the Anglo-French *entente* that had marked Conservative foreign policy between 1841 and 1846, under Aberdeen.[52] Given Malmesbury's long friendship with Napoleon and its almost adolescent roots, it was even closer than the Aberdeen–Guizot relationship. Anglo-French amity was Malmesbury's particular project, in the importance of which he fervently believed, not merely as a necessity of *realpolitik*. On the fall of the 1852 Government he regarded good Anglo-French relations – fostered despite the declaration of the Second Empire – as his proudest achievement. He would come to resent bitterly the way in which he believed that achievement to have been squandered by the Aberdeen coalition during 1853.[53]

Malmesbury's visits also indicate how Conservative views of the French leader's plans were beginning to develop. In 1852, Disraeli would acknowledge to his colleague 'yr. acumen & knowledge of circumstances and persons' in France.[54] As a result of Malmesbury's relationship with Louis Napoleon, and insights he could consequently offer, senior Conservatives had as clear an idea of French intentions as any in British politics. Malmesbury was under no illusion as to the nature of Napoleonic ambitions. After the coup in 1851, he would explain to Derby: 'I think it very likely that the President will, when once settled, try to have a European congress to remodel the treaties of 1815. That *was* always his hobby and a rather dangerous one'.[55] Via Malmesbury, the key Conservative foreign policy-makers were well acquainted with French aspirations and policies.

Malmesbury emphasised the fact that Britain's adherence to the Vienna settlement was the commitment which defined his position. Otherwise, in his view, Britain would avoid military involvement in continental affairs. Throughout the 1850s, the Vienna settlement would be at the centre of Malmesbury's worldview. His comments about only 'the interference of others' forcing Britain 'to execute the contracts of 1815' put him firmly in the tradition of Castlereagh,[56] who had been determined to avoid 'unnecessary Interference of the Government in events passing abroad'.[57] He had thought that the only time for British action was 'when actual danger menaces the System of Europe'.[58] Malmesbury's management of foreign policy would reflect the same assumption.

Stanley recognised the value of Malmesbury's French contacts in 1851 when, during his first ill-fated attempt to form a government, he seems to have considered Malmesbury for the Paris Embassy. Viscount Canning, alluding mischievously to Malmesbury's abilities with *les femmes*, related how he had seen 'a Protectionist Govt on paper ... in which you were put down for Paris. –How w[oul]d that suit? It was on the strength of your intimacy with L. Napoleon. and a general impression that you are not averse to Parisian habits'.[59] Whatever Malmesbury's personal habits, his work on Anglo-French relations and his views on policy would be of still greater significance once Louis Napoleon's *coup* effectively made him *l'inévitable* for the FO.

In the months after Malmesbury wrote his letter to Stanley, however, opposition to the Russell Government was not focused on Anglo-French relations. It was Palmerston's intervention in Greece that presented the Conservatives with one of their best opportunities to attack the Government.

Notes

1 British Library, London (hereafter BL), Aberdeen Papers, Additional Manuscripts (hereafter Add. MSS) 43055, fo. 258, Aberdeen to Princess Lieven, 3 March 1852.
2 For a detailed discussion of the party's internal difficulties in the period 1846–50, see, e.g., Stewart, *Foundation of the Conservative Party*, pp. 222–45.
3 Liverpool Record Office, Derby Papers, 920 DER (14) 177/2, fo. 76, Stanley to Croker, 7 June 1847.
4 *Ibid.*, fos 76–7.
5 Derby Papers, 920 DER (14) 178/1, fo. 49, copy, Stanley to Beresford, 2 September 1848.
6 *Ibid.*
7 *Ibid.*, fo. 64, copy, Stanley to Herries, 21 December 1848.
8 *Ibid.*, fos 82–3, copy, Stanley to Newcastle, 18 October 1848.
9 *Ibid.*, fo. 198, copy, Stanley to Granby, 7 January 1849.
10 *Benjamin Disraeli Letters* (hereafter *DL*), vol. 5, ed. M. G. Wiebe, J. B. Conacher, John Matthews and Mary S. Millar (Toronto, 1993), 1947, Disraeli to Lady Londonderry, 30 December 1849.
11 *Ibid.*, 1643, Disraeli to Lady Londonderry, 1 May 1848.
12 *Ibid.*, 1869, Disraeli to Lady Londonderry, 21 August 1849.
13 Muriel Chamberlain, *Lord Aberdeen: A Political Biography* (Harlow, 1983), p. 394.
14 See Monypenny and Buckle, *Disraeli*, vol. 3, pp. 168–95.
15 Brown, *Politics of Foreign Policy*, pp. 83–7.
16 Vincent, *Disraeli*, p. 4.
17 Derby Papers, 920 DER (14) 178/1, fo. 232, copy, Stanley to Beresford, 23 January 1849.
18 See e.g., *DL*, vol. 5, 1664, Disraeli to Ponsonby, 9 July 1848.
19 Brown, *Politics of Foreign Policy*, p. 84.
20 See, e.g., the diary of Edward Stanley, later the fifteenth Earl of Derby, in *DDCP*, 25 June 1850, p. 22. For an account of Malmesbury's role as the senior Protectionist Whip, see John Hogan, 'Party Management in the House of Lords 1846–1865', *PH*, 10 (1991), pp. 129–30.
21 Malmesbury, *Memoirs*, vol. 1, p. 27.
22 *The Diaries of Edward Henry Stanley*, 18 May 1889, pp. 845–6.
23 BL, Tracts, 2163, 'A nobleman' (Lord Fitzharris), *A reply to the pamphlet entitled 'The Policy of England towards Spain'* (1837).
24 For party differences over the Iberian peninsula, see e.g. Roger Bullen,

'Party Politics and Foreign Policy: Whigs, Tories and Iberian Affairs, 1830–6', *BIHR*, 51 (1978), pp. 37–59; Roger Bullen, 'The Great Powers and the Iberian Peninsula, 1815–48', in Alan Sked (ed.), *Europe's Balance of Power 1815–1848* (New York, 1979), pp. 54–78.
25 'A nobleman' (Lord Fitzharris), *A reply to the pamphlet*, p. 5.
26 *Ibid.*, p. 10.
27 For Stanley's speech, see Lords, 15 June 1847, *Hansard*, 93, cols 542–70.
28 Derby Papers, 920 DER (14) 177/2, fo. 83, copy, Stanley to Ellenborough, 16 June 1847.
29 *Ibid.*, fos 82–3.
30 BL, Peel Papers, Add. MS 40455, fo. 427, Aberdeen to Peel, 25 June 1847.
31 *Ibid.*, fo. 444, Aberdeen to Peel, 18 September 1847; Derby Papers, 920 DER (14) 177/2, fo. 319, copy, Stanley to Newcastle, 2 March 1848.
32 Peel Papers, Add. MS 40455, fo. 456, Aberdeen to Peel, 2 November 1848.
33 See Brian Connell, *Regina v. Palmerston: The Correspondence between Queen Victoria and Her Foreign and Prime Minister* (London, 1962), pp. 67–98.
34 Lords, 6 March 1849, *Hansard*, 103, cols 235–41.
35 Lords, 22 March 1849, *Hansard*, 103, cols 1086–103 and 1108–9.
36 Malmesbury, *Memoirs*, vol. 1, pp. 243–5 (1849); pp. 258–60 (1850).
37 Derby Papers, 920 DER (14) 144/1, Malmesbury to Stanley, 2 April 1850.
38 *DDCP*, 25 June 1850, p. 22.
39 *DL*, vol. 5, 1947, Disraeli to Lady Londonderry, 30 December 1849.
40 *Ibid.*, 1951, Disraeli to Count d'Orsay, 1 January 1850.
41 Derby Papers, 920 DER (14) 144/1, Malmesbury to Stanley, 2 April 1850.
42 *Ibid.*
43 *Ibid.*
44 *Ibid.*
45 *Ibid.*
46 *Ibid.*
47 *Ibid.*
48 *Ibid.*
49 *Ibid.*
50 *Ibid.*
51 *Ibid.*, Malmesbury to Derby, 5 January 1852.
52 For Aberdeen's policies while Foreign Secretary under Peel, see: Bourne, *Foreign Policy*, pp. 47–56; Roger Bullen, *Palmerston, Guizot and the Collapse of the Entente Cordiale* (London, 1974), pp. 25–50; Chamberlain, *Aberdeen*, pp. 297–388; Paul W. Schroeder, *The Transformation of European Politics* (Oxford, 1994), pp. 765–71.
53 See e.g., Bodleian Library, Oxford, Hughenden Papers, Dep. Hughenden 99/1, Malmesbury to Disraeli, 12 February 1853, fos 92–3; see also below, pp. 143–5.

54 Hampshire Record Office, Winchester, Malmesbury Papers, 9M73/457/1, Disraeli to Malmesbury, 2 January 1852.
55 Derby Papers, 920 DER (14) 144/1, Malmesbury to Derby, 27 December 1851.
56 *Ibid.*, Malmesbury to Stanley, 2 April 1850.
57 State Paper, 5 May 1820, reproduced in Temperley and Penson (eds), *Foundations*, pp. 48–63.
58 *Ibid.*
59 Malmesbury Papers, 9M73/456/2, Canning to Malmesbury, 24 February 1851.

3

Prelude to power, 1850–52[1]

[H]is hon. and learned Friend ... had distinctly called upon the House by his proposed resolution to choose deliberately and advisedly between two courses of policy ... the policy which he [Sir F. Thesiger] should call the policy of order against the policy of change. (Sir Frederic Thesiger, House of Commons, 24 June 1850)

The eighteen months before Derby formed his first Government were eventful ones. The period revealed much about Protectionist opinion and strategy; it also illuminated the preconceptions the party would bring to government in February 1852. The parliamentary furore over the Don Pacifico affair, in June 1850, provided an opportunity for a wide range of Conservatives to air their views on foreign policy. The Protectionist contribution has long been neglected. The debate, and its place in Protectionist strategy, illustrated both the nature and the political significance of Conservative opposition to Whig foreign policy. It also starkly exposed the extent to which Palmerston and responses to him defined party positions. The following year, the political atmosphere throughout Europe became increasingly febrile, while Russell's Government teetered from crisis to crisis. Conservatives everywhere fretted about the maintenance of stability, and, in December 1851, Louis Napoleon took the opportunity to supplant the institutions of the Second Republic in a *coup d'état*. The Protectionists' response to developments in 1851 revealed much about their perceptions both of foreign policy and of the Whig Government's apparent inadequacies.

Throughout this period, domestic concerns interacted with and helped define Conservative opinion on foreign policy, which played a significant part in a broader critique of Whig misrule – a part that has been underrated. For Protectionists, a dangerous foreign policy under Palmerston, compounded by Russell's ignorance on his Foreign Secretary's departure, mirrored an irresponsible domestic policy. The interventionist threat to European order and the resultant antagonism of other powers was a variant of the threat posed to stability and domestic order by Whig economic policy and parliamentary reform.

The Greek debate

By 1850, Europe seemed calmer than it had been during 1848–49. This was despite uncomfortable exchanges between Britain, on the one hand, and Austria and Russia, on the other, as a result of British protection being accorded to refugees who had fled Austria and Russia after 1848 (protection provided both in Britain itself and by the navy for those who had escaped to Turkey). In 1850, however, a number of longstanding disputes between Britain and Greece precipitated a crisis.

The Anglo-Greek relationship had been deteriorating for some years. One prominent bone of contention concerned the Ionian Islands, over which Britain exercised a protectorate. Greece and Britain had for some time been wrangling over control of two tiny islands close to the Ionian group, Cervi and Sapienza. To this ongoing tension had been added a number of petty disputes.[2] Restitution and apologies had been demanded by Britain for the Greek treatment of certain Ionian subjects and of sailors from a British ship, the *Fantome*. Demands for compensation from the Greek Government had also been made by two men who claimed British nationality. George Finlay, a British historian, was dissatisfied with money he had received for land that had been enclosed in King Otho's palace gardens. Most notoriously, 'Don' David Pacifico, who claimed British citizenship on account of his Gibraltarian origins, had made a number of exaggerated claims for compensation after a Greek mob had ransacked his house in 1847. The whole situation was further complicated by the fact that Britain was constantly manoeuvring for influence in Athens with France and Russia, its fellow-signatories to the 1832 treaty establishing Greek independence.

As a result of the pressing British claims, Palmerston had in 1849 given the Ionian authorities permission to assert British sovereignty over Cervi and Sapienza. Fortunately, perhaps, this had not been acted upon. More dramatically, in November 1849 the Foreign Secretary had ordered a British fleet (in the region protecting the Hungarian refugees in Turkey) to sail for Greece. There, in January 1850, the British minister Thomas Wyse authorised a blockade of Piraeus and other ports. The fleet was to persist with this action until the Greek Government would submit to British compensation claims in respect of Finlay, Pacifico, the *Fantome* and various Ionians.

A number of the other powers objected. Russia, already outraged at what it regarded as Palmerston's encouragement of European revolution in 1848–49, sent a particularly vigorous protest. When the French Government, supported by Russia, then offered to act as mediator, its offer was at first refused. French mediation having been accepted, the blockade lifted and an agreement brokered, Palmerston delayed dispatch of the news to his minister in Greece, which meant that the international compromise was superseded by a more punitive settlement obtained in the interim by Wyse, following his re-imposition of the blockade. France was offended and its ambassador withdrawn from London in protest at the apparent snub to French efforts. Palmerston had allowed a minor dispute with Greece to develop into a full-blown international row. He was obliged to apologise to France and to water down the settlement Wyse had reached.

Once the relevant papers had been presented and Anglo-French relations patched up, parliamentary criticism of Palmerston's policy in June 1850 delivered him first a blow and then a triumph. Led by Stanley, a broad range of parliamentary forces took the opportunity to condemn the Government's Greek policy in the Lords and its wider foreign policy in the Commons. On 17 June, the Lords voted 169 to 132 in favour of Stanley's motion that Palmerston's policy was 'calculated to endanger the continuance of our friendly relations with other Powers'.[3] But the subsequent four-day Commons debate on a resolution by Roebuck affirming confidence in the *whole* of Palmerston's policy ultimately let the Foreign Secretary off the hook. The Government obtained a victory, by 310 to 264, on 28 June, a triumph that was in part obtained as the result of Palmerston's *tour de force*.

The Foreign Secretary famously declared that 'as the Roman, in days of old, held himself free from indignity, when he could say *Civis Romanus sum*; so also a British subject, in whatever land he may be, shall feel confident that the watchful eye and strong arm of England will protect him against injustice and wrong'.[4] Though his speech made certain of a victory that was always likely, his opponents had been given an opportunity to criticise his current and previous foreign policy in a number of detailed attacks. The debates have attracted interest from scholars analysing Palmerston's policy, and from those examining the radical alternative.[5] The Peelite contributions have also attracted attention.[6] The Protectionist Conservative views have not. Yet, in addition to Stanley himself, almost all the leading Protectionists, and several minor ones, spoke out against Palmerston's policy.

Even allowing for opportunistic rhetoric, the Conservative contribution to the Greek debate was significant. The records of the debate furnish us with a rare and extensive example of front- and back-bench Protectionist opinion on foreign policy. They help demonstrate that there was a Protectionist position on foreign policy, even if it was largely defined at this juncture by what it was not (i.e. Palmerstonian). It also showed that the Protectionists were prepared publicly to oppose the popular Foreign Secretary as part of their campaign to provide an alternative government.

The established interpretation is slightly different. David Brown concurs with Robert Stewart's conclusion that Stanley, focusing primarily on Conservative reunion, did not want the popular Palmerston to be defeated in the Commons.[7] Brown has suggested that, in the Lower House, 'it would have been foolish to attack the most popular man in the country'.[8] As Brown's research has demonstrated, Disraeli was certainly unenthusiastic about attacking Palmerston; his speech was something of a damp squib. Disraeli's ambivalent attitude was not, however, representative of either Stanley or the party. Disraeli disobeyed orders from Stanley, who had stressed the importance of 'hitting hard and not sparing'.[9]

Stanley wanted to do more than merely wound the Foreign Secretary. Aberdeen was in no doubt that 'Stanley is certainly in earnest, and will do his best to break the Government'.[10] Prominent Protectionist MPs like Spencer Walpole, who attacked Palmerston even after his successful *Civis Romanus sum* speech, were more faithful to their leader's intentions than had been Disraeli.[11] Stanley was so hopeful of bringing down the Government that he drafted a possible Conservative Cabinet in which he included both Gladstone and Aberdeen.[12] Once again, foreign policy offered the best option for Conservative unity. Stanley felt that it was 'very desirable that we [Peelites and Protectionists] should act together'.[13] He consulted Aberdeen as to tactics[14] and he shared intelligence with the Peelites.[15] In the debate, senior colleagues such as Walpole and Disraeli made a point of praising Aberdeen's foreign policy.[16] It was assumed that Aberdeen would be Stanley's Foreign Secretary and Gladstone his Colonial Secretary, if the call came.[17] But the Protectionist leader was concerned about more than just relations with the Peelites.

Stanley wanted to ensure that there would be a significant Protectionist contribution to the debate: a genuinely broad Conservative front against Palmerston's foreign policy. Stanley explained to Disraeli that the likelihood of extensive Peelite contributions meant that 'the danger rather seems to be that it should bear *too much* the character of a Peelite debate'.[18] To that end, Stanley was keen that leading Protectionists such as Lord John Manners and

Walpole should speak.[19] He was less sure about the wider party, asking Disraeli: 'Have we any others who would not do us more harm than good?'[20] Sir Robert Inglis's condemnation of Palmerston for neglecting 'the maintenance of the religious interests of Christian truth' may have been exactly the sort of intervention Stanley wished to avoid.[21] Nevertheless, the party's determination to make an extensive contribution provided examples of a wide range of Protectionist opinion on foreign policy.

Protectionist condemnation of Palmerston's policy demonstrated consistent themes and concerns. It included four significant criticisms: of 'interference'; of the problems produced by a foreign policy supposedly based on 'liberal' or 'constitutional' principles; of disruption to the European status quo; and of disregard for international law and treaties.

First and foremost, like the Peelites and radicals, the Protectionists condemned interference in another country's affairs, just as they had in the debates about Portugal and Italy in the late 1840s. Stanley outlined what might be described as the definitive Conservative position: 'In any country the interference of a foreign Government in its internal administration is fatal to its prosperity and independence; it is fatal to its powers of development of its own resources, to its power of confirming its own constitution, to its maintaining the order and authority of its own Government'.[22]

His Commons colleagues followed his lead. Sir Frederick Thesiger felt that Palmerston's 'liberal acts ... with respect to the different Governments of Europe' had been 'likely to embroil us with all nations' and result in 'humiliation'.[23] He added that, during the 1848 upheavals, it must have been difficult for Palmerston to stop himself taking advantage and meddling, given 'the strong desire which the noble Lord had invariably manifested to interfere on every occasion with other nations'.[24] Walpole similarly felt that the principle behind Palmerston's policy was 'to interfere in the internal affairs of foreign countries'.[25] In his view that would lead to 'perpetual confusion and disquietude'.[26] To the Protectionists, the bullying of a weaker nation was particularly repugnant. In Stanley's view, the honour of the British flag was 'prostituted' by 'attacking a weak, unoffending people, interrupting harmless commerce, and plundering wretched, half-pauper fishermen of their sole means of subsistence'.[27] Almost every Conservative contributor expressed distaste for interference, particularly in weaker states.

In the Commons debate, Protectionists repeatedly condemned the notion of a foreign policy based upon the advancement of liberalism and constitutionalism. Roebuck's motion had opened up a wider debate on policy. Roebuck emphasised the role of liberal and constitutional principles in the conduct of foreign affairs. He described Palmerston's policy in glowing terms, suggesting that Britain had maintained peace by 'warning foreign Governments to make ready and proper and opportune concessions to the increasing enlightenment of the people'.[28] Conservatives rose again and again to object to the application of liberal principles in foreign policy. The Marquess of Granby, a veteran Protectionist, called it 'the support of propagandism all over the world',[29] pointing out the dangerous logic of interfering to support types of government of which Britain approved. As Walpole also observed, 'why should not Russia, Austria, France, or America, interfere in a similar manner in other countries to enforce their notions of freedom and government?'[30]

Attacks came from different angles, but all condemned the notion of a 'liberal' foreign policy. For the more extreme country gentlemen, the Foreign Secretary's espousal of liberalism abroad was positively malevolent. Alexander Baillie Cochrane (a Peelite who had moved back into the Derbyite fold) made up in outrage for what he lacked in accuracy. He denounced Palmerston 'for having supported revolutionary doctrines in every country, and for having tampered with the interests of every country'.[31] Sir John Walsh accused him of setting 'popular commotions and revolutions going', only, in the event, to reinforce despotism: 'the noble Lord's interference merely paved the way for Jacobinism and anarchy which eventually led to reaction'.[32] Lord John Manners, too, was dubious about much-vaunted liberal and constitutional principles. He felt it had been hypocritical for the British Government to support 'freedom' in Austrian-ruled Lombardy in 1848 by sympathising with another invasion of the country (by Piedmont-Sardinia).[33] He even suggested that Lombard sympathies were 'with the Emperor of Austria'.[34] Whether Palmerstonian interventions were really 'liberal' or whether liberalism was merely a useful popular justification for Palmerston's policy, Protectionists were equally suspicious.

The third, closely linked, criticism expressed in the Commons centred around the allegation that Palmerston's policy – cloaked in whatever language – connived at the disruption of the established European order. This was particularly significant for a party that feared Whig tampering with Britain's own political structure. In a telling phrase, Thesiger characterised the choice presented by Roebuck's motion as one between two policies: 'the policy which he [Thesiger] should call the policy of order against the policy of change'.[35] Much attention focused on Palmerston's supposed role in the revolutions in Italy in 1848–49. Disraeli attacked Palmerston for, allegedly, encouraging the rebels in Sicily who, in 1848, had offered the Sicilian crown to the Duke of Genoa (the younger son of King Charles Albert of Piedmont–Sardinia). Disraeli accused Palmerston of conduct counter to the accepted diplomatic norms: 'while we were maintaining intimate diplomatic relations' with King Ferdinand of Naples and Sicily, Palmerston was secretly 'entertaining propositions which ... would have deprived him of one of his crowns'.[36]

It is difficult to tell whether this was anything more than manufactured disapproval, given Disraeli's later pragmatism about Louis Napoleon's disruptive Italian policy. Nevertheless, he was clearly tapping into a vein of Conservative opinion on the matter. Walsh felt that Palmerston's dealings with the Sicilians 'were utterly irreconcilable with that character for honesty and plain dealing' which was 'the pride of England'.[37] Inglis felt that 'a great deal more ought to have been said' to King Charles Albert before he had led an army into Lombardy, 'in order to deter him from the unprovoked invasion of the territories of a Sovereign allied to him alike by blood and by treaty'.[38] Where Palmerston appeared to the Protectionists to have given encouragement, they would have preferred him to urge restraint.

Palmerston's alleged failure to abide by either international law or treaties was a particular focus for Conservative criticism. Unsurprisingly for a former Attorney General and future Lord Chancellor, Thesiger attacked Palmerston for disregarding the legal 'code' which regulated 'all civilised nations'.[39] Walsh felt that by contemptuously setting aside foreign (i.e. Greek) justice Britain 'would be violating the maxims of political and Christian morality'.[40] The Government was also criticised for allegedly failing to fulfil its legal obligations in the case of the disputed Ionian Islands. Britain, France and Russia, by the treaty of 1832, jointly guaranteed Greek borders. The contemplated British seizure of disputed territory would have been contrary to that treaty. Stanley alleged that the Government's course, 'by its abstinence from communication with other Powers – by its intrinsic injustice – has been calculated to endanger, and has endangered, the continuance of our friendly relations with other Powers'.[41] Walpole condemned Palmerston for issuing instructions to seize Cervi and Sapienza 'without the consent of France and Russia, the two other guaranteeing Powers'.[42] Manners felt that, if implemented, such orders would have led to war.[43] That view was widely shared. Inglis even suggested there might have been 'first a war with Russia, then with France, and perhaps a general European war'.[44] On the face of it, this was rather melodramatic, but events three years later would demonstrate how Near-Eastern issues could explode into a broader conflict.

The Protectionists were also concerned about Whig and radical distaste for Austria. Few went as far as Manners, who asserted that in Lombardy 'people were satisfied under the wise and paternal Government of Austria. [*Cries of* 'Oh, oh!']'[45] Conservatives were, however, suspicious of the notion that Austrian and British interests were necessarily opposed, as many of Palmerston's supporters believed. For Whigs and radicals, Austria – which, with Russian aid, had crushed rebellion in its dominions – was an opponent of the liberal principles Britain embraced. Roebuck thought British ministers should make it explicitly clear that 'we ... seek by that moral influence that is every day ruling Europe to favour the efforts of men who are rising up to govern themselves'.[46] Russell had pointedly described Palmerston as the 'Minister of England', not of Austria or Russia, to which Granby strongly objected: 'If that meant anything, it indicated that the interests of Russia and Austria were antagonistic to the interests of England. I hope that this is not the case'.[47] Disraeli condemned the Government for what he alleged was the Government's antipathy to Franco-Austrian friendship: 'surely there is no Power with whom we should witness her [France] cherish feelings of political sympathy with less jealousy than with Austria'.[48] The Protectionists saw no reason to discriminate between powers on the basis of their systems of government. In 1852, Malmesbury would accordingly attempt to breathe new life into 'our old Alliances' with the conservative powers.[49]

The Protectionists' criticism of Palmerston, which constituted only one part of the opposition attack, should be differentiated from the criticism by Peelites and Cobdenite radicals that has attracted more attention. While Peelite and Protectionist criticism of Palmerston had much in common, the Peelites were more concerned than their former colleagues about both the development of constitutional government and the iniquities of illiberal regimes on the Continent. Sidney Herbert, for example, spoke of the way in which he had 'long hoped to see constitutional and representative forms of government established in Italy', but Palmerston's foreign policy had endangered that goal.[50] He found it deplorable that revolutionary 'anarchy' in Rome and Sicily had 'only been relieved by the grinding oppression of military despotism'.[51] Few of Stanley's supporters were longing for constitutionalism in Italy. Neither did Austrian military despotism excite great concern on the Protectionist benches. As Malmesbury and

Derby's foreign policy would demonstrate, stability, of the kind enshrined in the Vienna settlement, mattered more to them than political ideals.

The debate also demonstrated that, while Peelite and Protectionist positions superficially converged on foreign policy, such unity was temporary and limited. Sir James Graham, formerly Home Secretary in Peel's administration, prefaced his speech on 24 June by referring to the fact that on the basis of domestic and economic policy – the 'general position of affairs' – he had supported the Whig Government.[52] Nor did he object in principle to intervention in the affairs of other states. He admitted that his part in Whig interventionism on the Iberian peninsula, while serving in Grey's administration, meant that he was not 'over chary with regard to the foreign relations of the country'.[53] His criticism was of the cumulative impact of Palmerston's policies since 1846. He deplored the way in which the Foreign Secretary's lecturing of foreign governments, his meddling in other nations' affairs, and his quarrelling with their rulers had alienated the other great powers. Nevertheless, the preface to Graham's speech revealed where his sympathies lay on domestic questions: he and other Peelites would have been most unwilling to support a Protectionist-led Conservative government.

Among the Peelites, Gladstone's position in particular requires comment. As Shannon has highlighted, he made scathing reference to the way in which Palmerston had provided Russia with an opportunity to criticise Britain.[54] Gladstone suggested that 'gentlemen of liberal politics ... must surely also say ... "If we are to receive public lessons upon our conduct, let us receive them from those who have from infancy drunk the milk and breathed the breath of freedom like ourselves"'.[55] His position, rather like Herbert's with regard to the Hapsburgs in Italy, was predicated on the distinctly liberal assumption that British interests were fundamentally different from those of the autocratic powers. Meanwhile, his reference to 'the moral supports which the general and fixed convictions of mankind afford' and the 'principles of brotherhood among nations' was an early indication of a very different philosophical and moral conception of foreign policy from that advocated by the Protectionists.[56]

Shannon has described the Peelites as 'peculiar custodians of the traditions of the Conservative concert ideal embodied in Aberdeen's policy'.[57] They certainly advocated the kinds of conciliatory policies pursued by Aberdeen when he had been at the FO between 1841 and 1846. But their criticisms of Palmerston were underpinned by a moral constitutionalism of a distinctly liberal hue. The Peelites' journey to a

'Liberal' government would be a long one, but they were already motivated by somewhat different concerns from those that exercised their former colleagues. They were, variously, more proselytising with regard to constitutionalism, more likely to be critical of powers such as Austria and Russia, and far less eager to bring down Russell's administration, of whose economic and domestic policies they generally approved.

The difference between Cobdenite and Protectionist positions was much more pronounced. Though Cobden was cheered from the Tory benches after he attacked Palmerston, it was on the basis that 'my enemy's enemy is my friend'. Cobdenite and Protectionist principles in foreign policy, like their economic instincts, were very different. Cobden believed that the 'the progress of freedom' depended more on 'the spread of commerce' than on 'the labours of cabinets and foreign offices'.[58] While, in general terms, Derby and his followers might well have welcomed the expansion of British commerce, the virtues of free trade – the basis of that commerce – were not likely to be extolled by any Protectionist politicians. Neither were they advocates of the 'no foreign politics' school. It was not the tools, structures and institutions of diplomacy that were decried from the Conservative benches, but the abuse of them. Except insofar as the Foreign Secretary's personal methods were targets, Conservatives did not share Cobden's opinion that 'the system at the Foreign Office is calculated to breed and perpetuate quarrels'.[59]

Conservative leaders would also have hesitated before publicly describing Russia, as Cobden did, as 'a semi-barbarous country'.[60] They recognised that Russia played a critical role in international affairs. They appreciated that Britain, strong at sea but militarily negligible on land, would sometimes need Russian support if it was to achieve its foreign policy objectives. That had been the case in 1841, and would again be the case in 1852, when it looked as if France might be on the point of invading Belgium. The radicals were happy to risk Russian enmity; the Protectionists were not.

Cobden also declared that, in international disputes, governments 'should resort to arbitration'.[61] While mediation (not arbitration, which was a more significant and formal process) had perhaps a greater appeal to Conservatives than to Palmerstonian Whigs, Derby's party did not share this internationalist approach to foreign policy. Radicals such as Molesworth meanwhile assumed that 'constitutional government and democratic institutions are the best forms of government for communities of our race in every part of the globe'.[62] Conservatives, especially ex-Whigs like Stanley, might respect constitutional government, but they had no particular love for democratic institutions.

One individual Protectionist contribution to the debate deserves separate comment. Although using arguments similar to his colleagues', Disraeli adopted a somewhat different position. It was distinctive both because of its ambivalent attitude towards Palmerston – which has been noted by historians – and because he employed a sort of inverted Palmerstonism himself. His attack on Palmerston was in the pattern of his rather strange relationship with the Foreign Secretary over the previous five years, and was generally rather subdued.

In his behaviour over Don Pacifico, Disraeli was the exception rather than the Protectionist rule. He had failed to follow Palmerston with a rhetorical onslaught, as Stanley had originally desired, instead producing at the last minute a speech that pulled several punches.[63] He attempted to engage with Palmerston's disputed policies on the Foreign Secretary's terms. Thus, interference *was* necessary, but in order to defend Britain's fundamental commercial and strategic interests rather than in the dubious pursuit of liberty. For example, he mischievously suggested that treaty obligations meant that Britain should have intervened in Schleswig–Holstein when the German states had annexed the disputed duchies in 1848: 'The right of England to interfere was obvious'.[64] This sort of statement took some of the sting out of his criticism. Brown has suggested that Disraeli's subdued contribution to the Don Pacifico debate was an example of his recognition of pro-Palmerstonian public opinion.[65] This populist instinct may well have been at the root of his slightly unusual rhetorical tack. If so, it was an early symptom of the Disraelian divergence from mainstream Conservative opinion on foreign policy that would become more and more evident throughout the 1850s.

Disraeli's unpredictability, his penchant for intrigue and his dalliance with Palmerston may well have been among the reasons why, when Stanley attempted to form a government upon Russell's brief resignation in February 1851, his chief Commons spokesman was not considered for the FO. Both Aberdeen and Viscount Canning (formerly Aberdeen's Under-Secretary) were offered it and declined. Even the elderly Wellington was considered. According to Gladstone's note of events (corroborated by Malmesbury's account in his *Memoirs*), he too was offered the position.[66] Stratford Canning, the Ambassador at Constantinople, eventually accepted, though even he was not an uncontroversial figure: he had assisted Palmerston in his defiance of Austria and Russia by protecting Hungarian refugees who had fled to Turkey after 1848.

Gladstone noted after his interview with Derby in February 1851 that 'Nothing was said of the leadership of the H. of Commons but his anxiety was evident to me to have any occupant but one for the Foreign Office'.[67] In the light of that note, Blake surmised that Disraeli was the man in question.[68] Whether or not that particular reference was to Disraeli, the latter was clearly not destined for the FO. The younger Stanley noted in his diary that Brunnow, the Russian minister in London, had 'several interviews' with his father during the 1851 ministerial crisis: 'He expressed in his own name and that of the diplomatic body, a strong desire that Lord Stanley should unite the offices of Premier and Foreign Secretary. They feared Disraeli's nomination to the latter post, and Brunnow was privately assured that this was not intended'.[69] In any case, it was clear that economic policy was always going to be the chief policy preoccupation of any incoming Conservative ministry. It must be doubted that Stanley really would have wanted his most able Commons speaker overwhelmed with FO business. If, as has recently been suggested, Disraeli's name was linked with that office, the source is most unlikely to have been Stanley or any influential Protectionist.[70] The Home Office was the job on offer to him.[71]

Nevertheless, if Disraeli was concerned about public perceptions of the Conservatives, it was understandable. There was clearly a strand of broadly 'liberal' opinion that was distinctly uneasy about Conservative principles being employed in foreign policy. Conservative non-interference and a desire for good relations with other powers was easily interpreted as *de facto* support for the domestic status quo in foreign countries, and thus of 'despotism'. The Conservatives were seen as supporters of despotic governments because they were not actively speaking or working against them. During the Greek debate, one MP tempered his criticism of Palmerston because of his concern about the Government's 'probable successors'; Thomas Chisholm Anstey was of the opinion that the Conservatives' first act 'would very probably be the betrayal of the brave Hungarian refugees'.[72] He thought they would 'stifle the cry of liberty in the Italian Peninsula' and 'attempt to check the Hungarians and Poles in their glorious efforts to raise the standard of independence in the land of their birth'.[73]

He was not alone in his views. Neither was suspicion about Tory sympathy for reactionary governments confined to Parliament. One Conservative described how he had seen, in a Charing Cross demonstration, 'the name of the noble Lord [Palmerston] identified with "liberal principles"; and the names of the right hon. Baronet the Member for Ripon [Graham], and the hon. Gentleman the Member for Buckinghamshire [Disraeli], placarded as connected with '"despotism"'.[74] Disraeli had experienced such public demonstrations. He later recalled how the London crowds had reacted to him in June 1850: 'I was ... pelted one afternoon when I was coming down here to express my opinion, and to give an honest vote'.[75]

The Greek debate may even have generated concern about Conservative principles beyond Britain. When Gladstone met with Neapolitan political prisoners, on his trip to the Kingdom of the Two Sicilies in 1850–51, one apparently told him: 'The present Govt. of Naples rely on the English Conservative Party. Consequently we [the Neapolitan prisoners] were all in horror when Lord Stanley last year carried his motion in the H. of Lords'.[76] This account may, of course, have been an exaggerated product of Gladstone's rage against the hated Neapolitan regime; in July 1851 he would publish his first open letter to Aberdeen about its iniquities.[77] True or not, the story echoed widespread unease in Britain. The younger Stanley would later recall that, in 1852, Malmesbury 'was daily spoken of as being in league with Napoleon and Count Buol to establish a despotic system throughout the Continent'.[78]

Such a view of Conservative foreign policy bore little relation to reality, as Stanley went on to observe (and as chapter 4 explores). But the Conservatives certainly did not see the world in the same way as did their opponents. Their 'mental maps' were shaped by rather different priorities and perceptions; their position was determined by more than outrage about Palmerstonian excesses.

'Papal aggression'

The political crisis that blew up in late 1850 and early 1851 as a result of the so-called 'Papal aggression' had little to do with Palmerstonian irresponsibility, though it had foreign roots. It did have some significance in foreign policy terms, however, not least because of the importance later accorded to Anglo-Roman discussions by Conservative ministers in 1852. A papal bull in October 1850 re-established the Roman Catholic episcopal hierarchy in Britain, appointed Cardinal Wiseman as Archbishop of Westminster and restored the Vatican as the direct authority over Roman Catholicism in England. As Saho Matsumoto-Best has described, this was met with public outcry in Britain.[79] The Government hastily drew up an Ecclesiastical Titles Bill, to appease Protestant opinion by restricting the Roman Catholic clergy's ability to hold territorial titles.

Whig relations with the Papacy made some Conservatives particularly uneasy. In the late 1840s, the ultra-Protestant wing of the party had been greatly perturbed by the efforts of the Russell Government to work with the apparently more liberal Pope Pius IX. The Whigs in the Diplomatic Relations (Court of Rome) Act of 1848 had legislated for the potential establishment of diplomatic links with the Vatican. It was the Conservatives' own future Lord Lieutenant of Ireland, Eglinton, who had been responsible for a prohibitive clause in that Act: the 'Eglinton Clause' prevented any priest being sent as an envoy to the Court of St James.[80]

While Stanley always had to consider his more militant Protestant colleagues, for him the 'Papal aggression' was not a serious threat, but an opportunity. Russell's fumbling with the Ecclesiastical Titles Bill, widely regarded as ill-conceived legislation, represented a chance for the Protectionists to exploit the Prime Minister's vulnerability. Stanley noted that diplomacy had again been maladroitly handled, observing to Disraeli that ministers had compounded their problems: 'I cannot help thinking that their difficulty is much increased by their having passed the Act enabling them to establish diplomatic relations with Rome, if they have not ... availed themselves of the power, for the purpose of remonstrating, either before the Act of the Pope, if they were aware of it, or immediately after, if it really took them by surprise'.[81]

The Protectionist leadership was not seriously concerned about the episode, and merely awaited an opportunity to exploit it. Malmesbury suggested that 'we shd follow the stream but not come forward as champions till we see the Govt. and the Catholics well by the ears'.[82] Stanley concurred.[83] The general weakening of Russell's position within his party after the introduction of the bill did, indirectly, help deliver Stanley his opportunity when Russell resigned in February 1851. But by October 1851, the 'Papal aggression' had largely served its purpose for the Protectionists. Derby, as he had become after the death of his father in June 1851, looked forward to discussing something that might 'vary the monotony of the session, and give us something to talk about besides Protection and Popery'.[84] For all the column inches and parliamentary time devoted to it, the 'Papal aggression' was small beer, if potent. More significant events were on the horizon.

Foreign instability and domestic danger

Foreign policy was not merely about political opportunity. The Conservative mindset perceived overseas developments in a broader context, in which European and domestic concerns were intertwined.

The shadow of revolution and disorder was still the backdrop to British politics. Conservatives responded to domestic politics amid wider European tensions; when they responded to foreign affairs they were at least partially focused on domestic radicalism. British sympathy for 'despotic' regimes was limited. Nevertheless, assaults on the continental ruling classes' power base represented an uncomfortable spectacle for the country gentlemen's party. Republicanism overseas was part and parcel of a decline in the power of the aristocratic class that had been the guarantor of domestic and European stability in the decades since the Napoleonic wars.

To Protectionists, Whig policies at home and overseas threatened to contribute to instability. Palmerston's foreign policy was one threat, as Granby noted during the Greek debate: 'It is not so much the immediate result of the noble Lord's policy of which we complain, as the unsettling of the institutions of every State in Europe'.[85] Whig–Peelite economic policy was another manifestation of the same dangerous tampering with the established order. For the Protectionists, the economic liberalism symbolised by repeal of the Corn Laws was the thin end of the republican wedge. It was a Whig–Peelite assault on the landed and agricultural interest, and John Russell's policies were, in Stanley's opinion, set to take Britain 'to the brink of the precipice'.[86] Though less pessimistic than some, he had noted in August 1850 that if a 'Free Trade Government' got a majority at the next election then 'the game is up; and I firmly believe we shall be in rapid progress towards a republic in name as well as in reality'.[87] This was not indicative of a particular fear for the position of the monarch: concerns about the apparent erosion of the landed interest and any resultant loss of political power dominated Conservative minds. This, in turn, affected the way in which they perceived European developments. Their views on foreign policy in the months before they took power cannot be viewed in the abstract.

For Protectionists, autumn and winter 1851 brought particular concerns about the interaction between the British domestic position and European political instability. Prospective parliamentary reform and a visit by the Hungarian rebel leader Louis Kossuth were both regarded with deep suspicion, given the unstable condition of Europe. Russell, despite his colleagues' misgivings, had pledged himself to introduce a measure of reform in the 1852 session. The bill that was drawn up would, if passed, have reduced the property qualifications for the franchise in counties and boroughs, while also redistributing the borough seats.[88] Proposed reductions in the property qualifications troubled most Conservatives and many Whigs, while not going far enough for radicals. A reform bill would have been controversial at the best of times; it seemed all the more so in the unstable condition of Europe.

In the tense political climate, Conservatives were more than usually aware of the dangers of public agitation. Aberdeen, reflecting on Russell's 'unfortunate and mischievous' pledge on reform, feared that Louis Napoleon's activities would help stimulate a British desire for democratic change: 'if the French President should succeed in restoring universal suffrage, the appetite of our people for the franchise may be increased'.[89] Derby was also suspicious about reform, but believed aristocratic self-interest would make the Whigs pause: 'John Russell & the Whigs have as little cause as we have to desire the whole power of the country to be thrown into the hands of the great towns'.[90] Nevertheless, Russell's policies seemed unnecessarily provocative. Disraeli would note in December 1851, given the political drama then unfolding in Paris, that 'for an English Minister to bring in a reform bill, in deference to the clamor [sic] of a very weak movement party, at the present moment is preposterous'.[91]

In late 1851, therefore, there was widespread expectation of political upheaval. When the Hungarian rebel leader Kossuth visited in November, Palmerston – to the delight of radicals – made no secret of his sympathy for him. Though Palmerston had been forbidden by the Cabinet to receive him, on 19 November the Foreign Secretary provocatively met a delegation of radicals instead. They presented him with an address in honour of his support for the Hungarian refugees in Turkey. Malmesbury described the unsettled atmosphere in bleak terms: 'The Ides of March are supposed to be the epoch looked forward to by the 'Rouges' throughout Europe. – You will see that Palmerston is laying himself out for a Radical move. It is remarkable how people of all classes talk of a coming republic as of a matter of course & of no great consequence'.[92] Disraeli recorded particular qualms about Kossuth's visit: 'I view what is going on with apprehension and disgust. He ought never to have been permitted to land, by any government, in the present state of Europe – but in the present state of England, in addition, with a new Reform Bill unnecessarily agitating the public mind, it is really tempting our fate'.[93] This was an uncomfortable time for the Protectionists. Events in France were about to concentrate their minds still further.

On 2 December 1851, Louis Napoleon dispensed with the National Assembly and assumed complete power in a *coup d'état*. Much has been written about the way in which the Queen, Palmerston, Russell and the Whigs responded.[94] Although the Cabinet agreed not to comment on the *coup*, Palmerston privately expressed his approval to the

French ambassador, Count Walewski, on 3 December. Russell asked him to explain why, but to no avail. Reports of Palmerson's indiscretion reached the Queen at Osborne House by way of the French Foreign Minister, the Marquis de Turgot, the British Ambassador at Paris, the Marquess of Normanby, and Normanby's brother, Colonel Charles Phipps (Prince Albert's secretary). On 17 December, spurred on by furious missives from Victoria, Russell finally dismissed his Foreign Secretary.

Exactly why Russell chose to do so at that moment, having for so long tolerated Palmerston's controversial behaviour, was (and remains) a matter for speculation. It seems likely that the indiscretion simply gave Russell the opportunity to do something he had wanted to do for some time. Palmerston was both an irritant and a threat. As A. J. P. Taylor put it, he had for a number of years been 'deliberately playing Russell off the centre of the stage'.[95] The Foreign Secretary's antipathy to reform was also notorious; he was likely to pose the most serious obstacle to Russell's new plans. The Protectionists' reaction to all these developments has been ignored; yet, in government within months, they too would have to deal with the consequences of the changes in France. Their analysis of events tells us much about their perceptions and assumptions.

The Protectionist leadership was of one mind. A misunderstanding of the French President was at the root of the imbroglio: Russell had been panicked by events in France. Malmesbury observed to Derby: 'I can't help feeling that from ignorance of the man, & reasoning merely by analogy from the history of his uncle[,] Johnny took into his head that this revolution meant war to England, & that he made as much haste as he could to recover our old alliances by kicking out Palmerston'.[96] He wrote to Disraeli in a similar vein: 'Johnny urged by Aberdeen[,] Brunnow and [Count] Bruhl [von Martinskirchen, Saxon Minister in London] saw in this coup d Etat [sic] war with France ... He got in a funck [sic] & hastened to secure the good will of Austria and Russia by sacrificing Pam'.[97] Disraeli, too, believed that Russell had 'resolved to dismiss P. at all hazards' because he was 'terrified at the prospect of a war with France with[ou]t allies, & [was] acted on by the foreign ministers & by Aberdeen through the Court'.[98] Derby concurred: 'The account you send of the causes, and the manner, of Palmerston's expulsion tally very much ... with those I have received from other quarters'.[99]

It seemed that Russell was being panicked into a new policy. As H. J. Baillie asked the Commons when Parliament returned:

Prelude to power, 1850–52 55

Was there any Member of the House who doubted what the real grounds were? Was there any one of them who could doubt that, in consequence of the recent changes in France and on the Continent of Europe, the mind of the noble Lord at the head of the Government had at length become convinced that his foreign policy had been a failure, and that ... it would be dangerous to persevere in it.[100]

Disraeli agreed: 'The fact is, the government have entirely changed their foreign policy'.[101] The Protectionists evidently anticipated that the Government, seeing the ranks of continental despotism expanded by the presence of the ruler of Britain's closest, most dangerous neighbour, would rush to the other great powers for comfort and security.

It seems unlikely that the Whigs saw French developments in quite the way the Protectionists thought they did. The instructions sent by the Prime Minister at the end of December to his new Foreign Secretary, Lord Granville, do not particularly suggest Whig 'funck'. Though concerned for the integrity of Belgium, Russell displayed no particular signs of panic: 'The President's assurances are hardly to be trusted, but I think he has no interest in going to war'.[102] His view was shared by senior colleagues such as Granville and the Marquess of Lansdowne, the veteran Whig leader in the Lords. The latter observed to the new Foreign Secretary: 'I am strongly inclined to think with you that it is the President's wish, to keep well with England'.[103] This did not preclude the possibility that Russell had panicked initially. Be that as it may, the Protectionists' commentary was much more revealing about them than it was about the Government.

Malmesbury and his colleagues had fastened on what they perceived to be Russell's misunderstanding about Louis Napoleon. Whether this was an accurate conclusion was neither here nor there. The Prime Minister appeared to the Protectionist leaders to be assuming, wrongly, that the French President was hostile to Britain. The Conservative leaders believed they understood Louis Napoleon and his intentions. In contrast, Whig foreign policy was displaying its usual, dangerous, Palmerstonian traits. It was also ill-informed about the most important foreign policy question: the Anglo-French relationship. On foreign policy, Conservative contempt for Russell's judgement was added to distaste for Palmerston's methods. On the one occasion the Foreign Secretary had acted on an assumption they shared – that Louis Napoleon's inclinations were pacific – Russell had dismissed him.

Underscoring Malmesbury's views in particular was his assumption that he, and by extension the Protectionists, understood the new French regime and could do business with it. As Louis Napoleon's power advanced, Malmesbury's significance in the context of Anglo-

French relations was increasingly evident to his colleagues. In foreign policy matters, the hitherto junior spokesman was gradually moving to Conservative centre-stage. Disraeli made a point of expressing his gratification that Malmesbury had 'sanctioned' his conclusions about Russell's misjudgement.[104] Derby would shortly demonstrate his high opinion of Malmesbury, and the value of Malmesbury's close relationship with Louis Napoleon, by appointing him as Foreign Secretary.

Non-interference was again a Conservative guiding principle. Derby asserted that Bonaparte's actions should be 'acquiesced in' partly because of 'general principles of non-interference with the purely internal affairs of another country'.[105] On the face of it, he did not differ greatly from the Prime Minister. In the House of Commons, Russell justified his dismissal of Palmerston by pointing out the dangers of his ex-Foreign Secretary's interventionism: 'If England were to allow her Foreign Secretary to pronounce an opinion of that kind, it could no longer be said that she had no interference with the internal affairs of France'.[106] But Russell was being disingenuous. He had for nearly six years publicly supported Palmerston's policies and his rhetorical attacks on the morality of foreign governments. As he ostentatiously pointed out, Palmerston was 'a Colleague ... whose abilities I admired, and whose policy I had approved'.[107]

The non-interference apparently advocated by both Russell and Derby stemmed, in reality, from different conceptions of foreign policy. The Whig Cabinet's officially neutral position with regard to the *coup* acknowledged the dangers of pronouncing on the politics of such a close neighbour. But was the Government as uncomfortable about intervention in other states' affairs as Russell implied? It seems unlikely that the Cabinet would have been so ready to jettison Palmerston had such a *coup* taken place in a location more geographically remote from Britain, or had Palmerston condemned dictatorial government rather than approving it, or had he not so often courted controversy by ignoring the Queen and his colleagues. Breaking the rules on non-interference was a useful justification for ejecting Palmerston, but it was not the totem of Whig policy Russell pretended. Derby and the Protectionists, by contrast, had consistently argued for non-interference as a tenet of foreign policy.

The principle of non-interference neatly dovetailed with a desire to restrain the forces of disorder. Derby and Malmesbury thoroughly approved of the way in which the French leader had dealt with political instability. With the tide of revolution stemmed, and no doubt happy to see his friend 'Louis' secure, Malmesbury was positively cock-a-hoop. Like Palmerston, he privately expressed to Louis

Napoleon his approbation and even pleasure. As he explained to Derby, 'I wrote ... to the President about a week ago to wish him joy of having overcome his personal enemies'.[108] He had told Napoleon: 'I happened to know that our city men were unanimous in believing his coup d'état had saved France & Europe from violence still worse and more prolonged'.[109] Russell explained to the Commons that 'it was necessary on our part not to do what we heard that the Austrian and Russian Ministers had done, namely, to go at once and congratulate the President on what he had done'.[110] Malmesbury had no such qualms, though he certainly would not have perceived or defined his letter-writing as 'interference' (there was, in any case, a world of difference between the private act of an opposition peer and that of the Foreign Secretary).

Derby, like Malmesbury, was under no illusions about the necessity of the President's course: 'The promptitude of his measures and the adherence of the army have saved France from a sanguinary civil war, and perhaps for the present suppressed a general European outbreak, which would have followed upon the success of the Reds'.[111] Derby's position, unlike Palmerston's, was entirely consistent with his long-maintained stance on foreign policy. His assessment of French politics was brutal and shorn of Whig references to morality or parliamentary government: 'France and Frenchmen are incapable of rational self-government ... sooner or later they will give themselves a master. I do not think we have anything to do with the morality of the transaction'.[112] In contrast, Whig foreign policy had, as Russell asserted, 'been continually giving the moral support and the moral sympathy of England to constitutional Parliamentary government'.[113]

The leading Protectionists' sanguine reaction to French events did not mean they were content or unsuspicious: the state of France emphasised to them the need for vigilance abroad and at home. While 'heartily' wishing Napoleon 'a continuance of his power', Derby entered the caveat that 'if, for the purpose of conciliating the army, he finds it necessary to adopt a warlike policy, I should look upon him as the most dangerous neighbour we could have'.[114] French events had domestic application. When Parliament reassembled in February 1852, Derby took the opportunity to play on Conservative (and conservative) fears in the wake of events in France.

In a defiantly aristocratic speech, Derby presented foreign revolution and despotism as a salutary warning of what happened when the landowning class were undermined. By examining contemporary British society through the prism of French politics, he managed to imply that both Peelite–Whig economic policy and domestic reform threatened the freedom and wealth of Britain, observing that

> there may be one lesson which we may learn from the state of things in Paris – we may consider for our own advantage how nearly the two extremes of unlimited republicanism and unlimited despotism approach – we may draw from the history of France and the state of other countries, that any country which weakens and destroys the influence, whether in or out of the Legislature, of that great permanent body, the territorial possessors of the land ... of the country gentlemen of England, who are spread throughout the length and breadth of the land ... exercising a conservative influence (not in the sense of party, but of conserving the institutions of the country) each in his own immediate neighbourhood – I say, if you weaken and destroy that body – if you take away the power of that class, which is intimately and indissolubly connected with the soil of the country, you may produce a republic, you may produce a despotism, you may produce a violent oscillation between the extreme of popular frenzy and the extreme of military despotism, but you destroy the possibility of the existence of a limited and constitutional monarchy, and take away the best and only security for the well-regulated liberties of the country.[115]

Radicals saw Protectionist fears and drew their own conclusions. When, within weeks, Derby formed his first government, Clarendon's radical brother Charles Villiers gave his own warning to Disraeli:

> The right hon. Gentleman will probably refer to the present state of Europe in support of his theory of reaction. The people of the Continent made a gallant effort, but a short time since, to obtain their political rights; but now the people are again trampled under foot, and are in a more prostrate condition, comparatively, than they have ever been known to be in the history of the Continent ... The state of Europe should be a warning to the people of England. The people of the Continent are now watching to see whether the people of this country – the last asylum of freedom – would allow their liberties, in like manner, to be filched from them.[116]

For all political factions, the implications of European events for Britain, and Britain's role in European developments, were recurrent concerns and of central importance.

Appointing a Conservative Foreign Secretary: policy imperatives

On 20 February 1852, the debate on the Militia Bill, re-organising British defensive preparations, gave Palmerston the opportunity to get his revenge on Russell. He and some of his supporters voted with the opposition. Russell was defeated, and Derby accepted the commission to form a government. The appointment of a Foreign Secretary was one of the new Prime Minister's most significant duties.

Malmesbury's relationship with Louis Napoleon made Derby's close ally a rather more obvious choice for the FO than some have suggested. Blake rather cruelly observed that he 'seems to have owed his position more to a distinguished diplomatic heredity and the fact that he shot with Derby than to any obvious talent for the post'.[117] But Britain's most significant neighbour was ruled by a man who had just seized more power in a *coup*; Malmesbury was that man's closest contact and friend in British politics (and for that matter Derby's too). His selection as Foreign Secretary in 1852 seems to have been fairly straightforward. In the context of Derby's ongoing correspondence with Malmesbury on French politics it was a perfectly logical one. Malmesbury was an unknown quantity to the public, but not to Derby. He represented the antithesis of the danger and unpredictability of Palmerston, whose qualities Derby thought 'pernicious for the conduct of foreign affairs'.[118] Beyond the odd rumour about Stratford Canning, there is little evidence connecting any name other with the FO than Malmesbury's in 1852.[119]

Documents generated by the appointment process illuminate Derbyite assumptions about foreign policy. Prince Albert recorded a conversation with the Conservative leader on 22 February:

> He [Derby] could not propose Lord Aberdeen for the Foreign Office, as from what had passed last year, he felt he could not induce him to accept. He could not propose Sir Stratford Canning whom he had offered it then ... because he was aware that, besides his violent temper, several of the Courts of Europe, with whom it was most important for us to stand well at this conjuncture, entertained the strongest prejudices against him ... The least objectionable person he could name was Lord Malmesbury(!), a man of fair abilities and a personal friend of his, for whose obedience he could vouch. On the Queen's expressing her doubts as to Lord Malmesbury's abilities, he said he would undertake to control the Office himself and hoped to keep the Under Secretaryship open for his son.[120]

The fact that Derby did not mention Malmesbury's friendship with Louis Napoleon in no way lessened its significance. Had he done so, it might have negated his point about Stratford Canning being unpopular with the Austrians and Russians; those courts might also have had concerns about a man close to the Bonapartist dictator. More importantly, there was every likelihood that the Queen would have looked unfavourably on Malmesbury's friendship with a man with whom she felt 'one can never be for one instant safe'.[121] Sure enough, a few days later, when Victoria was informed about Malmesbury's communications with the President, she was concerned: 'Ld Malmesbury, it appears, is a great friend of Louis Napoleon's & corresponds with him, which might be dangerous'.[122] Had she known about her new Minister's frank correspondence after the *coup*, she would no doubt have been even more concerned.

Fortunately, the new Prime Minister was fast learning how to head off the Queen at the pass. After the embarrassing round of refusals in 1851 he could ill afford to lose another potential Foreign Secretary. On 26 February, the Queen expounded to Derby 'on the character of Louis Napoleon, & expressed our hope that Ld Malmesbury was aware how little he was to be trusted'.[123] In defence of his Foreign Secretary, Derby drew on his advice. Malmesbury had earlier observed to Derby that Louis Napoleon was 'a man d'idées fixes more than any body I ever met except poor George Bentinck'.[124] In answer to the Queen's concerns, Derby said 'that he (Ld M) knew this [i.e. how little he was to be trusted] perfectly, & said that all Louis Nap'.s views were contained in his book "Idées Napoleoniennes" written in [18]39, for that he was more a man of "idées fixes", than anyone'.[125] In making that point to the Queen, and using Malmesbury's own words to do so, Derby evidently thought his colleague's views on Bonapartist France worth noting.

Malmesbury's other great strength was that he was not Stratford Canning. Derby's reasons for not choosing Canning were equally telling about his intentions in foreign policy. Russia and Austria, at least, were clearly among the 'Courts of Europe' to which Derby referred when he explained why he had not appointed Canning. Neither power appreciated Canning's habit of dabbling in Ottoman affairs, nor his role as Palmerston's ambassador in the disputes about refugees. Derby was determined to engage positively with the conservative powers; Canning might have been an obstacle. In 1851, he had been the option of last resort; by 1852, Malmesbury's value was much more obvious, and Canning's much less so. Derby had also avoided appointing a minister who might have been every bit as troublesome as Palmerston. As Malmesbury later observed, the risk with Canning was that 'there could have been no peace with Russia or in the Cabinet'.[126]

The Conservatives were not turning to the non-French powers in fright at Bonapartist pretensions, as they had suspected Russell of doing. Louis Napoleon's *coup* was obviously Derby's 'conjuncture' necessitating good relations with those powers, but that was not sufficient to explain the new Prime Minister's tactics. As the conduct of Conservative foreign policy in 1852 would demonstrate, Derby and Malmesbury sought a good relationship with the other powers as a key objective in its own right. In pursuing such an objective, the Conservatives were consciously rejecting a number of Palmerstonian and liberal ideas.

Peel had declared, in the Don Pacifico debate, his principle in foreign policy: 'The principle for which I contend ... is the principle for which every statesman of eminence in this country for the last 50 years has contended – namely, non-interference with the domestic affairs of other countries, without some clear and undeniable necessity arising from circumstances affecting your own country'.[127] The policy of Derby's first administration would be firmly in the tradition to which Peel had subscribed. The relative moral virtues or vices of foreign regimes were to be set aside in the construction of Conservative foreign policy. That policy would be, to borrow from Derby's condemnation of Palmerston on the same occasion, to avoid 'rashly and unnecessarily to disturb that harmony which ought to prevail between all ... great Powers'.[128] It would not always be a popular policy, but it would be evident from the Government's first days in power.

Notes

1 My grateful thanks to the editor and staff of *International History Review* (*IHR*) for allowing me to reproduce, unaltered, a number of sections of this chapter from an article that appeared in 2004: Geoffrey Hicks, 'Don Pacifico, Democracy and Danger: The Protectionist Party Critique of British Foreign Policy, 1850–1852', *IHR*, 26 (September 2004), pp. 515–40.
2 For a detailed account of all these disputes see, in particular: Ridley, *Lord Palmerston*, pp. 366–76; David Hannell, 'Lord Palmerston and the "Don Pacifico Affair" of 1850: The Ionian Connection', *European History Quarterly*, 19 (1989), pp. 495–507.
3 Lords, 17 June 1850, *Hansard*, 111, col. 1332.
4 Commons, 25 June 1850, *Hansard*, 112, col. 444.
5 See, e.g., Brown, *Politics of Foreign Policy*, pp. 101–18; A. J. P. Taylor, *The Troublemakers*, pp. 53, 56–7.
6 See, e.g., Muriel Chamberlain, *'Pax Britannica'? British Foreign Policy, 1789–1914* (Harlow, 1988), pp. 98–9.
7 Stewart, *Politics of Protection*, pp. 166–7; Brown, *Politics of Foreign Policy*, pp. 103–6.
8 Brown, *Politics of Foreign Policy*, p. 106.
9 Hughenden Papers, Dep. Hughenden 109/1, fo. 47, Stanley to Disraeli, 22 June 1850.
10 Aberdeen Papers, Add. MSS 43054, fo. 338, Aberdeen to Princess Lieven, 11 June 1850; Stewart also quotes this letter, but goes on to draw a different conclusion about Stanley: *Politics of Protection*, p. 166.

11 Commons, 23 June 1850, *Hansard*, 112, cols 644–52.
12 *DDCP*, 25 June 1850, p. 22.
13 Hughenden Papers, Dep. Hughenden 109/1, fo. 49., Stanley to Disraeli, 22 June 1850.
14 See, e.g., Aberdeen Papers, Add. MSS 43072, fo. 173, Stanley to Aberdeen, undated.
15 See *ibid.*, fo. 172, Stanley to Aberdeen, 5 June 1850.
16 Commons, 28 June 1850, *Hansard*, 112, cols 649–51 (Walpole); 721–2 (Disraeli).
17 *DDCP*, 25 June 1850, p. 22.
18 Hughenden Papers, Dep. Hughenden 109/1, fo. 47, Stanley to Disraeli, 22 June 1850.
19 *Ibid*.
20 *Ibid*.
21 Commons, 27 June 1850, *Hansard*, 112, col. 496.
22 Lords, 17 June 1850, *Hansard*, 111, col. 1297.
23 Commons, 24 June 1850, *Hansard*, 112, col. 263.
24 *Ibid.*, col. 262.
25 Commons, 28 June 1850, *Hansard*, 112, col. 649.
26 *Ibid*.
27 Lords, 17 June 1850, *Hansard*, 111, col. 1321.
28 Commons, 24 June 1850, *Hansard*, 112, col. 232.
29 Commons, 27 June 1850, *Hansard*, 112, col. 498.
30 Commons, 28 June 1850, *Hansard*, 112, col. 649.
31 Commons, 25 June 1850, *Hansard*, 112, col. 373.
32 Commons, 27 June 1850, *Hansard*, 112, col. 486.
33 Commons, 25 June 1850, *Hansard*, 112, col. 352. For Palmerston's Italian policy in 1848, see, e.g., Southgate, 'The Most English Minister...', pp. 251–6; George J. Billy, *Palmerston's Foreign Policy: 1848* (New York, 1993), pp. 85–109; Matsumoto-Best, *Britain and the Papacy*, pp. 71–136; for the situation in Italy in 1848, see: Dennis Mack Smith, *Victor Emmanuel, Cavour and the Risorgimento* (Oxford, 1971); Harry Hearder, *Italy in the Age of the Risorgimento 1790–1870* (London, 1983), pp. 13–21, 200–9; Lucy Riall, *The Italian Risorgimento: State, Society and National Unification* (London, 1994).
34 Commons, 25 June 1850, *Hansard*, 112, col. 352.
35 Commons, 24 June 1850, *Hansard*, 112, col. 262.
36 Commons, 28 June 1850, *Hansard*, 112, col. 732.
37 Commons, 27 June 1850, *Hansard*, 112, cols 487–8.
38 *Ibid.*, col. 496.
39 Commons, 24 June 1850, *Hansard*, 112, col. 266.
40 Commons, 27 June 1850, *Hansard*, 112, col. 480.
41 Lords, 17 June 1850, *Hansard*, 111, cols 1294–5.
42 Commons, 28 June 1850, *Hansard*, 112, col. 645.
43 Commons, 25 June 1850, *Hansard*, 112, col. 347.
44 Commons, 27 June 1850, *Hansard*, 112, col. 495.

Prelude to power, 1850–52 63

45 Commons, 25 June 1850, *Hansard*, 112, col. 353.
46 Commons, 24 June 1850, *Hansard*, 112, col. 232.
47 Commons, 27 June 1850, *Hansard*, 112, col. 503.
48 Commons, 28 June 1850, *Hansard*, 112, col. 729.
49 Malmesbury clearly understood Austria to be one of Britain's 'old' allies: see, e.g., Derby Papers, 920 DER (14) 144/1, Malmesbury to Derby, 28 December 1851; and below, pp. 75; 78–80.
50 Commons, 27 June 1850, *Hansard*, 112, col. 531.
51 *Ibid.*, col. 532.
52 Commons, 24 June 1850, *Hansard*, 112, cols 303–4.
53 *Ibid.*, col. 306.
54 Richard Shannon, *Gladstone: Peel's Inheritor* (London, 1982), p. 223.
55 Commons, 27 June 1850, *Hansard*, 112, col. 580.
56 *Ibid.*, col. 589.
57 Shannon, *Gladstone: Peel's Inheritor*, p. 223.
58 Commons, 28 June 1850, *Hansard*, 112, col. 673.
59 *Ibid.*, 112, col. 667.
60 *Ibid.*, col. 664.
61 *Ibid.*, col. 665.
62 Commons, 27 June 1850, *Hansard*, 112, col. 508.
63 Commons, 28 June 1850, *Hansard*, 112, cols 720–39; the ambivalent nature of Disraeli's attack is explored in Brown, *Politics of Foreign Policy*, pp. 104–6.
64 Commons, 28 June 1850, *Hansard*, 112, col. 733.
65 Brown, *Politics of Foreign Policy*, p. 105.
66 Note by Gladstone, 22 April 1851 ('written from 27 February'), reproduced in *The Gladstone Diaries*, vol. 4, ed. M. R. D. Foot and H. C. G. Matthew (Oxford, 1974), p. 310; Malmesbury, *Memoirs*, vol. 1, p. 277. Blake suggested – although it is unclear on what basis – that Gladstone was offered any post 'except the Foreign Office': Blake, *Disraeli*, p. 303.
67 Note by Gladstone, 22 April 1851, *Gladstone Diaries*, vol. 4, p. 310.
68 Blake, *Disraeli*, p. 303.
69 *DDCP*, 1 March 1851, p. 51.
70 According to Brown, *Politics of Foreign Policy*, p. 106, 'Disraeli's name was the one most often associated with the Foreign Office in Conservative circles over the coming months'; he cites Blake as his source.
71 Edward Stanley's diary accorded Disraeli the Home Office in the provisional Cabinet list, which matches Disraeli's later recollection: *DDCP*, 27 February 1851, p. 49; Swartz and Swartz (eds), *Disraeli's Reminiscences*, p. 44; and *DL*, vol. 5, p. 536. Yet, later in the entry for the same day, Stanley also noted that Walpole was allotted that post. On 25 February, Prince Albert merely recorded that Disraeli would be 'one of the Secretaries of State': *The Letters of Queen Victoria: A Selection from Her Majesty's Correspondence between the years 1837 and 1861*, ed. A. C. Benson and Viscount Esher, 3 vols (1907), 1911 edn (hereafter *LQV*), vol. 2, p. 303.

72 Commons, 25 June 1850, *Hansard*, 112, col. 357.
73 *Ibid*.
74 Sir Robert Inglis, Commons, 27 June 1850, *Hansard*, 112, col. 497.
75 Commons, 3 February 1852, *Hansard*, 119, col. 137.
76 *Gladstone Diaries*, 4, note by Gladstone, 13 February 1851, p. 307.
77 'A Letter to the Earl of Aberdeen on the State Prosecutions of the Neapolitan Government', a publication which attracted a good deal more attention later than it did at the time: mention of it is noticeably absent from the correspondence of the Conservative leaders (in Stanley's case perhaps because he was preoccupied by the death of his father and succession to the Derby title). Granville, too, admitted some while later that he had not read it: BL, Gladstone Papers, Add. MSS 44165, fo. 4, Granville to Gladstone, 9 February 1852.
78 *DDCP*, 'June' 1852, pp. 70–1; Count Buol was the Austrian minister in London, later Vienna's Foreign Minister.
79 Matsumoto-Best, *Britain and the Papacy*, pp. 143–71.
80 Eglinton's amendment was made, and passed by three votes, on 18 February 1848: *Hansard*, 94, cols 876–96.
81 Hughenden Papers, Dep. Hughenden 109/1, fo. 57, Stanley to Disraeli, 15 November 1850.
82 Derby Papers, 920 DER (14), 144/1, Malmesbury to Stanley, 27 November 1850.
83 *Ibid.*, fo. 1, copy, Stanley to Malmesbury, 2 December 1850; extract reproduced in Malmesbury, *Memoirs*, I, p. 67.
84 Hughenden Papers, Dep. Hughenden 109/1, fo. 109, Derby to Disraeli, 26 October 1851.
85 Commons, 27 June 1850, *Hansard*, 112, col. 500.
86 Stanley to Croker, 18 August 1850, in *The Croker Papers*, ed. Louis J. Jennings, 3 vols (London, 1884), vol. 3, p. 218.
87 *Ibid*.
88 For the reform plans, see Prest, *Lord John Russell*, pp. 331–40; Mandler, *Aristocratic Government*, pp. 272–4.
89 NA, Cardwell Papers, PRO 30/48/48, fo. 22, Aberdeen to Cardwell, 3 November 1851.
90 Hughenden Papers, Dep. Hughenden 109/1, fo. 121, Derby to Disraeli, 11 December 1851.
91 *DL*, vol. 5, 2214, Disraeli to Lady Londonderry, 28 December 1851.
92 Derby Papers, 920 DER (14) 144/1, Malmesbury to Derby, 17 November 1851.
93 *DL*, vol. 5, 2194, Disraeli to Ponsonby, 4 November 1851.
94 For the most detailed accounts, see Brian Connell, *Regina v. Palmerston, 1837–1865* (London, 1962), pp. 131–7; David Brown, 'The Power of Public Opinion: Palmerston and the Crisis of December 1851', *PH*, 20 (2001), pp. 333–58.
95 A. J. P. Taylor, 'Palmerston', in *Essays in English History* (Harmondsworth, 1976), p. 108.

96 Derby Papers, 920 DER (14) 144/1, Malmesbury to Derby, 28 December 1851.
 97 Hughenden Papers, Dep. Hughenden 99/1, fo. 28, Malmesbury to Disraeli, 28 December 1851.
 98 *DL*, vol. 6, ed. M. G. Wiebe, Mary S. Millar and Ann P. Robson (Toronto, 1997), 2219, Disraeli to Derby, 4 January 1852.
 99 Hughenden Papers, Dep. Hughenden 109/1, fo. 123, Derby to Disraeli, 7 January 1852.
100 Commons, 3 February 1852, *Hansard*, 119, cols 117–18.
101 *DL*, vol. 6, 2218, Disraeli to Malmesbury, 2 January 1852.
102 NA, Granville Papers, PRO 30/29/18/6, fo. 3, Russell to Granville, 30 December 1851.
103 Granville Papers, PRO 30/29/18/4, fo. 8, Lansdowne to Granville, 1 January 1852.
104 *DL*, vol. 6, 2218, Disraeli to Malmesbury, 2 January 1852.
105 Derby Papers, 920 DER (14) 179/1, fo. 329, copy, Derby to Croker, 22 December 1851.
106 Commons, 3 February 1852, *Hansard*, 119, col. 94.
107 *Ibid.*, col. 99.
108 Derby Papers, 920 DER (14) 144/1, Malmesbury to Derby, 28 December 1851.
109 *Ibid*.
110 Commons, 3 February 1852, *Hansard*, 119, col. 100.
111 Derby Papers, 920 DER (14) 179/1, fo. 327, copy, Derby to Croker, 22 December 1851.
112 *Ibid.*, fos 326–7.
113 Commons, 3 February 1852, *Hansard*, 119, col. 98.
114 Derby Papers, 920 DER (14) 179/1, fo. 330; fos 329–30, copy, Derby to Croker, 22 December 1851.
115 Lords, 23 February 1852, *Hansard*, 119, col. 23.
116 Commons, 15 March 1852, *Hansard*, 119, col. 1051.
117 Blake, *Disraeli*, p. 313.
118 *LQV*, vol. 2, p. 370, Prince Albert, Memorandum, 22 February 1852.
119 Some of the press expected that Stratford Canning would again be proposed, but no such suggestion seems to have emanated from Derby himself. Blake, *Disraeli*, p. 311, also mentions 'some sort of rumour current that Disraeli was to have the Foreign Office'. He dismisses it, and it does not seem to have had that wide a circulation.
120 'Changes of Government, Cabinet Reconstructions and Political Crises, 1837–1901' (Brighton, 1980), RA C27/14, Prince Albert, Memorandum, 22 February 1852. Stanley's diary, 'June' 1852, is at variance with this account, recording that 'the failure of negotiations with Lord Aberdeen and Sir S. Canning' had 'compelled Malmesbury's withdrawal to the F.O.' (rather than the Colonial Office): *DDCP*, p. 71. But Stanley's account is not borne out elsewhere. In a letter of 5 March to Stratford Canning, Derby made a particular point of explaining, on the grounds of

time and distance being an impediment, why he had not offered him the FO: Derby Papers, 920 DER (14) 180/2, fos 1–2, copy. Given that Stanley's journal was written some months afterwards, and that he had been in India at the time, one can safely assume his account was confusing the order of events in 1852 with those of 1851.
121 *LQV*, vol. 2, p. 362, Queen Victoria to King Leopold, 3 February 1852.
122 'Changes of Government', unfoliated, Queen Victoria's Journal, 25 February 1852.
123 RA C27/46, Queen Victoria, Memorandum, 26 February 1852.
124 Derby Papers, 920 DER (14), 144/1, Malmesbury to Derby, 5 January 1852.
125 RA C27/46, 'Changes of Government', Queen Victoria, Memorandum, 26 February 1852.
126 Malmesbury, *Memoirs*, vol. 1, p. 307.
127 Commons, 28 June 1850, *Hansard*, 112, col. 689.
128 Lords, 17 June 1850, *Hansard*, 111, col. 1295.

4

1852: foreign affairs, domestic problems

> I believe that peace will be best maintained by observing to all Foreign Powers – whether powerful or weak – a calm, temperate, deliberate, and conciliatory course of conduct, not in acts alone, but in words also. (Derby, House of Lords, 27 February 1852)

> The dispatches today from Russia declare Nesselrode to be most anxious for our reconciliation with Austria ... I can't help thinking that if we are in long enough we shall get our *old friends* right. (Malmesbury to Derby, 29 February 1852)

On acceding to office, Derby found himself in a particularly complicated situation, one which had implications for foreign policy, though the root of his problems lay elsewhere. He was at the head of a minority Government theoretically committed to protection, but relative prosperity and popular support for free trade made that commitment rather a hollow one. All but the most rampant 'ultras' recognised that the new administration would find it extremely difficult to turn back the clock to 1846. While Granby explained to the Commons that he 'confidently believed' Derby's Government would 'endeavour to carry out' a protectionist policy, even he accepted it would only happen 'if the country would support them'.[1] He admitted that 'it would be absurd and ridiculous ... to attempt to reverse a policy which had been the law of the land for upwards of five years, if the people of this country were convinced that that policy was just and advantageous'.[2]

The caveat about popular feeling was significant. Derby led a party which had campaigned strenuously on a protectionist platform for over five years. Peel had been viciously condemned by his former colleagues for his reversal of the policy to which he and his party had been committed. It would have been extremely difficult for Derby to do likewise and discard protection without an electoral mandate to justify his retreat either to his party or to the country. Deploying his classical scholarship in a jibe at Peel, he had made it clear to Disraeli that he would not countenance hypocrisy on such a scale: 'the game is, I believe, in our hands; but ... it must be played honestly and manfully; and to take office with the purpose of throwing over, voluntarily, the main object of those who have raised us to it is to follow too closely an "exemplar vitiis imitabile", to which I never can submit'.[3] Nevertheless, the fact remained that he was espousing a nominally protectionist policy while at the same time expecting ultimately to deliver the opposite. Derby would have to play 'the game' very carefully indeed if he was to remain Prime Minister and retain his party's support.

This left him in a delicate position, with ramifications across all policy areas. He could not formulate economic policy in detail or make any definitive pronouncement about it prior to the general election which he had publicly stated was necessary. He could not be explicit about what he was asking voters to support in an election, because his policy would depend on the extent of that support. Derby's accordingly vague public pronouncements about public finance – what Greville called his 'studied ambiguity' – were not likely to decrease suspicion about his administration's objectives at a time when reactionary government was in the ascendant across Europe.[4] An alarmed Sidney Herbert, hardly a radical, noted that 'maintaining a strong body of independent Liberal-Conservatives to contest the ultra-Tory element and tendencies of the present Government is more than ever necessary for the safety of the country'.[5]

Derby therefore had to convince the country that he and his untried ministers represented safe, responsible conservatism. This was also more likely to deliver Peelites like Herbert back into the bosom of the party to which many still hoped they would return. The Prime Minister's Mansion House speech on 12 April displayed his overriding concern: 'I do not presume to speak of any political course of action; but this I say, that I hope I see indications ... in this metropolis, that we are not looked upon as a set of reckless or careless men, likely to endanger the credit of the country and its great commercial and mercantile interests'.[6] Foreign policy had its part to play in demonstrating that the Conservatives were not 'reckless or careless'.

With a political tightrope to walk, the Government's approach to foreign affairs was defined in part by domestic preoccupations, just as it had been in opposition. A minority administration in power as a result of its enemies' divisions was by its very nature low in political credit, if not already in deficit. It could not afford disputes and controversies of the sort fomented by Palmerston. Its vulnerability, particularly prior to the election, meant that one eye was always on its domestic position. Diplomacy was tangled up with domestic priorities, even when – as with the briefly notorious Mather case – ministers particularly tried to avoid controversy. In one of the most interesting developments of the year, although it has been ignored by historians, the Conservatives even tried to bolster their domestic political position via secret diplomacy with the Pope.

The opposition was constantly searching for opportunities to attack, and if foreign policy was mishandled, opportunities would be provided. As far as the Prime Minister's son was concerned, diplomacy was 'essentially defensive' and 'ought not to challenge publicity'.[7] Many years later, his caution would prove his undoing, but his reasoning was sound: there were plenty of people ready to accuse the Government of incompetence, and of the extremism they perceived in its economic policy. Any association with the 'despotic' regimes in Austria, Russia or Prussia therefore carried a risk. Even mild-mannered Granville could not resist the temptation to label the Conservatives 'the party in England which ... had for the last four years generally adopted the complaints of Austria against the actual Government of this country'.[8]

Bad publicity was not the only danger. Any policy which led to increased international tension was potentially also an expensive policy, if it affected British commerce or if it inflated military spending. That was particularly undesirable for the party which included many of those who would have to stump up for extra expenditure, and who were unlikely to be compensated by regaining preferential duties.

Britain's foreign relations accordingly had to be calm and uncontroversial. Britons and British interests, along with Britain's broader commercial and strategic position, could thereby be protected and the Government's critics pre-empted. Achieving all this would be no easy task. Foreign policy could not be glossed over until the election as economic questions could. Problems would invariably stem from the uncontrollable 'events' so wearying to one of Derby's twentieth-century successors. The other powers were bound to generate such events sooner or later, and a definite policy response would be required.

Derby's domestic balancing act has nevertheless led many to assume that he had no policies at all. In August 1852, Newcastle judged the Conservative ministers to be 'men presuming to hold the reins of office with *no* principle – *no* plan – *no* policy – except that of continuing to hold them'.[9] Posterity has largely drawn the same conclusion. One early twentieth-century writer observed that Derby led 'a stop-gap Government without a majority and without a policy'.[10] Michael Bentley has put it more bluntly: 'the government had no thought ...

about anything'.[11] In foreign affairs, such an assessment overlooks the subtlety of a position which was only partially outlined in public, without Palmerston's flourishes, and more frankly discussed in private. Derby and Malmesbury stamped their imprint on diplomacy, but they did so quietly.

Derby was at the heart of the policy-making process in 1852. He was in a very strange position, with vastly more experience than his Cabinet. Only J. C. Herries and the Earl of Lonsdale had held ministerial office, and they were hardly names with which to conjure. Herries had not held office for 17 years, and then only for 6 months; Lonsdale had last served as Postmaster-General. Both Ramsay MacDonald and Tony Blair would succeed to the premiership with similarly novice cabinets; however, they would not take on as much of the burden of government as Derby did in 1852. The Prime Minister was also the Government's voice in the Lords, where half his Cabinet colleagues sat but – other than Malmesbury – said little.[12] Only Disraeli in the Commons had to tackle as wide-ranging a brief.

There was a paucity of front-bench talent. So many of the party's most able men had been lost over the Corn Laws: Gladstone, Herbert, Cardwell, Graham, Newcastle and Aberdeen were all gone. One of Derby's Cabinet colleagues admitted, shortly after the Government fell, that 'we were destitute of Parliamentary talent compared with the allies opposed to us'.[13] On one occasion when Disraeli was to be absent, the Prime Minister privately expressed his relief that Commons discussion would be limited: 'if we are to have 'interpollations' [*sic*], I should not be sorry that they took place in *our* House'.[14] Years later, after Derby's retirement, Malmesbury noted that the new Lord Chancellor, Cairns, was 'a very efficient addition to our strength in the Lords where our bench is comparatively weak in oratory[,] Ld Derby having always discouraged speaking by his friends & colleagues who have had consequently no practice'.[15] The Prime Minister dominated the Government, and foreign policy in 1852 would be as much Derby's as it was Malmesbury's.

What would be the principles guiding that policy? Following Russell's resignation on 21 February 1852, the new Prime Minister delivered a ministerial statement, as convention demanded. In this speech, to the Lords on 27 February, Derby outlined his intentions across a range of policy areas. Though the most keenly awaited section was that dealing with economic matters, the first substantive subject to which he turned his attention was foreign policy. This was no surprise, given the bitter controversies of the Palmerston years.

The Prime Minister's statement needs to be read in context: it was a product of what had gone before as much as a harbinger of what was to come. Nevertheless, it publicly set the tone that would be evident in policy formation. It did not address the details of European affairs: neither the Prime Minister nor his Foreign Secretary could have been expected to be familiar with them at that stage. Instead, it picked out general themes. It had three purposes: to reject what the Conservatives regarded as the irresponsible elements of Whig foreign policy; to assuage fears about Protectionist extremism; and to give some sense of Conservative principles.

Derby first rejected extremism of both belligerent and 'Utopian' varieties.[16] These were not throwaway comments. Louis Napoleon's coup had led to a somewhat hysterical war scare and widespread demands for increased defences. The late 1840s and early 1850s had also seen a burgeoning peace movement. Radicals such as Cobden and Bright were its parliamentary standard-bearers. The fifth International Peace Conference had been held in London in 1851, and Cobden had introduced parliamentary motions on disarmament. Derby contemptuously dismissed such 'Utopian theories'.[17] He had no desire to suggest any fellow-feeling with the radicals, into whose company opposition to Palmerston had occasionally brought him.

The Prime Minister's central concern, however, was to distance the Conservatives from Whig irresponsibility. He stressed the importance of 'observing to all Foreign Powers – whether powerful or weak – a calm, temperate, deliberate, and conciliatory course of conduct'.[18] When Derby emphasised the importance of applying principles equally in Britain's dealings with less powerful states, the implication was obvious in the wake of the Don Pacifico affair. Such a policy clearly contrasted with that pursued by Palmerston.

Derby's comments about treaties also recalled Palmerston's general interference in European affairs. Conservative foreign policy, Derby stressed, would pursue peace 'by adhering with strict fidelity to the spirit and the letter of the obligations imposed upon us by treaty'.[19] Circumvention of treaties, as over Greece in 1850, constituted an affront to the system which maintained European stability, and within which Derby was determined to work. For the Conservatives, the most important treaties were those of 1814–15. The Vienna settlement provided a stable, secure diplomatic structure, within which Britain could prosper. Nevertheless, Derby's reference to treaties was also an assurance of the Conservatives' intention to observe other commitments. The consequences of Palmerston's 1839 guarantee to Belgium would soon test that resolve.

Perhaps the most significant phrase in this section of Derby's speech was that which dealt with the nature of foreign governments. His initial comments on the subject sugared a rather different pill from that which Parliament had been asked to swallow by the Whigs. Derby first emphasised the fact that he was a wholehearted supporter of the British parliamentary system. In his opinion, the British Constitution was 'the best adapted to secure the happiness and the liberty of the greatest number'.[20] This was unsurprising from a former Whig who had sat in Cabinet with the men who had passed the Reform Act. Indeed, he declared that he should be 'glad to see our example diffusing itself through other nations and countries'.[21] Here was reassurance for those who feared an 'ultra' foreign policy.

The way in which he qualified that statement was, however, important. The relative liberalism of other countries was to be accorded no importance in his foreign policy. Derby declared that

> we have no right as a nation, to entertain particular prejudices, or particular sympathies, for this or that course of government that other countries may think fit to adopt, be these courses or forms of government the most absolute despotism, limited monarchy, constitutional republic, or, if such a thing could endure, absolute red republicanism; that which is the choice of a nation, so far as it affects its individual and internal concerns alone, it is the duty of a British Government to recognise.[22]

While the principle was one to which most politicians would have paid obeisance, in practice this represented a shift from the position staked out by the Russell Government.[23] The Conservatives would rapidly move to improve relations with continental governments of whom the vast body of Whigs and liberals were deeply suspicious.

Derby continued with his implicit disavowal of Palmerston's methods. In international disputes, he stressed the importance of offering, 'without waiting to be asked for it, such reparation as the circumstances of the case, and our own conscience, may show to be right'.[24] Palmerston's inflammatory (but popular) responses in such circumstances were notorious. The Austrians still fumed about his grudging apology in 1850 after the London draymen had manhandled Marshal Haynau, the butcher of the Hungarians. And plenty could remember 1841, when Palmerston had left Aberdeen a host of problems to resolve.

Derby's final comments recalled Don Pacifico. If a British subject had cause to complain about another state, the Prime Minister outlined the appropriate response: 'frankly and temperately to state the complaint we have to make, not indulging in vituperation and intemperance of language, but submitting equally to honour and justice the claim we should be the first to acknowledge ourselves'.[25] Such an approach would soon be put into practice, in a minor dispute with Tuscany that would become a major controversy.

A document produced by Granville barely six weeks earlier enables the historian to juxtapose the Conservative position with that of its Whig predecessor. One of the consequences of Palmerston's dismissal the previous December had been a request by the Queen for a statement of her Government's principles in foreign policy.[26] Her new Foreign Secretary produced the desired document a few weeks before the fall of the Government.[27] Given the brevity of his tenure, Granville's memorandum of January 1852 is usually dismissed by historians – it has been described as a document that 'need not be taken seriously'.[28] This is to do it an injustice.

The memorandum was a useful indicator of the Russell Government's liberal principles, and all the more striking given that its author was an amiable Whig to whom few conservatives could reasonably have objected. The selection of Granville had met with widespread approval. Aberdeen had rejoiced at the news: 'I like Granville's appointment very much, and have no doubt he will do well'.[29] Ellenborough told Granville that, for the FO, 'you seem to me better qualified to perform the duties than any man I know'.[30] But the new Foreign Secretary could not disguise the liberal mission over which he presided.

The memorandum praised Palmerston with faint damns. Granville conceded that 'the foreign policy of England has obtained, whether justly or unjustly, the reputation of interfering too much'.[31] He paid tribute to the shibboleth Palmerston had ignored, noting that the Cabinet 'adhered to the principle of non-intervention in the affairs of other countries'.[32] This might have been more convincing had he not then rejected the notion that it was 'unnecessary for this country to ... take a part in what passes in other countries'.[33] Indeed, he noted that if something looked likely to have 'international consequences' a judgement would be necessary as to whether Britain 'shall interfere at once'.[34] The Government's principle was not to intervene, except when it decided to intervene.

Such elastic phraseology was perhaps understandable: no government wanted to be painted into a corner by the Queen. But there were more exalted principles to come. Granville asserted that 'it is the duty and the interest of this country ... priding itself on its advanced state of civilisation, to encourage moral, intellectual and physical progress among all other nations'.[35] This had consequences for the way in which policy-makers dealt with 'those countries which have adopted liberal institutions similar in liberality to our own': it would be 'the endeavour of H.M.'s Govt to cultivate the most intimate relations' with those governments.[36] In its most intriguing phrase, the memorandum noted that, with regard to these countries, Britain 'will exert its influence to dissuade other Powers from encroaching on their territory, or attempting to subvert their institutions, and there may occur cases in which the honour and good faith of this country will require that it should support such allies with more than friendly assurances'.[37] Here was a foreign policy which gave clear precedence to certain countries with certain types of government.

A Whiggish historiography has accepted this as unremarkable, yet the differences between Derby's speech and Granville's memorandum are revealing. To take merely one: the Whigs would 'encourage' progress in foreign nations; the Conservatives would let the British example 'diffuse'. The semantics mattered. In them was contained the difference between interference and non-interference: between Wellingtonian tolerance of conservatism in the Iberian peninsular in the 1830s and Palmerstonian sponsorship of liberalism; between Derbyite tolerance of Austrian rule in northern Italy and Russellite encouragement of Italian 'freedom'.[38] Both Derby and Granville believed in the ideal of the British Constitution, but their respective principles had very different implications.

The notion that the liberal nature of Britain's Constitution entailed drawing particularly close to others of a similar ilk, purely on the grounds of ideological principle, was simply alien to the new ministers. Derby had made it clear that 'we have no right as a nation, to entertain particular prejudices, or particular sympathies, for this or that course of government that other countries may think fit to adopt'.[39] This was not just rhetoric: Conservative foreign policy was to be defined by necessity and expediency, not ideology.

This would create problems. For Derby and Malmesbury, the conundrum of foreign affairs in 1852 would be how to conduct their consciously non-Whig and un-Palmerstonian policy while at the same time satisfying domestic needs and audiences. A similar task – in some shape or form – faces most governments, but a fragile minority administration would be particularly conscious of domestic difficulties. Despite this, it pursued its own distinctive policy. It was rapidly evident that the Conservatives really did intend to pursue a 'calm, temperate, deliberate and conciliatory course of conduct' irrespective of the 'forms of government' with which they did business.

Diplomacy with the conservative powers: co-operation with 'old friends'

The Whig Government had been on only intermittently amicable terms with most of its foreign counterparts, although Granville had worked harder than Palmerston to remove difficulties. The most recent diplomatic spat had been over the status and behaviour of political refugees in Britain. A number of European powers had complained about Britain's tolerance of their political exiles, suspected of conspiring in Britain against their home governments.[40] Although the others let the matter drop after some soothing words from Granville, Austria was less easily mollified.

Anglo-Austrian relations, marred by a series of altercations and disputes, had been sour for some years. Austria, and perhaps Russia, cannot have been far from Malmesbury's thoughts when he recorded, in a telling phrase, his hope that 'if we are in long enough we shall get our *old friends* right'.[41] The Government's first weeks were duly marked by reconciliation with Austria, while French animosity towards Belgium also necessitated close co-operation with the 'northern' powers. Collaboration over Belgium enabled the Conservatives to foster the warmest Anglo-Russian relationship since Aberdeen had left the FO.

A reduction in Anglo-Austrian tension was not immediate. There was an initial hiccup as Vienna got the measure of the new administration. This revealed some important features of Conservative foreign policy. On 2 March, Malmesbury's first meeting with Buol, the Austrian Minister in London, was difficult. On the subject of refugees, Buol had, rather irregularly, just attempted to deliver notes on behalf of Modena and the Papal States. These were all but Austrian puppets and were officially unrepresented in Britain. Granville had refused to accept the notes, and an angry Buol remonstrated with Malmesbury, who would not accept them either.[42] He was no more ready than the Whigs had been to concede Austria's right to speak for the smaller nations in its orbit or under its influence.[43] To Buol, Malmesbury's maintenance of Granville's position must have seemed an unexpected defence of Whig policy.[44] It was, paradoxically, in keeping with a rather different approach to foreign affairs.

Malmesbury's response to Buol was informed by a particularly Conservative perception of the rights of small nations. From time to time, Palmerston had of course battled on behalf of smaller states. Belgium had been a notable beneficiary of his diplomacy. But his stance was eminently flexible. For example, had Charles Albert been successful in his expansionist policy in 1848–49, the small northern Italian states would – with Palmerston's blessing – have been subsumed within a stronger nation to offset Austrian and French power.[45] The Conservatives had condemned Palmerston's tinkering in Italy. They had also, of course, decried his 'bullying' of Greece.

For the Derbyites, the smaller nation states played a fundamental part in the balance of power: their integrity and independence needed to be defended. Maintaining Granville's line on Modena and the Papal States was entirely in keeping with such an outlook. But the Conservatives went further. At the same time that Malmesbury was refusing to shift on the subject of Buol's undelivered notes, he was also determined to preserve at least the form of another Italian state's independence from Austria.

In a contentious case which would come to occupy a lot of ministerial time, a young Englishman, Erskine Mather, holidaying in Tuscany – another puppet state – had been injured (in somewhat confused circumstances) by an Austrian soldier on parade in Florence.[46] On behalf of the young man and his outraged father, Granville had been pursuing the case with Austria. In discussion with Buol, the Whig Foreign Secretary had asserted that 'occurrences such as these if they were not accompanied by ample reparation must estrange the two countries'.[47] These were strong words, and from the outset Malmesbury deprecated his predecessor's approach: 'It was a blunder of Granville', he noted, 'not to hold the Tuscan Govt.' – rather than the Austrians – 'entirely responsible from the beginning'.[48] This was not merely a difference over detail.

As Derby later explained to the Lords, accepting that Austria was solely responsible for the actions of its soldiers in another sovereign country had broader implications. It would imply an acceptance of secret treaties and undesirable alterations in the international status quo:

> It appears that these [Austrian] troops are in Tuscany by a treaty by which we are in no way bound, because it is not a patent, but a secret article. We have never recognised the presence of the Austrian army; the Tuscan Government thought it right to invite them to assist them in maintaining order; but as regards foreign nations, that army must be considered as acting under the orders and directions of the Tuscan Government, who are responsible for any injury these troops may do.[49]

Derby and Malmesbury may well have calculated that there were, in any case, more pressing priorities. Subtracting Austrian responsibility from the diplomatic equation over Mather would remove an obstacle to Anglo-Austrian reconciliation. With Derby's sanction, Malmesbury assured Austria that its apology would be adequate; Tuscany alone would henceforth be expected to provide reparation.[50] As the Government's critics pointed out, however, the reality of Tuscan dependence on Austria meant that this assertion of smaller states' independence made little practical difference. Aberdeen, notably, advocated a pragmatic recognition of Austrian power.[51]

The Government nevertheless held firm. To Malmesbury, Derby was emphatic: 'you cannot ... appear to concede the principle for which he [Buol] contends of recognising Austrian responsibility for acts done in Tuscany'. He was more inclined to this opinion 'because Count Buol rests his case in great measure on a treaty between Austria & Tuscany, which has never been communicated ... and which I do not wish should be, to this country; and to which, as being a secret treaty ... he has, as I should think, no diplomatic right to refer'.[52] On the question of smaller states' rights, no concessions could be expected from the new Government.

A second aspect of Conservative foreign policy was also evident in early exchanges with the Austrians. Like all British governments, this one would be constrained by the political realities of a semi-democratised State. On the underlying problem of the refugees' status and treatment in Britain, political considerations made concession to Austria impossible.[53] The weight of public and parliamentary opinion was clear, although in Conservative circles there was sympathy for Austrian frustration. The *Quarterly Review* expressed its outrage at Whig tolerance of refugees: 'England ceases to be the city of refuge of the Hebrews – it resembles rather one of those Barbary seaports from whence the robber and the pirate defied the ministers of justice, and waged a perpetual war on industry and civilisation'.[54] In Parliament, Sir John Walsh sprang to Vienna's defence with an equally picturesque intervention:

> When they [the refugees] came to this country to seek an asylum, they were not satisfied to remain quiet, and to sleep under the shade of the British oak, guarded by the British lion. They forgot that when they came to this country they should not disturb the tranquillity of foreign States, or attempt to excite revolutions in their own country. That was the grievance, indeed it was the strong point, of the foreign Powers.[55]

Nevertheless, Derby had forcefully declared that Britain was an 'ark of refuge'.[56] With regard to Austrian demands for more punitive British action against refugees, Malmesbury pointed out to Lord Westmorland, the British minister in Vienna, that 'no Government which complied with such demands could exist a month in England'.[57] There seems, in any case, little evidence to suppose that the Prime Minister's views were other than those attributed to him by Malmesbury, that he felt 'strongly' the 'injustice and impossibility of yielding to any demand for the expulsion of refugees from this country as long as they conform to its laws'.[58] On the question of refugees, Austria had to accept that none of the governments with which it remonstrated in 1852 could make concessions.

Notwithstanding initially unpleasant interviews with Buol, Derby and Malmesbury worked hard to pursue *détente* with Austria. After meeting the Austrian minister on 2 March, Malmesbury informed Derby about Buol's demands for concessions.[59] The Prime Minister intervened and drew up a paper for Malmesbury to read to Buol on 5 March.[60] Although no concessions could be made on refugees or the Modena and Papal States representations, the object was 'to put an end to these unseemly wrangles between us and our old ally' by proposing an exchange of notes closing the outstanding matters.[61] After further unsatisfactory discussion, Malmesbury simply proposed to 'drop any further correspondence' on the Modena and Rome notes or the refugees.[62] His proposal was to 'let bygones be bygones'.[63]

The assumption underpinning Conservative policy was that Austria, if given an opportunity for reconciliation, would seize it. Malmesbury calculated that Vienna saw the Whig Government, not Britain, as its enemy. He pointed this out to Westmorland when dealing with another Anglo-Austrian dispute inherited from Granville. In January 1852, the Austrian authorities in Pesth, Hungary, had expelled two Scottish missionaries. The Foreign Secretary felt he was once again dealing with the fall-out from Whig policy: '*We* are ... getting the contrecoup of a cut meant ... at the *last* Government'.[64] Whatever the differing domestic priorities in a reactionary empire and a constitutional monarchy, he was convinced that he could do business with the conservative powers.

Malmesbury's instincts were sound. Tone matters as much as substance in diplomacy, and news of Derby's ministerial speech on 27 February had pleased the Austrian Government. His moderate language signalled a more positive approach. Whatever Buol's irritation on minor issues, Austria took advantage of the change in personnel and party. Westmorland described the mood in Vienna: 'The speech of Lord Derby, and the language he holds as to foreign Governments, has had the best effect here both with the Government and the public'.[65] The Austrian *Minister-Präsident* (Prime Minister), Prince Schwarzenberg, sent his congratulations on the speech, concurring with the principles Derby had outlined: *nous nous félicitons de pouvoir souscrire sans réserve aux principes et aux intentions que le Comte de Derby a développés avec autant de franchise que de lucidité.*[66]

Malmesbury rejoiced that the line had been drawn under the Anglo-Austrian acrimony of the Palmerston years. He explained to Lord Cowley, Britain's Ambassador to France, that 'Austria has sent two *very* friendly notes upon our accession to office'; and, to Austria's representative in Paris, Cowley was therefore to convey British 'satisfaction ... at bygones being bygones'.[67] He was positively jubilant when he told Lord Bloomfield in Berlin that 'all our wrangles with Austria are terminated'.[68]

Derby and Malmesbury did not hesitate to respond to the Austrian overture. The Prime Minister privately expressed his satisfaction to Buol.[69] Malmesbury, in the Government's official response to Schwarzenberg, used language that would later create domestic political difficulties. It is worth quoting the controversial passage in full:

> In proportion to the value which H.M. Govt place upon the maintenance of a cordial relationship with Austria, the oldest ally of England, cemented not only by the tie of mutual interest, but by the recollection of past efforts in a common cause, was the regret with which H.M.'s present Govt[,] on succeeding to office, found that the result of the events of the last few years had been found to substitute for those friendly relations a tone of mutual suspicion, if not of actual alienation, and to give to their diplomatic correspondence a character quite at variance with the dispositions which ought to subsist between them ... H.M.'s Govt feel assured that they shall have no difficulty in reconciling their duty, as Ministers of a Constitutional Sovereign[,] with the obligations which they owe to the just claims of any friendly Power, and the sentiments of sincere friendship with which they are actuated towards the Court of Vienna.[70]

Given the constraints of diplomatic language, it would have been difficult to have composed a more emphatic rejection of Whig foreign policy –or a clearer signal of a change in British attitudes. At the same time, Malmesbury went as far as he could go with regard to the refugees. He made sympathetic noises about the Government's aim of 'discouraging and repressing as far as the law and the constitution warrant, any attempt on the part of such exiles to abuse the hospitality they enjoy'.[71] Shortly afterwards, the Conservatives' change of focus on the Mather case, stressing Tuscan instead of Austrian responsibility, also enabled them to accept the apology (without reparation) offered by Schwarzenberg. In language markedly different from Granville's, Malmesbury told Westmorland:

Count Buol has read to me the despatch written to him by Prince Schwarzenberg ... expressing His Highness's regret at the unfortunate circumstances resulting in the severe injury of Mr Mather. It has given me the most sincere pleasure to inform Her Majesty's Government of the friendly spirit shewn [sic] by the Austrian Government towards this country.[72]

Such was Malmesbury's satisfaction, he wrote a week later to thank Austria again for 'the friendly tone of the Court of Vienna' with regard to the Mather case.[73] This change in atmosphere led the Foreign Secretary to hope that the Austrians would instead throw their weight behind British diplomacy and use their influence with the Tuscans to extract the desired reparations.[74] Whether or not that assistance would be forthcoming, Malmesbury and Derby had presided over a rapid and noticeable improvement in Anglo-Austrian relations. Granville publicly acknowledged – if in a not wholly complimentary manner – that Malmesbury had 'accomplished, without effort, that which he ... had failed to do'.[75]

This diplomatic success was matched by close co-operation with another of the autocratic powers. When Malmesbury took office, Russia was already pressing for exactly the sort of Anglo-Austrian *rapprochement* the Conservatives pursued. Shortly after his appointment, Malmesbury received despatches from Russia (aimed at Granville) which registered St Petersburg's 'most anxious' desire for Anglo-Austrian reconciliation.[76] It is difficult to imagine Whig policy coinciding as neatly with Russian desires. And it was just as well: at that juncture, French belligerence provided the Conservatives with a powerful new incentive to pursue Anglo-Russian amity.

In early 1852, France appeared to be threatening the independence of Belgium. Franco-Belgian relations were poor. Belgium owed its independence in part to Louis Napoleon's supplanted predecessor, Louis Philippe. Its king, Leopold, was no ally of the French President, and his late wife had been Louis Philippe's daughter. Belgium was host to a virulently anti-Bonapartist press, accessible to French readers. France had presented to the Belgians a long list of allegations about anti-French behaviour and demanded that action be taken. There was widespread apprehension that France was contemplating a military move against its smaller neighbour.[77]

Russia, Prussia, Austria and Britain had to take that threat seriously. They were bound to defend Belgium by a guarantee jointly made with France on 19 April 1839, signed at the time when the treaty of London had formally established Belgian nationhood. The Belgian guarantee would subsequently gain notoriety as the basis for the

British declaration of war in 1914. If aggression was to be deterred in 1852, great power co-operation was imperative. In this fraught atmosphere, Anglo-Russian relations took on a new significance.

There was a good basis on which to build. As would become evident in 1853, Nicholas I felt he had obtained some diplomatic satisfaction from the Conservatives over Near Eastern affairs in June 1844. On that occasion, the Russians believed they had negotiated a British undertaking to concert policy with St Petersburg in the event of the Ottoman Empire's imminent collapse.[78] This had been extracted from a Government of which Derby had, of course, been a prominent member. Nicholas may have hoped to be on equally good terms with the new administration. His veteran Chancellor, Count Nesselrode, was instinctively pro-Tory and keen to work with Britain. The increasing tension over French ambitions gave them both good reason to do so. Aberdeen, an experienced observer of Russian diplomacy, noted that Nicholas 'looks with much uneasiness and suspicion at the tendencies developed by the French Government; and ... this feeling increases every day'.[79]

Despite his unease, the Tsar also shared the Conservatives' desire to avoid provoking Louis Napoleon. The consonance of British and Russian views became increasingly evident as the two governments communicated over the Belgian question. The British representative in Russia, George Hamilton Seymour, conveyed encouraging news:

> Nesselrode ... observed to me that he had the great satisfaction of seeing that there was no shade of difference in the opinions of the English and Russian Cabinets as to French questions. The sincerity of the remark was borne out in a striking manner by the despatch relating to Baron Brunnow's conversation [in late March] with the Earl of Derby. On the margin of this paper, opposite to the passage in which M. de Brunnow states that Lord Derby is very anxious that in taking precautions against eventual dangers, no care should be omitted to prevent wounding the susceptibility of the French Government, the Emperor had written in his small clear hand, – 'ainsi nous sommes d'accord même eu cela'.[80]

Russian and British policies were fortuitously convergent just as Britain was looking for assistance in a difficult diplomatic situation.

Derby had made it clear that the Conservatives would adhere 'with strict fidelity to the spirit and the letter' of existing treaty obligations.[81] If France occupied Belgium, war was all but inevitable. The Conservatives would have to choose whether or not to abandon the 1839 treaty, and Belgium with it. Derby and Malmesbury therefore worked hard to achieve a European consensus to resist any potential French incursion. The Russian position was crucial. Britain had the naval power, but not sufficient resources for a land war. The Prussians (who rapidly promised assistance) and the Austrians would be far more vulnerable to French influence and aggression without Russia. A united front over Belgium would have to be underpinned by Russian power.

Derby believed St Petersburg was a vital check on France; that it was Russia's 'strong declarations' that were delaying the establishment of the widely anticipated new French Empire.[82] The Conservatives saw Britain and Russia as the joint and principal guarantors of European peace, as Malmesbury explained to Seymour:

> [I]n the present critical state of European politics nothing is so likely to prevent an interruption of the general peace, or to shorten the duration of any conflict ... as a close and cordial union between Great Britain and Russia; and Her Majesty's Government conceive that there can be nothing in the internal polity of the two countries, or in their views in regard to questions of general European interest, which should prevent them from freely communicating with each other, and from combining their efforts to ward off any interruption of the general peace in any quarter of Europe.[83]

Derby and Malmesbury accordingly focused on clarifying the Russian position, about which Brunnow had been evasive in response to Granville's enquiries.[84] On this issue, as with others, Malmesbury welcomed Derby's guidance. The Prime Minister drafted the significant despatches as well as checking correspondence.[85] He also took a very active part in negotiations, holding a 'long conversation' on key details with Brunnow on 28 March.[86] Derby wanted to be absolutely certain of Russian support, and that – given the delay in communications with St Petersburg – Brunnow was empowered to assert Russian policy in the event of Louis Napoleon acting without warning.[87]

This careful diplomacy paid off. Both on the principle of Russian support and on Brunnow's powers, Nesselrode was unexpectedly accommodating.[88] The Russians even talked about the numbers of troops they might mobilise.[89] In his diary, Seymour recorded his surprise at Russian readiness to comply with British requests: 'I had a long conv[ersatio]n with C[oun]t Nesselrode, & sec[urin]g from him what is quite an engagement that in the event of a French irruption into Belgium the armed opposition of Russia is to be counted upon'.[90] This diplomatic success was symptomatic of the general warmth that had characterised Anglo-Russian relations since the Conservatives had taken office.

On the face of it, this looked pragmatically Palmerstonian – searching for any port in a storm, as Palmerston had in 1841. But co-operation with Russia was a key part of the Derby–Malmesbury strategy for containing any threat to European peace. The Conservative leaders would again attempt to avert war via Anglo-Russian collaboration in 1859. Any similarity to Palmerston's foreign policy was misleading. It was Palmerstonian diplomacy, conceding a binding commitment of the sort the Conservatives were determined to avoid, which had left the Government in difficulties. The 1839 guarantee had, after all, been negotiated by Palmerston. Malmesbury conceded that, given Belgium's strategic significance and its role as a conduit for trade, Britain could not accept 'the Scheldt in the hands of France'.[91] But he regarded the Belgian guarantee with suspicion, as he later explained to Disraeli: 'Very few people know that by Palmerston's fatal policy *we* are bound to defend Belgium against all comers'.[92]

More than once in 1852 it looked as if Palmerston's treaty might leave Britain in trouble. The consensus that had been carefully built up in the spring looked decidedly shaky by the autumn, as Derby recorded in October: 'If France invade Belgium on any quarrel arising out of the liberty of the Press, it is quite clear that we shall have no cooperation from Austria; and I do not like the tone ... of the very last despatches, even from Russia'.[93] The preservation of Belgian integrity until 1914 suggests the treaty was a more powerful deterrent to aggressors than at times it appeared, or than Malmesbury believed. Nevertheless, central to Conservative policy was a desire to avoid commitments to other countries.

Despite the necessity for close co-operation with other governments and Malmesbury's enthusiasm about relations with the conservative powers, neither he nor Derby sought formal alliances. The Prime Minister's consideration of Austrian despatches had prompted him to warn Malmesbury not to get too close to Vienna: 'Our tone should be as cordial as possible, but we must take care what we say, for there is rather *too* great a desire to exhibit us as following exactly the same line as Austria, and I have no idea of committing the Government to another Holy Alliance'.[94] Even had such an alliance been desirable, the Conservative leaders were acutely aware of the political dangers to a Government that could be accused of being in league with autocrats. Derby's son recorded in his diary the 'vehemence' with which the 'popular journals' attacked the Foreign Secretary, who, they alleged, was 'in league with Napoleon and Count Buol to establish a despotic system throughout the Continent'.[95] As Stanley noted, there was 'no foundation for such charges'.[96]

Nevertheless, Malmesbury had to tread carefully. As Anglo-Austrian relations improved, he explained his delicate balancing act to

Cowley: 'Austria has certainly made a step in advance which we must meet with pleasure without committing ourselves to any identity with her despotic views'.[97] Relations with Russia and Prussia required the same care. When Brunnow had tried to persuade Derby to enter into negotiations as to the naval support Britain would offer if action was required on Belgium, Derby was emphatic: 'This of course I told him I was not prepared to do'.[98] The Government could not take the risk of making firm commitments in advance. In the context of the same question, Malmesbury urged Lord Bloomfield, Britain's Minister in Berlin, to 'take care that there is no such *secret understanding* [with Prussia] as to fetter our discretion as to the *extent* or even character of our interference in a supposed case, wh[ich] at present appears very improbable. We are not disposed to enter into any offensive & defensive alliances, altho' we shall readily acknowledge our responsibility as laid down by treaties'.[99]

Derby and Malmesbury sought instead to cultivate good relationships with all the European powers, irrespective of ideological stance or 'internal polity'.[100] This did necessitate diplomatic realignment, working closely with governments that would not have been regarded as natural allies by the Whigs, but a formal alliance was neither desirable nor politically sustainable. Other powers, however, did not entirely appreciate the nature of the Government's position, or the difficulties of British politics. With Anglo-Russian relations at the highest point they had been since Aberdeen was at the FO – or would be again until long after the Crimean war – St Petersburg offered exactly the sort of alliance the Conservatives wished to avoid.

In an episode all but neglected by historians, Derby turned down the Russian offer without hesitation. The exact details – even the date – of the offer are unfortunately very difficult to establish. Nevertheless, an alliance proposal seems to have been made, and the little evidence that has survived is clear about its fate. For some years, historians have been aware of a reference in Disraeli's draft memoirs,[101] in which he recalled that, soon after the Conservatives had formed the Government, Brunnow 'proposed to Lord Derby an alliance between England and Russia, offensive & defensive'.[102] The Prime Minister 'at once rejected the proposition', which the Cabinet was not invited to discuss.[103] The only other piece of evidence that has yet come to light lies in Malmesbury's Papers.

A message from Derby, filed with correspondence from March 1852, corroborates Disraeli's later recollection.[104] Malmesbury's note at the top refers, interestingly, to efforts by 'Powers' (plural) to 'force us to an alliance'.[105] Such a note suggests that it was not merely a

Russian initiative, although Brunnow was the messenger. Derby sent the Foreign Secretary a copy of a despatch and a 'report of what passed in conversation' between him and Brunnow. Given Malmesbury's note at the top, it seems likely – though one cannot be certain – that the despatch and the report related to the alliance proposal.[106] The Prime Minister's postscript certainly suggested that was the case: 'It would be useful that you should look up our old Treaty objections, that we may see whether we should act on them, or whether it would be expedient to establish any new basis'.[107] Whatever the exact details, Derby's 'steer' to Malmesbury was clear: he had already decided to reject the proposal. The only question to be resolved was the official basis for doing so.

As this episode demonstrated, the Prime Minister consistently determined the direction of policy, and often the detail. This would remain the pattern throughout his first two administrations. During the complex negotiations regarding Belgium, he had been closely involved in diplomatic minutiae. He had drafted and checked despatches, intervened and met with Brunnow, just as he had met with Buol over Anglo-Austrian questions. The Prime Minister disposed rapidly of the Russian alliance proposal and, apparently, almost without consultation. That any of his other colleagues would have disagreed with his handling of the matter seems unlikely, but he seems to have had no intention of asking them, having 'told him [Brunnow] he shall have an answer in an hour or two'.[108] This would be after Malmesbury had 'made what you think fit of the despatch'.[109] Disraeli was evidently also aware of the proposal, though he does not seem to have been consulted – unsurprisingly, given that it was well beyond his portfolio.

Derby's tight control over business did not indicate contempt for his colleagues. He took care to encourage his troops, paying Malmesbury quite a compliment a few weeks after the formation of the Government: 'I have read your private instructions with great interest – they are *excellent* – terse, clear, and admirably expressed. If all my young soldiers show as well, we shall exhibit a formidable line of battle'.[110] The Conservative line of battle would be attacked on several fronts over the coming months. Foreign policy would provide some ground for a possible advance, but it would also present a tempting target to the enemy.

The first onslaught came quickly. Publication of the Anglo-Austrian correspondence about refugees provoked howls of disapproval.[111] The Conservatives had presided over an improvement in foreign relations, but with the wrong state – one despised by liberal public opinion. Within and beyond Parliament there were objections to Malmesbury's description of Austria as 'the oldest ally of England'.[112] Palmerston gently teased ministers for their 'amicable Arcadian dialogue' with Austria.[113] Others were more vehement. Monckton Milnes suggested that 'such things seemed to establish a certain sympathy between the present British and Austrian Governments, which, he would take leave to say, would be anything rather than grateful to the feelings and opinions of the people of this country'.[114] Walpole, the Home Secretary, speaking in Disraeli's absence, protested unconvincingly that it was 'not a fair way of putting it ... that the renewal of our friendly relations with Austria had solely arisen from the assumption of office by the present Government'.[115] In the Lords, however, Malmesbury more confidently rejected suggestions that he was unreliable on the refugee question. His notorious letter to Buol was simply 'a civil answer to a civil despatch'.[116]

A row that blew up during the elections a few weeks later was less easily dispelled. It arose from the ongoing negotiations on the Mather case. The new Government's rather different approach to foreign policy unwittingly presented its enemies with a clear target. As the case revolved around an Englishman injured overseas, it proved fertile territory for those who had backed Palmerston over Don Pacifico.

The Mather negotiations had been far from straightforward. In March, Malmesbury had asked the father of the young man injured by the Austrian soldiers in Tuscany to name a suitable amount in compensation for his son's injuries.[117] Mather senior had suggested £5,000, which Malmesbury thought 'exorbitant'.[118] Redress by that stage being sought solely from Tuscany, the negotiations had been handled by the British representative in Florence, the Honourable Peter Campbell Scarlett, shortly to be succeeded by Sir Henry Bulwer. Malmesbury instructed Scarlett to inform the Tuscans that Britain would not be seeking Mather's suggested amount, proposing instead that Scarlett obtain a minimum of £1,000.[119] After long and grinding negotiations, an ailing Scarlett had on 5 May accepted from the Tuscans the rather lower sum of 1,000 *francesconi* – about £220. This was to be combined with the release of some British prisoners whose freedom Britain had in fact already agreed with Tuscany. With Scarlett becoming dangerously ill, the news of his settlement was conveyed by a junior diplomat, Henry Barron.[120]

Although disapproving of both the amount and the linkage with the prisoners' release, Malmesbury reluctantly agreed to the settlement. He drafted a despatch to Bulwer, en route to take over, on 21 May.[121] When Derby was sent the despatch to approve, he did so, re-wording it to his satisfaction.[122] The decision to accept Scarlett's deal was thus as much Derby's as it was the Foreign Secretary's. On 22 May, Malmesbury instructed Addington, Permanent Under-Secretary at the FO, to write to Mather's father, informing him of the acceptance of the Tuscan offer.[123] This Addington did on 24 May, the next working day.[124] He admitted that 'Her Majesty's Government do not consider that this sum is equivalent to the injury which Mr. Mather suffered, or to that which an English court would have awarded him'; however, he appealed to Mather's sense of patriotism to induce him to accept it.[125]

On 22 May, meanwhile, two further despatches had arrived from Tuscany.[126] Significantly, they revealed that Scarlett had agreed to waive the principle of Tuscan responsibility for the safety of British subjects in Tuscany, the fundamental point to which the Prime Minister and the Foreign Secretary had attached so much importance. But Malmesbury did not read those despatches until some later date. On 27 May, in answer to a question from Earl Fitzwilliam, he told the Lords that Scarlett had brought matters 'to a conclusion'.[127] Meanwhile, Mather senior, having received Addington's note of 24 May, indignantly rejected Scarlett's deal and sent copies of his correspondence to the press.[128] On 28 May, Malmesbury repeated his assertion that 'the case is now concluded'.[129] Having at some interim stage read the despatches that informed him of Scarlett's concession on the question of Tuscan responsibility, the Foreign Secretary then decided to rescind his previous acceptance of Scarlett's settlement. This he did in a series of despatches to Bulwer, dated 29 May.[130]

Derby and Malmesbury had left themselves open to criticism, which only increased when the relevant papers were published in 'blue book' form.[131] It was unwise of Malmesbury to have asked Mather senior to name a desirable amount in compensation rather than deciding the sum himself. It was equally unwise to have publicised Malmesbury's criticism of Mather senior's demands in the blue book, and to have accepted a deal that appeared unsatisfactory. It was even more inadvisable to have admitted to Mather senior that the deal was inadequate. From 28 May onwards, once Addington's letter was in the public domain, the administration's opponents had a rare opportunity to attack a clear decision by the Government. With an election imminent, they took full advantage.

Though the basic details of the case are trivial enough, the Mather affair repays examination in a wider context. Historians have hitherto focused on the handling of the case as the work of an inexperienced Foreign Secretary, rather than as a symptom of political differences over the conduct of foreign policy. Malmesbury has been singled out for condemnation, as he was by contemporaries. He has been criticised for being at best 'naïve', at worst 'clumsy, dilatory and negligent'.[132] It has been noted that his direction of policy 'was not marked by any great efficiency or firmness'.[133] Whether or not such criticism is justified, it leaves broader aspects of foreign policy unexplored.

Firstly, the case produced a small foretaste of later and more significant tension between Malmesbury and Disraeli. In 1852, Disraeli's part in diplomatic affairs was very limited. On this occasion, however, with a press campaign gathering pace in the wake of the publication of Mather senior's letters, Disraeli intervened. Perhaps alerted by an excoriating *Times* leader on 29 May, he wrote to Malmesbury, as well as to Derby and Stanley, fearing 'a British cry for the hustings'.[134] The Foreign Secretary did not welcome the Chancellor's intervention. Malmesbury had regularly expressed scepticism to Derby about Disraeli's mood-swings.[135] He was not about to accord them greater credence, as he explained to Derby: 'I have received a letter from Disraeli in a tremendous stew about the Mather case of which as yet he knows nothing'.[136] His words foreshadowed his response to Disraeli's interference in 1858–59.

It certainly seems unlikely that Disraeli knew much about the detail of the case or that he cared greatly about what happened to the Mathers. Nevertheless, the popular mood about such cases mattered in elections. Disraeli's comprehension of foreign policy was limited, but he understood how election campaigns worked. He was interested in foreign policy for what political advantage or disadvantage it brought. In 1852 he did not propose an alternative policy, as he would in 1859. Even at that stage, however, there was a tension between Disraeli's instinctive nervousness about public opinion – as he focused on the great goal of majority government – and Malmesbury's technocratic approach to diplomacy as a pursuit for the initiated. It would become a recurring theme throughout the 1850s.

Secondly, the Mather case further emphasised the way in which foreign policy was intertwined with domestic circumstances. In the furore that blew up about Mather, little was revealed about the successes or failures of Conservative foreign policy. The criticism was largely for electoral purposes, and exaggerated accordingly. All the parties recognised that the result of the 1852 election would be deeply significant. The preservation of free trade, and with it the broader Whig–Peelite legacy, potentially depended on denying Derby an overall majority. When the election results emerged over the summer, the Conservatives' gains left them as the largest party, with somewhere around 300 seats. This number was almost exactly equalled by the combined ranks of the Whigs and the reduced Peelites. The relative closeness of the results demonstrated the reality and the magnitude of the Conservative threat. For the opposition, therefore, all electoral ammunition was welcome: foreign-policy decisions stood proxy, at least in part, for Derby's elusive economic policy. This was a confusing time in politics, when it was by no means clear which leaders or what parties would be forming the next government. All the leading Whigs and Peelites were vying for position, and the only unifying theme was opposition to Derby's administration.

After the publication of the papers, debates in the Commons on 14 June and in the Lords on 21 June presented opportunities to embarrass ministers. Russell attacked select details of the published papers, and concluded with a sideswipe recalling Derby's criticisms over Don Pacifico: 'I beg leave to enter my protest against the conduct which seems to have degraded the Government in the eyes of all Europe; it could not degrade this country, because this country takes better and higher views than the Government of what is due to our national character'.[137] His motives were clear, as Granby pointed out: 'He [Russell] taunted the Government – "You have no policy; you have no opinion of your own." Well, Sir, I cannot say the same of the noble Lord, for I believe that the noble Lord has one opinion, which is this: that there is nobody fit for the government of this country except himself'.[138]

Such Conservative protests made little difference to the tide of criticism. The anti-Government journals and newspapers threw their weight behind the parliamentary opposition. *Fraser's Magazine* denounced Conservative foreign policy as 'the darkest chapter' of the Government's misdeeds.[139] Focusing on Malmesbury, its anonymous critic suggested that there was 'not a solitary instance in the history of administration in which an English statesman was convicted of so many grave and inexcusable errors within so brief a compass of time'.[140] *Punch*'s satirists described 'the most curious item' in the 'Protectionist Estimates' as 'the estimate that has been formed of our national honour, which (*vide* the Mather case) has been set down at two hundred and forty pounds'.[141] The leader-writer in *The Times* maintained that he had 'seldom read a more lame and feeble composition than that in which the Foreign-office communicates to the father of the wounded gentleman the result of these "long and vexatious negotiations"'.[142] The venom expended in such disproportionate attacks betrayed the seriousness with which the opposition and its organs regarded the election.

Thirdly, it was clear that no matter how hard the Conservatives sought to stamp their own imprint on foreign policy, debate about it would be conducted on Palmerstonian terms. In his *Memoirs*,

Malmesbury singled out what he believed to be the origin of the furore about Mather: 'a blustering speech made some time ago by Lord Palmerston, declaring that John Bull, wherever he was, or whatever he did, was to be as sacred as the ancient "civis Romanus"'.[143] Ironically, in 1852 Palmerston himself was remarkably un-Palmerstonian. Perhaps still toying with the possibility of joining Derby's ministry, he used restrained language in the debate about Mather.[144] But *Civis Romanus* cast a long shadow.

The Conservatives' opponents had realised that the Government was not going to conduct foreign policy with Palmerston's panache. In Parliament, Bernal Osborne lamented Palmerston's absence: 'The boast of *Civis Romanus sum* was gone now'.[145] *The Times* concluded its denunciation of Malmesbury by regretting that he had not had 'the spirit to defend private British interests and rights throughout the world'.[146] Not for nothing did *Punch* depict Malmesbury as a shoeblack polishing Austria's boots and Palmerston lurking behind, commenting 'Well I wouldn't clean that fellow's shoes at any price'.[147] Russell noted that Palmerston 'understood the business of his department'.[148] The implication was clear, but in case there was any doubt, he alleged that Malmesbury's handling of the case had 'degraded the Government in the eyes of all Europe', which was the more damaging because of the 'better and higher' behaviour that Britain expected of its leaders.[149] He singled out Gladstone's vilifications of Naples as evidence of more noble British behaviour.[150] But the sort of uncomfortable stalemate produced by Gladstone's polemical epistles and the controversy generated by the Don Pacifico affair was precisely what the Conservatives were attempting to avoid.

The Mather case demonstrated that Conservative foreign policy did not operate on the same basis as Palmerston's. Criticism of the Government on Palmerstonian grounds therefore had some validity, but it also missed the point. Certain assumptions, unaddressed by the historiography, underpinned Derbyite Conservative foreign policy and set it apart from the policies advocated by the Government's opponents. Malmesbury and Derby assumed that the way in which to deal with cases such as Mather's was to adopt precisely the opposite course to that which, for example, Palmerston had adopted over Don Pacifico: to proceed in the 'deliberate and conciliatory' manner Derby had advocated on assuming power. This was not pusillanimity: they simply assumed they were more likely to get the desired result that way. They had no interest in ostentatious displays of British power, as had been the Palmerstonian habit. A historiography still dominated by contemporary criticism has obscured this point.

It seems likely that the Conservatives were simply uninterested in cases like Mather's, which they regarded as an irritation and a distraction from more serious questions. Malmesbury was not an apologist for the Austrian regime or what he described as its 'studied rudeness' to British travellers.[151] He was, however, irritated by the series of minor Anglo-Austrian disputes generated by the misadventures of British travellers. His published journal includes a comment about 'freaks of travelling Englishmen who get themselves into scrapes abroad, and, being often deservedly punished or arrested, call upon their Government for protection'.[152] It was of a piece with a letter to Derby, in which he referred to 'the scrape wh[ich] that hothead has got us into'.[153] This was not merely personal pique over Mather. In August, when another case involving an Englishman (a Mr Newton) began to create difficulties, he displayed a similar exasperation:

> Considering the brutal nature of the Austrian soldiers & police, & the state of their country, & then the incurable snobbism of our young English travellers of the middle class, I see no end of these cases unless we openly say that if they choose to go for *pleasure* into a country so misgoverned we cannot go to war for the roughness they meet with.[154]

Malmesbury was not alone in his distaste for the diplomacy required by such cases, which was of necessity more confrontational than was normally desirable. Even at the height of the Mather furore, Derby stressed that the matter had to be kept in proportion, and backed Malmesbury in his search for a rapid conclusion: 'Regret for the past, and acknowledged responsibility for the future are all that we can require'.[155] Stanley's attitude was equally practical and unsentimental. He was keen to settle quickly and quietly over Newton, who, he felt, was 'bent on making himself as troublesome as he can'.[156] He could see no point in persisting with Austria: 'I don't expect that any better terms or more ample apology can be got out of Buol'.[157]

A desire to get such irritating matters dealt with as quickly and efficiently as possible would explain certain aspects of the Mather case, notably Malmesbury's delay in rescinding his original acceptance of Scarlett's deal and his less than consistent accounts of his actions. During the parliamentary debate he volunteered to the Lords a self-deprecating admission: 'I will candidly avow that in one part of this transaction I have been to blame. On a Saturday (the 22nd) I received what I believed to be the final despatch, settling the question not satisfactorily to me', but in which he concurred, as he believed that Scarlett 'had not waved [*sic*] the principle of the responsibility of the Tuscan Government'.[158] But then came the *mea culpa*:

Afterwards, other despatches arrived, one of which contained the important letter from the Duke of Casigliano [setting aside the question of Tuscan responsibility] ... I, in the meanwhile, had sent off a despatch to Sir Henry Bulwer, without having examined these last despatches. I take to myself blame for this ... My Lords, I will freely admit I did not open these despatches received on Saturday until the following Monday.[159]

His confessed mistake, for which he was roundly abused, neatly obscured a greater error. Malmesbury's concerns about Scarlett's abandonment of the principle of Tuscan responsibility seem, in fact, only to have been raised on 29 May.[160] This was *seven* days after the despatches had reached the FO, although Malmesbury told Parliament he had read the despatches on the 24 May.[161] The Foreign Secretary may have either not noticed or not cared sufficiently to address the matter, until he was forced to do so a whole week later, rather than the delay of a few days that he acknowledged (and to which historians have drawn attention). Without the public outcry, he would have quietly buried the episode. To Malmesbury and his colleagues, these cases involving British travellers were simply a nuisance.

Though it backfired badly, the way in which Derby and Malmesbury had handled the Mather case arose logically from their strategy of constructive engagement with the great and minor European powers. They saw no merit in hectoring or lecturing in the manner of Palmerston's more *active* diplomacy or Gladstone's public letters. Russell had suggested, while criticising Malmesbury, that 'immortal honour' attached to Gladstone for his denunciations of the Neapolitan regime.[162] It was very clear, however, that Gladstone's polemics had been unsuccessful in their primary object: the release of Neapolitan political prisoners. As Aberdeen had explained to Gladstone, Schwarzenberg felt that 'the publicity given to these accusations has entirely deprived him of the means of exercising any influence [at Naples], even in the most confidential manner'.[163]

Perhaps in part because of their own distaste for Whig moralising, the Conservative leaders appreciated that publicly lecturing foreign states was unlikely to achieve much: they regarded it as futile. When dealing with the Newton case, Malmesbury forwarded to Derby an article from the Austrian press which showed what he described as 'the feeling entertained against us by Palmerston's bluster & Haynau's case'.[164] In the Foreign Secretary's opinion, Britain 'would get nothing from Austria & the more we write the more incapable of obliging her to repair injustice & the more ridiculous shall we appear'.[165]

Moreover, the consequences of belligerence might be positively counter-productive. In the Commons debate over Mather, Bernal

Osborne had contrasted Malmesbury's conduct with that of Palmerston's in 1847.[166] On the occasion to which he referred, a British fleet had been sent to obtain the release of an imprisoned British consul in New Grenada. But such methods were anathema to the Derbyite leadership. Considering the Newton case, Malmesbury outlined the likely impact of pressuring Austria via a hypothetical blockade: 'Supposing Buol positively to refuse redress what can we do? ... blockade Trieste & Venice & stop a trade wh[ich] gives us a million sterling per ann[um]'.[167] The Government, as Derby had pointed out, did not wish to be seen as composed of 'reckless or careless men', to which charge they would have been exposed had they engaged in expensive public gestures over minor issues.[168]

Conservative ministers were consistently suspicious of interventionism. When, for example, another dispute (about British ecclesiastical jurisdiction overseas) threatened to draw in the Foreign Secretary, Derby noted with regret that the FO 'has already meddled in the matter under both Palmerston & Granville'.[169] He vetoed any further involvement. Stanley was, similarly, sceptical about Palmerston's handling of a Protestant *cause célèbre* involving an Italian couple. Francesco and Rosa Madiai, servants of English families, had provided a base for English Protestant proselytists, for which they had been imprisoned in Florence. Stanley thought a loud Palmerstonian intervention had been both cynical and futile: 'Palmerston undertook, if I recollect right, to defray the costs of their [the Madiai's] defence – an ostentatious piece of assistance, which gained him the publicity he wanted, and probably led to a severer sentence being passed on them, which he cared nothing about'.[170]

In short, the Conservatives in government deprecated and consciously avoided what they perceived to be Palmerston's methods, just as they had criticised them in opposition. Yet Malmesbury is often portrayed as a pupil of Palmerston. In his memoirs, Malmesbury revealed that, shortly after taking office, he had consulted Palmerston about foreign policy.[171] Perhaps because of this, one historian has even suggested that Malmesbury was 'an avowed protégé of Palmerston'.[172] The most recent study of Palmerston's foreign policy has again drawn attention to the fact that Malmesbury accepted the former minister's offer of advice.[173]

How much importance should be attached to the two men's discussion? It was logical enough for Malmesbury to record it in his *Memoirs*. He had a keen eye for what would now be described as 'celebrity appeal'. He was publishing his memoirs at a time when Palmerston was regarded more sympathetically than he had been twenty years earlier.[174] As far as the discussion itself was concerned, it was quite logical, as well as polite, for Malmesbury to meet with his predecessor-but-one. Palmerston was incontrovertibly the most experienced diplomatist in Britain. Malmesbury also met with Granville and Wellington.[175] In fact, the only ex-Foreign Secretary he did not meet was Aberdeen, no friend of the Derbyites. Palmerston also had personal connections with Malmesbury, whose grandfather had been Palmerston's mentor.[176] But Malmesbury's foreign policy displayed no evidence of any desire to follow Palmerston's example. No doubt Palmerston's guidance about office routine and procedure was useful. The gist of his policy advice, however, which was 'to keep well with France', can hardly have been a novel concept for Louis Napoleon's old friend.[177]

Only the uncontroversial aspects of Palmerston's foreign policy, which fitted with Conservative ideals, were adopted by Derby's administration. The Schleswig–Holstein agreement of May 1852 was the sort of measure that attracted bipartisan support. The treaty of London, patching up the ongoing territorial dispute between Denmark and the German states, was largely Palmerston's work.[178] While Malmesbury presided at the conference in London and concluded matters, the detailed negotiations had been carried out by the Whigs. Nevertheless, the patient settlement of complex disputes satisfied the Derbyite desire for a calm and peaceful resolution of difficulties. Malmesbury, with Derby's guidance, excelled at such work. He also took a leading part in the temporary settlements of the succession to the Greek throne and of the question of Neufchâtel, a Swiss canton which the treaty of Vienna had accorded to Prussia.[179] In all these matters, the Conservatives pursued a course which Palmerston in his less provocative moods might also have pursued. They had no desire to emulate other aspects of his diplomacy.

The Mather case demonstrates, finally, that Derby's role again repays examination. Without the Prime Minister, any analysis of Conservative policy is incomplete, and yet he has disappeared from the historiography. While he had not been as intimately involved in the negotiations as he had been over Austria and Russia, he had certainly directed policy. It was and is illogical to accord either praise or blame to Malmesbury alone. As the Foreign Secretary pointed out to Disraeli, Derby had closely followed all the negotiations: 'The Captain [Derby] saw all my despatches to Scarlett before the event'.[180] The Prime Minister assured the Lords that he had overseen matters: 'for the whole course of these proceedings I avow myself as fully and entirely responsible as my noble Friend ... I am just as much and as entirely open to censure as he from whatever quarter that censure may proceed'.[181] These were not empty words. Contemporary criticism of the Foreign Secretary, echoed in the historiography, has obscured the Prime Minister's role.

Turbulent priests: Ireland and Rome

Derby was also at the heart of the major foreign-policy initiative of the summer, which was every bit as caught up with domestic considerations. During the summer and autumn of 1852 the Government secretly made a concerted effort to establish diplomatic relations with the Papacy. With that objective, Bulwer was directed to 'retire' from Florence to Rome in an informal mission. When that mission was ultimately unsuccessful, an even more unofficial initiative was given the prime ministerial go-ahead. No aspect of foreign affairs in 1852 could be said to have received sufficient attention, but the negotiations with Rome have particularly suffered from under-exposure. Only one historian has, briefly, analysed this episode in a survey of Malmesbury's diplomacy; the few other references are to be found in studies of Disraeli.[182] But the search for a new diplomatic link with the Vatican cannot be adequately explored or explained simply in the context of the Foreign Secretary's career, and even less so as part of the Chancellor's.

Given the long history of Anglo-papal *froideur*, the British relationship with the Vatican had always been erratic and semi-official at best. The Whigs were not, of course, solely to blame for this state of affairs, but the 'papal aggression' furore, exacerbated by Russell, had hardly helped. This might not have mattered greatly, had it not had a bearing on a number of other issues. In purely diplomatic terms, the lack of a formal relationship with the Pope's government made it difficult to protect British interests in the Papal States. The existing informal and overlapping arrangements for British representation in Rome were less than satisfactory. Both William Petre, an attaché (whose role was somewhat vague), and the British consul, Freeborn, had some responsibilities. Malmesbury's opinion of the two men and their working relationship was not high, as he explained to Bulwer: 'Freeborn speaks of Petre as the pot did of the kettle – the kettle is the most noble instrument, and so is Petre of the two, but he is only fit to be used at the old ladies['] teatables in Rome'.[183]

Practical difficulties ensued. For example, when British national Edward Murray was convicted of murder by a Roman court and faced the death penalty, the case had at first to be overseen from Florence by

Bulwer. The Foreign Secretary was having to focus on this case just as the Mather affair was beginning to generate more work and problems. Malmesbury was therefore acutely aware of the necessity for effective working relationships with governments in that region. He may also have considered the fact that normalising relations with Rome would remove another bone of contention with Austria. A better diplomatic relationship with the Pope would be one more way of avoiding 'unseemly wrangles' like that in March over the question of Vienna's right to present notes to Britain on behalf of the Papal States.[184]

But the driving force behind the Rome mission was a domestic one. Pope Pius IX potentially had the power to suppress what Derby described as the 'spirit of turbulence' in Irish politics.[185] This was vital for the Prime Minister, who sought both calm and political advantage in Ireland. In the early 1850s, discontent over rural issues, sectarianism and widespread political agitation were producing tension and unrest across Ireland, just as they had in the 1840s. The long-term effects of the 1845 Famine were being felt in continuing demands for land rights. The Tenant League was pressing for its '3 Fs'.[186] The wave of anti-Catholicism stirred up by the 'Papal Aggression' crisis had added to a climate of sectarian ill-feeling.

With all these tensions contributing to violent agitation, the 1852 election campaign was particularly bitter in Ireland.[187] The active political intervention of significant numbers of the Roman Catholic priesthood added to difficulties. The Prime Minister was keen to reduce this clerical involvement and, in turn, the tensions in Irish politics. Throughout the 1850s the Conservatives were also aware of the potential for electoral advantage in Ireland. Russell's appeals to Protestantism during the 'papal aggression' had backfired badly on his party, and, in Clarendon's view, *slew* the Whig Party in Ireland'.[188] The former Lord Lieutenant's pessimism was justified. During the next decade the Conservatives worked assiduously, and with some success, to increase their Irish representation.[189]

In matters pertaining to the Pope and Roman Catholicism, Malmesbury was given strong guidance by the Prime Minister. From 1831 to 1833, under Grey, Derby had been Chief Secretary for Ireland, and he had spoken frequently on Irish matters thereafter. While Colonial Secretary in Peel's administration he had corresponded regularly with the Conservative leader about Irish education.[190] He had long favoured working with what he viewed as moderate Roman Catholicism. He had been a strong proponent of conciliation, via the employment of 'one or two *good* Roman Catholics' in Peel's Government.[191] As tended to be the case with Derby where Roman

Catholicism was concerned, however, this sentiment was tinged with doubt: 'I own I hardly know where to look for them'.[192]

When the question of better diplomatic relations with the Pope had been raised in the 1840s, Derby had agreed that this object was 'desirable'.[193] But the impetus and initiative came from Peel, and even at this early stage scepticism tempered Derby's instinct for conciliation ('the difficulties are very great'[194]). This was before Derby was more dependent on the Tory Protestant 'ultras' to whose influence Jones has attributed his later circumspection on religious matters.[195] Derby's willingness to engage with Roman Catholicism always had its limits, particularly in Ireland. Although it was written some eight years before his first premiership, a letter from Derby to Peel in 1844 summed up a position unchanged in 1852: 'I feel ... the necessity, if possible, of conciliating the moderate R. Catholics. I feel, at least as strongly, the necessity of not alienating the great body of Protestants. I know not whether these objects be compatible, but the attempt must be made'.[196]

In considering just such an 'attempt' through better relations with the Pope, which they began to contemplate from May onwards, Derby and Malmesbury were following in Conservative footsteps. During the 'papal aggression' crisis, Derby had deplored the Russell Government's lack of foresight in failing to establish relations with Rome, through which the crisis might have been averted.[197] In late 1851, the Whigs had laid plans for a mission to Rome, about which Malmesbury was subsequently notified.[198] Russell's Conservative predecessors had been rather more proactive, and Derby would have been well-informed about Peel and Aberdeen's efforts to improve relations. They had sent Petre to Rome in the first place, to establish better communications. As relations had warmed, Peel and his Home Secretary, Sir James Graham, had in 1844 succeeded in obtaining a papal intervention to restrain the political activities of the Irish Roman Catholic priesthood. Though its impact on the Irish clergy had ultimately been 'disheartening' to the British Government, Pope Gregory XVI had issued a Rescript in Ireland directed at politically active priests.[199]

It was this earlier political and diplomatic model that Derby and Malmesbury were to use as the template for their own unsuccessful attempt to improve Anglo-papal relations. The desired course of events was to be: an unofficial contact; a formalising of relations; a papal intervention to calm Ireland. From late May, Derby and Malmesbury discussed in detail how they might establish a formal diplomatic relationship, and from June onwards, Malmesbury and

Bulwer also corresponded on the subject. It was proposed that Bulwer should 'retire' from Florence to Rome as if on holiday. There, he would unofficially meet with Pius's Secretary of State, Cardinal Antonelli, and other senior Vatican officials. If some diplomatic *modus vivendi* could be agreed on, a layman would come to Britain as the Pope's envoy, and a combined Rome–Florence diplomatic mission would be created. In August, Bulwer was duly instructed to go to Rome, where he negotiated with the Papal Court from September to October. All communications were conducted in great secrecy, given their sensitivity.

Disraeli's involvement with Bulwer's mission was marginal and could be ignored altogether, were it not for the fact that the mission has become part of the broader Disraeli myth. Monypenny and Buckle suggested that the Chancellor was behind Bulwer's negotiations with Rome.[200] More recently, phrases of Bulwer's in a letter to Disraeli on 1 August, and a draft letter from Disraeli to Bulwer, have led the editors of the *Disraeli Letters* to conclude that Bulwer 'was in Rome on a mission for D[israeli]'.[201] This is another example of the historiographical tendency to place Disraeli closer to the centre of policy than he was.

Derby and Malmesbury had for two months prior to 1 August already been discussing the possibility of Bulwer going to Rome. The initial suggestion about establishing relations with Rome appears to have been made by Malmesbury, though it seems likely he and Derby had already discussed the matter. When the Murray case necessitated communications with the Vatican, Malmesbury spotted an opening to exploit: 'I was going to propose to you that we should make this case of Murray the opportunity for establishing diplomatic relations with Rome'.[202] As an old friend of Bulwer, Disraeli may well have had some influence in persuading him to undertake the journey, although it is difficult to see how a career diplomat could have refused the Foreign Secretary's instructions. Unfortunately, with the exception of one of Disraeli's drafts, it seems that only Bulwer's half of the correspondence with the Chancellor has survived. Nevertheless, the evidence in the extensive correspondence between Malmesbury, Derby and Bulwer suggests that the Disraeli–Bulwer letters were peripheral. Malmesbury, with Derby's support, was the co-ordinator of the mission. It was he who had to explain Bulwer's terms of reference to Disraeli, not the other way around.[203]

Disraeli's part, as an old acquaintance and correspondent of Bulwer, was a twofold one on the margins of foreign policy. Firstly, for Bulwer, Disraeli happened to represent a sympathetic and trusted point of contact with the Government, which could be used to assist with sensitive matters such as his allowance.[204] Secondly, in the latter days of the mission, he provided (at Bulwer's request) a letter which the diplomat could show to Papal staff, in an attempt indirectly to persuade Pius to agree to British terms.[205] This is the letter, only the draft of which survives, which has been presented as evidence of Disraeli's central role. But it mirrored one sent by Malmesbury on 22 September with the instruction: 'This letter to be shewn to Antonelli'.[206] Malmesbury's letter was uncompromising in its tone and evidently written with the intention of frightening the Vatican into co-operation. He hinted darkly at adopting 'measures which they [the British Government] would sincerely regret being obliged to execute' against Irish priests if the Pope was unco-operative.[207]

Disraeli's letter was more conciliatory and designed to demonstrate that, despite the dangerous religious tension in Britain, the Conservatives were keen to appease the Roman Catholics. It is unclear whether this was a co-ordinated effort by the Chancellor and the Foreign Secretary. Malmesbury's letter was sent two days after Bulwer penned his request for a letter to Disraeli. Bulwer may have anticipated strong words from the Foreign Secretary and hoped for gentler ones from the Chancellor. The production of a second letter so soon after the first for the same purpose may have been coincidental, though such a supposition stretches credulity a little. What *is* clear is that Disraeli was by no means the first, the only, or the main proponent of improved Anglo-papal relations.

The Prime Minister, in contrast, was the joint-architect of policy. His experience was critically important, as Malmesbury acknowledged: 'I am so absolutely ignorant of Irish politics & you are so completely experienced in them that I cannot do otherwise than require yr instructions for Bulwer in detail'.[208] The Foreign Secretary, as ever, willingly deferred to his leader. As he explained to Bulwer at the outset: 'I could add nothing to Lord Derby's able letter which I send you'.[209]

Derby was firmly focused on the Irish dimension, while Malmesbury seems to have been concerned with obtaining an improvement in Anglo-papal relations for its general political and diplomatic utility. Stanley made a note in his diary of the long conversations between Foreign Secretary and Prime Minister on the subject:

> Malmesbury hopes so to arrange matters, that we may have a permanent legation there [Rome], while the Pope has a layman acting as his representative in England. He thinks the effect of this friendly understanding on the R. Catholics of the U.K. would be considerable. My Father looks

to Ireland: wishes to lay before the Court of Rome the conduct of the Irish priesthood: and to obtain a condemnation of their proceedings from the highest spiritual authority.[210]

It was the political interventions of the Irish clergy that particularly incensed the Prime Minister. He explained this to Malmesbury when they first discussed the matter: '*Just at present* the great object would be to restrain the R.C. clergymen from making religious questions prominent at the elections – a course of proceeding which will infallibly kindle into tenfold fury the Protestant feeling which is always burning so fiercely'.[211] He accepted, however, that any fruits from Bulwer's mission would probably come too late to affect the election.

The mission could nevertheless have an important political impact. It was always domestic considerations that determined the course of this secretive diplomacy. As Malmesbury explained to Bulwer, 'if you succeed in your policy an important impression might be conveyed from Rome upon the minds of the *elected* before November when Parliament will meet'.[212] Although the election results were disappointing for the Conservatives, it was by no means clear that the Government would imminently fall. Clarendon, for example, thought that 'the Govt as yet is not *unpopular* ... the country at large being conservative wishes to keep the Govt in fear of worse things'.[213] Palmerston similarly observed that Derby 'might be able to struggle on for some considerable time'.[214] The Conservatives appeared to have a fair amount left to play for, and the independent Irish MPs effectively held the balance of power in Parliament.[215] Conservative self-interest and the general desirability of calm in Irish politics gave the Government every incentive to pursue a conciliatory policy in Ireland, and with Rome. It would produce legislation to deal sympathetically with the land question; foreign policy represented the other half of its two-pronged strategy.

For a British government, the Vatican was of course a rather different proposition from other European courts. The 'papal aggression' episode had generated such hysterical and rabid anti-Roman agitation that any negotiations could have backfired very badly with domestic opinion. Consequently, secrecy was imperative, as Malmesbury explained to Bulwer: 'You observe in a previous letter that my directions with respect to the place of your possible retirement were at variance in my public and private despatches. But I think you forgot that I could not mention *Rome* at all in my official document'.[216] The Foreign Secretary had to tread very carefully, with one eye always on the public opinion that had savaged him over the Mather affair. His instructions to Bulwer were framed accordingly: 'inform yourself, in such a manner as not to sacrifice the dignity of this country by any public refusal, whether an exchange of recognised diplomatic relations can be established'.[217]

Though Malmesbury doubtless was concerned about the 'dignity of this country', this was shorthand for the credibility and stability of the Government. Protestant opinion across the political spectrum, and not least among Malmesbury's colleagues, was deeply hostile to Rome. Virulent anti-Roman feeling secured the 'Eglinton Clause' in legislative concrete. Malmesbury knew that 'the Eglinton Clause ... cannot be repealed ... no Government could reverse that decision'.[218] The Prime Minister and the Foreign Secretary now had to circumvent their colleague's legislative success. Only a lay mission could be accorded to the British Court, and then representation could be ratcheted up by degrees.[219] But even so cautious a strategy posed potential domestic difficulties for the Government.

The negotiations with Rome, like all aspects of foreign policy, were conducted in the shadow of a parliamentary opposition and a press ready to pounce on every Conservative act. Opponents were determined to rid themselves of a Government whose survival, relative to the brief lifespan anticipated in certain quarters, was by the autumn dismaying many. Malmesbury followed press coverage closely and was very conscious of the damage it could do. Clearly influenced by the furore about the Mather case and the treatment of British citizens in Austria, he had promptly submitted to Derby the question of the British response to Murray's conviction when it arose.[220] The Mather affair was omnipresent. When the Duke of Wellington died in the autumn, Austria refused to send military representatives to his funeral because of the Haynau incident. The Foreign Secretary maintained that he was 'not sorry' about the Austrian insult, 'for *Mather* [senior] is capable of paying a dozen Hungarians, refugees, to boot the white coat, and they would do it cheap'.[221] Whether or not the remark had been made in jest, Malmesbury's baptism of fire was not going to be quickly forgotten.

Other potential publicity nightmares were closely monitored. As Malmesbury explained to Bulwer, it was 'of consequence' that the formal announcement of the commuting of Murray's death sentence to life imprisonment should be made 'before the meeting of Parliament'.[222] Malmesbury was evidently concerned about public reaction because within days he was pressing Bulwer about Murray, 'whose safety you *must* answer for officially before the meeting [of Parliament]'.[223] The exhausted envoy was likewise urged to great efforts when Shaftesbury started 'kindling the English public' about the case of Francisco and Rosa Madiai, as it was 'evidently to be made a great business'.[224]

It was the public interest and not the case itself that agitated Malmesbury. Such was the Foreign Secretary's concern about the fate of Francisco and Rosa Madiai that Bulwer was refused leave to return home after the Roman negotiations had petered out, and exhorted to 'apply yourself ... earnestly to the relief of these people'.[225] When, around the same time, Buol again raised the Neufchâtel question, the Foreign Secretary made it clear that the Government 'certainly shall not select the present moment' to consider a question that pitted Prussia against Swiss self-determination.[226] He had in any case no desire to re-open the question, but emphatically not with a new Parliament about to sit.

By late autumn, rumours of Bulwer's mission began to seep out, giving a flavour of the reaction the Government would face if its tightrope act went wrong. It was again vulnerable to accusations of consorting with illiberal foreign powers, this time in the capital of popery. In late September, *The Times* predictably took its opportunity: 'to treat with such a Power at this very time, when she has thrown aside her disguise and openly preaches treason under every form', it thundered, 'is a blunder and a weakness which we should hardly have supposed that even Lord Derby's Foreign Secretary would have committed'.[227] In a stern letter to Bulwer, Malmesbury showed his sensitivity to such accusations: 'Read an article in the Times of the 30th Septr. and you will see the line taken by the opposition on the *supposed* humiliation to which I have exposed the country by sending you with official authority to Antonelli'.[228] Disraeli told Bulwer that 'the accounts of yr. proceedings wh: appear in the journals ... have done no inconsiderable mischief'.[229]

Disraeli's comment may have been exaggerated because he knew it would be shown to the papal staff, but the situation was undoubtedly a delicate one. Lennox melodramatically recorded that 'there is a report that Bulwer is at Rome "to try & make terms with the Pope, about Bulls & about Ireland" ... knowing *the truth* I *trembled*[.] I trust to God we are not found out'.[230] It is unlikely that Derby's nerves were so easily affected, but he made it clear that nothing from Bulwer's discussions was to be publicly printed by the FO, 'both on the general principle that they *were* private, and also because one explanation will lead to another, and we should have to disclose more of our case than would be convenient'.[231]

Public suspicion of Rome contrasted with the Government's analysis. The conduct of the negotiations with the Vatican demonstrated the degree to which Malmesbury managed policy in a dispassionate, technocratic manner, to the extent that even a pragmatist like Derby had to veto the result. Throughout the negotiations, the Foreign Secretary was more optimistic than his leader, who had a cynicism born of an innate suspicion of Catholicism and a long immersion in Irish affairs. On the face of it, it is ironic that a political party so determinedly Anglican should have pursued *rapprochement* with the Pope. But such a position was entirely in keeping with Malmesbury's secular approach to politics.

Malmesbury's career, unlike that of many contemporaries, was unmarked by episodes of theological significance. His memoirs touched on religious matters only obliquely. He was remarkably free of philosophical baggage. A solidly Protestant Conservative, he was hardly pro-Roman; nevertheless, his stance during the 'papal aggression' had been that of the cynical politician, not the outraged Anglican.[232] Beyond the usual role of the Church in English aristocratic routine, religious and doctrinal questions held little inherent fascination for him. Clarendon was wrong in thinking that the Government was characterised by 'pure Orangeism'.[233] Even Gladstone recognised that the Conservatives were not as virulently Protestant as might have been expected. He condemned the Government's approach to religion 'much less strongly' than he had condemned 'the unheard of course pursued by Lord John Russell ... in 1850–51'.[234]

Malmesbury's deputy shared his dispassionate attitude to religion. Though a very different man and politician, Stanley was even less interested in such matters than his FO chief, and considerably less than his father. He mischievously proposed an alternative diplomatic option: 'My idea is ... that you must buy the Pope. I fancy £10,000 a year would be sufficient, and he would be cheap at the money'.[235] The suggestion may not have been serious, but the unsentimental logic was characteristic of the methods employed in Conservative foreign policy in 1852. The FO was run by men with little interest in religion, beyond its diplomatic utility.

When it came to matters involving the Vatican, Malmesbury was consistently prepared to give it the benefit of the doubt. When faced, for example, with the dispute about ecclesiastical jurisdiction, which involved Rome, he pointed out that 'the Vatican ... really is as liberal as possible to our countrymen in matters of religion at Rome itself'.[236] He was also more hopeful about the Pope's view of the Conservatives than was Derby, ascribing anti-British feeling to obstructionist Irish elements in the Vatican: 'the Pope is supposed to be rather friendly than otherwise towards our Government, but ... Irish influence and

Jesuitism are strongly working at him against us'.[237] He thought that the Pope's instinct for self-preservation should, pragmatically, propel him towards the Conservatives: 'It would not however appear difficult to persuade his Holiness that the peace of Europe and consequently of Italy depends not a little on a conservative policy'.[238]

Derby, consistently sceptical about the mission, drew the opposite conclusion to Malmesbury, though on the basis of a similarly pragmatic analysis. The Prime Minister was from the outset doubtful about the likelihood of Bulwer's success, on the grounds of pure *realpolitik*: 'It is difficult to say what he [Bulwer] is to urge the Pope to do or not to do, because what we really want is to abridge his own power and that of the priesthood his agents – in which he is not likely to assist us, especially as we have no quid pro quo to offer him, and no threat effectually to alarm him'.[239] By 3 October, as negotiations dragged on inconclusively, he was dismissive:

> It is clear that Bulwer will do nothing at Rome; and the last declaration of Antonelli, that in the business of the Irish priests they could not take the initiative, inasmuch as it would be an interference with the affairs of another country, is a declaration which it must have been difficult even for an Italian cardinal to make with a grave face.[240]

Although it was becoming clear that the obstacles in the way of formal diplomatic relations would be too great, Malmesbury remained hopeful that something would be achieved.

At the same time that Derby had concluded that Bulwer would 'do nothing', the Foreign Secretary was sending on to the Prime Minister 'very important letters' about the mission, including a proposal 'to give the Pope an opportunity of speaking for us in Ireland'.[241] The proposed initiative would require an Irish bishop to write to Pius, thus giving an opportunity for a papal intervention. The Foreign Secretary evidently considered the proposal serious enough to warrant correspondence direct from Achnacarry (his Scottish summer residence) to Knowsley during the shooting season: 'The subject is so important ... that I send you the letters straight from here'.[242] Given arrangements to make after Wellington's death on 14 September, and other pressing matters, Derby must have been busy; nevertheless, the fact that he took two weeks to answer suggested how much credibility he attached to the Vatican's offer.

When Derby did reply, his response verged on the polemical. His scepticism about the prospects for success with the Pope was underscored by his emphatic views on Irish affairs. His correspondence on foreign policy was almost always calm and measured; Catholicism in

Ireland, however, provoked him in a manner never equalled by recalcitrant foreign powers. On Bulwer's substantive point, he accepted that if Eglinton could find 'a R.C. Bishop whom he can trust, he should employ him to write such a letter as Antonelli suggests'.[243] The rest of the letter, however, described how inadequate such an epistle would probably be.

Unlike Malmesbury, Derby was sceptical about the compatibility of the objectives of a Conservative Protestant Government and a conservative Papal Court. Malmesbury had suggested to Bulwer that the Pope might appreciate the necessity for a 'conservative' policy in Europe, by implication clearly represented by governments such as Derby's. The Prime Minister, however, perceived a vital difference between English and papal definitions of conservatism. He doubted 'the sincerity of any desire on the part of Rome to repress that spirit of turbulence on the part of the Irish priesthood, which they see causes considerable annoyance to a Protestant – and [in] *their* eyes a *liberal* government'.[244] He believed that, if the Vatican was 'in earnest', it would not really be chary about taking the initiative in restraining its priests.[245]

He also thought 'a general exhortation to peace' would be useless because it would not be specific: 'unless it be directed to particular cases ... it will be taken by the Irish clergy just at its real worth, and will be treated with indifference accordingly'.[246] As Derby would have recalled, this was precisely what had happened when Pope Gregory had issued his Rescript in 1844. At the same time, a 'general exhortation' would give a propaganda victory to Rome; the Vatican would be able to point to it as 'proof of her moderation'.[247] Finally, he felt that it would be impossible to obtain something he considered essential: a condemnation and cessation of 'the crusade instituted by the R.C. priesthood against the temporalities of the Established Church'.[248]

The remainder of the letter was a diatribe against what he believed to be the unreasonable ingratitude and hypocrisy of priests in supporting candidates whose objective was to 'subvert' the established Church. He concluded with a flourish that left no doubt as to his views:

> How far the Pope & Cardinal Antonelli may be inclined to go in imposing a real check upon the aggressive spirit of Irish Catholicism I know not; but according not to their professions, but to the reality of their efforts in that direction, I for one, and the country with me, will judge of the sincerity of the friendly feelings they profess.[249]

Derby was once more the decisive voice in foreign policy.

Despite the Prime Minister's polemic, Malmesbury was determined to press on with his scheme for engaging with Rome. Derby had not explicitly vetoed further work on the Vatican's proposal, but with Eglinton similarly sceptical Malmesbury concluded that the Bulwer–Antonelli plan was dead in the water.[250] He was soon proceeding with a secondary plan on his own initiative. In Chelsea he met with a friendly Catholic priest, one Father Mahé, who suggested that an 'ecclesiastic' should 'be sent secretly to Rome' to meet with Antonelli and agree on two papal envoys to come and 'give a fair report of the material and moral condition of the Roman Catholic people'.[251] By this device, Mahé was 'certain that diplomatic relations can be brought about by degrees, by accepting here some inferior envoy from Rome'.[252]

Even Derby, notwithstanding his splenetic views on the Irish priesthood, had not lost sight of the potential value of improved relations. He considered the necessity for progress important enough to justify further consideration, inviting Malmesbury to St Leonards for more discussion.[253] Prior to that meeting, the Foreign Secretary wasted no time in suggesting that 'as you *both* [Eglinton and Derby] object to the course Bulwer & Antonelli agreed upon ... we must try some plan for establishing diplomatic relations like that proposed by my Chelsea friend whom you really ought to see some day'.[254] Despite all Derby's suspicions about Rome, Malmesbury's proposal clearly received prime ministerial approval. His 'Chelsea friend' reached Rome in December, though nothing more came of the initiative.[255] For a domestic prize, the Conservatives had been determined to pursue better relations, despite their own scepticism and the political risks.

Relations with the Pope had, however, slipped a long way down the foreign-policy agenda by the time the Government fell in December. An altogether more temporal prince was becoming a greater concern.

Notes

1 Commons, 19 March 1852, *Hansard*, 119, col. 1396.
2 *Ibid*.
3 Hughenden Papers, Dep. Hughenden 109/1, fo. 127, Derby to Disraeli, 10 January 1852. The Latin quotation is from Horace's *Epistles* 1.19, in which the poet discusses different forms of imitation. Horace deprecated being led astray by the misguided imitation of a bad example: 'decipit exemplar vitiis imitabile'. I am very grateful to Professor Christopher Harper-Bill for checking my translation.
4 BL, Greville Papers, diary, Add. MS 41119, fo. 202, 12 May 1852.
5 Lord Stanmore, *Sidney Herbert, Lord Herbert of Lea: A Memoir*, 2 vols

1852: foreign affairs, domestic problems

(London, 1906), I, Herbert to Mrs. Herbert, 31 March 1852, p. 151.
6 *The Times*, 13 April 1852.
7 Malmesbury Papers, 9M73/452/17/2, Stanley to Malmesbury, 12 September 1852.
8 Lords, 5 April 1852, *Hansard*, 120, col. 680.
9 Aberdeen Papers, Add. MS 43197, fo. 14, Newcastle to Aberdeen, 2 August 1852.
10 A. G. Gardiner, *The Life of William Harcourt*, 2 vols (London, 1923), vol. 1, p. 67.
11 Bentley, *Politics Without Democracy*, p. 95.
12 Seven out of thirteen Cabinet ministers were peers: Derby, Malmesbury, St Leonards, Lonsdale, Salisbury, Northumberland and Hardwicke.
13 *Croker Papers*, vol. 3, Hardwicke to Croker, 30 December 1852, pp. 259–60.
14 Malmesbury Papers, 9M73/451, Derby to Malmesbury, undated, 1852.
15 *Ibid.*, 9M73/79, Malmesbury, unpublished political diary.
16 *Ibid.*
17 Lords, 27 February 1852, *Hansard*, 119, col. 892.
18 *Ibid.*
19 *Ibid.*
20 *Ibid.*, col. 893.
21 *Ibid.*
22 *Ibid.*
23 See below, pp. 73–4.
24 Lords, 27 February 1852, *Hansard*, 119, col. 893.
25 *Ibid.*
26 *LQV*, vol. 2, pp. 351–2, Queen Victoria to Russell, 28 December 1851; Lord Edmond Fitzmaurice, *The Life of Lord Granville, 1815–1891*, 2 vols (London, 1905), vol. 1, pp. 47–9.
27 Granville Papers, PRO 30/29/18/4, fo. 1, draft, Granville to Russell, 12 January 1852; this document is reproduced in Bourne, *Foreign Policy*, pp. 310–12, although with an erroneous ms reference.
28 Agatha Ramm, 'Granville', in Wilson (ed.), *British Foreign Secretaries*, p. 85.
29 Aberdeen Papers, Add. MS 43055, fo. 236, Aberdeen to Princess Lieven, 1 January 1852.
30 Granville Papers, PRO 30/29/18/1, fo. 32, Ellenborough to Granville, 24 February 1852.
31 *Ibid.*, PRO 30/29/18/4, fo. 1, draft, Granville to Russell, 12 January 1852.
32 *Ibid.*
33 *Ibid.*
34 *Ibid.*
35 *Ibid.*
36 *Ibid.*
37 *Ibid.*

38 For the differences between Whig and Tory Iberian policies in the 1830s, see above, pp. 29–30.
39 Lords, 27 February 1852, *Hansard*, 119, col. 893.
40 See, e.g., Schwarzenberg to Buol, 4 February 1852, and Nesselrode to Brunnow, 26 January/7 February 1852 (Julian/Gregorian calendar dates), both communicated to Granville; reproduced in 'Further Correspondence Respecting the Foreign Refugees in London', *Parliamentary Papers* (1852), 54, pp. 1–7.
41 Derby Papers, 920 DER (14) 144/1, Malmesbury to Derby, 29 February 1852.
42 Malmesbury Papers, 9M73/50/6, copy, Malmesbury to Westmorland, 8 March 1852.
43 *Ibid.*
44 Granville himself was apparently surprised when he read about it in Malmesbury's *Memoirs*: Fitzmaurice, *Granville*, vol. 1, p. 77.
45 See above, pp. 43–5.
46 See de Groot, 'The Florentine Tragedy', *DUJ* (1952), pp. 95–106; Major, 'The Public Life', pp. 67–73.
47 NA, FO 7/397, private, draft, Granville to Westmorland, 13 January 1852.
48 Derby Papers, 920 DER (14) 144/1, Malmesbury to Derby, 1 March 1852.
49 Lords, 21 June 1852, *Hansard*, 122, col. 1056.
50 FO 7/397, no. 27, draft, Malmesbury to Westmorland, 23 March 1852. The draft was seen and approved by Derby; unlike most of the draft despatches to Vienna in March, it is clearly marked with his 'D'.
51 Lords, 21 June 1852, *Hansard*, 122, col. 1042.
52 Malmesbury Papers, 9M73/451, Derby to Malmesbury, 19 July 1852.
53 A detailed discussion of the political significance of refugees may be found in Bernard Porter, *The Refugee Question in Mid-Victorian Politics* (Cambridge, 1979), in particular chapter 5; the first Derby Government is briefly discussed on pp. 147–50.
54 Anonymous review, 'Farini's *History of the Roman States*', *Quarterly Review*, 90 (December 1851), p. 255; Walter E. Houghton (ed.), *The Wellesley Index to Victorian Periodicals 1824–1900*, vol. 1 (Toronto, 1966), p. 735, identifies the author as Edward Cheney.
55 Commons, 1 April 1852, *Hansard*, 120, col. 518.
56 Lords, 27 February 1852, *Hansard*, 119, col. 896.
57 Malmesbury Papers, 9M73/50/6, copy, Malmesbury to Westmorland, 8 March 1852.
58 *Ibid.*
59 *Ibid.*, fos 6–7.
60 *Ibid.*
61 *Ibid.*, fo. 7.
62 *Ibid.*
63 *Ibid.*

1852: foreign affairs, domestic problems

64 *Ibid.*, 9M73/50/57, copy, Malmesbury to Westmorland, 18 May 1852.
65 Malmesbury, *Memoirs*, vol. 1, Westmorland to Malmesbury, 4 March 1852, p. 311. Original not found.
66 Translation: 'we are happy to be able to adhere without reserve to the principles and intentions which the Earl of Derby has explained with so much candour and lucidity': FO 7/409, copy, Schwarzenberg to Buol, 5 March 1852, communicated by Buol, 10 March 1852.
67 Malmesbury Papers, 9M73/50/13, copy, Malmesbury to Cowley, 11 March 1852. Malmesbury edited this section out of vol. 1 of his *Memoirs*, where the rest of the letter is quoted (pp. 315–16).
68 NA, Bloomfield Papers, FO 356/31, Malmesbury to Bloomfield, 18 March 1852.
69 'Buol ... stated that he had seen the Earl of Derby after these [Austrian] despatches had been communicated ... and that he had equally expressed the satisfaction he had received from them': FO 7/401, no. 10, Westmorland to Malmesbury, 15 March 1852.
70 FO 7/409, draft, Malmesbury to Buol, 15 March 1852 (initialled by Derby).
71 *Ibid.*
72 FO 7/397, no. 27, draft, Malmesbury to Westmorland, 23 March 1852.
73 *Ibid.*, no. 32, draft, Malmesbury to Westmorland, 30 March 1852.
74 See, e.g., *ibid*, Malmesbury to Westmorland, between no. 25 and no. 26, private, draft, 20 March 1852.
75 Lords, 5 April 1852, *Hansard*, 120, col. 681.
76 Derby Papers, 920 DER (14) 144/1, Malmesbury to Derby, 29 February 1852.
77 For details of French allegations and Belgian apprehension see, in particular, FO 10/164, no. 23, Howard de Walden to Granville, 6 February 1852.
78 See Chamberlain, *Aberdeen*, pp. 379–81.
79 Aberdeen Papers, Add. MS 43055, fo. 252, Aberdeen to Princess Lieven, 19 February 1852.
80 The comment loosely translates: 'we agree exactly': FO 65/408, no. 48, Seymour to Malmesbury, 9 April 1852.
81 Lords, 27 February 1852, *Hansard*, 119, col. 892.
82 Aberdeen Papers, Add. MS 43072, fo. 187, Derby to Aberdeen, 22 March 1852.
83 FO 65/404, no. 8, draft, Malmesbury to Seymour, 16 March 1852, approved by Derby; the despatch is preserved as FO 181/268, no. 21.
84 See e.g., FO 65/404, no. 59, draft, Granville to Seymour, 18 February 1852; the despatch itself has not survived in FO 181/280.
85 See e.g., Derby Papers, 920 DER (14) 144/1, Malmesbury to Derby, 27 March 1852, requesting his advice on the response to Russia regarding Belgium; Malmesbury Papers, 9M73/451, Derby to Malmesbury, 28 March 1852.
86 Malmesbury Papers, 9M73/451, Derby to Malmesbury, 28 March 1852.

87 *Ibid.*; the despatch which Derby drafted on the question of Brunnow's powers, referred to in his letter to Malmesbury, was either FO 181/268, no. 30 or no. 31 to Seymour, 29 March 1852. Both asked essentially the same question. The drafts of both despatches were initialled by Derby: FO 65/404.
88 See, e.g., the extent to which Russia supported Britain, and on the powers given to Brunnow: FO 65/408, no. 47, Seymour to Malmesbury, 9 April 1852; no. 48, 9 April 1852; and no. 55, 14 April 1852.
89 *Ibid.*, no. 55, Seymour to Malmesbury, 14 April 1852.
90 BL, Seymour Diaries, Add. MS 60305, fo. 102, 29 March 1852.
91 Derby Papers, 920 DER (14) 144/1, Malmesbury to Derby, 27 March 1852.
92 Hughenden Papers, Dep. Hughenden 99/1, fo. 92, Malmesbury to Disraeli, 12 February 1853.
93 Malmesbury, *Memoirs*, vol. 1, Derby to Malmesbury, 3 October 1852, p. 353; original not found.
94 *Ibid.*, Derby to Malmesbury, 'March 1852', p. 312; original not found.
95 *DDCP*, pp. 70–1.
96 *Ibid.*, p. 71.
97 Malmesbury Papers, 9M73/50/13, copy, Malmesbury to Cowley, 11 March 1852.
98 *Ibid.*, 9M73/451, Derby to Malmesbury, 28 March 1852.
99 Bloomfield Papers, FO 356/31, Malmesbury to Bloomfield, 18 March 1852.
100 FO 181/268, no. 21, Malmesbury to Seymour, 16 March 1852.
101 See e.g., Jones, *Lord Derby*, p. 169.
102 *Disraeli's Reminiscences*, pp. 93–4.
103 *Ibid.*, p. 93.
104 Malmesbury Papers, 9M73/451, Derby to Malmesbury, undated (1852).
105 *Ibid.*
106 *Ibid.*
107 *Ibid.*
108 *Ibid.*
109 *Ibid.*
110 Malmesbury Papers, 9M73/451, Derby to Malmesbury, 15 March 1852.
111 The correspondence was published on 29 March 1852.
112 In his letter of 15 March, see above, p. 79.
113 Commons, 1 April 1852, *Hansard*, 120, col. 514.
114 *Ibid.*, col. 482.
115 *Ibid.*, col. 500.
116 Lords, 5 April 1852, *Hansard*, 120, col. 677.
117 FO Memorandum, 6 March 1852, 'Correspondence Respecting the Assault Committed on Mr. Erskine Mather at Florence', *Parliamentary Papers* (1852), 55, pp. 57–8.
118 FO 79/155, copy, Malmesbury to Scarlett, 9 March 1852.
119 *Ibid.*; he later told Bulwer that he had asked for 'not less than 500*l*': FO

1852: foreign affairs, domestic problems 111

     79/156, no. 7, draft, Malmesbury to Bulwer, 21 May 1852.
120 FO 79/159, private, Barron to Malmesbury, 9 May 1852.
121 FO 79/156, no. 7, draft, Malmesbury to Bulwer, 21 May 1852.
122 *Ibid*.; the amendment is clearly in Derby's hand; it was his version that was sent.
123 The date of Malmesbury's instruction was listed in his despatch to Bulwer: *ibid*., no. 16, draft, 29 May 1852.
124 *The Times*, 28 May 1852, Addington to Mather senior, 24 May 1852.
125 *Ibid*.
126 FO 79/159, no. 85, Scarlett to Malmesbury, 11 May 1852; FO 79/159, private, Barron to Malmesbury, 14 May 1852.
127 Lords, 27 May 1852, *Hansard*, 121, col. 1173.
128 *The Times*, 28 May 1852, Mather senior to Malmesbury, 27 May 1852.
129 Lords, 28 May 1852, *Hansard*, 121, col. 1264.
130 Malmesbury to Bulwer, FO 79/156, nos 14–17, 29 May 1852.
131 The four sets of papers were published in early June.
132 Major, 'The Public Life', p. 70; De Groot, 'The Florentine Tragedy', p. 104.
133 Hearder, 'The Foreign Policy of Lord Malmesbury', p. 24.
134 *DL*, vol. 6, 2296, Disraeli to Derby, 29 May 1852; *ibid*., 2297, Disraeli to Stanley, 29 May 1852. The letter to Malmesbury has not been found in Malmesbury's or Disraeli's papers, though one was clearly written: see Derby Papers, 920 DER (14) 144/1, Malmesbury to Derby, 30 May 1852.
135 See, e.g., Derby Papers, 920 DER (14) 144/1, Malmesbury to Derby, undated (1851?): 'I don't know what made D. so desponding [*sic*]'; 19 August 1851: Disraeli 'very much down, & full of fancies'; 5 January 1852: 'Dizzy more mopy than ever'.
136 *Ibid*., Malmesbury to Derby, 30 May 1852.
137 Commons, 14 June 1852, *Hansard*, 122, col. 633.
138 *Ibid*., col. 666.
139 'The Government and the Elections', *Fraser's Magazine*, 46 (July–December 1852), p. 124.
140 *Ibid*.
141 *Punch*, 22 (January–June 1852), p. 245.
142 *The Times*, 29 May 1852.
143 *Memoirs*, vol. 1, p. 335.
144 Commons, 14 June 1852, *Hansard*, 122, cols 666–78.
145 *Ibid*., col. 656.
146 *The Times*, 29 May 1852.
147 *Punch*, 23 (July–December 1852), p. 30.
148 Commons, 14 June 1852, *Hansard*, 122, col. 627.
149 *Ibid*., col. 633.
150 *Ibid*., col. 634.
151 Derby Papers, 920 DER (14) 144/1, Malmesbury to Derby, 2 September 1852.

152 *Memoirs*, vol. 1, p. 335.
153 Derby Papers, 920 DER (14) 144/1, Malmesbury to Derby, 30 May 1852.
154 *Ibid.*, Malmesbury to Derby, 21 August 1852.
155 Malmesbury Papers, 9M73/451, Derby to Malmesbury, 25 June 1852.
156 *Ibid.*, 9M73/452/27/1, Stanley to Malmesbury, 24 September 1852.
157 *Ibid.*, 9M73/452/18/2, Stanley to Malmesbury, 14 September 1852.
158 Lords, 21 June 1852, *Hansard*, 122, col. 1036.
159 *Ibid*.
160 In his despatches to Bulwer, see above, p. 87.
161 His account changed: he originally told Derby he had read them on the 25th: Derby Papers, 920 DER (14) 144/1, Malmesbury to Derby, 31 May 1852.
162 Commons, 14 June 1852, *Hansard*, 122, col. 634.
163 Gladstone Papers, Add. MS 44088, fo. 114, Aberdeen to Gladstone, 9 October 1851.
164 Derby Papers, 920 DER (14) 144/1, Malmesbury to Derby, 21 August 1852.
165 *Ibid*.
166 Commons, 14 June 1852, *Hansard*, 122, col. 657.
167 Derby Papers, 920 DER (14) 144/1, Malmesbury to Derby, 21 August 1852.
168 See above, p. 68.
169 Malmesbury Papers, 9M73/451, Derby to Malmesbury, 29 August 1852. The dispute is explored by J. E. Pinnington, 'The Consular Chaplaincies and the Foreign Office under Palmerston, Aberdeen and Malmesbury: Two Case Histories – Rome and Funchal', *Journal of Ecclesiastical History*, 27:3 (1976), pp. 277–84.
170 Malmesbury Papers, 9M73/452/33/2, Stanley to Malmesbury, 29 September 1852.
171 Malmesbury, *Memoirs*, vol. 1, pp. 317–18.
172 Keith A. P. Sandiford, *Great Britain and the Schleswig–Holstein Question 1848–64: A Study in Diplomacy, Politics, and Public Opinion* (Toronto, 1975), p. 28.
173 Brown, *Politics of Foreign Policy*, p. 138.
174 Even Gladstone had conjured up Palmerston's ghost in his Midlothian campaign of 1879–80.
175 *LQV*, vol. 2, Prince Albert, Memorandum, 27 February 1852, p. 375; Malmesbury, *Memoirs*, vol. 1, p. 318.
176 The first Earl has been described as 'the most important influence on the political emergence of the third Viscount Palmerston': Bourne, *Palmerston: The Early Years*, p. 4.
177 *Memoirs*, vol. 1, p. 317.
178 For a detailed analysis of the Schleswig–Holstein question, and the settlement of 1852, see e.g. Sandiford, *Schleswig–Holstein Question*, in particular chapter 2.

179 See, e.g., Major, 'The Public Life', pp. 93–8.
180 Hughenden Papers, Dep. Hughenden 99/1, fo. 51, Malmesbury to Disraeli, 29 May 1852.
181 Lords, 21 June 1852, *Hansard*, 122, col. 1057.
182 See, e.g., Major, 'The Public Life', pp. 74–6; Monypenny & Buckle, *Disraeli*, vol. 3, pp. 399–401.
183 Malmesbury Papers, 9M73/50/97, copy, Malmesbury to Bulwer, 15 August 1852.
184 See above, pp. 75–6.
185 Derby Papers, 920 DER (14) 144/1, Malmesbury to Derby, 3 October 1852.
186 Fixity of tenure, free sale and fair rent.
187 Hoppen has described it as 'one of the most violent of all nineteenth-century Irish elections': K. Theodore Hoppen, *Elections, Politics, and Society in Ireland, 1832–1885* (Oxford, 1984), p. 397.
188 BL, Lansdowne Papers, LANS 3/32, Clarendon to Lansdowne, 14 August 1852.
189 See, e.g., K. Theodore Hoppen, 'Tories, Catholics, and the General Election of 1859', *HJ*, 13 (1970), p. 65.
190 See, e.g., Peel Papers, Add. MS 40468, Stanley–Peel correspondence.
191 *Ibid.*, Add. MS 40467, fo. 41, Stanley to Peel, 4 August 1841; see also Jones, *Lord Derby*, p. 125.
192 *Ibid.*
193 Peel Papers, Add. MS 40492, fo. 130, Stanley, note on minute circulated by Peel, 8 November 1841.
194 *Ibid.*
195 Jones, *Lord Derby*, p. 125.
196 Peel Papers, Add. MS 40468, fos 132–3, Stanley to Peel, 18 February 1844.
197 See above, p. 51.
198 Matsumoto-Best, *Britain and the Papacy*, pp. 170–1.
199 Peel Papers, Add. MS 40450, fo. 439, copy, Peel to Graham, 24 December 1844; see also, in particular, *ibid.*, fos 434–6, Graham to Peel, 23 December 1844. A succinct account of this episode may be found in Oliver Macdonagh, *States of Mind: A Study of Anglo-Irish Conflict 1780–1980* (Oxford, 1983), pp. 96–7.
200 Monypenny and Buckle, *Disraeli*, vol. 3, p. 399.
201 Hughenden Papers, Dep. Hughenden 121/3, fo. 80, Bulwer to Disraeli, 1 August 1852; *DL*, vol. 6, 2409, note 1, draft, Disraeli to Bulwer, undated.
202 Derby Papers, 920 DER (14) 144/1, Malmesbury to Derby, 22 May 1852.
203 Hughenden Papers, Dep. Hughenden 99/1, fo. 76, Malmesbury to Disraeli, 3 September 1852.
204 See, e.g., *ibid*, fos 76–7.
205 *Ibid.*, Dep. Hughenden 121/3, fos 88–91, Bulwer to Disraeli, 20

September 1852; *DL,* vol. 6, 2409, draft, Disraeli to Bulwer, undated. The editors suggest early October as the date; it is unclear why they demur from Monypenny and Buckle's designation of 'latter half of September, 1852': *Disraeli,* vol. 3, p. 399.
206 Malmesbury Papers, 9M73/50/109–10, copy, Malmesbury to Bulwer, 22 September 1852.
207 *Ibid.,* fo. 110.
208 Derby Papers, 144/1, Malmesbury to Derby, 31 May 1852.
209 Malmesbury Papers, 9M73/50/77, copy, Malmesbury to Bulwer, 25 June 1852.
210 *DDCP,* 2 August 1852, pp. 78–9.
211 Malmesbury Papers, 9M73/451, Derby to Malmesbury, 1 June 1852.
212 *Ibid.,* 9M73/50/77, copy, Malmesbury to Bulwer, 25 June 1852.
213 Lansdowne Papers, LANS 3/32, Clarendon to Lansdowne, 3 September 1852.
214 *Ibid.,* fo. 36, Palmerston to Lansdowne, 14 October 1852.
215 J. H. Whyte, *The Independent Irish Party, 1850–9* (Oxford, 1958), p. 93.
216 Malmesbury Papers, 9M73/50/76–7, copy, Malmesbury to Bulwer, 25 June 1852.
217 *Ibid.,* 9M73/439/8, copy, Malmesbury to Bulwer, 3 August 1852.
218 *Ibid.;* see above, p. 51.
219 Malmesbury Papers, 9M73/439/8, copy, Malmesbury to Bulwer, 3 August 1852.
220 See Derby's comment in *ibid.,* 9M73/451, Malmesbury to Derby, 28 June 1852.
221 *Ibid.,* 9M73/50/131, copy, Malmesbury to Bulwer, 6 November 1852.
222 *Ibid.,* 9M73/50/111, copy, Malmesbury to Bulwer, 22 September 1852.
223 *Ibid.,* 9M73/50/118, copy, Malmesbury to Bulwer, 3 October 1852.
224 *Ibid.,* 9M73/50/117, copy, Malmesbury to Bulwer, 29 September 1852; see above, p. 93.
225 Malmesbury Papers, 9M73/50/117, copy, Malmesbury to Bulwer, 29 September 1852.
226 *Ibid.,* 9M73/50/115, copy, Malmesbury to Westmorland, 24 September 1852.
227 *The Times,* 30 September 1852.
228 Malmesbury Papers, 9M73/50/117–18, copy, Malmesbury to Bulwer, 3 October 1852.
229 *DL,* vol. 6, 2409, Disraeli to Bulwer, undated.
230 *Ibid.,* note 3, Lennox to Disraeli, 20 October 1852.
231 Malmesbury Papers, 9M73/2/255, Derby to Malmesbury, 'Friday Evg.'.
232 See above, p. 51.
233 Lansdowne Papers, LANS 3/32, Clarendon to Lansdowne, 14 August 1852.
234 Aberdeen Papers, Add. MS 43070, fo. 257, Gladstone to Aberdeen, 5 August 1852.
235 Malmesbury Papers, 9M73/452/22/2, Stanley to Malmesbury, 16

September 1852.
236 Derby Papers, 920 DER (14) 144/1, Malmesbury to Derby, 2 September 1852.
237 Malmesbury Papers, 9M73/50/89, copy, Malmesbury to Bulwer, 22 July 1852.
238 *Ibid.*
239 *Ibid.*, 9M73/451, Derby to Malmesbury, 1 June 1852.
240 Malmesbury, *Memoirs*, vol. 1, Derby to Malmesbury, 3 October 1852, p. 353; original not found. The sentiments expressed here are consistent with surviving Derby letters on the subject.
241 Derby Papers, 920 DER (14) 144/1, Malmesbury to Derby, 3 October 1852; this letter must have crossed with Derby's of the same date – it is clear neither was a response to the other.
242 *Ibid.*
243 Malmesbury Papers, 9M73/451, Derby to Malmesbury, 17 October 1852.
244 *Ibid.*
245 *Ibid.*
246 *Ibid.*
247 *Ibid.*
248 *Ibid.*
249 *Ibid.*
250 Derby Papers, 920 DER (14) 144/1, Malmesbury to Derby, 24 October 1852.
251 Malmesbury Papers, 9M73/79, unpublished political diary, 21 October 1852.
252 *Ibid.*
253 *Ibid.*, 9M73/451, Derby to Malmesbury, 'Sat.' – Saturday was 23 October. Malmesbury noted receipt of the letter in his unpublished diary on 23 October (9M73/79), and, according to his *Memoirs*, vol. 1, p. 359, went to St Leonards the day following.
254 Derby Papers, 920 DER (14) 144/1, Malmesbury to Derby, 24 October 1852.
255 NA, Russell Papers, PRO 30/22/10F, fos 73–6, Petre to Malmesbury, 17 December 1852, forwarded to Russell. Shortly afterwards, Russell dismissed Petre: *ibid.*, PRO 30/22/10H, fo. 77, copy, Russell to Petre, 15 February 1853.

5

Entente cordiale

Malmesbury, Earl age 49: was Foreign Sec under Ld Derby, never held office before. Known to me intimately, as I served under him at the F.O. ... goes at once to the point, has no illusions, no favourite theories; a good judge of character ... A personal friend of the French Emperor; contributed to bring about the Anglo-French alliance. (Stanley, undated character sketch, *circa* 1853)

From the summer of 1852, the most important foreign policy question facing the Conservatives was how Britain should respond to the anticipated declaration of a new French Empire, which finally occurred in December. The British recognition of the Empire, and with it Louis Napoleon's new title of Napoleon III, is the achievement for which the 1852 Government is chiefly remembered. It was certainly the one which Malmesbury himself later regarded with the greatest pride; it was a personal triumph for his vision of the Anglo-French relationship. He and Derby successfully maintained Britain's good relations with the 'northern' powers, and established a close alliance with the new French regime. While doing their best to reconcile Louis Napoleon to the European status quo, to which (as they were well aware) he was fundamentally opposed, they were able to keep on good terms even with the governments most suspicious of a new Empire, like that in St Petersburg. Their strategy was typical of their consistent search for compromise between Europe's rival powers. It was reminiscent of Aberdeen's efforts to maintain good relations with all the great powers between 1841 and 1846; indeed, much more so than the confused policies pursued by Aberdeen's own Government from December 1852.

Throughout 1852, European diplomats and politicians expected Louis Napoleon to take the next step in his self-defined walk with destiny and declare himself the head of a new French Empire.[1] There were persistent rumours that the Empire was imminent. As early as 10

April, the *Illustrated London News* observed that the 'only matter of doubt' about Louis Napoleon's intentions was 'the moment of fitting convenience when he may choose to assume the title of Emperor of the French'.[2] The accession of a Bonaparte to the French throne was, in theory, prevented by the treaties establishing the Quadruple Alliance, which Britain and the northern powers had signed in 1815.[3] It was not the letter of any particular treaty that concerned European diplomats and politicians, however, but the extent to which a new French Empire would affect Europe's stability. Derby and Malmesbury had long been resigned to an imperial declaration. Immediately after the *coup d'état* in 1851, Derby had assumed a new Napoleonic Empire would not be far behind. He hoped, however, that 'the President, or the Emperor, as I suppose he will be before long' would appreciate the importance of peace with Britain, and 'have sense and firmness to see and act upon the real interests of his country'.[4]

By the early summer, the great powers were having to move beyond hopes and hypotheses to consider what their response would be when the apparently inevitable Empire was declared.[5] Britain faced a particular conundrum. The Government wanted to maintain good relations with Russia, Austria and Prussia, with whom, thus far, it had worked well. But an accord with France, Britain's closest and most important neighbour, was equally vital. The Conservatives therefore avoided for as long as possible taking any particular line. This required some delicate manoeuvring. During the summer, even British ministerial attendance at a meal hosted by Walewski, in honour of the French President's birthday, was authorised by Derby only 'subject to an assurance … that nothing shall be said or done to give to the dinner any political significance, and especially nothing as regards the imperial title'.[6]

Relations with the other powers required equally careful handling. Malmesbury was keen to avoid offering a hostage to fortune by committing Britain to any particular course when the Empire arrived. A formal commitment to some sort of mutual pact, which the other powers would have welcomed, was anathema to the Conservatives. Malmesbury therefore sought to work, within the concert of Europe, for a formal reconciliation of the Empire to the geopolitical status quo. Stanley summarised the British policy: 'England will make her recognition of the Empire conditional: but she will co-operate with the other Powers in demanding from Napoleon a public pledge of his peaceable intentions, which they, when consenting to relax the provisions of a treaty in his favor [sic], have a clear right to ask for'.[7] In fact, as events transpired, Louis Napoleon offered an assurance to the other powers' sensibilities regarding his 'peaceable intentions' before they needed formally to demand one.[8] It was, instead, an argument about a superficially minor question of nomenclature that would produce the greatest difficulty prior to the imperial declaration.

The Conservative leaders meanwhile tried, whenever possible, to encourage the Bonapartist regime to work with Britain. In August, when Derby was considering the sensitive question of what to do about anti-Bonapartist plotting by French refugees in the Channel Islands, he proposed that Britain 'on the very ground of the number of the refugees, and their supposed projects, invite the President to send over some French police to cooperate with ours. It is a step which would mark confidence'.[9] Malmesbury had misgivings, but was nevertheless prepared to go to some lengths in order to promote good relations with France. He agreed with the spirit of Derby's proposal, but 'had ... intended to communicate the intentions of these persons to the President privately'.[10]

He put great store by his personal relationship with Louis Napoleon, but he had also learnt from the baptism of fire he had been given over the Mather case. He was anxious to avoid any word slipping out if Britain passed information on to France: 'we should equally deserve the confidence of the French Govt without risking the outcry wh[ich] will be made if we openly propose to them to join in a surveillance ... if the President were informed by some one viva voce the whole object w[oul]d be obtained without any risk of a debate in the H of Commons'.[11] Derby evidently took his Foreign Secretary's advice. Malmesbury's cousin and secretary, the staunchly reliable George Harris, was sent on a private mission to inform the President about the plots uncovered by Britain. When Louis Napoleon 'most cordially' thanked Malmesbury for the information, he had good reason: this was a British Government very eager to keep on good terms with him.[12]

Malmesbury had a good idea what would be the outcome of less friendly interventions in French affairs. The other powers' resistance to Louis Napoleon's projected marriage with Princess Caroline Stephanie de Vasa (or Wasa), a descendant, on her mother's side, of the Beauharnais family (that of Louis Napoleon's mother, and of the Empress Josephine's first husband), enraged Louis Napoleon: 'The President is very angry at the difficulties thrown in the way of his marriage by Austria &c. The lady says she will have him & Walewski & Persigny both agree that he never will forgive this interference'.[13] The other powers' hostility had, of course, benefits for the Foreign Secretary's policy of close co-operation with France. Malmesbury had noted the happy result of earlier rumours about a Holy Alliance treaty against France: 'In the meantime L. N. won't be pleased & will [be] more civil than ever to us'.[14]

The Conservatives also saw France as a useful economic partner, which they had no desire to antagonise. Throughout the summer Disraeli and Malmesbury had attempted to trump the free-traders and negotiate an Anglo-French commercial treaty. Their efforts foreshadowed the later, more successful, Liberal initiative.[15] They engaged in a series of exchanges about the goods that might have been covered by such an agreement. Had the treaty been concluded, it would have boosted the Conservatives' credibility on economic policy significantly, as well as further cementing the Anglo-French relationship. As Anthony Howe has pointed out, it would also have challenged the wisdom of the Peelite–radical embrace of unilateral free-trade measures, by obtaining mutual reductions in tariffs.[16] It would have been a triumph of pragmatism to compare with the Reform Act in 1867. Not for nothing was Disraeli 'charmed' at the prospect of a treaty that periodically appeared to be imminent.[17] Ultimately, though, the Conservatives ran out of time before their negotiations had got far enough.

British public opinion was less inclined than the Government to give Louis Napoleon the benefit of the doubt. By the autumn, criticism of the President was *de rigueur* in the liberal press. One publication, noting the triumph of 'despotism' on the Continent, described the French President as 'the evil spirit of the whole *imbroglio*'.[18] Such language was typical. On 6 November, the Earl of Donoughmore was so concerned about press attacks that he condemned them on no less an occasion than the address in answer to the Queen's Speech. He deplored the 'unmeasured abuse from a large portion of the public press'.[19] He suggested that, while the British might be greatly attached to their system of government, that was no reason to force others to adopt it, 'or to cover them with invectives because they preferred their own'.[20]

Louis Napoleon was not just criticised for his despotic tendencies: talk of a French invasion was widespread. As Clarendon noted: 'Even the Frenchmen in London talk with confidence of the "descente" before another year is over'.[21] Brougham, in response to Donoughmore's condemnation of press attacks, agreed that Britain had no right to interfere in other countries' affairs, but warned that 'we lie under no obligation to regard the words rather than the acts of any Government'.[22] He reminded the Lords that, in case 'evil times' came, it was 'our imperative duty, to make timely provision against them'.[23] Sidney Herbert thought that even Palmerston, broadly sympathetic to the French leader, 'has no confidence in the pacific intentions of his friend the Emperor'.[24]

Malmesbury nevertheless continued to be optimistic about his old friend's intentions. As he told Cowley: 'I see a presentiment in both countries [Britain and France] that L.N. means mischief – Lord Derby gets letters every day to say so. I alone do not believe it as he studiously shuns every cause of offence to England – but still we must be ready'.[25] Derby was less sure of Louis Napoleon's long-term reliability; in the short term, though, he too thought peace could be preserved. He predicted that the time would come when Napoleon would 'want another coup de théâtre', but, 'if he meditates any such project at present, I must give him credit for the *most consummate* hypocrisy'.[26] He thought the crisis over the establishment of the Empire would pass: 'The *Empire* is fast approaching; but I conclude L.N. will give the assurances required by the Northern Powers, [and] that they will recognize him personally'.[27] He and Malmesbury correctly calculated that the French President was not, at that stage, interested in provoking a war (which would, after all, have potentially been against all the old allies from 1815) and that the other powers would also appreciate that fact.

The Conservative leaders had concerns nonetheless. Derby had noted earlier in the year that 'it is a precarious position, when the peace of the world depends on the will of one man, & that man dependent in great measure ... on the good will of a numerous, ambitious, well appointed army'.[28] He told Malmesbury that 'we must continue to make all "snug" at home, in case of a sudden outbreak'.[29] Malmesbury agreed. He suggested that, if 'general opinion' was proved to be correct about French intentions, 'all we can do is de rester dans notre droit and & be prepared at the *Admiralty*'.[30] Defensive preparations continued apace.[31]

Some of those who would soon take up ministerial office in the next government were even more pessimistic. A typically gloomy Clarendon told Lansdowne in October that the President's 'pacific declarations make me feel more than ever sure of his warlike intentions'.[32] Aberdeen had been concerned for some time, noting in August: 'Should the President finally determine to make himself Emperor, it will not lead to immediate hostilities; but I fear they will not be far distant'.[33] These assessments did not augur well for a good cross-Channel understanding when Derby and Malmesbury left office.

Recognition of the Second Empire

It was only at the beginning of November that Britain finally had to adopt a definitive policy on the Empire. All the chancelleries of Europe had to respond to important developments in France. On 4 November, the President of the French Senate, Prince Jerome Bonaparte (Louis Napoleon's uncle), formally requested the establishment of a Second Empire. It was decided that the proposition to create the Empire was to be put to the French people in a plebiscite. It was clear that the would-be emperor intended to call himself 'Napoleon III'. To the other powers, this implied a hereditary right to the throne, in succession to the first Napoleon, and his son the King of Rome (later the Duc de Reichstadt), who had briefly been proclaimed 'Napoleon II'. It raised the possibility that, if the other powers approved, they would, in effect, retrospectively nullify their recognition of the restored Bourbons and the Orleanist regime, their relations with those governments, and, by implication, significant chunks of the Vienna settlement.

Throughout the 1850s, it remained an article of faith for Derby and Malmesbury that the arrangements of 1814–15 constituted the bedrock of European stability; any potential threat to the Vienna settlement was always their greatest concern. Louis Napoleon's acknowledgement of its primacy was of great symbolic importance, even if – as many people suspected – his intentions towards it were less than honourable. Stanley recorded the way in which the foreign diplomats attached an importance to the question of the numeral III 'to an extent that is ludicrous'.[34] But Stanley's own colleagues also attached great significance to the title: in their analysis, by adopting it, Louis Napoleon appeared to be publicly disregarding the settlement. In October, Derby had hoped that the President would 'be content, for the present, to drop the question of hérédité'.[35] When the announcement of the title appeared to suggest that this would not be the case, he and Malmesbury felt they were unable to set aside precedent so blatantly. Just before the announcement to the Senate, Malmesbury told Cowley how he had responded when Walewski had informed him about the title: 'I said I thought it would give rise to difficulties. [Walewski asked if that meant] With us? Yes even with us as I did not see how we were to stultify all our acts for the last 37 years'.[36]

The Conservatives would have to devise the response they had avoided, until then, contemplating in too much detail. They had to ensure that their concerns about the implications of the title were met in a satisfactory manner, that they kept on good terms with France and that they did so without alienating the other powers, whose support they might need. During November and early December, Malmesbury and Derby guided policy in tandem; the Prime Minister's political skills were combined with Malmesbury's careful wooing of the French. Their strategy in the last months of 1852 was not dissimilar to Neville Chamberlain's in the 1930s: compromise with a resurgent and unpredictable European power while preparing a defensive safety-net. Unlike Chamberlain, however, they also kept a diplomatic 'grand alliance' in reserve. The fact that they avoided diplomatic isolation or political damage was a triumph for their cautious, conciliatory approach.

This external complication came at a time when the Government faced the greatest domestic pressure it had yet encountered. With concerns closer to home, the Cabinet seems to have played very little part in constructing foreign policy: ministers were preparing the crucial financial measures on which their survival depended. The new parliamentary session commenced in the same week that the French President announced his intention to re-establish the Empire, and the political classes were waiting to hear about one issue above all others: the fate of protection. When Greville recorded rumours of Cabinet 'dissentions [sic]' over 'the great question', he did not mean foreign policy.[37] Disraeli – temperamentally the most likely to go beyond his own portfolio – was preoccupied with financial questions. Comment on foreign affairs is noticeably absent from his surviving correspondence for the period. Greville had even heard that the Lord Chancellor (Lord St Leonards) believed that 'the Govt were quite satisfied with L N's pacific assurances, and saw no danger'.[38]

Disraeli and his colleagues certainly seem to have been content to let Malmesbury get on with his job undisturbed. The Foreign Secretary commanded the affection of his colleagues during the short-lived administration. When a rumour had circulated in the summer that Lonsdale (Lord President of the Council) would be replaced by the previously snubbed Stratford Canning, Disraeli dismissed the idea: 'If he be brought in to be a Sec of State in disguise, the arrangement will end in speedy disaster, & will destroy that feeling of union & camaraderie wh[ich] is one of our main sources of strength. Malmesbury w[oul]d feel degraded, & all spirit w[oul]d evaporate'.[39] The Chancellor reminded Stanley that the unity of the Cabinet was one of their strengths: 'At least your father has an united cabinet, & he has experience enough to appreciate such a blessing'.[40] Stanley himself privately recorded his high opinion of his superior at the FO, whose 'certain awkwardness in speech and writing', in his opinion, did not 'do justice to his real ability'.[41]

In the autumn, when it seemed as if Palmerston might convert benevolent neutrality into support for the Conservatives, the Prime Minister told Malmesbury in no uncertain terms that the former Foreign Secretary would not be returning to his old post: 'He said Palmerston was ready to join us as soon as he saw we were safe [i.e. through the Budget] but that neither he nor the Queen would ever consent to his having the For. Office. – "I never wd deal with him on those terms."'[42] Perhaps Malmesbury exaggerated, but there would have been little point in doing so in his private diary (and he did not publish that entry in his *Memoirs*). Derby certainly made a point of singling out the Foreign Secretary for praise at the end of 1852. He observed, of Malmesbury, that 'no one has been more unsparingly, and, I venture to say, more unjustly maligned'.[43] He maintained that he 'had no cause for anything but self-congratulation in having obtained ... the services of one who ... has brought to bear an ability, a diligence, and a good judgement on the affairs of his department, which reflect the highest credit upon him'.[44] Derby was a loyal friend, but there is no evidence to suggest he did not mean what he said. From his point of view, of course, there was a clear advantage in having Malmesbury at the FO: Derby could intervene in a way that would never have been possible if Palmerston had been running policy.

In the crucial days before and after Napoleon's speech to the French Senate, there were at least three Cabinet meetings.[45] There was discussion about the developments in France during at least the first two.[46] If the Cabinet quibbled about Malmesbury's policy with regard to the Empire, he evidently did not feel there was any discussion significant enough to record in his diary; neither did Stanley. This was in sharp contrast to later Cabinet disagreements about defence, which both diarists noted.[47] The policy Malmesbury outlined to his Cabinet colleagues was precisely the policy that was pursued.[48]

It was on the would-be emperor's new title, not his future intentions, that their attention was focused. Although, in the summer, ministers had outlined their desire for a pledge from Louis Napoleon of his good intentions, this seems to have been dropped by the autumn. This may, in part, have been because he had made every effort to appear peaceable in his public pronouncements. In a speech in Bordeaux on 11 October, he had dramatically declared that 'the empire is peace'.[49] After receiving news of the Senate's proceedings on 4 November, Malmesbury noted that, whatever might be ministers' private concerns, they 'must act upon what is officially said and done', and that what had been said publicly was unobjectionable.[50] He assumed, for instance, that references in the Senate to the conquests of 1789 meant 'popular liberties not territory as no territory was gained for France in that year'.[51] Perhaps the wish was father to the thought. He had told Derby a few weeks earlier that the French leader was 'convinced that war with England lost his uncle the throne, and that he *means* to try *peace* with us'.[52] It was unsurprising, then, that Malmesbury concluded that the public announcement of Bonaparte's intentions did not give 'an advantageous ground of protesting'.[53] An even 'better' reason for not protesting was that no 'positive assurances' had been received about the intentions of the other powers.[54]

Immediately after the French Senate's deliberations, therefore, the Conservatives played for time. While they did so, they attempted to establish the line that would be taken by the northern powers, just as they had over Belgium earlier in the year. The previous week, Aberdeen had told Gladstone that the other powers were 'estranged' from Britain, but the Government certainly did not see things that way.[55] The northern powers occupied a central place in Conservative strategy. Malmesbury warned the Cabinet on 6 November that it was unwise to protest too hastily or publicly about events in France until they were certain about the line that would be taken by the others:

> I then raised the question of the Empire ... Cowley took in his private letters an exaggerated view of it & wanted an immediate protest. – This is not necessary for the time, & not expedient until we are sure of the 3 Great Powers. – I proposed that when L. N. announced the title we should recognise it with *a protest* against a recognition of his retrospective right to the throne.[56]

The Cabinet agreed that this was an appropriate response, and on 8 November Derby himself duly took the lead and drafted a memorandum to be sent to Russia, Austria and Prussia. It was an intervention of almost unparalleled length and detail, which it would be difficult to imagine many other prime ministers emulating. His despatch outlined the British position and enquired about the other powers' views. When transmitted to Vienna, St Petersburg and Berlin, it ran to dozens of pages. Malmesbury was awestruck: 'L[or]d Derby writes an elaborate memorandum on the new titles of L. N. One of the most extraordinary papers I ever read. Addington and Mellish, the oldest and ablest rédacteurs at the Foreign Office, said that neither Canning nor Palmerston could have done the like, & without a single erasure'.[57]

The memorandum, which was sent to Austria, Russia and Prussia on 9 November, was certainly elaborate, referring in detail to diplomatic precedent. It made three key points: that while the establishment of the Empire *per se* was no business of the great powers, it had implications which the powers could not ignore; that they should not respond precipitately; and that they should co-operate in defending the Vienna settlement, and thus in rejecting the President's claim (implied in the title 'Napoleon III') that he had a hereditary right to the imperial throne.[58]

From the outset, Derby employed the usual non-interventionist principles. He made it clear that Britain, as far as the internal government of France was concerned, had no desire to counteract 'the will, clearly and practically expressed', of the French population.[59] He nevertheless thought that the President's message to his people 'is calculated to give rise to serious reflection'.[60] He focused on the President's reference to restoring the Empire overturned by the European powers in 1815. In Derby's view, it 'gives to the message a different character' from that which would have been the case had the president simply been an announcing an 'internal arrangement'.[61]

He suggested it was, as yet, unnecessary to make an official response to developments in France. In his view, 'to notice it now, would have the appearance of unnecessarily interfering in affairs purely French'.[62] From a British perspective, a delay was desirable. Firstly, it would reduce the likelihood of a precipitate act by any other government. The apparent hostility of the other powers to the new Empire could hardly be ignored, even if Malmesbury was rather melodramatic in his assessment of their mood: 'The temper of the Great Powers is now such that if I was minister of a despotic state, we would rush upon France & crush her'.[63] Secondly, as rapidly became clear, Britain would have time to explore all available avenues in pursuit of compromise with France.

The principle of co-operation between the great powers lay at the heart of the memorandum, as it had been at the heart of foreign policy throughout the year. Derby asserted that 'it is of vital importance that a common course of action, or at least an assertion of a common principle, should be agreed on by all the Great European Powers'.[64] It was important that 'there should be a thorough understanding between all the Great Powers' and that 'large discretion' be given to representatives in Paris or London, 'to act as circumstances may require'.[65] This last arrangement was exactly the one that had been adopted with regard to Belgium in the spring, though on this occasion it was to prove a less significant element in British strategy.

The memorandum suggested that there needed to be great power co-operation on two points. Firstly, there needed to be a collective affirmation of the importance of the Vienna settlement. The powers could not tolerate a repudiation of Vienna: the 'new order of things must recognise a present change, & not a retrospection annulling the past'.[66] There might need to be notes 'similar in purport, but not identic[al] in language' that the powers would stand by the settlement of 1814–15.[67] Derby had no desire that it should appear as if Britain was building a coalition against France. If necessary, however, *in extremis*, a 'collective note' should convey 'the determination of Europe that the settlement of 1815 shall not be annulled'.[68] The terms of such a note were not outlined in detail.

Co-operation, Derby suggested, was also necessary on the interlinked question of the title 'Napoleon III'. The implication of the title, that the Empire rested 'upon hereditary right' was 'wholly inadmissible'.[69] On that point, in particular, Europe needed to be 'unanimous'.[70] It could not be dismissed in vague terms, as the question of imperial intentions could. It would rapidly become the focus of correspondence between the powers.

It would have been an unusual diplomatic crisis if British royal sensibilities had not at some point been affected; at this point ministers were delayed by their own ruler. True to form, the Queen was alarmed when she saw Derby's draft memorandum on the Empire. It is possible that the Conservative leader had gone further in the direction of great power unity than his Whig counterparts might have done in the same circumstances. The Queen wrote to the Prime Minister on 8 November to tell him that she was not prepared to let the memorandum be sent 'without having had some verbal explanations about it'.[71] She was concerned that Britain should not draw too close to the other powers on the question of the title. A royal letter was also despatched to Malmesbury the same day, urging on him 'the importance of our not committing ourselves on this point, and not giving our allies to understand that we shall join them in not acknowledging Napoleon III'.[72] The Queen warned the Foreign Secretary that 'our object should be to leave France alone, as long as she is not aggressive'.[73] It seems unlikely that the Francophile Malmesbury or the experienced Derby needed such a warning, but the Queen clearly thought her ministers were taking a dangerous risk.

Derby was rather put out by this 'most inconvenient' intervention, but he and Malmesbury duly travelled to Windsor on 9 November, to calm a nervous monarch, who was '[f]rightened at first but afterwards satisfied'.[74] Neither Malmesbury nor Derby recorded what arguments they used to assuage her fears, but they evidently persuaded the Queen they had not gone too far. They may well have assured her that their co-operation with the other powers was strictly limited. Significantly, the Foreign Secretary had told Cowley on 5 November that, once an assurance had been obtained that the northern powers would 'oppose the *numeral*', Britain must 'after this one act of coalition separate ourselves as to the form of disapprobation'.[75] Nevertheless, Derby and Malmesbury both considered that some sort of co-operation with the 'despotic' states was imperative.

Despite the lengths to which Derby had gone, his memorandum was superseded by events before the other powers had time to respond. Malmesbury had been pursuing matters with France. He tried to impress on Louis Napoleon the significance Britain attached to the difficulty of the imperial numeral: 'with great hesitation I took the step of making our opinions known to him *unofficially* & as an old friend'.[76] Whether this was simply through Cowley's private conversations with Louis Napoleon or if another medium was involved is unclear. On 6 November, Malmesbury certainly informed Cowley of the Government's intentions in no uncertain terms: 'The feeling of the Govt is decidedly to oppose the recognition of the title of Nap III because it infers a stultifying of our former acts & treaties'.[77] It was on this point that British efforts centred.

Malmesbury also sought to mollify Louis Napoleon, arranging for the first Napoleon's will to be returned to France. In his unpublished diary, the Foreign Secretary noted that 'I announced my intention' of giving back the will; in his *Memoirs*, the policy appeared a rather less personal one: 'Agree to give back Napoleon's will to the French government'.[78] The difference was slight, but the latter obscured the extent to which he was engaged in a very personal mission to promote Anglo-French amity.

Whether Louis Napoleon was influenced by these diplomatic sticks and carrots or whether he was persuaded more by a general concern about relations with Britain, the matter was resolved to British satisfaction. On 11 November, the President assured Cowley that, for three reasons, he did not consider his Empire hereditary: firstly, he did not call himself 'Napoleon V', as he might have done, given that his uncle Joseph (the ex-King of Spain, the first Napoleon's older brother) and his own father, Louis (the ex-King of Holland, Napoleon's younger brother), had outlived Napoleon's son, the Duc de Reichstadt; secondly, he did not date his reign from his cousin's – Reichstadt's – or his father's death, which he would have done if he was an hereditary monarch; thirdly, he had called an election, which would have been unnecessary if his title was hereditary.[79]

Malmesbury thought these assurances would 'save our honour without risk of a quarrel'.[80] Derby agreed, and Malmesbury told Cowley to inform the President 'personally from me & L[or]d Derby that this explanation ... gave us the greatest pleasure'.[81] He wanted the French leader to be assured that 'I have always *smoothed* difficulties for him', and that he and his colleagues wanted relations with the President to be 'on the most friendly footing of alliance'.[82] Malmesbury rarely missed an opportunity to ingratiate himself with his old friend.

From 12 November onwards, the aim of British policy was simply to incorporate these assurances in some more substantive written form in order to save face publicly, as Malmesbury noted on 17 November: 'If the President[']s assurances to Cowley are officially given & voluntarily expressed we should allude to them as rendering questions unnecessary wh[ich] w[oul]d otherwise have been indispensible [sic]'.[83] It took some time to persuade the French of the necessity of providing some official record. After much wrangling, the official expression of the French clarification on the question of the title was eventually obtained on 1 December, the day before the imperial proclamation.[84]

Schroeder has suggested that Britain, during November, formed part of a 'conservative entente', a united front with the northern powers, from which Malmesbury then separated Britain by being the first to recognise the new Emperor.[85] But Derby and Malmesbury had always been careful to avoid drawing too close to the other powers. Once Britain had assurances about the numeral, it needed no more. Russia, Austria and Prussia were fully aware of the nature of Britain's position, even if they did not share its Government's interpretation of the title. Malmesbury continued to keep in close contact with them about the declaration. The Foreign Secretary recorded in his diary that the Prussian Minister, Bunsen, thought 'we ought to be quite satisfied with Louis Napoleon[']s declarations to Lord Cowley'.[86] If Malmesbury's record is to be believed, Brunnow, too, told him that 'my view is the best for *England* & that the declaration I shall get from L. N. will be of the greatest use to the other Powers'.[87] Apparently, the Russian Minister also assured the Foreign Secretary that 'nothing can have been more honourable & friendly than our [Britain's] conduct to all of them, & he even added that ours was the most practical & statesmanlike view of the subject'.[88] The Conservative leaders certainly remained on good terms with Brunnow.[89]

The explanation about the numeral, a device for saving face, was what mattered to Malmesbury and Derby: it was important for the President to be *seen* to acknowledge the significance of the Vienna settlement. In practice, of course, this meant very little. But, in Malmesbury's opinion, any French promises about policies, such as an announcement of Louis Napoleon's adherence to treaties, would have been worthless 'moonshine'.[90] What was more, he observed: 'The

Great Powers have not their own hands clean enough to handle the subject with advantage'.[91] Nevertheless, the diplomatic relationship with the other powers was maintained.

The Government persisted with its scheme, outlined in Derby's despatch of 8 November, to produce a joint response with the London ministers of the other great powers after the imperial declaration. On 3 December, to the Queen's consternation, Malmesbury and the representatives duly signed a secret memorandum affirming the importance of the European status quo: 'a proof that altho' I could not persuade them that the French interpretations respecting the numeral III were satisfactory we nevertheless remained of one mind on the more essential subjects relating to our common interests'.[92]

As this continued co-operation with the other powers suggested, the Foreign Secretary was by no means complacent about the French threat in the medium and the long term. On 23 November, he explained his analysis to Derby: 'It seems to me of vital importance to spend the next 4 months actively in our preparations... These months are invaluable & are to us what the peace of Amiens was to Napoleon the 1st when it gave him time to create his artillery'.[93] Despite his basic optimism about Louis Napoleon, the information Malmesbury was receiving about French naval preparations concerned him: 'My *opinion* still is that L. N. will avoid a war with us if he can, but I now *know* that he is preparing it'.[94]

Derby was similarly concerned that Napoleon might at some stage risk war. In December, he suggested to Prince Albert that 'our danger is not so much from desire on the part of the new Emperor for war, but from the necessity which may, and probably will arise, for finding occupation for his army, and excitement for his people'.[95] Whether Derby's reasoning was accurate, his prediction was proved broadly correct: within seven years Napoleon would fight both Russia and Austria, while he would later rise to Bismarck's bait and, fatally, take on Prussia.

Given ministers' concerns, defence expenditure was the logical accompaniment to Malmesbury's foreign policy. Disraeli, in response to royal and Cabinet pressure, proposed a significant increase in naval spending.[96] Parry has suggested that the pressure exerted on Disraeli by his colleagues was representative of their desire to over-compensate for political weakness by showing 'vigour' in defence.[97] This may have been true of some of those Cabinet members whose views on defence were disparagingly recorded by Stanley in December. The Duke of Northumberland, 'an old sailor, and an ignorant politician', was responsible – as First Lord of the Admiralty – for a substantial portion of the increase in defence spending, and 'the country party, as represented in the cabinet, shared his fears, and supported his demand'.[98] Even Northumberland accepted that the spending increase was a 'grievous charge'.[99] But it would have been difficult for any government to avoid doing something about defence in the circumstances. Both Derby and Palmerston would find it equally necessary to increase national defences in the wake of another scare in 1858–59.

Derby, like Palmerston in the 1860s, also genuinely believed that defence required more investment, irrespective of the nature of the French regime. As early as 1848 he had corresponded with Ellenborough about inadequacies in the national defences, 'the importance of which it is impossible to overlook'.[100] In 1852 the Conservative leader was no less concerned. Stanley noted that his father, 'though not believing in the likelihood of war, had always held the opinion that our military and naval defences were too much neglected in peace'.[101] Derby was not alone in that opinion. Aberdeen had told Princess Lieven earlier in the year that 'we have undoubtedly let our means of defence become very insufficient, and I can see no objection to propose now, whatever would have been prudent in the time of King Louis Philippe'.[102] Palmerston apparently also thought 'that upon our preparation or the want of it will turn the decision of the French Govt. as to the policy towards us'.[103]

At no point, however, does it seem that Derby, Malmesbury or Disraeli – the three men whose views mattered the most in late 1852 – seriously believed that the Second Empire represented an imminent threat or necessarily any threat at all. Defence spending merely supplemented the central policy of conciliating France. If anything, the war scare reinforced the importance of the 'calm, temperate, deliberate and conciliatory' policy the Government had pursued all year. As Derby explained to the Queen, the anti-French public mood might become a self-fulfilling prophecy: 'just in proportion as this country entertains a just jealousy of the designs of France, and feels called on to take measures for her own protection, it is the more desirable to hold conciliatory language, and to make it evident that the measures which are in progress are measures of precaution, and not of hostility'.[104]

Disraeli, while having to expand defence expenditure, certainly displayed little concern about danger from France. Immersed in his budget, the Empire did not distract him; he was, as usual, uninvolved in foreign policy in any direct sense. For him, the new defence commitments were a necessary *political* act, not of vital strategic or diplomatic importance. On the one hand, he assured a sceptical Queen Victoria, the most senior and significant advocate of increased expenditure, that 'in making the financial arrangements, he has left a very large margin for the impending year ... wh[ich] will permit the fulfilment of all yr. Majesty[']s wishes, with respect to the encreased [sic] defence of the Country'.[105] On the other hand, to a no less sceptical John Bright (in a rather desperate bid to garner radical support), 'he mentioned those *damned defences*, and said that he had cut and slashed them to bring the estimates for them to a more moderate sum'.[106] That was a more accurate indication of his views.

When Disraeli was faced with more demands for naval and military expenditure, in the latter stages of his budget preparation, he protested vehemently to Derby:

> We are pledged to the Queen, as far as the seamen and marines are concerned, & we must not seem to waver, but I think you must exert yr. utmost authority, that there shall be retrenchment, no matter at what inconvenience, in all in wh[ich] her honor [sic] & safety are not concerned. I think Hardinge [the new Commander-in-Chief of the British Army] also ought to give up his extra 1000 men.[107]

Greville, whose Government contacts were extensive, thought that, although 'national defence occupies every body's mind', it was 'v[er]y doubtful if any important measures will be taken'.[108] The last thing the Government needed was further large expenditure on defence when it already faced a delicate balancing act if the budget was to pass. It was widely accepted that the fate of the Government was inextricably linked with the success or failure of Disraeli's financial measures. For financial reasons, as well as diplomatic and political ones, a conciliatory foreign policy was advisable.

Even though the imperial declaration was made without widespread consternation in Britain, Malmesbury's desire to foster good Anglo-French relations made him a target when he formally announced British recognition of the new Empire on 6 December. He over-egged the pudding in his desire to impress on people the importance of good Anglo-French relations. He explained that the Empire had been recognised on the basis 'that a people have a right to choose their own Sovereign without the interference of any foreign Power'.[109] But not a little admiration for his old friend seeped through. He described, at length and in poetic terms, the respect which was accorded to the Bonaparte name in France: 'a name which, in the great power it exercises, in the magic with which it acts upon the people of France, experience alone has been able to make Europe understand'.[110]

Malmesbury asserted that, seeing 'this immense demonstration of feeling on the part of the French people, it was impossible for Her

Majesty's Government ... not to have advised Her Majesty immediately and cordially to accept and recognise the Empire'.[111] He skated disingenuously over the difficulties relating to the imperial title, stating that the French 'frankly took the initiative' to inform Britain that they 'adopt the title with no intention of claiming any hereditary right from the first Emperor'.[112] He concluded by saying that, in his dealings with France, he had found 'nothing but fairness and fair play ... and wishes to maintain an unbroken friendship with this country'.[113] In his opinion, the French Government appreciated 'the great folly and crime which it would be on either side to provoke war'.[114]

According to Prince Albert's recollection, a few months later, Derby 'confessed to me he covered his face with both hands when he heard his colleague's laudatory speech'.[115] The Prince, a staunch supporter of the new Aberdeen Government, reckoned it 'a mistake, to be buried along with others'.[116] Derby certainly felt that Malmesbury 'overdid' the 'Napoleonist tone', while his son thought Malmesbury had accompanied his recognition of the Empire with a 'perhaps needlessly elaborate' description of Napoleon's pacific intentions.[117] The Foreign Secretary's remarks led to a bad-tempered, but revealing, parliamentary exchange.

Viscount Canning, Aberdeen's former Under-Secretary, rose after Malmesbury had finished and delivered a scarcely veiled rebuke: 'I feel convinced that the sense of the House would condemn any noble Lord who, in following the noble Earl, should express any opinion, or offer any observations of his own, upon this subject.'[118] An irritated Malmesbury enquired as to what Canning regarded as 'being in bad taste'.[119] He was, predictably (and pompously), told that it was 'deemed advisable ... to abstain from any comment on the conduct of neighbouring Powers in their own affairs, whether it be the conduct of the people or of their rulers'.[120] Malmesbury replied that he hoped that he had not said 'a single word to excite the slightest disagreeable feeling'.[121] He 'rose with the most earnest wish to say of France and the French all that France and the French would wish to say of themselves'.[122] The parliamentary spat was terminated, but the controversy was not.

Canning was not alone in being unhappy with the handling of the imperial declaration. His kinsman, Derby's putative Foreign Secretary in 1851 – by that stage ennobled as Lord Stratford de Redcliffe – also made it clear in 'half a dozen disagreeable remarks' to Malmesbury in December that he disapproved of the latter's course.[123] He told the Foreign Secretary that, had he been in the Lords, he would have 'remarked' on his speech.[124] A *Quarterly Review* columnist, probably Croker, also condemned 'the want of statesmanlike reserve and of national dignity in which the recognition of the French Emperor was announced'.[125] Referring to Malmesbury's comments about Napoleon, the essayist suggested that 'acquiescence in the choice of the *French people* should have been ... kept distinct from all *personal* allusions'.[126] At the same time, he condemned Napoleon for what he described, rather improbably, as 'the most extravagant and despotic usurpation the world has ever seen'.[127]

In 1853 the liberal *Fraser's Magazine*, rejoicing in any sign of Tory disunity, sarcastically summed up Malmesbury's predicament: 'Poor Lord Malmesbury! It is his singular fate to displease all parties, and now that he is given up by the *Quarterly*, his career as a public man may be considered at an end'.[128] Criticism by the *Quarterly*, however, revealed little about foreign policy. It said rather more about the bitterness of 'ultras' like Croker over the abandonment of Protectionism. Stratford was bitter too, and there was no love lost between him and Malmesbury, who professed unconcern, wishing that the Ambassador *had* remarked on the speech, 'for I sh[oul]d have recalled him'.[129]

Criticism from the disaffected and the slighted was not of great political significance in itself, but it did illuminate the undercurrent of distaste for the new Emperor in British political circles. Stanley's concern was not about what Malmesbury had said, but that his speech 'had the demerit of provoking hostile criticism from those who might disagree, hazarding thus the use of language which coming from persons of influence, might injure the alliance'.[130] The Anglo-French relationship was fragile, and – paradoxically – the reaction to the speech had emphasised the utility of having at the FO a man who was determined to work with the new regime; Stanley also recorded that he had heard how the French Minister in Russia boasted of '*une entente parfaite*'.[131] When the Government was forced to resign after the failure of Disraeli's budget on 16 December, and the party returned to opposition, the state of the French *entente* it had established remained a great concern to Malmesbury and the Conservatives.

The incoming Government, a Whig–Peelite coalition led by Lord Aberdeen, was to generate concern about far more than merely Anglo-French relations. It was Aberdeen's ministry, and not its much-maligned predecessor, that would be responsible for the greatest failure of nineteenth-century foreign policy.

Notes

1 For analyses of Louis Napoleon's political ideas and ambitions, see: J. M. Thompson, *Louis Napoleon and the Second Empire* (Oxford, 1954), pp.

112–14; Roger Price, *The French Second Empire: An Anatomy of Political Power* (Cambridge, 2001), pp. 15–19 and generally.
2 *Illustrated London News*, 10 April 1852, p. 282.
3 Article 2 of the three identical treaties of 'Alliance and Friendship', between Great Britain and, respectively, Austria, Prussia and Russia, 20 November 1815, stated that: 'Napoleon Bonaparte and his family ... have been for ever excluded from Supreme Power in France': Michael Hurst (ed.), *Key Treaties for the Great Powers, 1814–1914*, 2 vols (Newton Abbot, 1972), vol. 1, p. 122.
4 Derby Papers, 920 DER (14) 179/1, fo. 330, copy, Derby to Croker, 22 December 1851.
5 There is a useful account of Malmesbury's French policy during 1852 in Major, 'The Public Life', pp. 77–93, though it is primarily concerned with the Cowley–Malmesbury exchanges.
6 Malmesbury Papers, 9M73/451, Derby to Malmesbury, 11 August 1852.
7 Derby Papers, 920 DER (15) 37/2, unpublished diary, 15 July 1852.
8 See below, p. 123.
9 Malmesbury Papers, 9M73/451, Derby to Malmesbury, 20 August 1852.
10 Derby Papers, 920 DER (14) 144/1, Malmesbury to Derby, 21 August 1852.
11 *Ibid.*
12 Malmesbury, *Memoirs*, vol. 1, Harris to Malmesbury, 2 September 1852, p. 346.
13 Derby Papers, 920 DER (14) 144/1, Malmesbury to Derby, 27 August 1852.
14 *Ibid.*, Malmesbury to Derby, 30 July 1852.
15 There has been no detailed study of the Conservative negotiations, but a very useful short account may be found in Anthony Howe, *Free Trade and Liberal England, 1846–1946*, (Oxford, 1998) p. 87.
16 *Ibid.*
17 NA, Cowley Papers, FO 519/196, fo. 171, Malmesbury to Cowley, 11 October 1852.
18 *Illustrated London News*, 6 November 1852.
19 Lords, 11 November 1852, *Hansard*, 123, col. 22.
20 *Ibid.*, col. 23
21 Lansdowne Papers, LANS 3/32, Clarendon to Lansdowne, 15 October 1852.
22 Lords, 11 November 1852, *Hansard*, 123, col. 42.
23 *Ibid.*, col. 43.
24 Gladstone Papers, Add. MS 44210, fo. 64, Herbert to Gladstone, 21 October 1852.
25 Cowley Papers, FO 519/196, fo. 174, Malmesbury to Cowley, 15 October 1852.
26 Derby Papers, 920 DER (14) 181/2, fos 35–6, copy, Derby to Malmesbury, 3 October 1852.
27 *Ibid.*, fo. 32.

28 *Ibid.*, 179/1, fos 376–7, copy, Derby to Beaufort, 27 January 1852.
29 *Ibid.*, 181/2, fo. 33, copy, Derby to Malmesbury, 3 October 1852.
30 *Ibid.*, 144/1, Malmesbury to Derby, 15 October 1852.
31 See below, pp. 129–30.
32 Lansdowne Papers, LANS 3/32, Clarendon to Lansdowne, 14 October 1852.
33 Aberdeen Papers, Add. MS 43055, fo. 285, Aberdeen to Princess Lieven, 11 August 1852.
34 Derby Papers, 920 DER (15) 37/2, unpublished diary, 19 November 1852.
35 *Ibid.*, 920 DER (14) 181/2, fos 32–3, copy, Derby to Malmesbury, 3 October 1852.
36 Cowley Papers, FO 519/196, fo. 183, Malmesbury to Cowley, 2 November 1852.
37 Greville Papers, Add. MS 41119, fo. 294, diary, 11 November 1852.
38 *Ibid.*, fo. 289, diary, 3 November 1852.
39 *DL*, vol. 6, 2374, Disraeli to Stanley, 29 August 1852.
40 *Ibid.*
41 *DDCP*, 'June' 1852, p. 70.
42 Malmesbury Papers, 9M73/79, unpublished political diary, 24 October 1852.
43 Lords, 20 December 1852, *Hansard*, 123, col. 1703.
44 *Ibid.*
45 See Malmesbury Papers, 9M73/79, unpublished political diary; and *Memoirs*, vol. 1, pp. 361–3.
46 Malmesbury, *Memoirs*, vol. 1, p. 361; Malmesbury Papers, 9M73/79, unpublished political diary.
47 See, e.g., Malmesbury Papers, 9M73/79, unpublished political diary, 1 December 1852; *DDCP*, 5 December 1852, pp. 86–7.
48 The policy he outlined on 6 November; see below, p. 124.
49 *The Times*, 13 October 1852.
50 Cowley Papers, FO 519/196, fo. 193, Malmesbury to Cowley, 6 November 1852.
51 *Ibid.*
52 Malmesbury, *Memoirs*, vol. 1, p. 357, Malmesbury to Derby, 8 October 1852; original not found.
53 Cowley Papers, FO 519/196, fo. 194, Malmesbury to Cowley, 6 November 1852.
54 *Ibid.*
55 Gladstone Papers, Add. MS 44088, fo. 149, Aberdeen to Gladstone, 31 October 1852.
56 Malmesbury Papers, 9M73/79, unpublished political diary, 6 November 1852.
57 *Ibid.*, 8 November 1852 (slightly altered when published: see Malmesbury, *Memoirs*, vol. 1, p. 363).
58 FO 120/270, 'Memorandum for communication to the Governments of

Austria, Prussia and Russia', 8 November 1852, enclosed in Malmesbury to Howard, no. 30, 9 November 1852; a draft, presumably the original which so impressed Malmesbury, is in Derby Papers, 920 DER (14) 37/2.
59 Ibid.
60 Ibid.
61 Ibid.
62 Ibid.
63 Malmesbury Papers, 9M73/79, unpublished political diary, 5 November 1852.
64 FO 120/270, 'Memorandum for communication to the Governments of Austria, Prussia and Russia', 8 November 1852, enclosed in Malmesbury to Howard, no. 30, 9 November 1852.
65 Ibid.
66 Ibid.
67 Ibid.
68 Ibid.
69 Ibid.
70 Ibid.
71 Malmesbury Papers, 9M73/451, Queen Victoria to Derby, 8 November 1852, enclosed in Derby to Malmesbury, 'Tues' (9 November 1852).
72 LQV, vol. 2, Queen Victoria to Malmesbury, 8 November 1852, p. 397.
73 Ibid., p. 398.
74 Malmesbury Papers, 9M73/79, unpublished political diary, 9 November 1852.
75 Cowley Papers, FO 519/196, fo. 100, Malmesbury to Cowley, 5 November 1852.
76 Derby Papers, 920 DER (14) 144/1, Malmesbury to Derby, 12 November 1852.
77 Cowley Papers, FO 519/196, fo. 194, Malmesbury to Cowley, 6 November 1852.
78 Malmesbury Papers, 9M73/79, unpublished political diary, 8 November 1852; *Memoirs*, vol. 1, p. 363. It is unclear where Malmesbury 'announced' his decision – it was not in the Lords.
79 FO 27/939, no. 672A, Cowley to Malmesbury, 11 November 1852.
80 Derby Papers, 920 DER (14) 144/1, Malmesbury to Derby, 12 November 1852.
81 Cowley Papers, FO 519/196, fo. 197, Malmesbury to Cowley, 12 November 1852.
82 Ibid., fo. 198.
83 Derby Papers, 920 DER (14) 144/1, Malmesbury to Derby, 17 November 1852.
84 FO 27/940, no. 687, Cowley to Malmesbury, 1 December 1852,
85 Paul W. Schroeder, *Austria, Great Britain and the Crimean War: The Destruction of the European Concert* (Cornell University, 1972), p. 6.
86 Malmesbury Papers, 9M73/79, unpublished political diary, 22 November 1852.

87 Derby Papers, 920 DER (14) 144/1, Malmesbury to Derby, 28 November 1852.
88 *Ibid.*
89 See, e.g., *ibid.*, 182/1, fos 38–41, copy, Derby to Brunnow, 2 January 1853 (misdated 1852).
90 *Ibid.*, 144/1, Malmesbury to Derby, 12 November 1852.
91 *Ibid.*
92 FO 93/11/28, Minute, Secret Memorandum, 'Relations with the Imperial Government of France', 3 December 1852; *LQV*, vol. 2, Queen Victoria to Malmesbury, 8 December 1852, p. 408.
93 Derby Papers, 920 DER (14) 144/1, Malmesbury to Derby, 23 November 1852.
94 *Ibid.*
95 *Ibid.*, 181/1, fos 303–4, copy, Derby to Prince Albert, 8 December 1852.
96 See e.g., Blake, *Disraeli*, pp. 337–8.
97 Parry, 'The Impact of Napoleon III', *TRHS* (2001), p. 159.
98 *DDCP*, 5 December 1852, p. 87.
99 Hughenden Papers, Dep. Hughenden 138/1, fo. 31, Northumberland to Disraeli, 4 December 1852.
100 NA, Ellenborough Papers, PRO 30/12/21/4, fo. 31, Derby to Ellenborough, 16 January 1848.
101 *DDCP*, 5 December 1852, p. 87.
102 Aberdeen Papers, Add. MS 43055, fo. 262, Aberdeen to Princess Lieven, 25 March 1852.
103 Gladstone Papers, Add. MS 44210, fo. 64, Herbert to Gladstone, 21 October 1852.
104 Derby Papers, 181/2, fos 123–4, Derby to Queen Victoria, 21 November 1852.
105 *DL*, vol. 6, 2438, Disraeli to Queen Victoria, 14 November 1852.
106 *The Diaries of John Bright*, ed. R. A. J. Walling (New York, 1931), 15 December 1852, p. 129.
107 *DL*, vol. 6, 2453, Disraeli to Derby, 30 November 1852.
108 Greville Papers, Add. MS 41119, fo. 289, diary, 3 November 1852.
109 Lords, 6 December 1852, *Hansard*, 123, col. 971.
110 *Ibid.*, col. 972.
111 *Ibid.*, col. 973.
112 *Ibid.*, col. 974.
113 *Ibid.*, cols 974–5.
114 *Ibid.*, col. 975.
115 *Letters of the Prince Consort 1831–1861*, trans. E. T. S. Dugdale, ed. Kurt Jagow (London, 1938), Prince Albert to Prince William of Prussia, 23 February 1853, p. 187.
116 *Ibid.*
117 Hughenden Papers, Dep. Hughenden 109/2, fo. 3, Derby to Disraeli, 17 February 1853; Derby Papers, 920 DER (15) 37/2, unpublished diary, 6 December 1852.

118 Lords, 6 December 1852, *Hansard*, 123, col. 975.
119 *Ibid.*
120 *Ibid.*, col. 976.
121 *Ibid.*
122 *Ibid.*
123 Malmesbury Papers, 9M73/79, unpublished political diary, 18 December 1852.
124 *Ibid.*
125 'The Budget', *Quarterly Review*, 92 (December 1852), p. 274.
126 *Ibid.*
127 *Ibid.*
128 'The Government & the Country', *Fraser's Magazine*, 47 (February 1853), p. 238.
129 Malmesbury Papers, 9M73/79, unpublished political diary, 18 December 1852.
130 Derby Papers, 920 DER (15) 37/2, unpublished diary, 6 December 1852.
131 *Ibid.*, 12 December 1852.

6

From peace to war: opposing Aberdeen, 1852–55

[I]f *we* had remained in office the Eastern question would have assumed a very different appearance – at all events, no mismanagement of ours could have made it look worse than it does at present. (Derby to Malmesbury, 24 September 1853)

The years after 1852, from the formation of the Aberdeen coalition until its downfall in January 1855, were marked by Conservative frustration, in foreign affairs no less than any other area. In the Conservatives' view, their successors were responsible for, on the one hand, endangering the relationship they had nurtured with France and, on the other, fatally mishandling relations with Russia.

Aberdeen's stewardship failed to prevent Britain plunging into the quagmire of the Crimean war. During 1853, a dispute blew up between Russia and Turkey over the protection of the Christian holy places in the Near East. It was exacerbated by French dabbling, as Napoleon sought domestic political advantage. Russia re-asserted the right it claimed to protect Orthodox Christians in the Ottoman Empire. The Tsar also perceived that the Ottoman Empire might be prodded into its long-awaited collapse, from which all sorts of benefits might flow to Russia. The other powers – with their own economic and strategic interests in the eastern Mediterranean – were gradually drawn in to the row. Britain and France sent fleets to the region, while they and the Austrians attempted to defuse the diplomatic crisis. Ostensibly, they sought to preserve peace and protect Turkey, although Napoleon's motives were questionable.[1]

It was ironic that the Aberdeen coalition, headed by an experienced diplomat, should founder on foreign policy; but it was not surprising. The coalition was a domestic expedient; it contained ministers who had long been opposed on foreign policy. It was a recipe for disaster: the Government was split between those who advocated a firm line against Russia in order to prevent war and those led by Aberdeen – instinctively sympathetic to Russia – who favoured more conciliatory methods of preserving peace. It pursued alternately one policy and then the other, and it prevaricated for long periods.[2] If Aberdeen's vacillation over the 'Eastern question' in 1853–54 represented Peelite foreign policy, it was as unwelcome to the Conservatives as Whig interventionism. Russia meanwhile persisted with an antagonistic policy. In October 1853, the Turks declared war on Russia. After a series of unsuccessful attempts to stop hostilities, Britain (maintaining its policy of upholding the Ottoman Empire) was drawn in, with France, on the Turkish side in March 1854. Once Britain was at war with Russia, there ceased to be normal debate about foreign policy.

From December 1852, the Conservatives found themselves in a new and unpredictable situation. They had been ejected from office and, while they had not been decisively defeated at the polls, they had hardly received a clear endorsement from the electorate. There could be no early expectation of forming another ministry. Worse, the party was faced with a Cabinet incorporating nominally 'Conservative' elements. Opposition to Aberdeen was going to be a different business from opposing the Russell Government. Derby summed up the situation in early 1853: 'I apprehend ... that for the present at least, the position of the Conservative party must be that of armed neutrality, awaiting the development of the extraordinary association which has taken place'.[3] This did not imply passivity. The dangers posed by the Whig–Peelite combination and its potential instability meant that 'for the safety of the country it is essential that, if it can be done, our party should be kept together, well in hand and awaiting the course of events'.[4]

Derby's 'armed neutrality' would, effectively, remain the party's position for another three years. The onset of war less than eighteen months after the advent of Aberdeen's coalition meant that the opportunities for bringing down the Government and replacing it with a Conservative one were limited. Often ill, Derby himself made far fewer appearances. The Conservative failure to form an administration after Aberdeen fell in January 1855 would be a graphic illustration of the practical difficulties faced by the party while it remained in a parliamentary minority. During the war, for a variety of reasons, Derby was reluctant to attack the Government too harshly or directly. Nevertheless, the party remained 'armed' and attacked when it could.

Derby, Malmesbury and Disraeli continued to follow foreign affairs closely, though few of their colleagues did. For the Conservative leaders the subject now had a personal dimension which it had not previously possessed. They had briefly been the arbiters of foreign policy, and regarded the peaceful condition of Britain's foreign relations with some pride. Derby explained to Brunnow in early 1853 that it was 'very gratifying to me that at the close of my short administration, I am enabled to hand over to my successors the foreign relations of the country with all the Great Powers in a state to say the least, fully as satisfactory as that in which I found them'.[5] In February 1853, Disraeli reminded the Commons of the French *entente*: 'during the period that we occupied office nothing took place that at all impaired that cordial understanding between the two countries'.[6] The Conservatives observed Britain's subsequent diplomatic difficulties and its descent into the Crimean war with dismay.

The Peelite presence in the Aberdeen coalition might have been expected to reduce tension over foreign policy. Not an order paper could have been inserted between Derbyite principles and the Peelite ideal outlined by Newcastle in 1852, of 'a foreign policy at once respecting the rights of other countries and firmly maintaining our own'.[7] Yet the opposition leaders rarely found themselves agreeing with Aberdeen, whose policy was far from the conventional Conservative one he had pursued in the 1840s.

Despite this, during 1853 there was not a broad, sustained Conservative Party assault on the management of foreign affairs. This lack of enthusiasm for attacking the coalition may, in part, have stemmed from the fact that the party was demoralised after its exit in 1852. In foreign policy debate, however, the importance of this factor should not be over-emphasised. Opposition politics was in some ways returning to the *status quo ante bellum*. Beyond the leadership there had never been that many Conservative politicians focusing on foreign affairs. A lack of front- and back-bench interest was not specifically a Conservative problem. Except at times of crisis, there were not that many parliamentarians of any party interested in speaking on foreign policy. Derby did not exaggerate much when he noted in 1856 that it was a subject which '9 in 10 of the H. of Commons care nothing about'.[8]

Nevertheless, the Conservatives suffered from a particular shortage of parliamentary representatives with foreign policy expertise, which was concentrated on the government benches. From February 1853 (when Clarendon took over after Russell's brief tenure at the FO) until Russell's resignation in 1855, there were four former Foreign Secretaries in the coalition Cabinet: Aberdeen, Palmerston, Russell and Granville. Disagreements could be contained within the tent. This was one reason why the Cabinet became the most important forum for debate on foreign affairs in the months prior to the Crimean war.[9] Serious Conservative consideration of the subject for much of the mid-

1850s, in the form of public interventions or substantial private correspondence, seems to have been confined to Derby, Malmesbury and Disraeli, although others from time to time made contributions.

But if there was 'little by way of an effective alternative to the Government's foreign policy presented in Parliament', it was not entirely the Conservatives' fault.[10] During 1853, the coalition very effectively managed to restrict parliamentary debate on the subject. To avoid discussion of the developing Near Eastern crisis in the first half of the year, the Government regularly used the excuse that it would have been inappropriate to consider matters while it was still actively engaged in various negotiations with other powers. In such a situation, it was unclear what exactly constituted British policy or how it could be debated.

It was extremely difficult to pin down the Government. When Russell made a statement on 16 August, for example, he gave very little warning that he would do so.[11] Sir John Pakington, Derby's Colonial Secretary in 1852, was the only Conservative front-bencher available.[12] He was inexperienced (and perhaps uninterested) in foreign policy discussion. Conacher has noted the particular absence of opposition speakers in that 'odd' debate.[13] Given that it was mid-August, however, and the shooting season had started, it was not really odd that members of the party of the country gentlemen were thin on the ground. Even Disraeli had left London.[14]

The Conservatives, of course, could have sought more opportunities to attack the Government's foreign policy throughout the 1853 session, but there was little incentive to do so. With no expectation of an early return to power, there was no obvious reward for the effort that would have been expended. What was more, coalition disunity was notorious; the Cabinet was quite capable of providing its own challenges to foreign policy. By late 1853, Palmerston had even concluded that the perpetuation of disunity was one of his principal duties: 'the presence in the Cabinet of a person holding the opinions which I entertain as to the principles on which our foreign affairs ought to be conducted is useful in modifying the contrary system of policy, which, as I think, injuriously to the interests & dignity of the country there is a disposition in other quarters to pursue'.[15] There was a lot to be said for giving ministers enough rope with which to hang themselves.

The Eastern question also happened to enter a critical phase while Parliament was in recess for five months. Opportunity for debate – and the supply of information with which to contribute to it – was therefore even more restricted. In early 1854, when the opportunity came, the Conservative leadership made spirited assaults on the

Government. By then, the incentives to do so were greater. Divisions in Cabinet, over new Russellite reform plans and foreign policy, led the Conservatives to consider that a return to office might be imminent. Stanley noted on 28 February 1854 how he had returned home to find Derby 'confident of victory, planning future measures and framing his cabinet'.[16]

Despite the difficulties in 1853, the Conservatives were neither silent nor uncritical as the coalition flailed about in the Near Eastern morass. Malmesbury's role in this period was of particular significance. He continued to be a close confidant of Derby and – at least until the Crimean war introduced tensions – Stanley and Disraeli too. He was the only surviving ex-Foreign Secretary outside the Cabinet, and his colleagues drew on his knowledge. When Disraeli was preparing to attack the coalition in February 1853, he used details supplied in a 'very good letter' from the former Foreign Secretary.[17] Derby looked to him for information about French views.[18] Malmesbury kept up his connection with Napoleon, visiting Paris twice in 1853.[19] He continued to feel that he had a particular appreciation of French sensibilities. Though he hardly possessed the authority that Palmerston or Aberdeen had wielded in opposition, he was by 1853 the Conservatives' unchallenged expert on foreign affairs.

As the position in the Near East deteriorated, Malmesbury effectively operated as shadow Foreign Secretary. During the summer of 1853, supported by Hardwicke, he kept up the pressure on the Government. In May it was he who finally extracted some information from Clarendon about great-power negotiations.[20] On 12 August, he ambushed the Government with a long speech outlining what he perceived to be the flaws in their foreign policy.[21] He was, in his turn, subjected to a broadside from *The Times*, which accused him of speaking 'of his relations with France as if no English Minister had ever before lived on terms of good neighbourhood with that Government'.[22] By focusing on Malmesbury's criticism of the Government, and in such a vigorous manner, the newspaper testified to the danger represented by a hostile ex-Foreign Secretary. Malmesbury was one of the few with a consistent, sustained critique of Aberdeen's policies.

Of what did that critique consist? The Conservative leadership regarded the foreign policy of the Aberdeen coalition as fundamentally flawed, on two grounds. Firstly, the Government seemed to be threatening the Anglo-French relationship, which in turn left British interests vulnerable in the East. Secondly, it appeared supine in its handling of the Eastern question, misleading Russia and precipitating war.

The Conservatives deplored what they regarded as the coalition's general antagonism towards France and, in particular, Napoleon. Within weeks of their resignation, the Conservatives were raising concerns about Anglo-French relations. Early in 1853 two Cabinet ministers, James Graham (First Lord of the Admiralty) and the Francophobe Charles Wood (President of the Board of Control), made controversial speeches about France, Wood's being especially antagonistic. In language very different from that adopted by the Conservative ministers in 1852, Wood condemned Napoleon for suppressing opposition: 'Such a despotism never prevailed in France even in the time of Napoleon the First'.[23] He listed Napoleon's crimes: 'The press gagged; liberty suppressed; no man allowed to speak his opinions; the neighbouring country of Belgium forced to gag her press'.[24] Warming to his theme, he declared that there was 'no press in Europe free but ours, which, thank God, he cannot gag. (Cheers)'.[25]

The speech enraged Malmesbury, who feared its effect on Napoleon. Malmesbury felt that in 1852 he had detached him from Russia, Austria and Prussia, with which countries the Emperor might have otherwise worked in opposition to Britain: 'Our Govt had successfully separated France from them & when we recognised the Empire there was no one thing she would not have done *for* us and *with* us'.[26] He feared that the 'conceited insanity of this man Wood' would destroy Anglo-French amity.[27] When Malmesbury visited Napoleon in March 1853, he recorded in his private diary that the Emperor had referred to the Wood and Graham speeches.[28] Malmesbury's anger at what he perceived as ministerial obtuseness was in the same vein as criticisms of Russell for misjudging Louis Napoleon in 1851. The Conservative leaders' concern was the more pronounced because they believed they had a better understanding of French sensibilities.

The Aberdeen–Napoleon relationship caused particular disquiet in Conservative ranks. Aberdeen, with his Orleanist contacts, was widely supposed to be hostile to Napoleon. Malmesbury told Derby in September that his correspondence with Walewski led him to believe that Napoleon 'does not trust Aberdeen to be a sound comrade, should a war be necessary'.[29] Disraeli feared the Emperor's reaction to the coalition's handling of Anglo-French relations: 'the conduct of our government to him has been so inconsistent, & often so mistrustful, that we have absolutely encouraged him to leave us in the lurch'.[30] When Palmerston briefly resigned from the Government in December 1853 over reform, Malmesbury noted that 'his resignation will very much alarm Louis Napoleon who looked entirely to him to stand to his guns'.[31] In early 1854, he recorded an interview with Palmerston, in which he apparently learnt that 'A[berdeen] is despised & that pressure was put on P. to return by the *French* Govt. as well as ours'.[32]

The Conservatives were not just concerned about the Anglo-French relationship for its own sake: the problem with endangering that alliance, as they feared the Government was doing, was that it would impact on the British position in the deteriorating Near East. Britain would be left impotent and without her most significant ally in a region where it had vital strategic interests. As early as February 1853, Malmesbury outlined the problem to Disraeli. He noted that the 'counterpoise against Russia & Austria in Turkey is England and France',[33] but that if the latter were alienated from Britain, then the consequences of any emergent St Petersburg–Paris–Vienna axis could be grave: 'Why should not the three omnipotents part the Ottoman monarchy as Poland was parted[?]'[34] Malmesbury, like Palmerston, was focused on the preservation of Turkish power.

Derby was similarly worried that any mishandling of Anglo-French relations would affect the Near East. By September 1853 he was concerned that Aberdeen might have 'succeeded in disgusting France into a withdrawal from her union with us'.[35] He feared that, 'if any credence is to be given to John Russell and Palmerston [the more bellicose members of the coalition] … we shall be drawn into a war with Russia, in which it will only depend on the good faith & firmness of France whether we are left without an ally except the Turk'.[36] As it transpired, the Anglo-French relationship was more durable than it appeared, but the Conservatives' corresponding alarm about Aberdeen's relationship with Russia proved to be well-founded.

The Conservatives deplored Aberdeen and Peel's collaboration with the Tsar in 1844, which had produced the secret memorandum agreeing to concert British policy with Russia and Austria if Ottoman power were to collapse.[37] Nesselrode's memorandum, which the Conservative leaders had apparently been shown when they were in office during 1852, represented exactly the sort of commitment they had sought so carefully to avoid. Early in the crisis, they identified it as a significant problem: they felt that it left Aberdeen in a very weak position from which to oppose Russian demands. They suggested – as many others would later – that it was the existence of that personal guarantee which had encouraged the Tsar to pursue an aggressive policy in the East once Aberdeen was Prime Minister. In July 1853, some months before the memorandum was published, Malmesbury wrote to remind Derby about it: 'It shews [*sic*] at once the whole difficulty of Aberdeen's position with Russia & is the key to all his hesitations & fears'.[38] With Britain's entry into the war imminent in March 1854,

Disraeli privately railed against 'the complicity of Aberdeen wh[ich] is the real crime'.[39]

The existence of the Nesselrode memorandum nevertheless represented a political opportunity; potentially, it left Aberdeen compromised. In August 1853, confidential FO papers were apparently used by *The Times* to attack Malmesbury. He responded with some low politics of his own, reminding Clarendon of Aberdeen's vulnerability if 'some body a partisan of mine was to send [to the press] an account of his secret conversation ... in 1844'.[40] Malmesbury was not the bumbling lightweight his enemies liked to depict him as being. His threat had the desired result, producing a grudging quasi-apology in the next day's edition.[41] With the memorandum becoming public knowledge in 1854, as hostilities loomed, the opposition grabbed the opportunity to use it as a stick with which to beat the coalition.

In 1854, the Conservatives alleged in public what they had previously maintained in private, that if it had not been for the Foreign Secretary of 1844 becoming Prime Minister there would have been no war. The fault was with Aberdeen, not the Tsar. In the Lords on 31 March, Derby suggested that, on Aberdeen's appointment, the Tsar 'was led, and most naturally, to believe that the time had arrived to carry into operation the understanding entered into in 1844'.[42] Aberdeen retorted that the memorandum had 'no other practical effect in the world than that there should be no separate action, in the event of that calamity taking place which the Emperor of Russia anticipated would happen to Turkey'.[43] Malmesbury was stung by that response into a renewed attack on the Prime Minister, returning to what he considered the central point, namely,

> that within five or six days after the intelligence of the accession to office of the noble Earl opposite [Aberdeen] the Emperor [Nicholas I] took up the thread of the propositions as broken off since 1844 – that is, I think, sufficient evidence to convince almost any mind that the Emperor considered the noble Earl as ready to act upon the policy embodied in the memorandum.[44]

Disraeli followed up in a similar vein in the Commons, suggesting that 'the Emperor, systematically, candidly, with almost fatal frankness, required that agreement to be fulfilled, and endeavoured to work it out in all its provisions'.[45] These public attacks on the Government were not merely rhetorical devices. The Conservative leaders believed Aberdeen bore a personal responsibility for war. Russian confusion about British foreign policy had, in their opinion, flowed inevitably from a commitment of the kind they had avoided in 1852.

From peace to war: opposing Aberdeen 147

Malmesbury pointedly noted that Aberdeen's absence from Derby's Cabinet had meant that the Tsar 'had no hold over *us*'.[46]

The Conservatives also alleged that, by failing to adopt a clear position from the outset, the Government had misled Russia about the extent to which Britain would oppose the Tsar's ambitions in Turkey. Malmesbury feared that the Sultan would be forced to give in to Russian demands because of a lack of British support: 'if the Turk admits the demands of Russia … it is the most signal & disgraceful diplomatic defeat that this country has sustained for a century. Worse than all this it will prevent the present ruler of France from ever trusting an English alliance & he will turn to the other Powers from wh I separated him'.[47]

It was thus the Government, not the Russians, which attracted Conservative ire. In August 1853, Hardwicke had warned of the danger posed by British vacillation: 'the pacific character of the communications which had taken place between this country and Russia, and between this country and Turkey, would ultimately tend to produce more difficulty than if they had been of a more serious and determined character'.[48] Pakington also drew attention to the Cabinet's prevarications. He suggested that Parliament needed to consider 'whether the blessings of peace might not have been better secured and more surely maintained if the Government had thought fit to follow a more vigorous and decided policy at an earlier period of these negotiations'.[49] As war became imminent in January 1854, Derby put it much more strongly: 'My Lords, I think that the Emperor of Russia has great cause to complain. I think that Her Majesty's Government deceived and deluded him with regard to the course which he might have expected them to pursue'.[50] Stanley asked Seymour, on his ejection from St Petersburg, if greater firmness from Britain might have prevented war. Britain's former minister agreed it might well have done.[51]

Attacking the Government, rather than Russia, provided an important collateral benefit: it avoided offending pro-Russian Conservatives. There was a significant minority ready to give the Tsar the benefit of the doubt. Even at the height of the war, Lord Claud Hamilton criticised the ministerial assumption that 'the danger which threatened the Sultan came wholly from Russia'.[52] That, he thought, 'was known to be totally the reverse of the fact. No one who read the Blue-books could fail to see that the real danger of Turkey arose from its own internal mismanagement and the recklessness of its Government'.[53] Granby was outraged by British war aims. He thought that Britain 'had no right to tell Russia what number of ships she should build in her ports'.[54] As Disraeli planned the Conservative parliamentary strategy on the outbreak of war, he observed that there was 'no necessity for any personal attacks on the Emperor of Russia'.[55] He appreciated that 'there are many personal friends of the Emperor [Nicholas] on our side'.[56] Malmesbury later noted that 'some of our 250 ... are very Russian & cannot be depended upon[,] viz Granby, Lovaine, Claude Hamilton, Hilliard &c'.[57]

The Conservatives' criticism of the Government was underscored by personal ill-feeling towards Aberdeen, notably absent from their attacks on Palmerston or Russell. The Conservatives criticised the Prime Minister heavily, in private and in public. Though they had once been colleagues, and until 1852 had from time to time co-operated, Derby had little respect for the Peelite who had succeeded him as Prime Minister. His comments after one parliamentary skirmish summed up his general contempt for Aberdeen, who was 'more old-womanish, ill-conditioned & impotent than usual'.[58] His feelings were shared by many of his colleagues, who saw the Peelites' participation in government as another great betrayal, second only to their free-trade heresy. In May 1853, when an Irish MP attacked the Government, Stanley noted how the bitterness on the Conservative benches manifested itself: 'it seemed strange to see the English country gentlemen cheering and vehemently encouraging an Irish Roman Catholic of the ultra-radical party ... but the circumstance shows how strong is their feeling against Lord Aberdeen and his colleagues'.[59]

At Malmesbury's meeting with Napoleon in March 1853, the Emperor had enquired about Aberdeen's views on Anglo-French relations. Malmesbury, having already vouched for Clarendon and Russell being in favour of alliance with France, replied rather stiffly that he 'would only answer for the two I had mentioned[,] not having had any relations with the others'.[60] When war was declared, Aberdeen's leadership was the focus of Conservative criticism. His lack of control over his Cabinet was one target. Given Palmerston's resignation and reinstatement in December 1853, Derby suggested that the public would 'have to inquire ... who is, in point of fact, the guiding genius of the Cabinet'.[61] Disraeli held Aberdeen personally responsible for war. Privately he described him as 'the real criminal' who had precipitated the conflict.[62] In public, he alleged that 'the war has been produced by one man ... who occupies the most eminent post in the country'.[63]

In an ironic reversal of earlier relations, Conservative contempt for Aberdeen's premiership was matched by a much improved relationship with Palmerston during 1853 and 1854. Palmerston's flirtation with Derby's Government had established a better basis for relations. Palmerston did nothing to discourage Conservative expectations that he would yet join them. In early 1854, Stanley recorded in his diary how Palmerston hinted at co-operation, 'playing fast and loose, throwing out hints that might mean much or nothing'.[64] Disraeli, according to Stanley, relied on 'Palmerston's secret support'.[65] There appeared to be a good basis for co-operation. Palmerston's well-known antipathy to reform was an asset in Conservative circles, while as the coalition's Home Secretary he was far less likely to offend Tory sensibilities than he would have been at the Foreign Office.

But there were other reasons for a *rapprochement* with Palmerston. Among rank-and-file Conservatives, Disraeli's own unpopularity during the years in opposition made Palmerston an attractive alternative. Walpole noted in November 1853 that 'there is & has been much distrust of Disraeli', while Malmesbury observed that 'if Palmerston left the Govt there is no doubt that many of our staunchest supporters w[oul]d follow him as leader of the Commons'.[66] The risk and then expectation of conflict made the experienced former Secretary at War and ex-Foreign Secretary more palatable. After Palmerston's brief resignation in December 1853, Malmesbury felt that the Government had 'lost the man to whom the whole country looked in the event of a war'.[67] At the outset of hostilities, Granby was not the only one who believed that 'if Her Majesty's Government had been more of one mind, or … if the noble Lord the Member for Tiverton … had been at the head of the Government, there would have been no war'.[68]

Once the conflict had begun, however, the nature of opposition changed. The Conservatives were no longer simply attacking the mismanagement of foreign policy. They were confronted instead with the difficulties of commenting on a national war effort. Criticising the management of a war has always been a difficult business for politicians. The Conservatives still needed to be ready for government if the opportunity came, but had to avoid the appearance of being unpatriotic.

War with Russia

Derby set the Conservative tone at the declaration of hostilities. While he lambasted the coalition's pre-war foreign policy, he talked of 'the necessity of giving an active support to Her Majesty's Government in the prosecution of that war which, however lamentable and however much to be deprecated … is … a just war, and which, in the present state of things, however different it may have been originally, is also a necessary war'.[69] But the party had a difficult balance to strike. After six months of war Malmesbury would tell Disraeli that his 'only fear' about the Conservative position was that 'some of our *hungry* ones may betray a fatal satisfaction at national calamities'.[70] He worried that, if this happened, 'we sh[oul]d become execrated forever'.[71] The party was perhaps more aware of the dangers than Malmesbury feared. Once the mistakes leading to war had been deplored, the party leaders and a significant chunk of the parliamentary party publicly supported its vigorous prosecution.

That is not to say the party was united; far from it. Stanley, who thought 'that we should have done better to keep out of it', noted the range of views at the declaration of war:

> Of the country gentlemen, some joined in the war cry out of mere thoughtlessness, some out of fear of Russia, some in order to annoy the Government, some to stave off Reform: a few because they liked the prospect of popularity ... but there remains a large number who dislike prospective disturbance in Europe, who object to fight where England has nothing to gain: and who in their hearts agree with Cobden.[72]

Stanley was deeply concerned about the consequences of war, and inclined towards as early a peace as was possible. He argued strongly for that in the *Press*, the newspaper that had been established to give the Conservatives a voice (though its main achievement was to give Disraeli and his allies an even louder one). While Stanley's articles were anonymous, his views were well-known. More seriously, in the latter stages of the conflict Disraeli would challenge Derby's strategy of support for the war. At no stage, however, was Derby prepared to let the Conservatives become a 'peace party'.

It was, as ever, Derby who determined party policy, although the historiographical focus on Disraeli has led some to assume that the Conservative leadership was more pro-peace than it was. One of Edward Bulwer Lytton's biographers, for example, has suggested that Lytton, by speaking out against the conduct of the war while pressing for its vigorous prosecution, was 'at odds with the Tories'.[73] In fact, Lytton – who was becoming a prominent Conservative – was making speeches that were merely a variation on a Derbyite theme. When Derby explained to the Lords his reasons for refusing to form a government in January 1855, he singled out Lytton as one of the men who would have been in his Cabinet, with his 'unrivalled eloquence and commanding talents'.[74]

Other leading Conservatives adopted a critical but essentially pro-war stance. Malmesbury, despite his attacks on pre-war foreign policy, was particularly bellicose throughout the conflict. In 1855, he would tell Derby how he had complained to Napoleon that 'whilst we were negotiating at Vienna our admirals ought to be shelling Odessa'.[75] Stanley would note that, by the latter stages of the conflict, 'both Lord Derby and Malmesbury inclined decidedly to the party of war. Most, though not all, the country gentlemen, connecting the idea of war with prosperity and high prices, supported them to a man'.[76]

Between 1854 and 1856, therefore, foreign policy had little independent existence beyond the diplomacy of war or peace. The period of the Crimean war was consequently an anomalous one. Malmesbury recorded in his *Memoirs* that, when he met with Palmerston in early May 1854, they 'agreed perfectly on all points of foreign policy'.[77] Nevertheless, the Conservatives continued to harass the Government in Parliament, and at the close of the 1854 session Disraeli felt that they had conducted a 'satisfactory campaign'.[78] Malmesbury recorded that the coalition 'gets beaten almost every night in the House of Commons'.[79] Not for the first or the last time, however, Disraeli was privately exasperated by Derby's leadership: 'As for our Chief', he complained to Lady Londonderry, 'we never see him. His house is always closed; he subscribes to nothing, tho his fortune is very large; & expects, nevertheless, everything to be done'.[80]

Whether or not this outburst was a fair reflection on Derby's leadership, Disraeli's frustration was of longer term significance. His desire for a more vigorous campaign in 1854 was expressed in terms that summed up his broader political strategy: 'There cannot be too much vigilance, too much thought, & too much daring. All seem wanting'.[81] Disraeli's desire for bold risk-taking in opposition would subsequently manifest itself in government, not least in attacks on Malmesbury's management of foreign affairs. Ultimately, in another Russo-Turkish crisis nearly a quarter of a century later, it would help produce the final triumph of Disraelian over Derbyite politics.

In the mid-1850s, however, Conservative policy was still determined by Derby, whose strategy remained essentially that of the 'armed neutrality' he had adopted in 1853. He awaited the breakdown of the disparate forces that made up the coalition, rather than chancing a full-frontal attack which might damage the Conservatives and/or strengthen the Government. In early 1855 he warned Eglinton that 'it is not my policy to hazard a division, though I may any day be forced into one'.[82] He expanded on his policy in his instructions to the Chief Whip, Jolliffe: 'I am very much inclined to think that we should ... not risk an assault leading to a great action, in which we should probably be beaten, & in which, if not, one success would be very embarrassing to ourselves, & still more so to the country'.[83]

Derby thought that a victory could be embarrassing because the strength of the Conservative Party was 'not sufficient to form a Govt'.[84] He added that, if the Conservatives initiated a division in which the coalition was defeated, it would make it very difficult to find any defeated ministers who would serve in a Conservative-led administration. If, on the other hand, the coalition defeated the Conservatives, it would strengthen the Government and 'patch up their internal differences', by which he set great store.[85] Derby's 'masterly inactivity' may have been reinforced by a personal lack of enthusiasm for a fight in what he viewed as such unpropitious circumstances. He told Disraeli in November 1854: 'I can hardly say that I am eager for the fray'.[86]

In such circumstances, even Malmesbury, while accepting Derby's analysis, feared losing the initiative to opposition figures such as Ellenborough, 'the great outsiders' over whom the Conservative leadership had little control.[87] He pressed Derby to keep himself in the public eye. He worried about the consequences if the Conservatives were 'silent, or only play second fiddle to Grey &c', and stressed the importance of Derby taking a clear parliamentary lead: '*You* ought I think to be at the head of every demonstration even if you don't *charge*'.[88] But it was Disraeli's growing differences with Derby over the political response to the war that would prove to be of greater importance than any of Malmesbury's concerns. When the Aberdeen coalition, battered in the Commons and increasingly weakened by internal tensions, did fall apart, Derby's failure to form a ministry provided further grounds for Disraelian discontent.

In January 1855, as war dragged on, and British deficiencies became more and more obvious, the coalition was increasingly attacked at home. Finally, it was overwhelmingly defeated in the Commons, on Roebuck's motion for a committee to inquire into the conduct of the war. The coalition resigned on 30 January. The Queen duly called Derby to form a government, a task which he eventually declined when it became clear that Palmerston would not serve. As far as foreign policy was concerned, the political crisis of early 1855 had little immediate significance. It did, however, re-affirm Malmesbury's place in the Conservative hierarchy and demonstrated his leader's satisfaction with the job he had done in 1852.

Malmesbury was again Derby's preferred candidate for the FO. A royal memorandum of 31 January recorded the Conservative leader's intention to 'return to Lord Malmesbury, who, he thought, had done well before, and had now additional experience'.[89] Derby's attitude to alternative suggestions was instructive. Though Palmerston would have been well aware of mutual antagonism between Derby and

Clarendon, he suggested that Derby 'ought to try, by all means, to retain Lord Clarendon at the Foreign Office'.[90] Derby conveyed to the Queen his particular displeasure at this suggestion.[91]

It seems possible that Palmerston suggested the retention of the coalition's Foreign Secretary as a quasi-condition of his acceptance of office in the hope that it would help discourage Derby from forming a government. Palmerston was a master of the art of appearing reasonable while making his support contingent on conditions he knew would prove unacceptable. He would play the same game, with the same successful result, against Granville and Russell in June 1859. Later, on 31 January, ranging across his various difficulties in a long letter to the Queen, the Conservative leader said that Clarendon was unacceptable to 'Lord Derby's friends', unless he received 'a special injunction' from the Queen to include the Whig minister.[92] Both Malmesbury and Stanley recorded that Derby did at some point accept that Clarendon might be a necessary addition, although there is confusion on this point.[93] The fact remained that Malmesbury was Derby's first choice for the FO. He would return to that office in 1858, while in 1866 it would not be offered to Stanley until Malmesbury had formally disclaimed his interest in it.[94]

It was the Government now formed by Palmerston, however, and not a hypothetical Derby Cabinet, that would have to be the Conservative focus for the foreseeable future. Palmerston would be no easy target. But when opportunities came, they would be provided by foreign policy.

Notes

1 For a detailed discussion of the origins of the Crimean war see, e.g., Andrew D. Lambert, *The Crimean War: British Grand Strategy Against Russia, 1853–56* (Manchester, 1990), pp. 1–82; David M. Goldfrank, *The Origins of the Crimean War* (Harlow, 1994).
2 See, e.g., J. B. Conacher, *The Aberdeen Coalition 1852–55* (Cambridge, 1968), pp. 137–287.
3 Derby Papers, 920 DER (14) 182/1, fos 47–8, copy, Derby to Lambert, 4 January 1853.
4 *Ibid.*, fo. 48.
5 *Ibid.*, fo. 40., copy, Derby to Brunnow, 2 January 1853.
6 Commons, 18 February 1853, *Hansard*, 124, col. 261.
7 Aberdeen Papers, Add. MS 43197, fo. 12, Newcastle to Aberdeen, 2 August 1852.
8 Derby Papers, 920 DER (14) 183/2, fo. 135, copy, Derby to Malmesbury, 15 December 1856.

9 See, e.g., Brown, *Politics of Foreign Policy*, p. 177.
10 *Ibid*.
11 Commons, 16 August 1853, *Hansard*, 129, cols 1760–9.
12 *Ibid*., cols 1780–3.
13 Conacher, *Aberdeen Coalition*, p. 177.
14 He had left for Torquay on 15 August.
15 Lansdowne Papers, LANS 3/42, fo. 39, Palmerston to Lansdowne, 8 December 1853.
16 *DDCP*, 28 February 1854, p. 122.
17 *DL*, vol. 6, 2487, Disraeli to Stanley, 14 February 1853.
18 See e.g., Derby Papers, 920 DER (14) 182/2, fo. 79, copy, Derby to Malmesbury, 24 September 1853.
19 From 18 March to 1 April, and from 22 November to 3 December, according to his *Memoirs*, vol. 1, pp. 386–96, 410–14.
20 Lords, 27 May 1853, *Hansard*, 128, cols 651–4.
21 Lords, 12 August 1853, *Hansard*, 129, cols 1605–24.
22 *The Times*, 17 August 1853.
23 *Ibid*., 7 February 1853, speech at Halifax, 3 February 1853.
24 *Ibid*.
25 *Ibid*.
26 Hughenden Papers, Dep. Hughenden 99/1, fo. 93, Malmesbury to Disraeli, 12 February 1853.
27 *Ibid*.
28 Malmesbury Papers, 9M73/79, unpublished political diary, 20 March 1853.
29 Derby Papers, 920 DER (14) 144/1, Malmesbury to Derby, 29 September 1853.
30 *DL*, vol. 6, 2558, Disraeli to Londonderry, 26 September 1853.
31 Derby Papers, 920 DER (14) 144/1, Malmesbury to Derby, 21 December 1853.
32 Hughenden Papers, Dep. Hughenden 99/1, fos 119–20, Malmesbury to Disraeli, undated (? 2 January 1854).
33 *Ibid*., fo. 93, Malmesbury to Disraeli, 12 February 1853.
34 *Ibid*.
35 Derby Papers, 920 DER (14) 182/2, fo. 79, copy, Derby to Malmesbury, 24 September 1853.
36 *Ibid*., fo. 78.
37 See above, p. 81.
38 Derby Papers, 920 DER (14) 144/1, Malmesbury to Derby, 11 July (1853).
39 *DL*, vol. 6, 2644, Disraeli to Carrington, 27 March 1854.
40 Bodleian Library, Oxford, Clarendon Deposit, c.103, fo. 166, Malmesbury to Clarendon, 16 August 1853.
41 *The Times*, 17 August 1853.
42 Lords, 31 March 1854, *Hansard*, 132, col. 157.
43 *Ibid*., col. 176.

44 *Ibid.*, col. 183.
45 Commons, 31 March 1854, *Hansard*, 132, col. 297.
46 Derby Papers, 920 DER (14) 144/1, Malmesbury to Derby, 11 July (1853).
47 Hughenden Papers, Dep. Hughenden 99/3, fo. 155, Malmesbury to Disraeli, undated.
48 Lords, 12 August 1853, *Hansard*, 129, col. 1643.
49 Commons, 16 August 1853, *Hansard*, 129, col. 1783.
50 Lords, 31 January 1854, *Hansard*, 130, col. 74.
51 *DDCP*, 27 May 1854, p. 125.
52 Commons, 4 June 1855, *Hansard*, 138, col. 1375.
53 *Ibid.*
54 Commons, 24 May 1855, *Hansard*, 138, col. 1030.
55 *DL*, vol. 6, 2644, Disraeli to Carrington, 27 March 1854.
56 *Ibid.*
57 Hughenden Papers, Dep. Hughenden 99/1, fo. 134, Malmesbury to Disraeli (? 24 March 1854).
58 Derby Papers, 920 DER (14) 182/2, fo. 208, copy, Derby to Malmesbury, 11 February 1854; the parliamentary exchanges to which he referred were in the Lords: 10 February 1854, *Hansard*, 130, cols 396–402.
59 *DDCP*, '5–6 May' 1853, p. 106.
60 Malmesbury Papers, 9M73/79, unpublished political diary, 20 March 1853.
61 Lords, 31 January 1854, *Hansard*, 130, col. 86.
62 *DL*, vol. 6, 2644, Disraeli to Carrington, 27 March 1854.
63 Commons, 31 March 1854, *Hansard*, 132, col. 301.
64 *DDCP*, 23 February 1854, p. 121.
65 *Ibid.*, 24 March 1854, p. 123.
66 Worcestershire Record Office, County Hall Branch, Worcester, Hampton (Pakington) MSS (viewed on microfilm), 705:349/4732/2/vi/29, Walpole to Pakington, 22 November 1853; Derby Papers, 920 DER (14) 144/1, Malmesbury to Derby, 8 September (1853).
67 Derby Papers, 920 DER (14) 144/1, Malmesbury to Derby, undated 'Thursday night' (probably 15 December 1853).
68 Commons, 31 March 1854, *Hansard*, 132, col. 270.
69 Lords, 31 March 1854, *Hansard*, 132, col. 153.
70 Hughenden Papers, Dep. Hughenden 99/1, fo. 145, Malmesbury to Disraeli, 26 November 1854.
71 *Ibid.*
72 *DDCP*, 20 February 1854, p. 120.
73 Leslie Mitchell, *Bulwer Lytton: The Rise and Fall of a Victorian Man of Letters* (Hambledon, 2003), p. 201.
74 Lords, 8 February 1855, *Hansard*, 136, col. 1338.
75 Derby Papers, 920 DER (14) 144/1, Malmesbury to Derby, 14 April 1855.
76 *DDCP*, 'November 1855', p. 135.

77 Malmesbury, *Memoirs*, vol. 1, p. 433.
78 *DL*, vol. 6, 2666, Disraeli to Sarah Brydges Williams, 29 July 1854.
79 Malmesbury, *Memoirs*, vol. 1, p. 438.
80 *DL*, vol. 6, 2669, Disraeli to Lady Londonderry, 7 August 1854.
81 *Ibid.*
82 Derby Papers, 920 DER (14) 183/1, fo. 111, copy, Derby to Eglinton, 9 January 1855.
83 *Ibid.*, fo. 116, copy, Derby to Jolliffe, 14 January 1855.
84 *Ibid.*
85 *Ibid.*, fo. 117.
86 Hughenden Papers, Dep. Hughenden 109/2, fo. 62, Derby to Disraeli, 28 November 1854.
87 Derby Papers, 920 DER (14) 144/1, Malmesbury to Derby, 5 December 1854.
88 *Ibid.*, Malmesbury to Derby, 19 January 1855.
89 *LQV*, vol. 3, Queen Victoria, Memorandum, 31 January 1855, p. 82.
90 *Ibid.*
91 *Ibid.*
92 *Ibid.*, Derby to Queen Victoria, 31 January 1855, p. 83.
93 Malmesbury, *Memoirs*, vol. 2, pp. 6–7; *DDCP*, 31 January 1855, p. 130. Stanley suggested 'my Father assented without difficulty' to retaining Clarendon. But, according to Malmesbury, Derby also told him the Queen 'has expressed a wish that I should return to the Foreign Office, to which I agreed'.
94 See below, p. 248.

7

From war to peace: opposing Palmerston, 1855–58

> I am afraid I shall be repeating what I have so often said before to your Lordships in expressing my want of confidence in the discretion and the prudence with which the foreign affairs of this country have been conducted ... I see that the noble Viscount continues ... all that mischievous interference with the affairs of foreign countries which I have so constantly deprecated here. (Derby, House of Lords, 16 March 1857)

Once Palmerston was at the head of affairs, with a significant element of popular support, the business of opposition was even more difficult. From the formation of the Palmerston Government until the conclusion of the 'Peace of Paris' in April 1856, the new Prime Minister's agile political footwork, his personal following, the Conservatives' fear of being considered unpatriotic and their very public failure to provide an alternative administration continued to restrict the party's options. Nevertheless, once the war was over, it was Palmerston's handling of international relations that began to provide significant political opportunities. The search for political advantage in opposition produced tensions within the Conservative leadership which would become more pronounced in government.

Peace or war?

In May 1855, after the failure of peace negotiations in Vienna, Palmerston's coalition faced a sustained attack in both Houses. The Conservatives stuck to Derby's preferred tactic: supporting the war but criticising its conduct. In the Lords, Derby backed Ellenborough's proposal for an address to the Queen, which did precisely that.[1] Disraeli had private doubts about the conflict, but in the Commons on 24 May he presented the Conservatives as the patriotic champions of the war effort.[2] His resolution attacked the 'ambiguous language and uncertain conduct' of the Government.[3] Neither motion was carried. What was more, Palmerston had avoided the danger of an opposition united on a peace platform. John Vincent has described the debates as 'the most important of the war'.[4] He has suggested that Palmerston cleverly prevaricated. This forced Disraeli, in the hope of political advantage, wholeheartedly to support the conflict.[5] Andrew Lambert, on the other hand, has concluded that Palmerston was simply 'weak' and that Disraeli fortuitously provided 'temporary relief'.[6]

Palmerston may or may not have been weak, but the Conservatives certainly were. However many cards he held, they held none. Criticising Aberdeen for ambivalence and uncertainty, after two years of his leadership and a stalled war effort, was all very well. Castigating the populist Palmerston for the same sins, when he had been three months only in charge, was always likely to be problematical. Malmesbury later noted that 'throughout the whole debate it struck me that we had no case, and that the attack was not on the present Government, but on the last'.[7]

The dating of that diary entry in Malmesbury's *Memoirs* is inaccurate and perhaps was added subsequently to emphasise his patriotism. Nevertheless, it neatly summed up a significant problem for the Conservatives. The fledgling Government had weaknesses, but it occupied a very different position from its predecessor. Even the minority administration of 1852 had been permitted to survive ten months. There was little enthusiasm for swapping ministers again in May 1855, and the comings and goings at Windsor in January had very publicly demonstrated the lack of alternatives.

Had Disraeli advocated making peace, a more radical tactic for harrying Palmerston, it would have been a dangerous gamble. Wartime opposition was still, as it has always been, a world away from attacking foreign policy in peacetime. Foreign policy was accepted as a legitimate subject for partisan debate; for many, a European war was not. On 14 May, Derby had signalled that he would oppose Earl Grey's forthcoming motion in favour of peace.[8] If Disraeli had demanded peace, Derby's support must have been extremely doubtful. His reaction when Disraeli proposed such a course later in the year does not suggest that he would have responded positively.

Nevertheless, there were Conservatives who sought peace. The party was hobbled by divisions in its own ranks. After Disraeli had launched his attack on the Government in May, Clarendon guessed that 'Dizzy's declaration of war ag[ain]st. neg[otia]t[io]ns. won't please the peace à tout prix people who, if Derby speaks truth, abound in his party'.[9] Whether there were, beyond radical ranks, that many who wanted peace at *any* price, there was certainly a wide variety of Conservative opinion about the war. In the debate on 25 May, Stanley made a curious speech which was all but a clarion call for peace, full of dire warnings about the dangers of war, but ending with a call to support Disraeli's bellicose resolution.[10] Walpole, in his turn, suggested that the Government ought not to have broken off negotiations, given the conciliatory offer made by Russia at Vienna.[11] In contrast, Whiteside, having dismissed the negotiations, declared that he 'placed no faith in Russian treaties because it was part of the history of Russia that she had never kept a treaty when it was her interest to break it'.[12] Granby, on the other hand, opposed Disraeli's motion and outlined his belief that negotiations 'might yet end in a just and honourable peace'.[13]

When the Commons discussed amendments, the lack of unity was just as obvious. Lord Claud Hamilton declared that he 'did not wish to involve himself in any responsibility for continuing the war, as he, indeed, had never been able to approve of going to war at all'.[14] Other backbenchers firmly supported the war. John Lloyd Davies thought that 'the House should give the Government as much aid and moral energy as it could'.[15] Henry Ker Seymer observed that there was 'no reason to think that any tinkering on the part of Austria would induce Russia to propose anything more favourable until the result of a resort to arms was decided in favour of the Western Powers'.[16]

The one important point on which the Conservatives were more or less united, contrary to Clarendon's observation, was that they represented something distinct from the conventional 'peace party'. From a variety of directions the Conservatives assaulted those who really appeared to be the advocates of peace at any price: men such as Cobden, Bright, Milner Gibson and, sporadically, Gladstone.[17] An increasingly belligerent Bulwer Lytton attacked Milner Gibson's assertion that peace would be better for British interests: 'the continuance of the war is as yet essential to the vindication of the national honour, and ... the national honour is the bulwark of the national interests'.[18] Walpole dismissed proposals for a return to peace negotiations after they had failed: 'it would not be becoming in this country to make overtures to Russia for a renewal of them'.[19] Henry Drummond vented his spleen on the apostles of liberalism at home and overseas. Having asserted that Cobden, in pursuit of his liberal ideas, had exaggerated Russian aggressiveness and was thus partly responsible for war, he denounced him as second only to Palmerston 'in deluding the people on the subject of Russia'.[20]

Whatever their views, the country gentlemen could not resist a chance to pick at the scab of 1846. Whiteside suggested that a treacherous Russia had long worked against British interests, even in the eighteenth century when there had been an Anglo-Russian commercial treaty, 'an instructive lesson which the hon. Member for Manchester had sadly misunderstood'.[21] George Bentinck doubted the applicability of the free-trade radicals' 'one nostrum which ... was to cure all evils'; in other words, 'a measure tending to procure the importation of cheap cotton in a raw state, and at the same time enable the manufacturers of that raw cotton to export it'.[22] Ker Seymer deplored the morals of commercial men, condemning the radicals as 'men who would sacrifice every ally and abandon every treaty rather than diminish to any extent the sale of cotton goods'.[23] Even Stanley made an explicit pronouncement that 'I do not speak the language of the Peace Society', and pointedly quoted Machiavelli.[24]

As the year and the war progressed, the Conservatives' own Machiavelli was increasingly frustrated. Despite his bullish stance in May, by late 1855 Disraeli was having doubts about supporting the conflict.[25] After the Russians were forced to evacuate the fortress at Sebastopol, Disraeli became convinced that it was time for the Conservatives to change direction and 'prepare the public[']s mind for a statesmanlike peace'.[26] He persuaded himself that such a stance was a political necessity. He explained to Lytton that 'I do not very clearly comprehend how a war ministry & a war opposition can coexist. An opposition must represent a policy, & if it represents the policy of the minister, it ceases to be an opposition'.[27] He had used almost exactly the same phrase with the Chief Whip Jolliffe (coincidentally staying with him at Hughenden), who had conveyed it to Derby.[28] Disraeli still felt keenly his frustration at Derby's failure to form a ministry, believing that the Conservative Party 'has shrunk, or ... at any rate, is believed by the country to have shrunk, from the responsibility of conducting the war'.[29] If the Conservatives would not run a war, they must advocate peace.

Disraeli's logic was hardly unassailable; at the very least, it ran counter to his strategy in May. Like Gladstone, however, he had an infinite capacity for designing new clothes to cover the nakedness of his opportunism. As he explained to Malmesbury, 'the only thing that can ever give us a chance is that the war should finish'.[30] His goal was power. In pursuit of it, his logic sometimes had to take implausible turns. Ann Pottinger Saab has suggested that while his position 'might seem like a startling reversal', it followed 'naturally from the idea of all-out war for limited objectives', and he argued for peace because the Ottoman Empire had been saved.[31] He did reverse his position, and there was indeed nothing startling about it, but it had little to do with saving the Turks. That may have provided a useful excuse for a *volte face*, but it was not the argument he outlined to his allies. He was bitter about January's disappointment, had long been sceptical about the war, dreaded a longer one and saw that Napoleon wanted peace. It all added up to a perfect opportunity for an attack.

It was a step too far for his colleagues. Lytton, for one, was firmly opposed to any change in the Conservatives' position: 'there never was a period in which a party comprising men who boast so large a stake in the country should more carefully distinguish its policy and acts from the character of faction'.[32] More importantly, Derby was deeply concerned. He feared the consequences for the party. A succession of pro-peace articles in Disraeli's *Press* newspaper, advocating his proposed change in policy, had produced unusually heated responses from Knowsley.

Writing to Jolliffe on 19 October, in a letter he instructed him to show Disraeli, Derby had expressed his opinion that the *Press* articles were 'eminently calculated to injure the Conservative party'.[33] Hints of concord with the anti-war elements horrified him. He thought 'nothing could be more fatal' to the Conservatives 'than a suspicion ... of an intention to combine with the various subdivisions of the Peace Party ... for the purpose of embarrassing the Government by urging upon them an impossible peace'.[34] What Derby knew, or maintained he knew, of the Tsar's views led him to believe 'that unless driven to far greater straights [sic] than he has yet been, there is no chance of his submitting, under defeat, to any terms which would give real security to Europe'.[35] Derby regarded the conflict in much the same way as Clarendon, who had similarly noted that 'Russia is not *generally* beaten enough to come to terms'.[36]

When it became clear that Disraeli had not been persuaded by Jolliffe, Derby penned a long letter directly to his deputy. He categorically rejected Disraeli's analysis, on the grounds that,

> having been, in common with the country at large, parties to entering into it [the war], and having blamed previous governments for want of vigour in carrying it on, we cannot with honor [sic], or even with regard to party interests, constitute ourselves a peace opposition, merely because we have a war ministry; and I will never consent to weaken an administration to which I am opposed, by increasing their difficulties in carrying the country through what has become an inevitable war.[37]

He accepted that the Conservative position was 'one of extreme difficulty', particularly because of the lack of 'some definite object to aim at'.[38] But he could not support Disraeli's pro-peace position. This was not because he was unprepared to oppose the Government, but because, as he had explained to Jolliffe, a peace policy would be fundamentally unworkable: 'I can be no party to urging upon the Government ... a course of action which I think they neither ought to pursue, nor could pursue with success, and which, if I were in office tomorrow, I could not hope to bring to a conclusion satisfactory to myself or to the country'.[39]

Derby even suggested that a Conservative agitation for peace might prolong war: 'the more she [Russia] is led to believe that there is in the country and in the legislature a growing disinclination to the war ... the more impracticable she is likely to prove'.[40] He categorically denied the suggestion that the Conservatives had 'shrunk' from responsibility for the conflict: 'I cannot admit that we shrunk from *conducting the war*'.[41] He had maintained in February that his inability to form a sustainable government, not a lack of desire to lead the war effort, had been behind his declining the Queen's invitation.[42] On that question, Disraeli had clearly touched a raw nerve; such vehemence reflected either genuine anger or an underlying sense that the charge was justified. Whichever was the case, Derby concluded his letter with a veiled threat to retire if a peace policy was pursued.

Recognising their mutual dependence, Derby and Disraeli patched up their quarrel. Disraeli reluctantly agreed to keep his views to himself.[43] Derby meanwhile appreciated that Disraeli was indispensable, that the Conservatives 'could not do without him even if there were any one ready and able to take his place, and if he could be with any justice thrown over'.[44] Relations between them nevertheless remained distinctly cool for some time.

Disraeli was not alone in his desire for a peace policy. Stanley, as Derby noted, was 'more pacifically inclined than I am ... and would be satisfied with worse [peace] terms than I should be prepared to accept'.[45] It was, however, highly unlikely that Stanley would risk an open breach with his father. Another future Cabinet minister, Northcote, certainly sounded as if he was pursuing a Disraelian strategy when, in early December, he told his constituents that it was 'not a right thing to carry on the war for the purpose of getting more, if they could get enough. The object of the war was a satisfactory, safe, and durable peace, and that ought to be attained'.[46] In 1855, though, Northcote and other more junior advocates of peace wielded no meaningful authority in the party.

Malmesbury, whose role was rather more important, emphatically did not support Disraeli's views. Significantly for future relations, this seems to have been the point at which the two men's respect for one another began seriously to diminish.[47] Malmesbury regarded his colleague's opinions about the war with great suspicion, as he explained when, in November, he wrote to tell Derby about his latest visit to the French Emperor. Napoleon had apparently begun their interview 'by asking me the state of parties & your opinion & my own as to the questions of peace & war'.[48] Malmesbury contemptuously recalled that he had 'told him Disraeli's *views*, not being able to call them *opinions*'.[49]

He was as adamant against Disraeli's proposed line as Derby had been. His analysis, however, was slightly different. Perceiving, like Disraeli, the likelihood of an imminent peace agreement, he spotted an alternative political opportunity:

> He [Napoleon] *will* have peace if he can. *France is blown* ... Now for the Conservative Party in England. It is of the greatest consequence that we should act from the very first day of the session on a system upon this great question, & above all not allow either Peelite or Radical to take the initiative. It is quite on the cards that Palmerston will be forced by France into a peace before February. If he is, & we choose to condemn it *we* can do so *consistently* & with *popularity*.[50]

But he was concerned to restrain his colleague: '*Disraeli must not prate peace beforehand*. He will perhaps save Palmerston as it is by the opinions already put forth in his cursed *Press*'.[51]

To Disraeli himself, Malmesbury delivered a slightly different version of his message: 'I don't believe peace will be made, but if it is Pam will be *forced* into it by *France*. Should this happen he will be most unpopular in this country for his prestige exists on his supposed standing as to war ... It is therefore in my opinion unwise in our party to preach peace beforehand – as it will assist him when he is obliged to take this unpopular measure'.[52] Malmesbury shared his views with Stanley, who noted that the former Foreign Secretary 'naively' advised him to 'keep silent on the war' in order to leave open the possibility of attacking Palmerston for whatever he did.[53] Malmesbury was indeed rather naive in attempting to convince Stanley, who recorded his distaste for such opportunism: 'I thought comment on the morality of this proposal needless and inconvenient, therefore said nothing'.[54]

Disraeli was not as reticent. He repeated to Malmesbury the point he had made to Derby and others, that a party that had 'shrunk from the responsibility of conducting a war' could not criticise a Prime Minister over the terms of a peace treaty.[55] Disraeli agreed with Malmesbury that 'as a general rule silence and inactivity should be our tactics'.[56] He believed, however, that 'anything which indicates a desire to conclude the war on honourable terms in this country assists the [French] Emperor and distracts and enfeebles Palmerston'.[57]

Malmesbury retorted that, if peace was concluded, the Conservatives should, rather, 'gather round us the masses who are against any peace at all'.[58] He delivered a stern warning: 'You, Stanley, others who are for ending the war now shd not open their lips on it till the session as our tactics must depend on the discussions now proceeding'.[59] Disraeli did not reply.

The developing rift between Disraeli and his fellow Conservatives was not easily bridged. After their correspondence in November and early December 1855, the relationship between Disraeli and Malmesbury never fully recovered. They do not seem to have exchanged more than a few lines until they returned to government in February 1858. Greville's account of a meeting with Disraeli in January 1856, as peace negotiations were underway, indicated the extent to which their friendship had deteriorated. Although Greville was no ally and thus never an entirely reliable witness, his account certainly does not seem out of place next to the exchanges of the previous months:

> He [Disraeli] ... talked of Derby and the blunders he had made in spite of all the advice he had given and the remonstrances he had made to him, that he had written to him and told him what he knew from undoubted authority must and would happen about peace, and implored him not to commit himself to the continuance of the war, but that Derby with all his great talents had no discretion, and suffered himself to be led and influenced by some of the weakest and least capable men of his party – Malmesbury in particular, who had predicted that peace was impossible.[60]

If Greville's account is accurate, Disraeli's outburst is instructive. He had – wilfully or otherwise – misunderstood his colleagues. Derby's objections to Disraeli's proposed policy sprang, principally, not from doubts about the likelihood of peace, but doubts about its potential quality. Malmesbury, on the other hand, had wanted to take the initiative just as much as Disraeli had, but in a different way. He had never predicted that peace was 'impossible'. He had proposed a political strategy that could be adopted whether peace was made or not. Not for the last time, Disraeli also failed to appreciate that Derby might take more notice of Malmesbury, a personal friend of Louis Napoleon, than of vague, anonymous sources. Whatever the relative merits of their strategies, this episode had chipped away at the mutual respect between Derby's senior lieutenants.

The treaty of Paris brought the Crimean war formally to an end on 30 March 1856. Its most significant elements were punitive restrictions on Russian defences: the notorious 'Black Sea clauses'. Although the Conservatives did attack the peace terms, they made little headway.[61] Derby was nevertheless concerned about the nature of the peace, observing to Malmesbury that, in the post-war diplomatic manoeuvres, 'Russia is playing us false as far as she dares'.[62] He was also suspicious of Napoleon and an apparently speedy improvement in Franco-Russian relations: '"our august ally" is less to be depended on than might be desirable. It is quite evident to me that there is a great desire on both sides for a *rapprochement* between the two Emperors, at our expense ... it will not be long before our Government will have cause to be heartily ashamed of the terms and results of the peace they have "patched up"'.[63]

Derby, generally a shrewd judge of diplomatic developments, had perceived the significance of the changes wrought by the war. Russia, like France, now had a vested interest in altering the European status quo. Derby's error was to suppose that it was the British who would be the principal victims of any *rapprochement* between Paris and St Petersburg. In fact, as it transpired, Austria was far more vulnerable.

His letter was not, however, representative of any particular Conservative focus on foreign affairs during 1856. Survival as a significant party of opposition was of greater concern. The condition of the party was poor. Disraeli was widely distrusted on the Conservative benches, a situation exacerbated by his outspoken *Press* articles during the war. His relationship with Derby was not much better than with Malmesbury, while Derby himself put in only rare parliamentary appearances.[64] Such was the low level of morale by late 1856 that even Malmesbury observed that 'for the first time in my life I own that I feel discouragement in regard to our political position'.[65]

Derby blamed the Conservative position on Palmerston's skill: 'he has adroitly played his cards, so as to avoid ... making any attack upon our institutions, or affording much ground for censure from a Conservative Opposition'.[66] In the circumstances, Derby thought the fact that the Conservatives 'should have held together at all ... is rather to be wondered at'.[67] He did, however, hold what amounted to a crisis meeting with prominent Conservatives at Knowsley in January 1857. As Angus Hawkins has noted, it was held at a time when it was known that Disraeli would be unable to attend.[68] Along with issues such as the perceived iniquities of the income tax, the party leaders perceived that foreign policy might once more be a useful rallying-point. The next year would again demonstrate its centrality in British domestic politics.

In late 1856, Derby had observed that one of the ways in which Palmerston had hitherto deflected criticism within his own party was by 'keeping up the show of Liberalism in his foreign policy, which 9 in 10 of the H. of Commons care nothing about'.[69] Nevertheless, foreign policy was a double-edged sword. It was always more likely to expose Palmerston's flank than his conservative domestic policy. By early 1857, for the first time since the early 1850s, tempting Palmerstonian targets were appearing around the globe.

In Europe, France and Britain had broken off relations with King Ferdinand of Naples, after strongly criticising the nature of his regime.[70] Disputes festered on about the provisions of the treaty of Paris, not least with regard to the fate of the Turks' Danubian principalities. In the Near East, the Government had sanctioned an intervention in Persia.[71] Developments in the Far East were worse.[72] In October 1856, the Chinese had arrested the crew of a small boat, the *Arrow*. Although the crew had subsequently been released, the British authorities in Hong Kong had become involved because the boat had been flying the British flag. Sir John Bowring, the Governor, had ordered the bombardment of Canton. The full extent of the British role became clear in early 1857, when Palmerston retrospectively approved Bowring's actions.

In late December, Malmesbury had written to Derby outlining ways in which the party might attack Palmerston. He suggested that 'Naples[,] China & the necessity of a second Congress at Paris' were all vulnerabilities.[73] During the winter of 1856–57, Disraeli had been away on a visit to Paris. When he returned, Derby recommended an attack on foreign affairs, and echoed Malmesbury's points.[74] Disraeli, however, had a rather different card up his sleeve.

Disraeli's political network had at that point been boosted by the addition of Ralph Earle, a junior official and Tory sympathiser at the Paris Embassy, who had already established contact with Pakington.[75] It seems plausible, as most historians have assumed, that Disraeli's winter visit to the French capital was the occasion for their first meeting.[76] The ambitious Earle evidently came to some arrangement with the equally ambitious politician. The relationship would be long and mutually advantageous. Soon after Disraeli's return, Earle began to send over information that might be put to political use. In the second Derby administration, Earle would become Disraeli's private secretary, and would act as his intermediary with Napoleon. Earle's extra-curricular activities remained secret from Derby and Malmesbury, who were still unaware of his role in 1859.

Disraeli wasted no time in using Earle's reports.[77] In February 1857, he lobbed a parliamentary grenade at Palmerston. It produced decidedly mixed results. Supplied with details by his new informant, he

From war to peace: opposing Palmerston 167

alleged that, while Clarendon had been negotiating the treaty of Paris, all along there had been a secret treaty between Austria and France.[78] With Palmerston's encouragement and approval, that treaty had apparently guaranteed Austrian possessions in Italy. The arrangement contrasted with the Government's public criticism of Austria: 'all this time ... will it be believed that a secret treaty was in existence guaranteeing to Austria the whole of her Italian dominions?'[79] Palmerston denied its existence.[80]

Both he and Disraeli unwittingly misled Parliament. The treaty did exist. It had been produced at the height of the Crimean war, to prepare the way for Austria to join the allies. If the Austrians had come in, it would have provided safeguards for their exposed position in Italy. But it had been negated by Austria's withdrawal from negotiations and continued neutrality. As Malmesbury noted, 'the facts which he [Disraeli] stated were correct, but do not bear the same intentions and consequences which he had put upon them'.[81]

Disraeli nevertheless returned to the question, having received further details from Earle.[82] This time, he ignored Clarendon's peacemaking, which was probably just as well. The 1854 treaty, as he had now been told by Earle, was a dead letter by the time of the Paris Conference in 1856. His allegations of Clarendon's hypocrisy would have been difficult to sustain. Disraeli instead elaborated on the details of the treaty, telling the House that it had been 'executed' and giving the date.[83]

Notice of his intention to revisit the matter had prompted a flurry of correspondence between Palmerston, Clarendon and Cowley.[84] Unfortunately, the Ambassador had misunderstood the answers he had obtained from Walewski (who had been elevated to become Napoleon's Foreign Minister). Supplied with erroneous information, Palmerston confirmed the existence of a 'convention', but denied that it had been signed.[85] The Commons accepted Palmerston's statement. The situation in the House, Greville recorded, 'was v[er]y bad for D[israeli]'.[86] Clarendon noted with satisfaction how he had heard from Conservative peers that Disraeli 'was much damaged[,] at which some of his own Party seem to be well pleased'.[87] Disraeli was, however, partially vindicated on 12 February when he was able to turn the situation into what Greville described as 'something like a triumph'.[88] Palmerston, supplied with corrected details about the treaty, performed an embarrassing u-turn about the signature: he admitted that 'in point of fact it was signed'.[89] In a scrappy exchange, the Prime Minister lost his temper and the House.

Disraeli had gained a few feet in his war of attrition, but it was a small achievement for the effort, and at the cost of some embarrassment. One Conservative backbencher, the young Robert Cecil, was singularly unimpressed.[90] Anonymously recounting events for the *Saturday Review*, Disraeli's future foreign secretary and successor thought that his 'excessive taste for startling dramatic situations' had led him into a 'ridiculous position'.[91] Not only that, Disraeli had become dull, having 'of late years discovered a narcotic for the most resolute attention'.[92] Harsh words indeed to level at a man whose reputation had been made by his verbal destruction of Peel. Cecil dismissed the small victory over Palmerston, pointing out that whether or not the treaty had been signed was a small detail compared with the fact that the whole treaty was defunct: 'The [Prime Minister's] disadvantage was ... more apparent than real; for the marrow of Mr. Disraeli's original charge lay in the existence of a permanent guarantee, not in the nature of the instrument by which it was conveyed'.[93]

It has long been noted by historians that Disraeli's persistence over the treaty cast some doubt on his political judgement, but it was also revealing abut his relationship with his colleagues.[94] Derby did not set any greater store by Disraeli's opinions than he had during the war. After the first attack on Palmerston, the Conservative leader sent a friendly warning. His capacity for recalling the detail of foreign policy was undiminished. He had guessed what the 'treaty' in question might be:

> It has crossed my mind whether you may have been misled by an offer which I believe certainly was made by France, when Austria was on the point of joining her forces to ours, that she would guarantee her Italian dominions, *during the time the Austrian troops might be so engaged*, against the consequences of their withdrawal, but the expedition to the Crimea was resolved on, Austria withdrew the offer, and the whole agreement fell to the ground.[95]

Derby hoped that this was '*not* your informant's basis'.[96]

Nevertheless, Disraeli ignored him and returned to the attack. The following day, Derby noted the strategy's failure: 'Your treaty appears to have been what I was afraid it would turn out to be – the old arrangement limited to the war'.[97] The admonition was gentle, but it was there none the less. Cowley's misunderstanding and Palmerston's misjudgement rescued the situation, but Disraeli was not enhancing his standing with his leader or his party on such questions.

Malmesbury continued to be unimpressed. In April 1857, he made one of his regular trips to Paris. His description of Disraeli's reputation there was rather different from the latter's own ebullient reports of his winter visit.[98] In a 'long talk' with Malmesbury, Napoleon apparently outlined his concerns about Disraeli's behaviour: 'He [Napoleon] seems to have a very moderate opinion of D. who passed last winter at Paris & [Napoleon] had been much annoyed about the mare's nest about the secret treaty'.[99] According to Malmesbury, 'D[israeli]. was so positive [about the existence of the treaty] that P[almerston]. began to believe there *really* was some secret convention between France & Austria. Cowley was blown up for not knowing it & went sweating off to Walewski. He was furious at being suspected'.[100]

It is, of course, difficult to tell whether Malmesbury was exaggerating Napoleon's views in order to maintain the importance of his own links with the Emperor and/or to discredit Disraeli. One thing is clear, however: Disraeli *had* created difficulties in Anglo-French relations during the 'secret treaty' affair. In one of his interviews with the British Ambassador in February, Walewski had told Cowley that the Emperor 'thought that Lord P's sentiments had latterly somewhat cooled towards him [Napoleon]'.[101] Clarendon noted that this stemmed from 'what D[']Israeli had reported to him [Napoleon] about P's feelings'.[102] Palmerston appreciated the danger of any rift in Anglo-French relations, and hurried to assure Napoleon that 'my sentiments towards him and about him have not changed ... I have the fullest confidence that the British Govt may intirely [sic] rely upon him [Napoleon] as a loyal ally'.[103]

Had Disraeli known about any difficulties he had made for Palmerston and Cowley, he probably would not have cared. Difficulties for the Whig leaders would doubtless have given him some satisfaction, especially if he had convinced himself that his own stock was high in France. If Malmesbury's report is even half true, however, then Disraeli was not as well regarded by the Emperor as he had supposed. He might have been rather more concerned about that. The 'mare's nest' may well have negated any good that his trip to Paris had done.

None of this mattered unduly in 1857; such was the small change of opposition. But the episode was representative of long-term trends. It had shown, not for the first time, the extent to which Disraeli could create as many problems as he solved while he pursued political advantage. His ill-advised rhetorical contributions on diplomatic questions would increasingly create problems for the Conservatives. More seriously, these accumulating differences over foreign policy were reinforcing mutual doubts about judgement within the party leadership. The tension between Disraeli, on one side, and Derby and Malmesbury, on the other, over both the place of foreign policy in strategy and – ultimately – the nature of the policy itself would have greater implications in government.

In late February and early March 1857, it was Palmerston's support for Bowring in China, rather than secret treaties, that – as Derby and Malmesbury had foreseen – provided the more fertile territory for a parliamentary offensive. By supporting Cobden's censure of the Government, and taking advantage of Russell's and the Peelites' estrangement from Palmerston on the question, the Conservatives were able to contribute to his defeat in the Commons on 3 March. The defeat was followed by the announcement of a general election.

The Conservatives' participation in the debate was, of course, highly opportunistic, and it is impossible to tell how many really cared about the Chinese slaughtered by Bowring. It must also be remembered that not all Conservative MPs were prepared to act against the Government in combination with radicals or Peelites. What was more, Palmerston decisively won the election. Nevertheless, the China debate was the first real opportunity since 1852 for many Conservatives to reaffirm principles that separated them from Palmerston. Such differences had been obscured for a significant period by the war. The Conservatives now had an opportunity to dissociate themselves from the Government. As Samuel Warren explained in opening the second night's debate, it was the 'acts and objects' of the Government in China that led him to disregard his previous stance of 'generous though guarded support' for Palmerston.[104]

Conservative contributions to the debate were consistent with the party's attacks on Palmerston in the early 1850s. Just as the Conservatives had condemned the 'bullying' of Greece in 1850, so they attacked Palmerston for supporting aggressive British commerce in 1857. In the Lords, for example, Ellenborough warned that 'it is not safe to assume the tone of bullying the weak; least of all is it safe ... to undertake foreign operations of a dangerous nature without adequate preparations and without adequate means'.[105] His Commons colleagues expanded on the theme. Warren emphasised that he was 'no member of the peace-at-any-price party', but warned that 'if we are bent blindly and obstinately on persevering in war for a sinister and unhallowed object, we shall attract to ourselves the reprobation of the whole civilized world'.[106]

Bulwer Lytton accused the Government of supporting measures 'that equally violate the laws of nations and the spirit of English honour'.[107] He lectured ministers on what he considered to be appropriate behaviour: 'In dealing with nations less civilized than ourselves, it is by lofty truth and forbearing humanity that the genius of commerce contrasts the ambition of conquerors'.[108] Whiteside suggested that the British flag 'is degraded and disgraced when it is upheld for the purpose of screening crime, of tyrannizing over the weak, or of attacking the defenceless'.[109] Pakington maintained that he could not 'conceive any doctrine more monstrous than that we should act the character of a despot or a bully under any circumstances'.[110] Cecil, suspicious of allowing merchants to drive policy, outlined what he took to be the dangers inherent in British imperialistic aggression. Nations such as China, he suggested, understandably 'looked upon the trade of England as the mere precursor of her dominion'.[111]

Just as Malmesbury and Derby had long used financial justifications for a conciliatory attitude towards other states, Palmerstonian policy was also deplored for its potential economic consequences. This had the utility of connecting directly with the Conservatives' campaign against the income tax. Ellenborough reminded the Lords of the financial implications of Bowring's actions. Bowring, Ellenborough suggested, 'must have known the great difficulties under which the finances of India and of England laboured'.[112] He detailed what he believed was the consequence: 'One million, that is, one penny in the pound of the income of the country is already gone for that war – and for what? No progress has been made'.[113]

In the Commons, Cecil similarly drew attention to financial questions. He pointed out that 'colonial merchants did not pay for these wars' and that, therefore, 'there never was any one so warlike as the merchant of the British colonies'.[114] Disraeli condemned a 'turbulent and aggressive system which I believe must increase the burdens of the people, and ultimately endanger and diminish the power of the nation'.[115] He noted, in contrast, the virtues of 'a foreign policy which, while it maintains the true interests and dignity of the country, is conciliatory to all other States'.[116] This was a phrase that might have come straight from Derby's ministerial speech in 1852, though the policy Disraeli described was hardly the one he himself would pursue as Prime Minister in the 1870s.

In the period prior to the general election, Derby used a debate on the income tax to pull together these various points and again condemn Palmerston's attitude to international relations. He delivered a wide-ranging philippic. While he pointedly praised Palmerston's wartime leadership, he made it clear that policy in peacetime was a different case, outlining his 'want of confidence in the discretion and the prudence with which the foreign affairs of this country have been conducted by the noble Viscount'.[117] He had two clear targets: Palmerston's interventionism and the increased expenditure it entailed.

Both were classic Conservative themes.

He pointed out that 'the expenditure of this country ... depends upon the system of policy that is to be pursued, and more especially upon the system of foreign policy that is to be pursued by the Government'.[118] He delivered an apocalyptic warning that the danger of Palmerston's interventionist policies was such that 'you must be ready to provide on the shortest notice for a war that may spread over the whole face of the world'.[119] In places he sounded almost Cobdenite in his comments about the financial implications of Palmerstonian policy. Denying that there was an 'unprincipled combination' of Conservatives and radicals, however, he took particular pains to dissociate himself from Cobden, 'a gentleman with whom I have not the least acquaintance, and have never, I believe, exchanged a word either upon this or any other subject'.[120]

Derby's point was not a radical one; it was profoundly conservative, with a small and a large 'C'. In contrast to Cobden, or what was popularly supposed to be Cobden's position, he was not proposing commerce as a panacea for international ills. The interests of middle-class merchants and industrialists were, unsurprisingly, not Derby's principal concern. Instead, he focused on the financial problems faced by his aristocratic colleagues, who had 'that slight interest in taxation which is involved in having to pay it'.[121] He also described his distaste for interference on the basis of liberal principles, dear to the hearts of some of Palmerston's more radical supporters. He raised Palmerston's suspension of relations with Naples, an act which he branded 'as mischievous and as unjustifiable as any I ever heard of'.[122]

The action against Naples was incompatible with the Conservative conception of the international order, at the heart of which still lay the independence of sovereign states, however small the nation or unjust the regime: 'Were the Neapolitans your subjects? What mattered it to you how the course of justice ran in Naples ...?'[123] It was a familiar theme, recalling Conservative condemnations of Palmerston's blockade of Greece and Granville's involvement in Tuscan affairs. Bowring's aggressive intervention in China and the Naples policy were identified as part and parcel of the same Palmerstonian liberal 'meddle'.[124] Derby condemned 'all that mischievous interference with the affairs of foreign countries which I have so constantly deprecated here'.[125]

It is unclear whether the parliamentary attacks on Palmerston's handling of international relations made any significant difference, one way or the other, to the Conservative share of the vote in the election that followed. Foreign policy was, in any case, merely one of a range of issues raised by the Government's opponents. Hawkins has demonstrated that the 1857 election was not simply a plebiscite on Palmerston, and it was very far from being a plebiscite on his foreign policy.[126] The course of the 1857 election did, however, illustrate the particular difficulties involved in opposing Palmerston's handling of international relations.

To articulate a Conservative alternative to Palmerston's 'patriotic' stance was fraught with danger. Brown has described the way in which Palmerston's view of society 'emphasised national prestige and patriotic honour above all else'.[127] His stance was that of the patriotic minister, robustly defending liberty and British honour. It is striking that, in 1850 and 1857, when this stance led to him being condemned for recklessness in foreign affairs, his opponents reaped few tangible benefits. In 1858 and 1874, on the other hand, when the Conservatives could level at a Prime Minister the charge that he was unnecessarily *conciliatory* to foreign powers, there were more fruitful pickings to be had.

In the aftermath of the Crimean war, the Conservative position on international affairs was, moreover, not a straightforward one to defend. One Conservative MP summed up the opinions of his Lincolnshire electors in April 1857:

> Taking the feelings of the constituency generally as to 'leaders', I may put them 'Palmerston', 'Derby' (not popular)[,] 'D'Israeli' (unpopular)[,] 'Lord John' (very unpopular)[,] 'Gladstone' (*extremely* unpopular). Lord Palmerston *very popular because* he carried out the Russian war. – Lord Derby unpopular *because* he did not carry out the Russian war, & *because* the *farmers* think he *dropped them* in /52 ... D'Israeli, not trusted.[128]

This was, of course, merely a snapshot of one constituency, and Russell and Gladstone were even less popular than the Conservative leaders. It nevertheless demonstrated that the Conservatives ran a serious risk when they opposed a 'patriotic' leader. If attacking Palmerston's handling of international relations in 1857 had produced so few tangible benefits, then Derby and Malmesbury had been wise to oppose Disraeli's anti-war policy in 1855.

The necessity of not appearing unpatriotic was as important in peacetime as it had been during the war. If the Conservatives' patriotism could be called into question, it would affect their credibility in foreign affairs. This was of particular significance, as both sides recognised. The party had very little to gain from attacking Palmerston's conservative domestic policy; it was all the more important that it appeared credible on foreign policy. Palmerston appreciated the point, and in his address to his Tiverton electors seized the opportunity to describe his opponents as men 'who have endeavoured to make the humiliation and degradation of our country the stepping stone to power'.[129]

Malmesbury publicly demonstrated Conservative concern. Lacking an election platform, he wrote an open letter to Palmerston, via *The Times*. He returned to the China question, accusing Palmerston of 'electioneering claptrap' and deploring the fact that Palmerston had found it necessary 'wantonly to accuse those who have, like myself, often supported you in maintaining the honour of England and defending her best institutions of sacrificing these to the basest personal motives'.[130] Palmerston brusquely responded, also in a public letter, that he had 'neither time nor inclination to renew the China debate'.[131] Clarendon thought Palmerston's response to Malmesbury was 'capital – it was so much the best way of treating him'.[132] Accusing one's opponents of being unpatriotic, however, and underlining the point by refusing to apologise for doing so, carried with it dangers that Clarendon did not fully appreciate. It meant that the Government had to maintain a monopoly on patriotism, which it would not be able to do in 1858.

For neither Government nor opposition was this a matter on which concessions could be made. Palmerston's supporters at *The Times* took the dangers of Malmesbury's broadside seriously enough to devote a long leading article to a counter-attack. They likened Malmesbury's stance on Bowring to the justice meted out by Judge Jeffreys, describing Malmesbury's Lords speech on the question as 'a tissue of the greatest abuse of Sir John Bowring'.[133] For their part, Malmesbury and Derby agreed that, if the question was raised when Parliament returned, they would accept the necessity of pressing military action in China to a successful conclusion. It would be vital, however, to reaffirm their opposition to the Government's original policy of supporting Bowring, as Derby explained: 'Such a course on our part would be the most dignified answer to the absurd charges which the Prime Minister of the country, with a view to electioneering claptrap, did not think it beneath himself to bring against his political opponents'.[134]

At home, the remainder of the 1857 political session was quiet, though the latter part of the year was dramatically marked by the mutiny of the Indian Army. One point, however, is worth noting: Disraeli continued to be the focus for tension in the parliamentary party. Derby, seriously ill, entrusted the Lords in his absence to the ever-reliable Malmesbury. He warned him to 'impress upon all our friends in both Houses, & especially on Disraeli, the necessity in my mind of being very guarded in their language on the subject of reform, & of not committing the Party hastily to the adoption of any course'.[135] The ill-feeling between Malmesbury and Disraeli, however, had not gone away.

In Derby's absence, the two disagreed about strategy. Malmesbury was driven to complain to the leader about Disraeli: 'I could not prevail upon him to call together our usual knot of councillors to go over the [Queen's] Speech'.[136] Malmesbury and the other leading Conservatives had been forced to outmanoeuvre him: 'D[israeli] said it was sufficient for *him* and *me* to agree upon what was to be done. I w[oul]d not however take that responsibility with his single backing & I found that Eglinton & Hardwicke were quite of my opinion. We have therefore made him ask Walpole[,] Pakington & Lytton to meet us at Eglinton's house ... to go over the Speech'.[137] This was not the stuff of great political controversy, but it was more evidence of Disraeli's growing tendency to disregard his colleagues.

Derby remained typically sanguine, despite electoral defeat, severe gout and squabbles between his lieutenants. He was still playing a long game, as he explained to Lord John Manners after the election: 'On the whole ... considering the Palmerston fever now raging, we have not done badly, & shall still be able, I hope, to show a good compact front, while Pam and Johnny fight it out for the liberal leadership'.[138] Derby later outlined his strategy in more detail to Disraeli: 'to foment divisions and jealousies between the discordant elements of the Government majority, must be our first object, while we should carefully avoid multiplying occasions for their voting in concert, in opposition to motions brought forward by us'.[139] He advised Disraeli to avoid attacking the Government, and Palmerston in particular: the election had demonstrated the danger of full-frontal assaults on the Prime Minister.

None of this really constituted a new strategy, of course; it was a reaffirmation of one that had served the Conservatives well for five years. It had produced Aberdeen's resignation in 1855 and Palmerston's parliamentary defeat in 1857. And it was foreign policy that had offered the most fruitful opportunities for exploiting the Government's internal tensions. Directly or indirectly, Britain's foreign relations had brought about the downfall of every government since 1846, except Derby's own (depending on how one assesses the budget vote in 1852).[140] It was unsurprising that it was developments abroad that would bring Derby his reward for five years of patiently awaiting liberal self-destruction. What was surprising was that the Conservatives' best chance would come when a radical motion criticised Palmerston for appeasing France, rather than the radicals providing grounds for Conservatives and conservative supporters of Palmerston to unite. Neither Derby nor Disraeli, however, was going to throw away the opportunity that fell into their laps in February 1858.

The relative quiescence of European affairs in 1857 gave way in January 1858 to a serious crisis in Anglo-French relations. The events of early 1858 have attracted much attention and may be briefly recounted.[141] On 14 January 1858, an Italian nationalist, Felice Orsini, attempted to assassinate Napoleon and the Empress with a bomb. The bomb turned out to have been manufactured, and the attack planned, by refugees in Britain. This prompted the French to renew their calls for action against political refugees in Britain who plotted against foreign governments.

On 20 January, Walewski penned a highly critical despatch, which Clarendon received the following day, but to which he did not formally respond. The Cabinet did decide, however, to strengthen existing British law, and drew up a Conspiracy to Murder Bill. Meanwhile, France's official newspaper *Le Moniteur* raised the political temperature by printing inflammatory addresses by officers of the French Army. On 6 February the British diplomatic correspondence was published. On 9 February, the Conservatives supported the first reading of the Conspiracy Bill, although Disraeli's carefully worded speech reserved the party's future position.[142]

With Anglo-French tension increasing, a significant number of politicians on both sides of the House were uncomfortable about appearing to pass legislation in response to French menaces. More importantly, disaffected liberals and radicals, led by Russell and Graham, were waiting for a chance to move against Palmerston. On 19 February, Milner Gibson used the opportunity provided by the debate on the second reading of the Bill to make a shrewd tactical move. He proposed a resolution which criticised not the Bill itself, but the Government's failure to respond to Walewski's despatch. This opened the floodgates for a range of speakers to attack the Government for being insufficiently firm against France. Most of the Conservatives present supported Milner Gibson's resolution, which passed by nineteen votes. Palmerston resigned the following day, and Derby accepted the Queen's offer to form a government. This was, ironically, one of the few occasions on which no differences of principle separated ministers from their opponents. The Conservative role in Palmerston's defeat was entirely opportunistic.

Analysis of the episode does reveal two points of significance: firstly, about perceptions of France; secondly, about the centrality of Derby. The Conservatives were just as eager as the Government to placate France. Their concern about great-power sensibilities had underscored their diplomacy in 1852. They, too, wished to avoid a dangerous split with their neighbour, to whom – moreover – Britain had recently been closely allied in war. In response to French demands, Derby and Clarendon had therefore confidentially agreed to concert their efforts.[143] On 30 January Derby assured Clarendon 'that the question was a national & not a party one & that if we liked it he w[oul]d be prepared to consider with us beforehand any measure wh[ich] the Govt determined upon introducing'.[144] Disraeli apparently told Persigny that he had promised to come '*á l'appui de l'Empereur* to the best of his power' if a measure was introduced to Parliament.[145]

The Conservatives were genuine in their desire to deflect French wrath. That they did not fundamentally disagree with their predecessors' policy was clear when, after the fall of Palmerston's Government, they evidently intended to press on with the Conspiracy Bill. A few days after taking office, Malmesbury recorded in his diary that he had assured Persigny 'we sh[oul]d proceed with Palmerston's Bill'.[146] The Queen also noted that the legislation would continue on its way after the matter of the despatch had been resolved, and then 'the Conspiracy Bill will pass'.[147]

The Conservatives also continued to see Napoleon as a natural ally. Throughout the crisis in early 1858, while reaping the political benefits of Francophobia, senior Conservatives doubted that Napoleon himself was fundamentally aggressive. Instead, they felt he had fallen amongst thieves. Malmesbury, ever willing to give his old friend the benefit of the doubt, felt that 'the pluck & sound common sense of Nap. III sown and ripened in adventure ... are rotting under the unceasing obsessions of an Eugenie [the Empress], a Walewski, & such like average minds'.[148] Walpole, in a rare intervention from the Home Office shortly after the Conservatives took power, came to a similar conclusion: 'the greater part of this stir in France is a ministerial move to keep themselves popular with the Emperor & with the French people at our expense, rather than a serious apprehension on his part that we shall not do what is just and right as regards himself ... We must be firm with them [the ministers] and conciliatory with him'.[149] This interpretation would be more publicly and damagingly outlined by Disraeli in his 1858 re-election speech.[150]

The historiographical emphasis on Disraeli extends to the marginalisation of Derby as an opposition leader, but the latter's role in exploiting the Anglo-French crisis was of central significance. Derby's instructions to Disraeli before the critical debate on 19 February have been used as evidence of the former's reluctance to engage Palmerston and the latter's boldness by comparison.[151] The evidence suggests otherwise. The Conservative leader certainly cautioned Disraeli that Milner Gibson's motion '*must* not' come in 'on Friday' (i.e. 19 February) because of the necessity that 'you and I should understand each other before attempting to commit the party, or allowing it to commit itself'.[152] This does not prove that Derby was reluctant to engage the Government. He was concerned that the party should be adequately prepared and that it should strike at the most propitious moment. He clearly saw the potential in the situation. Derby observed to Disraeli, in the most telling phrase of the letter: 'C'est le commencement de la fin'.[153]

There were good reasons for Derby to be cautious. For mundane but practical reasons, it was not an ideal time. As he pointed out to Disraeli, he was intending to be out of town for two days. Malmesbury, who might be needed quickly, was in Hampshire. The expected division and its consequences were unpredictable. As Stanley noted, 'the result surprised both victors and vanquished'.[154] If the Conservatives supported Milner Gibson's motion and it was defeated, the party was vulnerable. The Conservatives would have been exposed to all sorts of charges of treachery and of gambling with foreign policy. They would appear irresponsible and unprincipled, and would perhaps provide an opportunity for the disparate liberal elements to unite against them: the very opposite of the objectives Derby had been patiently pursuing. Derby had only to look back to the previous year and the China debate to see how the Prime Minister could recover after defeat in the Commons.

Finally, no-one knew better than Derby that Disraeli, too, was unpredictable. His natural enthusiasm for attacking the Government might get the better of him. Lonsdale had once noted that 'Disraeli has extraordinary confidence in his powers of speech. He thinks always he is going to put the question, and he will carry the whole House with him. He has been deceived so often that he ought to be wiser'.[155] Disraeli's self-confidence was undiminished, and it required careful management if an opportunity was to be effectively exploited.

Evidence is scanty as to exactly who – if anyone – made the crucial decision for the Conservatives to join the disaffected liberal factions in opposing the Government. What evidence there is points to Derby, either at the meeting with Disraeli that he had requested in his letter or during the debate on 19 February. Palmerston laid the blame for his defeat firmly at the door of the Conservative leader. To the Queen, he

From war to peace: opposing Palmerston 179

expressed his opinion that Derby had counted potential votes and taken his chance.[156] Derby wrote to Palmerston on 22 February, noting that the vote 'took me and my friends so entirely by surprise'.[157] The outgoing Prime Minister scrawled a sarcastic comment:

> The surprize was just this. L[or]d Derby was under the gallery … and seeing the effect produced by Milner Gibson[']s speech he sent to Disraeli & Walpole to say they ought to vote with Gibson, though by so doing they would be voting against the Conspiracy Bill which they had before supported *but* by doing so they might put the Government in a minority. The surprize therefore would not have been great.[158]

It was a highly plausible account. Derby was in the chamber observing the debate, and it seems extremely unlikely that Disraeli would not have consulted him. If any message went to Conservative MPs to vote against the Government, it would have been sent – or at the very least approved – by Derby. It is by no means certain that instructions *were* sent by the Conservative leaders. Nevertheless, it seems likely. It has been estimated that only twenty-nine Conservative MPs voted with Palmerston.[159] If there was confusion among MPs about how they should have been voting, it was limited. Robert Stewart asserted that Derby's advice was to back Palmerston, but there seems to be no evidence to support this.[160] In the absence of a contradictory first-hand account, we must assume that Disraeli acted with Derby's full approval, and perhaps at his instigation.

If the events were confused, the outcome was clear. Palmerston was impaled on exactly the sort of strident affirmation of English interests he had so often wielded against his opponents. It was hardly a great triumph for Conservative principles; nevertheless, the single most important obstacle in the way of a Conservative Government had been removed. Fortunately for the new administration, Palmerston would represent little danger for the next eighteen months. Unfortunately, he was by no means alone in his taste for foreign-policy theatricals.

Notes

1 Ellenborough, Lords, 14 May 1855, *Hansard*, 128, col. 483.
2 For his doubts, see, e.g., *DL*, vol. 6, 2747, Disraeli to Sarah Brydges Williams, 1 May 1855.
3 Commons, 24 May 1855, *Hansard*, 128, col. 973.
4 J. R. Vincent, 'The Parliamentary Dimension of the Crimean War', *TRHS*, Fifth Series, 31 (1980), p. 41.
5 *Ibid.*, pp. 41–3.
6 Lambert, *Crimean War*, p. 237.

7 Malmesbury, *Memoirs*, vol. 2, p. 23: '12 May 1855'. The date cannot be accurate, as Derby's speech – to which Malmesbury refers – was on 14 May: Lords, 14 May 1855, *Hansard*, 128, cols 514–36.
 8 Lords, 14 May 1855, *Hansard*, 128, col. 517. Professor Vincent interprets Derby's speech differently. He suggests Derby only came 'off the fence' on 28 May: Vincent, 'Parliamentary Dimension', p. 43.
 9 Southampton University Library, Palmerston (Broadlands) Papers, GC/CL/637, Clarendon to Palmerston, 24 May 1855.
10 Commons, 25 May 1855, *Hansard*, 128, cols 1241–1251.
11 Commons, 8 June 1855, *Hansard*, 128, cols 1701–1702.
12 Commons, 25 May 1855, *Hansard*, 128, col. 1205.
13 Commons, 24 May 1855, *Hansard*, 128, col. 1032.
14 Commons, 4 June 1855, *Hansard*, 128, col. 1378.
15 Commons, 8 June 1855, *Hansard*, 128, col. 1688.
16 Commons, 24 May 1855, *Hansard*, 128, col. 1026.
17 For Gladstone's tergiversations, see Shannon, *Gladstone: Peel's Inheritor*, pp. 314–15
18 Commons, 4 June 1855, *Hansard*, 128, col. 1378.
19 Commons, 8 June 1855, *Hansard*, 128, col. 1705.
20 Commons, 7 June 1855, *Hansard*, 128, col. 1583.
21 Commons, 25 May 1855, *Hansard*, 128, col. 1206; it is unclear whether he meant Milner Gibson or Bright, both of whom represented Manchester.
22 Commons, 8 June 1855, *Hansard*, 128, col. 1689.
23 Commons, 24 May 1855, *Hansard*, 128, col. 1027.
24 Commons, 25 May 1855, *Hansard*, 128, col. 1246.
25 For a discussion of Disraeli's views at this point, see: Pottinger Saab, 'Foreign Affairs and New Tories', *IHR* (1997), pp. 286–311.
26 *DL*, vol. 6, 2787, Disraeli to Bulwer Lytton, 6 November 1855.
27 *Ibid.*
28 See *DL*, vol. 6, 2788, note 1, Disraeli to Derby, 7 November 1855; for Derby's views, see Somerset Record Office, Taunton, Hylton Papers, DD/HY, box 18, bundle 1, fos 14–20, Derby to Jolliffe, letters of 19 October 1855, 2 November 1855, 6 November 1855, 20 November 1855, 2 December 1855.
29 *DL*, vol. 6, 2787, Disraeli to Bulwer Lytton, 6 November 1855.
30 *Ibid.*, 2797, Disraeli to Malmesbury, 30 November 1855.
31 Pottinger Saab, 'Foreign Affairs and New Tories', p. 306.
32 *Speeches of Edward Lord Lytton*, ed. Robert Lytton, 2 vols (Edinburgh and London, 1874), vol. 1, p. lxxii, Lytton to Radcliffe, 12 November 1855.
33 Hylton Papers, DD/HY, box 18, bundle 1, fo. 14, Derby to Jolliffe, 19 October 1855.
34 *Ibid.*
35 *Ibid.*
36 Palmerston (Broadlands) Papers, GC/CL/693/2, Clarendon to

From war to peace: opposing Palmerston 181

   Palmerston, 16 September 1855.
37 Hughenden Papers, Dep. Hughenden 109/2, fo. 91, Derby to Disraeli, 25 October 1855.
38 *Ibid.*
39 Hylton Papers, DD/HY, box 18, bundle 1, fo. 14, Derby to Jolliffe, 19 October 1855.
40 Hughenden Papers, Dep. Hughenden 109/2, fo. 92, Derby to Disraeli, 25 October 1855.
41 *Ibid.*, fo. 91.
42 See Derby's speech in the Lords, 8 February 1855, *Hansard*, 136, cols 1332–50.
43 *DL*, vol. 6, 2788, Disraeli to Derby, 7 November 1855.
44 Derby Papers, 920 DER (14) 183/2, fo. 135, copy, Derby to Malmesbury, 15 December 1856.
45 Hylton Papers, DD/HY, box 18, bundle 1, fo. 14, Derby to Jolliffe, 19 October 1855.
46 *The Times*, 8 December 1855, speech at Dudley, 5 December 1855.
47 According to Stanley, the problems in their relationship dated from 1852: diary entry for 15 November 1869, *DDCP*, p. 345. But the two had co-operated amiably enough in opposition prior to and during the Crimean war: e.g. 'I have been revelling in your speech ... Many thanks for the handsome way in which you mentioned me': Hughenden Papers, Dep. Hughenden 99/1, fo. 94, Malmesbury to Disraeli, 20 February 1853; and 'You have done *two* great deeds this year – for to you we owe the suffocation of the Peelites & the abasement of Johnny': *ibid.*, fo. 162, 22 July 1855
48 Derby Papers, 920 DER (14) 144/1, Malmesbury to Derby, 25 November 1855; this letter is quoted in part in Monypenny and Buckle, *Disraeli*, vol. 4, pp. 23–4.
49 *Ibid.*
50 *Ibid.*
51 *Ibid.*
52 Hughenden Papers, Dep. Hughenden 99/1, fos 170–1, Malmesbury to Disraeli, 27 or 29 November 1855.
53 *DDCP*, 30 November 1855, p. 141.
54 *Ibid.*
55 *DL*, vol. 6, 2797, Disraeli to Malmesbury, 30 November 1855.
56 *Ibid.*
57 *Ibid.*
58 Hughenden Papers, Dep. Hughenden 99/1, fo. 173, Malmesbury to Disraeli, 1 December 1855.
59 *Ibid.*, fo. 174.
60 Greville Papers, Add. MS 41121, diary, fo. 349, 26 January 1856.
61 Lords, 5 May 1856, *Hansard*, 141, cols 1947–2029; Commons, 5 May 1856, *ibid.*, cols 2037–114; Commons, 6 May 1856, *ibid.*, 142, cols 18–138. The Commons attack was led by Manners, and was noticeably

short of big-hitters.
62 Malmesbury, *Memoirs*, vol. 2, Derby to Malmesbury, 25 August 1856, pp. 50–1; original not found.
63 *Ibid.*
64 For the Conservatives' difficulties in this period see Hawkins, *Parliament, Party*, chapter 2, in particular pp. 47–50.
65 Derby Papers, 920 DER (14) 144/1, Malmesbury to Derby, 7 December 1856.
66 *Ibid.*, 183/2, fos 134–5, copy, Derby to Malmesbury, 15 December 1856.
67 *Ibid.*, fo. 134.
68 Hawkins, *Parliament, Party*, p. 50.
69 Derby Papers, 920 DER (14) 183/2, fo. 135, copy, Derby to Malmesbury, 15 December 1856.
70 See 'Correspondence relating to the Affairs of Naples', *Parliamentary Papers* (1857), Session 1, 18.
71 See 'Correspondence respecting relations with Persia', *ibid.*, Session 2, 43.
72 See, e.g., W. C. Costin, *Great Britain and China 1833–1860* (Oxford, 1937), 1968 edition, pp. 206–30.
73 Derby Papers, 920 DER (14) 144/1, Malmesbury to Derby, 15 January 1857.
74 Hughenden Papers, Dep. Hughenden 109/2, fo. 99, Derby to Disraeli, 23 January 1857.
75 See, e.g., Hampton (Pakington) MSS, 705:349/4732/2/vii/13, Earle to Pakington, 2 December 1855; for more on Earle, see G. B. Henderson, 'Ralph Anstruther Earle', *EHR*, 58 (1943), pp. 172–89.
76 The editors of the *Disraeli Letters*, vol. 6, 2795, note 5, on the grounds of handwriting analysis, have suggested that it may have begun as early as November 1855. This seems unlikely, given the lengths to which Earle was going to flatter Pakington in December 1855. Probably Pakington put them in contact. It was he who provided a reference when Earle became Disraeli's private secretary in 1858: Hughenden Papers, Dep. Hughenden 96/1, fos 170–2. Henderson suggested that this was to disguise the Disraeli–Earle connection: 'Ralph Anstruther Earle', p. 179.
77 For an account of the exchanges over the 'secret treaty', see Henderson, *Crimean War Diplomacy*, pp. 249–66.
78 Commons, 3 February 1857, *Hansard*, 144, cols 110–11 and 138–9.
79 *Ibid.*, col. 110.
80 *Ibid.*, col. 164.
81 Malmesbury, *Memoirs*, vol. 2, p. 58.
82 Commons, 10 February 1857, *Hansard*, 144, cols 458–67; Hughenden Papers, Dep. Hughenden 96/1, fos 28–36, Earle to Disraeli, 5 February, and fos 42–8, Earle to Disraeli, 8 February.
83 Commons, 10 February 1857, *Hansard*, 144, col. 465.
84 Between 6 and 20 February 1857, the three exchanged a total of seventeen letters and telegrams about the affair.

85 Commons, 10 February 1857, *Hansard*, 144, col. 471.
86 Greville Papers, Add. MS 41122, diary, fo. 150, 12 February 1857.
87 Palmerston (Broadlands) Papers, GC/CL/1011, Clarendon to Palmerston, 11 February 1857.
88 Greville Papers, Add MS. 41122, diary, fo. 150, 12 February 1857.
89 Commons, 12 February 1857, *Hansard*, 144, col. 535.
90 Cecil had been elected to Herries's old seat, Stamford, in August 1853.
91 'The House of Commons Mare's Nesting', *Saturday Review*, 3 (1857), p. 152; see Michael Pinto-Duschinsky, *The Political Thought of Lord Salisbury 1854–1868* (London, 1967), Appendix 1, 'Published Writings of Lord Salisbury', p. 162.
92 'The House of Commons Mare's Nesting', p. 152.
93 *Ibid.*, p. 153.
94 See, e.g., Monypenny and Buckle, *Disraeli*, vol. 4, pp. 67–8; Blake, *Disraeli*, p. 370.
95 Hughenden Papers, Dep. Hughenden 109/2, fos 110–11, Derby to Disraeli, 8 February 1857.
96 *Ibid.*, fo. 111.
97 Hughenden Papers, Dep. Hughenden 109/2, fo. 113, Derby to Disraeli, 11 February 1857.
98 For the latter, see, e.g., *DL*, vol. 6, 2882, Disraeli to Lennox, 26 December 1856.
99 Derby Papers, 920 DER (14) 144/1, Malmesbury to Derby, 25 April 1857.
100 *Ibid.*
101 Clarendon Deposit, c.73, fo. 300, Cowley to Clarendon, 10 February 1857.
102 Cowley Papers, FO 519/175, fo. 260, Clarendon to Cowley, 12 February 1857.
103 Clarendon Deposit, c.69, fo. 118, Palmerston to Clarendon, 11 February 1857; copy forwarded in Cowley Papers, FO 519/175, fo. 260, Clarendon to Cowley, 12 February 1857.
104 Commons, 27 February 1857, *Hansard*, 144, col. 1496.
105 Lords, 26 February 1857, *Hansard*, 144, col. 1364.
106 Commons, 27 February 1857, *Hansard*, 144, col. 1502.
107 Commons, 26 February 1857, *Hansard*, 144, col. 1446.
108 *Ibid.*
109 Commons, 27 February 1857, *Hansard*, 144, col. 1528.
110 Commons, 2 March 1857, *Hansard*, 144, col. 1643.
111 Commons, 27 February 1857, *Hansard*, 144, col. 1541.
112 Lords, 26 February 1857, *Hansard*, 144, col. 1363.
113 *Ibid.*, col. 1364.
114 Commons, 27 February 1857, *Hansard*, 144, col. 1539.
115 Commons, 5 March 1857, *Hansard*, 144, col. 1898.
116 *Ibid.*
117 Lords, 16 March 1857, *Hansard*, 144, col. 2333.
118 *Ibid.*, col. 2316.

119 *Ibid.*, col. 2324.
121 *Ibid.*, col. 2312.
122 *Ibid.*, col. 2334.
123 *Ibid.*, col. 2335.
124 *Ibid.*, col. 2317.
125 *Ibid.*, col. 2334.
126 Hawkins, *Parliament, Party*, pp. 64–5.
127 Brown, *Politics of Foreign Policy*, p. 20; Brown has analysed this aspect of Palmerstonian politics in detail; see, in particular, pp. 20–45.
128 Hughenden Papers, Dep. Hughenden 114/1, fo. 3, copy, J. Banks Stanhope to Colonel Taylor, 17 April 1857.
129 *The Times*, 24 March 1857.
130 *Ibid.*, 26 March 1857, Malmesbury to Palmerston, 25 March 1857.
131 *Ibid.*, 30 March 1857, Palmerston to Malmesbury, 25 March 1857; copy in Palmerston (Broadlands) Papers, GC/MA/193.
132 Palmerston (Broadlands) Papers, GC/CL/1031/2, Clarendon to Palmerston, 30 March 1857.
133 *The Times*, 26 March 1857.
134 Derby Papers, 920 DER (14) 183/2, fo. 239, copy, Derby to Malmesbury, 6 May 1857.
135 *Ibid.*, fo. 234, copy, Derby to Malmesbury, 30 April 1857.
136 *Ibid.*, 144/1, Malmesbury to Derby, 4 May 1857.
137 *Ibid.*, Malmesbury to Derby, 4 May 1857.
138 *Ibid.*, 183/2, fo. 204, copy, Derby to Manners, 31 March 1857.
139 Hughenden Papers, Dep. Hughenden 109/2, fo. 121, Derby to Disraeli, 24 April 1857.
140 The defeat in December 1852 may be attributed to foreign affairs only if one accepts, as Parry suggests, that the increase in defence spending was the principal reason for votes against Disraeli's budget: Parry, 'The Impact of Napoleon III', p. 157. Others attribute his defeat to a broader range of factors: Blake, *Disraeli*, pp. 347–8; Peter Ghosh, 'Disraelian Conservatism', *EHR*, 99 (1984), p. 281; K. Theodore Hoppen, *The Mid-Victorian Generation, 1846–1886* (Oxford, 1998), pp. 150–1.
141 The most thorough accounts may be found in: Porter, *Refugee Question*, pp. 170–99; Hawkins, *Parliament, Party*, pp. 96–106; see also Robert Woodall, 'Orsini and the Fall of Palmerston', *History Today*, 26 (1976), pp. 636–43.
142 Commons, 9 February 1858, *Hansard*, 148, cols 1053–63.
143 See, e.g. Clarendon Deposit, c.82, fo. 51, Palmerston to Clarendon, 21 January 1858, and, fo. 66, Palmerston to Clarendon, 28 January 1858; *ibid.*, c.103, fo. 726, Derby to Clarendon, 2 February 1858.
144 Palmerston (Broadlands) Papers, GC/CL/1146/1, Clarendon to Palmerston, 30 January 1858.
145 *Ibid.*, GC/CL/1143/2, Clarendon to Palmerston, 21 January 1858.
146 Malmesbury Papers, 9M73/79, unpublished political diary, 25 February 1858.

147 *Dearest Child: Letters Between Queen Victoria and the Princess Royal*, Queen to Princess Royal, 24 February 1858, p. 58.
148 Clarendon Deposit, c.103, fos 768–9, Malmesbury to Clarendon, 10 February 1858.
149 Malmesbury Papers, 9M73/6, Memorandum by Walpole, 2 March 1858, Walpole to Malmesbury, 3 March 1858.
150 See below, pp. 189–90.
151 See e.g. Monypenny and Buckle, *Disraeli*, vol. 4, p. 113; Blake, *Disraeli*, p. 379.
152 Hughenden Papers, Dep. Hughenden 109/2, fo. 306, Derby to Disraeli, undated.
153 *Ibid*.
154 *DDCP*, 20 February 1858, p. 154.
155 *Croker Papers*, vol. 3, p. 448, Lonsdale to Croker, 25 December 1852.
156 Palmerston to Queen Victoria, 19 February 1858, *LQV*, vol. 3, pp. 265–6.
157 Palmerston (Broadlands) Papers, GC/DE/66, Derby to Palmerston, 22 February 1858.
158 *Ibid*.; Palmerston recorded an abridged version of the same events in his diary: Palmerston (Broadlands) Papers, D/18, 19 February 1858.
159 See, e.g., Gurowich, 'Party and Independence', pp. 239, 251.
160 Stewart, *Foundation of the Conservative Party*, p. 317.

8

Disraelian undertones, 1858

> Blow Dizzy, blow thy sounding horn, thine own horn, loud and high ...
> ('Disraeli's Glee', *Punch*, 5 June 1858)

In November 1858, after the Conservative Government had survived for nine months, Clarendon recorded, for Palmerston's benefit, details of a visit to the Salisburys at Hatfield. He described an encounter with Derby, noting in particular 'a long talk with him upon foreign affairs to wh[ich] he seems to devote much attention'.[1] It was not fully appreciated at the time, nor has it been since, that Derby indeed continued to follow foreign affairs closely during his second ministry. Given Malmesbury's greater experience, he was certainly able to leave much more of the detail to his Foreign Secretary, but the Prime Minister oversaw Malmesbury's work and once more intervened at critical moments. Conservative foreign policy was in precisely the same 'conciliatory' mould as it had been in 1852.

For the party leadership, however, the period was marked by a striking new feature. Disraeli was beginning to develop alternatives to the Malmesbury–Derby approach: first of style, then of substance. While the Foreign Secretary and the Prime Minister directed foreign policy in the manner they had always adopted, their most prominent colleague had different ideas. As the European situation deteriorated by the beginning of 1859, this difference turned into a direct challenge to Malmesbury. This Disraelian role requires reassessment.

The politics of Conservative foreign policy, 1858

When Derby outlined his Government's foreign-policy objectives in his ministerial statement on 1 March, he needed to demonstrate that – given the crisis in Anglo-French relations – foreign affairs were safe in Conservative hands. In order to do so, he returned to familiar Conservative themes. He described how the Government intended to 'maintain friendly relations with all powers, great and small, with which we are brought into contact'.[2] In a sideswipe at Palmerston he expressed his hope that 'we shall maintain those relations without adopting either a tone of haughty intimidation or a tone of servile submission towards any Government'.[3] It was not an explicit condemnation of either Palmerston's China policy or his response to French pressure, but it cannot have taken much imagination to perceive his point.

Just as he had throughout the 1850s, Derby outlined his intention to abstain 'from any interference whatever with the purely domestic affairs' of foreign powers.[4] In early 1858, Palmerstonian policy over Naples was one obvious target of Derbyite disapproval; in 1859, however, non-interference would take on a greater importance as France, Piedmont and Austria plunged into war. Derby also made it clear, as he had done in 1852, that international disputes should be resolved by 'frank and unreserved but amicable communications'.[5] He made a point of registering his hope that relations with Russia 'may speedily resume – if, indeed, they have not already resumed – the friendship and cordiality by which they were formerly marked'.[6]

Derby understandably dwelt on the subject of Anglo-French relations at some length. He made a particular point of stressing the value which he placed on the relationship between the two countries: 'if there be one country with which, more than another, it is necessary for our mutual welfare and for the advantage of the world, that we should maintain a permanent good understanding, that country is our nearest and most powerful neighbour – the great empire of France'.[7] He was ambivalent about the question of whether it would be necessary to continue with the Conspiracy to Murder Bill; it was already becoming clear that there would be significant political difficulties in doing so.[8] He emphasised instead his 'sanguine hope' that Malmesbury's reply to the despatch that Clarendon had left unanswered would be 'such as to remove from the minds of the people of this country all irritation, and enable us calmly and deliberately to proceed to the consideration of the important question of the amendment of the law'.[9]

The mollifying of French anger was necessary for practical as well as political reasons. Britain's defensive position was such that no government could have afforded any further antagonism. In the wake of the Indian Mutiny, British resources were thinly spread, as Derby later noted: 'I should fear there are no spare troops in Ireland. If there had been, they would have been despatched to India'.[10] The French naval base at Cherbourg was in the process of being substantially expanded; it was clear that there was only one great power that was likely to be a target from that point on the French coast.[11] Technological changes in naval warfare were also rapidly making sections of the British fleet obsolete.[12] Charles Wood, the outgoing First Lord of the Admiralty, may have assured Malmesbury that a significant naval force could be deployed in the event of any hostilities ('enough to make one very secure as to any attack'), but ministers were well aware that Britain's defensive position was less than entirely adequate.[13]

Throughout 1858 and 1859, Britain's apparent vulnerability to attack, even invasion, created widespread concern. The Government meanwhile had to control costs and reduce tension with France, while accepting, as the Prime Minister acknowledged, that 'the utmost activity consistently with not attracting observation ought to be shown in placing in a state of readiness for immediate action (not at the end of a fortnight or three weeks, but 48 hours or 3 days) as large a portion as possible of our naval force at home, and especially our line of battle ships'.[14]

Derby's colleagues, whose appointments to ministerial roles meant that they had to stand for re-election, appreciated that they had to avoid inflaming the international situation. In their election campaign speeches, in February and March 1858, they duly echoed their leader's sentiments. Like the Prime Minister, they had to square a circle and promote the virtues of Anglo-French relations without acknowledging that it was their opposition to Palmerston's Conspiracy Bill that had exacerbated tensions with France. To do so required some dexterity.

Stanley (who had agreed, after much soul-searching, to take the Colonial Office) told his Kings Lynn electors on 4 March, in a typically dispassionate analysis, that 'men of all parties agree, looking at it as a matter of reason rather than of feeling, that upon a close and intimate alliance between England and France the best hopes of European civilisation depend'.[15] He enlarged on that theme by presciently predicting the rise of Russia and America as the principal rivals to traditional European economic and political interests, suggesting that this made it all the more important that Britain and France remained on good terms. He gave his assurance, however, that the Conservatives would have 'nothing to do' with the Conspiracy Bill.[16] The same day, General Peel, at Huntingdon, expressed the view that 'there was something due to the Honour of England which Her Majesty's Ministers had left undone'.[17] Nevertheless, he reminded his electors that Derby had communicated 'the deep anxiety which his Government felt ... to maintain unimpaired those cordial relations, the continuance of which the best interests of those two great nations as well of Europe and the world demand'.[18]

Other ministers made similar points. Lord John Manners, at the north Leicestershire election on 8 March, commented that

> fair warning was given to Her Majesty's Ministers, that the honour of England must be vindicated from the aspersions which had ... been cast upon it, and which would continue to attach to it so long as the despatch of Count Walewski remained unanswered. That warning was given in vain.[19]

On 5 March, Sotheron Estcourt (a junior minister but, within the year, Home Secretary), had condemned Palmerston because he 'did not stand up resolutely against foreign dictation'.[20] But he had made a point of aligning himself with 'those who utterly reprobate the conduct of those refugees who ... live here hatching conspiracies against foreign Powers, and bring disgrace and discredit on this country'.[21] These rhetorical acrobatics were somewhat disingenuous, given that the pro-French Conservatives had obstructed the Conspiracy Bill purely in order to defeat Palmerston. Only the speech made by Disraeli, however, actually worsened Anglo-French relations.

Stanley had already noted, while dithering about whether to join the Government, that 'the character of Disraeli ... does not command general confidence, either in parliament or among the public'.[22] At the same time, Malmesbury had worried about the Chancellor's involvement in foreign policy. When pressing Derby about the appointment of a suitable under-secretary at the FO, he stressed that 'it is impossible to *cram* a Chancellor of the Exchequer with ready answers or even of the bearing, of a case wh[ich] may have gone thro' a dozen phases'.[23] What was more, though the Foreign Secretary hardly needed to remind Derby, Disraeli's judgement was poor. If Malmesbury wished to avoid involving his colleague in foreign policy, his caution was justified: Disraeli's forays into that area during 1858 hindered British diplomacy and created political difficulties.

Just as it had during the years in opposition, Disraeli's desire to turn foreign policy into an electoral and political weapon backfired: it ran counter to the careful strategies employed by Malmesbury and Derby. Much has justifiably been written about Disraeli's desire to maintain Anglo-French relations as the cornerstone of British foreign policy.[24] His first notable act after the formation of Derby's second Government, however, was to make a speech that alienated the French. On 8 March, using tactics he had originally adopted in the Commons during the Conspiracy to Murder Bill debate, he attacked not the Emperor but the men around him:

> I feel persuaded that when the Emperor himself brings ... his personal investigation and supervision to all the circumstances of this difficult

case, he will not hesitate to recognize the original error of his Ministers ... then I am sure the Emperor of the French will not send dictatorial messages or menaces; he will leave them to Counts and Colonels (laughter).[25]

Public mirth at the expense of French ministers, army officers and, by implication, the Emperor was never likely to be welcome in Paris. It was even less so in the heightened atmosphere of 1858. Unhelpful interventions were tolerated when made by opposition politicians, as was the case with Disraeli's 'secret treaty' in 1857. It was a different matter when the intervention was by a leading government spokesman in the middle of a diplomatic crisis. Walewski wrote, complaining of 'le singulier discours de M d'Israeli'.[26] The ongoing Anglo-French negotiations were set back.

Cowley described to Malmesbury the effect of the speech: 'I do not write to you in such good heart as yesterday – Walewski sent for me this afternoon ... he hinted that his position had been much spoiled by D'Israeli's speech to his constituents, which (between ourselves) is thought very offensive'.[27] Malmesbury also received a note from a Paris informant, much perturbed: 'I was sorry to see D'Israeli's attack ... and *that*, after he had been elected! When there was no object to catch a few stray votes'.[28] Malmesbury dealt with it calmly, noting that, on seeing Disraeli's speech, 'I knew what to expect. W[alewski] has written me a letter expressing his distaste and D. has ... sent him an epistle of explanation'.[29] Knowing, though, that the diplomatic contretemps would have 'got my colleague Dizzy into hot water', the Foreign Secretary had to hide it from the Queen.[30]

Notwithstanding the temporary difficulties created by Disraeli, relations with France were rapidly restored after patient negotiation by Derby and Malmesbury in London, and by Cowley in Paris. Malmesbury felt that the Conservatives were better guarantors of future peace than Russell, their likely successor if they, in turn, lost power. He told Cowley, in a passage he encouraged him to share with Napoleon, that 'if Lord Derby is allowed to remain in ... then at all events there is a chance of not having ... a certain war with somebody or other'.[31] A polite exchange of despatches by Malmesbury and Walewski drew a line under the disagreements of January and February.[32] As Cowley explained, the Emperor and his ministers were 'resigned' to the failure of the Conspiracy Bill, given the political situation in Britain, and therefore they 'let matters take their course'.[33] The rapidity with which the French Government was prepared to heal the breach, despite histrionics from Persigny, suggested that there was no appetite in Paris for any escalation of the crisis.

France was not the only concern. Soon after taking power, the Conservatives had to turn their attention to a dispute with the Neapolitan Government. The Kingdom of Two Sicilies had imprisoned two British engineers when the Sardinian ship *Cagliari* on which they were working was involved in acts of piracy against Naples. The previous Government had made little progress in the case.[34] Derby blamed the Whigs' ideological approach to diplomacy for the imbroglio, and encouraged Malmesbury in his efforts to mend relations with the hated King 'Bomba': 'The sooner we can get France to join us, on any plausible pretext, in renewing diplomatic relations with Naples, the better. The truth is that, in theory, our ground of rupture was indefensible; and, in practice, we never should have had these difficulties to contend with, had we had a resident minister at Naples'.[35]

The Conservatives embarked on the sort of 'frank and unreserved but amicable communications' that Derby had publicly advocated.[36] In the absence of official British representation at Naples, a young diplomat, Richard Lyons, was sent on a mission to try to resolve matters. He obtained the release of both prisoners. In the mean time, the Conservatives had learnt from the controversy over the Mather case in 1852. Although legal opinions had several times been expressed to Clarendon, the Law Officers were asked to produce a further report with regard to the question of compensation for the engineers.[37]

When the report was produced, Derby – perhaps, again, mindful of the difficulties over Mather – intervened with a long letter to Malmesbury. He outlined in great detail how matters should be handled. His suggestions for 'the substance of a despatch' were duly followed by Malmesbury, and a detailed despatch requesting compensation was very much a joint effort of the two men.[38] Eventually, the stick of ever more forceful British communications combined with the carrot of improved relations produced compensation in June 1858. Lyons's efforts did not go unrecognised. This was the beginning of a fruitful relationship between the diplomat and the Conservatives. Stanley would appoint him as Ambassador to France in 1867, and Salisbury would even offer him the FO in 1886.[39]

As Malmesbury and Derby dealt with the *Cagliari* affair in the spring, the Chancellor's involvement once more concerned the Foreign Secretary. He noted in his diary, after a Cabinet meeting discussing the matter, that Disraeli was 'as usual alarmed'.[40] Palmerston recorded the Foreign Secretary's irritation: 'Clarendon told me that L[or]d Malmesbury in speaking to him about Disraeli had called him "that fellow"[,] it was about Disraeli having against Derby[']s orders promised to lay before Parliament Law Officers['] opinions about [the] Cagliari case'.[41]

This may have been relatively minor stuff, but it illustrated the brittle relationship between Derby's two most senior Cabinet colleagues, and the potential for misunderstandings and disagreements. There continued to be tension over Disraeli's role, just as there had been in opposition. He was not going to be bound by his Treasury portfolio; he regarded his Commons leadership as a licence to roam over whatever political ground he chose. The leadership gave him the opportunity to dive into detail beyond the call of duty, and it was an opportunity he relished. It soon produced more difficulties.

Responsibility for foreign affairs in the Commons lay with the Parliamentary Under-Secretary Vesey Fitzgerald. He did not have the presence or profile to rival that of the Chancellor, although at least one senior parliamentarian suspected that Fitzgerald was 'a much safer card on a delicate foreign question than Dizzy'.[42] In Disraeli's opinion, however, foreign affairs was his province. He assured the Chief Whip that 'the For: Und Sec: does not represent the F.O. in the Ho[use] of Commons, except in matters of petty detail. The Leader of the House always represents the F.O.'.[43] One suspects that this owed more to Palmerstonian precedent than any constitutional authority, but he wasted no time turning theory into practice.

Disraeli did not merely expound in the House on issues of political significance and delicacy such as the *Cagliari* case and Anglo-French relations. He discussed matters as varied as passport arrangements, the proposed Suez Canal, Mediterranean telegraphs, Tibet, the Danubian principalities and the envoy at Turin. Hearder has suggested that he made Fitzgerald's job 'less arduous'.[44] Fitzgerald did not see it that way. Such was the extent of Disraeli's contributions that Malmesbury had to intervene on his deputy's behalf: 'Fitzgerald is very much hurt at your not letting him answer any questions ... If you take the [case of the] Cagliari you can safely give him the others'.[45] There is no doubt that Disraeli was the lynchpin of the Conservative Party in the Commons, as Smith has described, 'all the time in his place in the House, attentive and resourceful', who wore himself out with his 'exhausting servitude' there.[46] At least some of this servitude, however, was self-imposed.

With his own portfolio, the Chancellor scored a significant success by producing an uncontroversial and relatively popular budget. With foreign affairs quiescent and opponents divided, the Conservatives found themselves in a much more secure domestic position than they had been in 1852. Manners passed on news from Liverpool that 'the

Budget is universally approved of down here by all parties'.[47] The Marquess of Salisbury, Lord President of the Council and party grandee, received similar reports. They were rapturous. The sense of satisfaction must have been the greater given the failure in 1852. One correspondent wrote that he could not resist 'the impulse of telling you how *universally popular* ... the Budget is'.[48] Another informed him that 'general opinion down here is that at the next election we shall get an absolute majority tho perhaps small'.[49]

The only significant domestic difficulty arose over the reform of Indian governance and some unfortunate mistakes by the Colonial Secretary Ellenborough.[50] But the latter's resignation and opposition divisions ensured the spectacular withdrawal of a censure motion tabled by Edward Cardwell. By August, Russell grudgingly recorded: 'Public events have been favourable to this country & consequently to the govt.'.[51] Palmerston, too, thought the prospects were generally good for the Conservatives: 'If I was to make a book about the Govt['s] chances, I would rather back them in, than out, for next session'.[52]

Rhetorical forays by Disraeli, buoyed by personal and party success, nevertheless continued to produce problems for his colleagues. One such controversy – an episode that has attracted little attention from historians – stemmed from a speech he made in May 1858.[53] It is of interest not least because it was a rare parliamentary discussion of foreign affairs at a time when no particular crisis loomed. It indicated the difficulties that Disraeli created with his tactics; it also hinted at the differences between his approach and the sort of foreign policy pursued by Derby and Malmesbury.

On 26 May, at a banquet in Slough, after the withdrawal of Cardwell's motion, Disraeli made a triumphant speech to some of his constituents, the content of which attracted a great deal of controversy. It included an assault on his political opponents, a personal attack on the Earl of Shaftesbury and an implied denunciation of J. T. Delane, editor of *The Times*. Unusually for a non-parliamentary speech, it gave rise to three separate discussions in Parliament – two in the Commons and one in the Lords. The speech itself, as well as reflecting on the failure of Cardwell's motion, was a three-pronged critique of the late Government: of its foreign policy, its management of the nation's finances and its response to the Indian Mutiny.

With regard to foreign affairs, Disraeli focused on two areas: the Orsini crisis and the British sailors imprisoned by the Neapolitans over the *Cagliari* affair. With regard to Orsini, he asserted that 'the question of peace or war when we acceded to office was not a question of weeks or days, but of hours'.[54] Nevertheless, because of Conservative efforts, 'peace has been preserved, while the honour of the country has been vindicated'.[55] In addition, 'two of your fellow-subjects were lingering ... in a foreign dungeon, and ... the efforts of a Government which boasted of being irresistible in its domestic strength and in its foreign policy had not succeeded in relieving the misery of their position'.[56] But, he pointed out, 'the Government of Lord Derby ... did succeed in freeing these two neglected and suffering Englishmen'.[57]

Disraeli then attacked what he described as 'a cabal – a cabal which has no other object but to upset the Government of the Queen', and which 'consists of some scheming English politicians and some foreign intriguers'.[58] To this barely veiled assault on the leading Whigs was added a condemnation of the press: 'leading organs now are place-hunters of the cabal, and ... the once stern guardians of popular rights simper in the enervating atmosphere of gilded saloons'.[59]

The nature of Disraeli's presentation was important. In order to highlight the differences between Whig and Conservative policy, he employed a tactic that would become familiar in Disraelian strategy: he attempted to appropriate patriotism for the Conservatives. Palmerston had made it his battleground, so Disraeli attempted to take the fight to the enemy. Continuing to draw on the Conspiracy to Murder controversy, he capitalised on the opportunity to attack Palmerston for subservience to foreigners: 'Let the cabal be successful, and in foreign affairs you would have a truckling foreign policy'.[60] He outlined his vision of Conservative policy: 'we shall still pursue that determined, but yet prudent and conciliatory system which, while it will in our opinions maintain peace, will do so with honour'.[61]

This foreshadowed by more than a decade his attacks on Gladstone's foreign policy, but it is clearly in the same vein – for example – as his denunciations of the Liberal response when Russia abrogated the 'Black Sea clauses'.[62] Famously, 'peace with honour' was a theme to which Disraeli would return in 1878, after the Congress of Berlin. He would be more successful with this tactic in the 1870s than he was in the 1850s, but the speech was a clear attempt to delineate party differences.

Derby was initially unperturbed: 'Your speech reads well – but I have only had time to glance over it'.[63] Nevertheless, he saw the potential dangers: 'I think you will be attacked for having taken too much credit for ourselves on the India question'.[64] In fact, Disraeli was attacked for taking too much credit for the Conservatives on a range of issues. The Government's opponents, frustrated at Conservative success, thought they had spotted an opportunity to exploit. In a passage as exaggerated in its claims as the speech itself, *The Times* alleged that the prospect for foreign affairs was much darker than Disraeli had suggested:

> So agreeable are some of these inventions that really our only wish is that they were indeed true. Would to Heaven ... we could persuade ourselves that our relations with France are better at this moment than when an adverse vote of the Commons released Lord Palmerston from all further responsibility in the affair! We can only say it is not the impression of anybody who knows anything about it, and we hope and trust Mr. Disraeli does not himself believe that which he says.[65]

Hammond, the Permanent Under-Secretary (a Whig sympathiser and appointee) at the FO, told Clarendon his opinion of Disraeli's claims: 'I was certainly as much astonished as you could be at learning that when you left office we were within an hour of war with France'.[66] He blamed the Conservatives for Britain's difficulties with France: 'If we were, it was not that you left us so, but that the advent of the present Government to power, inaugurated by a breach of faith with the Emperor in regard to the Conspiracy to Murder Bill, brought us into that predicament. The state of things was theirs not yours!'[67] Cornewall Lewis thought the speech 'a marvellous piece of impudence – such a vainglorious boast was never before uttered by any body, in such a position'.[68] He encouraged Palmerston to 'take some notice of it' in the Commons.[69]

The opposition certainly tried to turn the speech to account in Parliament. Greville recorded the mood: 'The Whigs were stung to madness, and two or three nights were occupied in both Houses, principally by Palmerston & Clarendon, in answering this speech, & demonstrating its falsehood'.[70] He thought that the Whigs 'might just as well have left it alone[,] particularly as nobody cared much what D. said'.[71] Having so palpably failed to defeat the Government over India, however, the opposition did not take kindly to having insult added to injury. Almost all the opposition leaders spoke during the debates.

The most controversial point was Disraeli's suggestion that an Anglo-French war had been imminent in February. Russell suggested that France 'might have felt aggrieved at the conduct of our Government; but that is very different from the two countries being on the brink of war'.[72] Clarendon indignantly declared: 'I am as ignorant as probably most of you are of the cause which is supposed to have led to the danger which has now passed away, and of which we knew nothing and heard nothing until last Wednesday at Slough'.[73] On the question of a 'cabal', Palmerston professed his desire 'to know who these foreign intriguers are who are conspiring with us for the purpose of dispossessing hon. Gentlemen opposite from their seats'.[74] He also 'utterly and entirely' denied the charge 'that there was any imminent probability of war between England and France'.[75]

On the face of it, this was a problem of style and a battle of words, not of substance. But a minority Government courting credibility could not afford to provoke battles through post-prandial point-scoring. Disraeli's intervention was a distraction the Government could have done without, as the radical MP Trelawny noted: 'The Slough speech damaged [the] govt.'.[76] Though Derby and Malmesbury defended their colleague in Parliament, some thought Disraeli damned with faint praise. Palmerston noted in his diary that 'Derby only half defended him'.[77] Trelawny went further: 'The chief danger of the Derby–Disraelites lies, I think, in the number of Orators they have among them – some of whom are apparently covert rivals. On dit that Derby laughed as much as any one at Palmerston's successful tilt at Disraeli'.[78] Neither diarist was necessarily *au fait* with the exact relationship between the Conservative leaders, and both were likely to put the worst possible gloss on the affair, but rumours about the difficulties Disraeli created for his colleagues were never far away (and not always from Whig sources).[79]

Defending his lieutenant, Derby conceded that the 'precise terms' used by Disraeli were 'perhaps a little inflated'.[80] Obliquely, he referred to the possibility that Disraeli had engaged in 'unnecessary discussion of topics which had better not been entered into at all'.[81] Granville drew attention to what he thought was 'the evident difficulty' the Prime Minister displayed in his defence of Disraeli.[82] There was truth in Granville's charge that, with regard to the imminence of war, Derby 'more less evaded' the question.[83] Malmesbury certainly did not speak for long in Disraeli's defence, though he was rarely given to lengthy orations.

Derby glossed over the question of war with a rhetorical sleight of hand, and used the opportunity to give a paean of praise to Napoleon.[84] He defended Disraeli in three other ways. Firstly, on the release of the British sailors from the *Cagliari*, he pointed out the firm but constructive way in which Britain had engaged the Neapolitan Government.[85] The Whigs had not been active enough, he implied, and had created extra difficulties by breaking off relations with Naples the year before: Malmesbury 'naturally thought that a person filling an important diplomatic situation, though not at Naples, would probably have more influence with the Neapolitan Government than a mere acting consul'.[86] Secondly, in a passage that brought him closest to Disraeli, he emphasised the importance of sound finance and avoiding an increase in income tax, which he suggested the ousted Government had been planning.[87] Finally, he stressed the importance of the Conservatives' lenient and moderate settlement in India after the Mutiny.[88]

The speeches made by Malmesbury and Derby were revealing about their approach to foreign policy, differing from both that outlined by the Whigs and from Disraeli's. The substance of Derby's points was not markedly different from Disraeli's, but his emphasis and presentation were. His description of constructive engagement with the great and minor powers was notably different from Disraeli's quasi-Palmerstonian references. Conservative foreign policy as defined by Derby and Malmesbury continued to be, above all else, *anti-*Palmerstonian.

They explicitly noted the hypocrisy of Whigs criticising ill-advised public speeches. Malmesbury objected to what he described as Clarendon's 'lecture ... on the necessity of cultivating habits of public discretion'.[89] He enlarged on the theme of Palmerston's irresponsibility in foreign affairs:

> [T]here is a homely but apposite proverb, 'Let those who live in glass houses take care how they throw stones'; and truly the late Prime Minister may be said to live in a crystal palace ... I think that the speech of the Chancellor of the Exchequer ... could not, either in its tone, or taste, or probable consequences, be compared with the speech[,] in a discretionary point of view, of the noble Viscount on the occasions to which I have alluded.[90]

Yet, in defending Disraeli, Derby and Malmesbury demonstrated their reluctance to employ the rhetorical tactics the Chancellor had used. Derby eschewed the kind of references to English 'honour' that his colleague had repeatedly made at Slough. He stated that he would not deal with the question of foreigners and 'cabals'.[91] He did not repeat the assertion that the Whigs and their allies were unpatriotic. His foreign policy was not built on establishing a divide between 'foreigners' and England. Conservative foreign policy, whether in the conduct or presentation of Derby, Malmesbury or Disraeli, was defined in a Palmerstonian context; for the first two, however, Palmerston represented something against which Conservative foreign policy could define itself, while for Disraeli Palmerston represented something to mimic.

Disraeli's political role was, of course, critically important; Derby and Malmesbury consequently worked hard to conciliate and restrain their colleague. Within a few weeks, the Foreign Secretary was writing to sympathise with Disraeli's difficulties: 'What between gamblers & reporters ... you have a very odious task'.[92] He congratulated him on 'the course you have so ably kept', which he suggested would lead to 'a Party better disciplined than any I ever recollect even in Peel's time'.[93] Malmesbury and Derby worked hard to avoid further damage. The experience of Slough and the earlier 'counts and colonels' speech had left their mark. When there was discussion about postponing the Lord Mayor's dinner in Derby's absence, Malmesbury suggested that allowing the Chancellor to speak was inadvisable: 'God knows what D. will say'.[94]

And Derby took no chances. When Disraeli was again about to address his constituents, Derby observed: 'I need not urge on you the advantage of saying *nothing* in your speech'.[95] The Prime Minister needed to conceal the Government's plans for reform: his first attempt to 'dish' the Whigs.[96] But the warning applied to all policies. The storm after Slough cannot have been far from his thoughts when he exhorted Disraeli specifically even to 'abstain from taking credit to ourselves for what I believe to be the prosperous condition of our affairs'.[97] That tactic had been at the root of the problem in May. Feuchtwanger has suggested that, despite his secondary position after Derby in 1858–59, 'it would make no sense to write down Disraeli's vital role'.[98] To gloss over the difficulties Disraeli created for his colleagues would be similarly illogical.

Not all the differences between the leading Conservatives over diplomatic matters were about policy or its presentation; the personal flavour of the bad relations between Malmesbury and Disraeli made it less likely that differences could be amicably resolved. When an ally of Disraeli was searching for a diplomatic post in the summer of 1858, Malmesbury was adamant in his refusal to appoint him, provoking bitterness in the Disraeli camp. The Chancellor's confidant Lord Henry Lennox, interested in the post vacated by Howard in Florence in 1858, was a notable non-beneficiary of Malmesbury's largesse.[99] Instead of the plum post of Florence, he was offered, but refused, the Secretaryship at Brussels.[100] The Disraeli camp was in high dudgeon at Malmesbury's refusal to co-operate. Earle referred darkly to Malmesbury's 'personal prejudice'.[101] Lennox recorded that 'Disraeli ... is *very much annoyed* and *still* thinks, though Florence is gone, that Malmesbury ... must be brought to book ... he considers Malmesbury has behaved shamefully'.[102]

This may have been a minor tiff over patronage, but it was symptomatic of the poor relations between Foreign Secretary and Chancellor. In August, when Stanley and Disraeli were discussing leaked information that had appeared in *The Times*, Disraeli told Stanley he knew the source: 'The *only* person, I believe, who *communicates* with the "*Times*", who is, in anyway [sic], connected with the Government, is Mr Drummond Wolf, a private secretary of Lord Malmesbury. I saw the paragraph with astonishment & disgust'.[103] Stanley added a sceptical footnote: 'I know this to be untrue, & believe the report came from D[israeli]'.[104] The continuing tensions in the higher echelons of government increased the potential for a serious falling-out over policy, which was not long in coming. The various minor differences of 1852–58 were a prelude to the more significant differences that emerged in 1859.

In foreign-policy terms, it was, however, the French Emperor, who – as usual – generated the most serious concerns. In 1858–59, Derby and Malmesbury regarded Napoleon's schemes with great caution, just as they had in 1852. The expansion of the naval base at Cherbourg, completed in 1858, was viewed with apprehension in Britain. French naval plans became the particular focus for British attention – and alarm. In August, the Queen and Prince Albert, accompanied by Malmesbury, on a state visit were shown the Cherbourg dockyard. While Malmesbury went with the royal couple to France, and thence to Prussia, it was Derby who ran the FO.

At that time, not least because of the Cherbourg development, both Prime Minister and Foreign Secretary became increasingly suspicious about Napoleon's future plans. While Derby ran the FO, with his usual close attention to detail, he kept Malmesbury and Cowley informed about French military preparations. He drew their attention to the unusually large French imports of British saltpetre, which could be used in the production of munitions.[105] Although Derby did not believe that 'our trusty ally has any hostile feelings or intentions at this moment', he thought that Napoleon 'means to place himself in a position to make his power be felt, whenever its suits him that we should feel it'.[106] The Cabinet increased the pace of naval construction, but Malmesbury worried that Britain was 'very deficient in materials of war' and that 'our population is defenceless'.[107]

By the autumn, Derby and Malmesbury were even more concerned about Napoleonic intentions. A squabble between France and Portugal about the *Charles et Georges*, a French slave-ship captured off Mozambique (a Portuguese colony), drew in Britain. As an ally of both nations, and the chief opponent of the slave trade, Britain was in a difficult position, and Malmesbury attempted to mediate. France was, however, almost intractable; Derby noted that 'Walewski's tone is so haughty and unaccommodating, as hardly to leave a loop-hole'.[108] Malmesbury thought that the 'moral of all this' was that 'if we are to hold our own we must have more ships at our command in the Channel'.[109] Derby agreed: 'We must, at all hazards, keep up our strength in the Channel'.[110]

The *Charles et Georges* affair also threatened to provide opportunities for the Opposition. Derby thought Palmerston might 'take up this question to make political capital out of'.[111] Though there were no serious political difficulties in late 1858, Palmerston was quietly waiting in the wings. He was, by this time, closer to Napoleon than was Malmesbury. In a partisan gesture, Napoleon invited Palmerston and Clarendon to meet him at Compiègne in November 1858.

It was, however, Napoleon's plans for territorial redistribution, not his interventions in British politics, that were about to produce serious difficulties. In August, Derby had noted that one of the newspapers 'had rather a good simile' for Napoleon, 'when it said that he kept the gates of the Temple of Janus neither open nor shut, but creaking day & night on rusty hinges, so that nobody could get a wink of sleep'.[112] In 1859, in Italy, the creaking gates would be smashed open.

Notes

1 Palmerston (Broadlands) Papers, GC/CL/1177, Clarendon to Palmerston, 25 November 1858.
2 Lords, 1 March 1858, *Hansard*, 149, col. 28.
3 *Ibid.*
4 *Ibid.*, col. 29.
5 *Ibid.*
6 *Ibid.*
7 *Ibid.*
8 The previous night, Malmesbury had already told Persigny it was 'impossible' to continue with the Bill: Malmesbury Papers, 9M73/79, unpublished political diary, 28 February 1858. This was earlier than has previously been appreciated: H. Hearder, 'Napoleon III's Threat to Break Off Diplomatic Relations with England During the Crisis Over the Orsini Attempt in 1858', *EHR*, 72 (1957), pp. 478–81; Porter, *Refugee Question*, pp. 187–8.
9 Lords, 1 March 1858, *Hansard*, 149, col. 38.
10 Derby Papers, 920 DER (14), 184/2, fo. 91, copy, Derby to Malmesbury, 2 May 1858.
11 See, e.g., M. J. Salevouris, *'Riflemen Form': The War Scare of 1859–1860 in England* (New York, 1982), pp. 37–40.
12 See, e.g., C. I. Hamilton, *Anglo-French Naval Rivalry, 1840–1870*

(Oxford, 1993), pp. 64–105.
13 Malmesbury Papers, 9M73/447/4, Wood to Malmesbury, 1 March 1858.
14 Derby Papers, 920 DER (14) 184/2, fo. 90, copy, Derby to Malmesbury, 2 May 1858.
15 *The Times*, 5 March 1858.
16 *Ibid.*
17 *Ibid.*
18 *Ibid.*
19 *Ibid.*, 9 March 1858.
20 *Ibid.*, 6 March 1858.
21 *Ibid.*
22 *DDCP*, 21 February 1858, p. 155.
23 Derby Papers, 920 DER (14) 144/2, Malmesbury to Derby, 23 February 1858.
24 See, e.g., Monypenny and Buckle, *Disraeli*, vol. 4, p. 215; Ghosh, 'Disraelian Conservatism', *EHR* (1984), pp. 284–5; Smith, *Disraeli*, p. 122; Feuchtwanger, *Disraeli*, p. 112; Parry, 'The Impact of Napoleon III', p. 159.
25 *The Times*, 9 March 1858.
26 Malmesbury Papers, 9M73/6, Walewski to Malmesbury, 10 March 1858.
27 *Ibid.*, Cowley to Malmesbury, 10 March 1858.
28 *Ibid.*, 9M73/22/40, 'B' (presumably an agent; the index entry for that folio is blank) to Malmesbury, undated 1858.
29 *Ibid.*, 9M73/53, copy, Malmesbury to Cowley, 11 March 1858.
30 *Ibid.*, copy, Malmesbury to Cowley, 12 March 1858.
31 *Ibid.*, copy, Malmesbury to Cowley, 2 March 1858.
32 The most important despatches (Cowley to Malmesbury, 23 February 1858; Malmesbury to Cowley, 4 March 1858; Walewski to Persigny, 11 March 1858) are helpfully reproduced in 'Correspondence respecting Foreign Refugees in England', *Parliamentary Papers* (1857–58), 60.
33 Malmesbury Papers, 9M73/6, Cowley to Malmesbury, 9 March 1858.
34 See: 'Paper relative to the Imprisonment of the Engineers, Watt and Park, at Salerno'; 'Correspondence respecting the "Cagliari"'; 'Further Correspondence respecting the "Cagliari"', *Parliamentary Papers* (1857–58), 59. The most thorough account of this episode may be found in Carter, 'Sir James Hudson', pp. 9–27; no published account exists in English.
35 Malmesbury Papers, 9M73/20/4, Derby to Malmesbury, 12 April 1858.
36 Lords, 1 March 1858, *Hansard*, 149, col. 29.
37 'Further Correspondence respecting the "Cagliari" (Opinions of the Law Officers of the Crown, dated April 12, 13, and 17, 1858)', *Parliamentary Papers* (1857–58), 59.
38 Malmesbury Papers, 9M73/20/4, Derby to Malmesbury, 12 April 1858; FO 70/297, Malmesbury to Lyons, 15 April 1858, covering Malmesbury to Carafa, 15 April 1858.

39 Lord Newton, *Lord Lyons: A Record of British Diplomacy*, 2 vols (London, 1913), vol. 2, pp. 371–5.
40 Malmesbury Papers, 9M73/79, unpublished political diary, 13 March 1858.
41 Palmerston (Broadlands) Papers, D/18, diary, 17 March 1858.
42 Granville Papers, PRO 30/29/18/6, fo. 25, Herbert to Granville, 31 August 1858.
43 Hylton Papers, box 24, bundle 13, fo. 31, Disraeli to Jolliffe, 24 February 1858.
44 Hearder, 'The Foreign Policy of Lord Malmesbury', p. 405.
45 Hughenden Papers, Dep. Hughenden 99/2, Malmesbury to Disraeli, 15 April 1858.
46 Smith, *Disraeli*, p. 130.
47 Derby Papers, 920 DER (14) 161/7, Manners to Derby, 21 April 1858.
48 Salisbury Papers, unfoliated, Colonel Samuel Wilson to Salisbury, 28 April 1858.
49 Salisbury Papers, unfoliated, Samuel Triscott to Salisbury, 10 June 1858.
50 See Hawkins, *Parliament, Party*, pp. 123–44.
51 Granville Papers, PRO 30/29/19/23, fo. 43, Russell to Granville, 27 August 1858.
52 *Ibid.*, PRO 30/29/18/6, fo. 24, Palmerston to Granville, 30 August 1858.
53 For brief references, see: Monypenny and Buckle, *Disraeli*, vol. 4, pp. 150–4. Blake, *Disraeli*, p. 381; Feuchtwanger, *Disraeli*, p. 114.
54 *Selected Speeches of the Earl of Beaconsfield*, ed. T. E. Kebbel, 2 vols (London, 1882), vol. 2, speech at the Slough Banquet, 26 May 1858, p. 459.
55 *Ibid.*
56 *Ibid.*
57 *Ibid.*
58 *Ibid.*, p. 463.
59 *Ibid.*
60 *Ibid.*
61 *Ibid.*, p. 468.
62 See, e.g., speeches by Disraeli in the Commons: 9 February 1871, *Hansard*, 204, cols 82–8; 24 February 1871, *ibid.*, cols 839–54; 21 April 1871, *ibid.*, 205, cols 1496–9.
63 Hughenden Papers, Dep. Hughenden 109/2, fo. 211, Derby to Disraeli, 27 May 1858.
64 *Ibid.*
65 *The Times*, 28 May 1858.
66 Clarendon Deposit, c.561/2, Hammond to Clarendon, 30 May 1858.
67 *Ibid.*
68 Palmerston (Broadlands) Papers, GC/LE/113, Cornewall Lewis to Palmerston, 28 May 1858.
69 *Ibid.*
70 Greville Papers, Add. MS 41123, diary, fo. 55, 7 June 1858.

71 *Ibid.*
72 Commons, 28 May 1858, *Hansard*, 150, col. 1072.
73 Lords, 1 June 1858, *Hansard*, 150, col. 1272.
74 Commons, 31 May 1858, *Hansard*, 150, col. 1214.
75 *Ibid.*, cols 1206, 1215.
76 *The Parliamentary Diaries of Sir John Trelawny*, ed. T. A. Jenkins (London, 1990), 11 June 1858, p. 49.
77 Palmerston (Broadlands) Papers, D/18, diary, 19 May 1858.
78 *Parliamentary Diaries of Sir John Trelawny*, 11 June 1858, p. 49.
79 Later, on 26 February 1859, the American Ambassador Dallas recorded how he had heard from Lyndhurst, after Disraeli's announcement that the Government believed Austria and France would withdraw from Rome, 'that when Lord Derby in the House of Lords, was informed of what Disraeli had said ... he (Derby) remarked, "he has gone too far"...': *The Diaries of G. M. Dallas*, ed. S. Dallas (Philadelphia, PA, 1892), p. 313.
80 Lords, 1 June 1858, *Hansard*, 150, col. 1294.
81 *Ibid.*, col. 1287.
82 *Ibid.*, col. 1301.
83 *Ibid.*, col. 1302.
84 *Ibid.*, cols 1290–1.
85 *Ibid.*, cols 1293–4.
86 *Ibid.*, col. 1293.
87 *Ibid.*, cols 1296–7.
88 *Ibid.*, cols 1297–1300.
89 *Ibid.*, col. 1306.
90 *Ibid.*, cols 1306–7.
91 *Ibid.*, col. 1297.
92 Hughenden Papers, Dep. Hughenden 99/2, fo. 15, Malmesbury to Disraeli, 6 July 1858.
93 *Ibid.*
94 Derby Papers, 144/2, Malmesbury to Derby, 20 June 1858.
95 Hughenden Papers, Dep. Hughenden 109/2, fos 224–5, Derby to Disraeli, 4 October 1858.
96 For the broader context in which this letter was written, see Hawkins, *Parliament, Party*, p. 177.
97 Hughenden Papers, Dep. Hughenden 109/2, fo. 225, Derby to Disraeli, 4 October 1858.
98 Feuchtwanger, *Disraeli*, p. 113.
99 See, e.g., Malmesbury Papers, 9M73/22/67, Richmond to Malmesbury, 30 May 1858; *ibid.*, 9M73/54, Malmesbury to Richmond, copy, undated.
100 Even over that, Malmesbury expected 'a great deal of grumbling in the line & out of it': Derby Papers, 920 DER (14) 144/2, Malmesbury to Derby, 10 September 1858; see also *ibid.*, Malmesbury to Derby, 18 September 1858; 28 September 1858.

101 Hughenden Papers, Dep. Hughenden 96/1, fo. 190, Earle to Disraeli, 1 June 1858.
102 West Sussex Record Office, Goodwood MS, 1825/623, Lennox to Richmond, undated, 1858; also *ibid.*, 1825/624, Lennox to Richmond, undated, 1858.
103 Derby Papers, 920 DER (15), Additional Papers, Disraeli to Stanley, 13 August 1858.
104 *Ibid.*
105 Malmesbury Papers, 9M73/20/11 (enclosing copies of letters to Cowley, and from General Peel), Derby to Malmesbury, 13 August 1858.
106 *Ibid.*, 9M73/20/15, Derby to Malmesbury, 16 August 1858.
107 Derby Papers, 920 DER (14) 144/2, Malmesbury to Derby, 21 August 1858.
108 Malmesbury Papers, 9M73/20/37, Derby to Malmesbury, 16 October 1858.
109 Derby Papers, 920 DER (14) 144/2, Malmesbury to Derby, 27 October 1858.
110 Malmesbury Papers, 9M73/20/39, Derby to Malmesbury, 27 October 1858.
111 *Ibid.*, 9M73/20/37, Derby to Malmesbury, 16 October 1858.
112 *Ibid.*, 9M73/20/15, Derby to Malmesbury, 16 August 1858.

9

The Italian question

> By inheritance, by long continued possession, by the faith of treaties which, if once broken through, must cause incalculable mischief to the tranquillity of Europe – by all these ties Austria has acquired a hold over her Italian provinces, of which neither we, nor any nation, under any plea or upon any pretext, has a right to deprive her. (Derby, House of Lords, 3 February 1859)

The European crisis

The events that preceded the Austro-French (and Austro-Piedmontese) war of 1859 may be briefly summarised. Doubtless spurred on by Orsini's attempt on his life, Napoleon had decided to do something to appease Italian nationalists (and boost the French position to the south-east); he duly met Cavour, the Prime Minister of Piedmont–Sardinia, at Plombières, in July 1858. There, they secretly agreed to take advantage of the simmering discontent in northern and central Italy, and provoke a war with Austria. If Piedmont and France were victorious in a war, Piedmont would gain, at the very least, Lombardy and Venetia; France would get Savoy and Nice. A marital alliance between the King of Piedmont's daughter and Napoleon's cousin was arranged to cement the bargain. On New Year's Day 1859, Napoleon, in a widely reported incident, first signified his displeasure with Vienna by snubbing the Austrian Ambassador. Austro-French relations deteriorated rapidly in the first months of 1859.

Nevertheless, there were international efforts to resolve matters without a war. Malmesbury hoped to calm central and northern Italy by encouraging reform in the Papal States and persuading the Austrians to reconsider the way they engaged with Italian affairs. The Pope formally requested the evacuation of Austrian and French troops from the Papal States, where they had been since helping to quell revolution in 1849. Lord Cowley was sent off to Vienna in March to try to reach a deal with Austria. Meanwhile, the Russians and the French, after some months of negotiation, secretly concluded an agreement (though word of it slipped out quickly enough), by which Russia promised 'benevolent neutrality' in any Franco-Austrian war.[1] Cowley's mission was then superseded by a Russian proposal – probably made at French prompting – for a European congress to consider the situation in Italy. The Austrians played into the hands of Cavour and Napoleon, however, and – after much wrangling about when, how and if there should be disarmament prior to a congress – delivered an ultimatum to Piedmont to disarm. A conciliatory overture by Piedmont came too late to stop Austria declaring war, which it did on 29 April 1859. France went to Piedmont's aid on 3 May.

Before turning in detail to the events of 1859, it is worth assessing the framework of ideas and preconceptions within which Conservative foreign policy was determined during the crisis; in other words, what might be described as the Derbyite 'mental map'. Whatever its merits or flaws, the policy which the Government pursued in 1859 was consistent with the policy which Derby and Malmesbury had advocated since the late 1840s. It exhibited all the same features, and grew out of the same assumptions, that had marked Derbyite Conservative attitudes to foreign policy for a decade. Although it sought to preserve peace and/or limit war, it was determinedly non-interventionist; or, rather, it was not interventionist in the Palmerstonian sense of supporting dramatic change or risking war. It was very different from the brinksmanship later adopted by Disraeli during the Russo-Turkish crisis of 1877–78. From the outset, Malmesbury played honest broker between Austria and France, spending his time 'smoothing down the quarrels between Buol & Walewski'.[2]

Neither Prime Minister nor Foreign Secretary was prepared to risk British involvement in a conflict. When Buol wanted Britain to issue a stern warning to deter Napoleon from interference in Italian matters, Derby was adamant that such a statement 'would commit us far more than is prudent or safe'.[3] In February, he declared in Parliament that 'England has no direct concern' in the 'state of apprehensions under which Europe at the present moment labours'.[4] He accepted that Britain did have the concern 'which every great commercial and maritime power must always have in the general peace and prosperity of Europe'.[5] This, however, was an opportunity to demonstrate how the Conservatives could preserve British interests while avoiding the kind of interference for which they had so often condemned Palmerston (and the diplomatic mistakes for which they had condemned Aberdeen). Throughout the crisis Derby and Malmesbury were determined to avoid any risk of British military intervention, and it was this determination that underscored all their diplomacy.

As far as was possible within the bounds of diplomacy, they were also determined to preserve the European status quo. Malmesbury's and Derby's conception of the international order was based, as it always had been, on the existing balance of power. It did not admit of individual nations' or nationalities' rights to alter that balance significantly. Throughout the 1859 crisis, Derby and Malmesbury believed that reform of the central Italian states should be sufficient to calm the disquiet in the region. In early January, for example, the Foreign Secretary suggested proposing to Prussia that the two powers should accept 'any plan which would give the Roman States a better Govt.'.[6] Given Derby's views on Roman Catholicism, it was no surprise that he identified the 'unhappy portion' of the peninsula under the Pope's jurisdiction as 'the real plague spot of Italy'.[7]

Derby and Malmesbury were prepared to accept 'a redistribution of the territorial arrangements of the Papal dominions'.[8] That far, the Foreign Secretary thought Britain should approve of an 'infringement' of the treaties of 1815, 'but no further, and we should not be prepared to sanction any change of the present territorial distribution of Europe'.[9] This was the territorial settlement that had 'ensured the longest peace on record'.[10] Derby thought Malmesbury's approach 'quite the right one'.[11] In essence, it remained the British Government's approach throughout the crisis. The American Ambassador George Dallas noted shrewdly (if not wholly accurately) after the opening of Parliament in February that the Government 'insists upon maintaining inviolate the faith of treaties; among which, of course, are those of the Holy Alliance of 1815, which parcelled to Austria her possessions in Italy'.[12]

In the interests of upholding the Vienna settlement, the Conservatives attempted to help the Austrians to help themselves. There seems little evidence that this amounted to a 'partiality to Austria' that, as Jonathan Parry has described, some liberals believed they had identified, and duly criticised.[13] Nevertheless, the Conservatives were far from being instinctively anti-Austrian over Italy in the way that, for example, Palmerston and Russell were. Unlike the liberals, they took no pleasure from the discomfiture of Austria, whose situation, Derby noted in January, looked 'very anxious'.[14] Anglo-Austrian relations in this period have rarely received much historiographical attention; research has tended to focus on the Anglo-French and Anglo-Italian relationships. Nick Carter, for example, has concluded that Malmesbury adopted 'an unusually lenient attitude' towards Napoleon: the very opposite of the pro-Austrian tendencies of which contemporaries accused him.[15]

The constructive advice and cautious comfort offered to Austria indicate, however, that the Foreign Secretary was neither unduly nor exclusively sympathetic to France. Malmesbury apparently made it clear to Count Apponyi, Austria's representative in London, that there would 'never' be British intervention to support Austria against Italians in 'a purely Italian war'.[16] But he also advised him that Britain's position in a 'war of aggression upon Austria by France and Russia must depend upon the circumstances of the case & whether provocation had been given to justify it'.[17] The Foreign Secretary pointed out that, while British public opinion would support Italian nationalism, 'it would be equally strong against any wanton aggression of France or Russia, so Austria must take care to be forbearing & always in the right'.[18] He repeated this phrase again and again. He told Lord Augustus Loftus, Britain's Minister in Vienna, to inform Buol 'in explicit terms that the public feeling here and the consequent acts of the Govt. of whatever elements composed, will depend entirely on Austria being *in the right at first*'.[19] Buol was to 'put Sardinia and France in the *wrong* if he can'.[20] He told Bloomfield in Berlin 'to make Prussia urge Austria to *keep in the right, & put France in the wrong*'.[21]

It was only Vienna's determination to ignore this advice that forced the Conservatives to condemn Austria, for whose place in the balance of power they otherwise had much sympathy. When Austrian aggression was clearly going to precipitate war, the situation changed. Derby had no choice but to criticise Austria. This he did, in the strongest possible terms, in his speech at the Mansion House on 25 April: 'There was nothing ... to justify the hasty, the precipitate, and, because involving the horrors of war, the criminal, step which has been taken by Austria'.[22] That kind of condemnation was the more necessary because of widespread suspicions that the Conservatives awaited their opportunity to intervene on Austria's side. They did not; but their attitude was certainly more ambivalent than that of their opponents.

Their position could easily be misconstrued. A reasonable point was later made by *The Times* when it described one of Derby's pre-dissolution speeches. The newspaper observed that 'the spirit of the speech was evidently in favour of Austria, and [thereafter] the long silence of the Ministry was looked upon as a sign that Lord Derby meditated entangling the country in some inconvenient alliance'.[23] The Conservatives were happy to exploit such ambiguities when it suited them. When warning the Queen (who was certainly pro-Austrian) against too strong a condemnation of France during the war, Derby took up a Disraelian idea and played on the Queen's hopes: 'If ... Austria should sustain serious reverses, the jealousy of France will increase, and the feeling of the country will support your Majesty in a war, should such arise, against her aggression'.[24] No liberal could credibly have made the same suggestion. Even Russell, who was considerably more bellicose about Italy than most of his colleagues, would contemplate war on behalf of Austria only *in extremis*: 'if France & Sardinia attacked Austria in Venetia (unprovoked)'.[25]

The liberals viewed the balance of power very differently from the Government. While the Conservatives were reaffirming their faith in the treaty of Vienna, Russell thought that Austria should 'give up' large chunks of its Italian territory.[26] Palmerston told Granville in January 1859, in a phrase much beloved of historians, that he was 'very Austrian north of the Alps but very anti-Austrian south of the Alps'.[27] He would 'rejoice and feel relieved, if Italy up to the Tyrol were freed from Austrian dominion & military occupation'.[28] Even the more cautious Clarendon told Palmerston that he wished 'as heartily as you do that the Austrians were out of Italy'.[29] Many liberals, moreover, had long had a predilection for Italian nationalism of the 'liberal' variety represented by Cavour. As Carter's research has demonstrated, Malmesbury neither liked nor fully understood the nature of 'Italian' or Piedmontese national ambitions (despite his personal fondness for Italy and Italians).[30] That misunderstanding led the Foreign Secretary to believe that the Italian states could be appeased with reforms of the sort he envisaged in 1859.

But whether or not Malmesbury understood Italian nationalism was not really the point. Neither Italian national aspirations nor Piedmontese ambitions were new in 1859. The genie of nationalism had been periodically pushed back in its bottle (Greece and Belgium excepted; both special cases of particular strategic significance). Derby was sanguine about 'that enthusiastic dream of Italian unity which at all times and under all circumstances has been indulged in, but which is never likely to be fulfilled, simply because ... internal dissensions and internal differences of opinion among the Italian States ... would render such an union an absolute impossibility'.[31] That view of Italy was widely held among Conservatives. *Blackwood's* deemed 'Italian nationality, unity, or indeed political independence, to be among those wild chimeras and alluring phantoms which have long formed the stock in trade of certain noisy politicians'.[32]

The idea of adopting national aspirations as the basis for decisions about the territorial arrangement of Europe was one about which conservatives had been deeply suspicious since the French Revolution. In his classic analysis of Castlereagh for the *Quarterly Review* in 1862, the third Marquess of Salisbury approvingly described how that early nineteenth-century Foreign Secretary would have viewed such a philosophy:

> The idea ... scarcely seems to have dawned upon him that any one had laid it down as a political dogma, that no two peoples speaking different languages ought to be under the same government; and that any amount of revolutionary confusion was preferable to such an enormity ... If he had been more instructed in what has been recently called the new European law, he might have been embarrassed at being asked to proffer to it the sanction of England, who owns, without any consent of the peoples whatever, more nationalities than she can comfortably count.[33]

Derby and Malmesbury were as concerned about the implications of nationalism as Castlereagh or Salisbury. Malmesbury pointed out to Cowley – in a message that was passed to the Emperor, from whom it leaked to the liberal leaders – that 'Austria has the same right to Lombardy as England has to Ireland and India'.[34] Clarendon, who thought Malmesbury 'very stupid' to have told Napoleon this, nevertheless appreciated the point: 'if we are to engage in a crusade for oppressed nationalities it is a comparison we shd have to make privately to ourselves & we shall find that the Austrians cannot be more hated than we are'.[35]

It was thus by no means clear to Conservatives in 1859 that the great powers should defer to Italian nationalists. Even in 1848, despite what the Conservatives viewed as Palmerstonian meddling, the European status quo had been preserved. There was no obvious reason why Italian nationalism and Piedmontese aggrandisement should not again be contained. What was new in 1859 was French determination to encourage Italian nationalism, and – critically – Russia's passive connivance in that policy. With hindsight, it can be seen that Russia's defeat in the Crimea, by creating another dissatisfied power and destroying the last vestiges of the Holy Alliance, had fundamentally altered the European balance; in 1859, however, the full implications of that change were unclear.

Plenty of observers understood, of course, that Russia was now playing a very different international role. Palmerston told his electors in April that 'the scene has changed' and that 'an alliance between Russia and France ... is an alliance, I am afraid, that can only be founded upon the principle and with the object of aggression upon other Powers'.[36] Malmesbury, too, appreciated that Russia was both unpredictable and dangerous, noting in late April: 'Russia has taken such a decidedly French line that she is not a neutral Power'.[37] The

Franco-Russian agreement of March clearly signified some sort of anti-Austrian development, while the Russian congress proposal was widely believed to have been made at Napoleon's suggestion.[38] The Queen observed that Russia was 'evidently playing, as she always does, a double game'.[39] It was, nevertheless, by no means clear in 1859 exactly what 'game' the Russians were playing or what the impact would be on European borders.

It was not clear that a unified, independent Italian State would be the ultimate outcome of any Franco-Piedmontese disruption of northern Italy. Such a disruption might have presaged the establishment of a dangerous French client state and/or a diminution of Austrian power, both equally unwelcome for Conservatives. The former eventuality did not come to pass; the latter did, with many consequences. In what John Charmley has categorised as 'insular liberal logic', Palmerston thought that limiting Austria to her territories north of the Alps (and later supporting German national aspirations) – thereby supposedly strengthening her – was the way to preserve, rather than change, the balance of power.[40] Derby and Malmesbury were not prepared to accept that alteration of the status quo was the way to preserve it.

What might be described as 'conservative' logic was therefore utterly different from Palmerston's, if just as 'insular' in its unspoken assumption that others in Europe could be persuaded to preserve the Continent in the form that satisfied Britain. As late as 11 May, by which time many liberals were welcoming the apparently imminent expulsion of the Hapsburgs from Italy, Malmesbury was still hoping to persuade Austria to co-operate and thus preserve the existing European balance: 'we shd be ready ... to stop the war if possible by inducing them to take some large measure of reform as to Italy – wh[ich] Napoleon w[oul]d be either obliged to consent to, or declare himself for their total expulsion'.[41] It would have required the complete reconstruction of all Malmesbury's and Derby's 'mental maps' for them to have accepted the argument that the existing balance of power required alteration, still less that Britain should in some way assist in altering it.

There were also practical political and strategic considerations which, just as they had in 1852, suggested the advisability of the neutral, mediating role the Conservatives were already inclined to adopt. With electoral reform and self-preservation preoccupying a divided Cabinet throughout the first six months of 1859, and serious defensive inadequacies to address, the Government's neutral foreign policy made political sense. Palmerston's information was quite accurate when he recorded in his diary on 10 January that he had heard 'rumours of dissensions in Cabinet about foreign and domestic affairs'.[42] Ministers, disagreeing greatly between themselves, were attempting to devise a reform bill and secure their own survival as a Government.[43] The Conservative election addresses and speeches of 1859 focused by and large on reform, in most cases to the exclusion of foreign affairs altogether.

As the Italian crisis broke, Cabinet members were also engaged in intense discussions as to how to strengthen British defensive weaknesses, about the extent of which they were only belatedly becoming aware. From January 1859, as ministers haggled over the naval and military budgets, there were vigorous exchanges within government and between the Queen and her ministers. The Foreign Secretary was acutely conscious of the deficiencies. During the Cabinet's budget discussions, Pakington harried him with concerns about 'both about the ships and the *men*'.[44] After one of many ministerial meetings on the subject, Malmesbury told Derby that he thought there had never been a greater 'public iniquity' than 'that of the Whigs who left our Navy in the state shewn [sic] by the papers we discussed today'.[45]

Whether or not it was justifiable to blame the Whigs for such apparent weaknesses – given that the Government had already had a year in which to start addressing them – the awareness of them reinforced the need for sensitivity in foreign policy. The Conservatives therefore pursued, broadly, the same policy they had followed in 1852: seeking compromise in foreign affairs, while constructing a safety net of greater defence expenditure. Under internal and external pressure, this was not a Cabinet that could afford to indulge in a more active or interventionist foreign policy, even had it wanted to.

Right up until the Government's defeat in June, its foreign policy also seemed to make political sense because it appeared to be the only course that might satisfy the voting public. The Government was well aware that its preference for the European status quo sat very uneasily with public opinion, as Derby noted at the outset of the crisis: 'If Austria ... leads to war in Italy, our position would be a very embarrassing one – for public sympathy in this country would be on the side of France, or rather of Italy, and this country would never raise a finger of support of Austrian rule over Lombardy'.[46] Malmesbury made a point of warning Buol, via Loftus, that if Austria 'enters other countries but her own in Italy without concert, the opinion in England will be decidedly against her'.[47]

While public opinion may have been pro-Italian, however, that did not necessarily make it favourable to British military involvement of any sort, as Malmesbury explained to the Queen: 'whatever might be the ideas of individual ministers, not one in England would *dare* at present to leave a severe neutrality. There could be no doubt of the universal feeling on this point, which superseded every other question, both with candidates, & constituents in the present elections. In fact it was the *only one* which was ostentatiously expressed'.[48] Neutrality was the most popular option. After having described Austria as 'criminal' in his Mansion House speech, Derby noted triumphantly: 'I was *very* well received last night – the country is all for peace – almost a tout prix'.[49]

The problem was that there was a widespread suspicion that the Government was itching to go to Austria's aid; there were even public meetings to decry its pro-Austrian tendencies.[50] Malmesbury's belief that his policy – if it had been popularly understood – would have received more support, made him even more bitter about Disraeli after the Chancellor conspicuously failed to publish the foreign policy 'blue books' before the Government's final Commons defeat.[51] When they were finally published, the Duke of Bedford was not alone in noting that 'Malmesbury's despatches appear to be liked, and to have raised his reputation'.[52]

For a range of reasons, the Conservatives therefore consistently sought, in a range of European capitals, to prevent war, to limit it when it occurred and, above all, to keep Britain out of it. Malmesbury's policy was to be *actively* neutral, although he was not sufficiently active for Disraeli's taste. There was, of course, a fine line between promoting peace and intervening to do so. Russell observed in August 1859 that the Queen's definition of 'intervention' applied even to the Derby Government's foreign policy: 'In Her sense the whole of Malmesbury's conduct from Jan[uar]y to June was intervention – I shall wish to point out the difference between intervention & friendly advice'.[53] Conservative policy, however, constituted more than 'friendly advice': it was a determined and increasingly desperate search for peace accompanied by an almost paranoid fear of provoking war. Disraeli neither fully appreciated nor supported the way in which that policy was pursued.

Notes

1 There have been few detailed analyses of this strange alliance, but for further details, see: B. H. Sumner, 'The Secret Franco-Russian Treaty of 3 March 1859', *EHR*, 48 (1933); John Knox Stevens, 'The Franco-Russian Treaty of 1859: New Lights and New Thoughts', *Historian*, 28 (1966). The latter had access to some additional documents released by the USSR.

2 Derby Papers, 920 DER (14) 144/2, Malmesbury to Derby, 2 January 1859.
3 Malmesbury Papers, 9M73/20/50, Derby to Malmesbury, 27 January 1859.
4 Lords, 3 February 1859, *Hansard*, 152, col. 42.
5 *Ibid.*, cols 42–3.
6 Derby Papers, 920 DER (14) 144/2, Malmesbury to Derby, 4 January 1859.
7 Lords, 3 February 1859, *Hansard*, 152, col. 45.
8 Derby Papers, 920 DER (14) 144/2, Malmesbury to Derby, 4 January 1859.
9 *Ibid.*
10 Cowley Papers, FO 519/196, fo. 696, Malmesbury to Cowley, 7 January 1859.
11 Malmesbury Papers, 9M73/20/48, Derby to Malmesbury, 5 January 1859.
12 Diary, 3 February 1859, reproduced in *Diaries of G. M. Dallas*, p. 306. Strictly speaking, it was not the Holy Alliance (which, in any case, Britain had not joined), but the 1814 treaty of Paris and the 1815 treaty of Vienna which had delineated Austrian possessions in Italy. It is interesting to note, however, that the Conservative stance put Dallas in mind of the Holy Alliance.
13 Parry, 'The Impact of Napoleon III', p. 159.
14 Malmesbury Papers, 9M73/20/47, Derby to Malmesbury, 4 January 1859.
15 Carter, 'Administering the Constitutional Pill', p. 57.
16 Derby Papers, 920 DER (14) 144/2, Malmesbury to Derby, 28 December 1858.
17 *Ibid.*
18 *Ibid.*
19 Malmesbury Papers, 9M73/54, copy, Malmesbury to Loftus, 5 January 1859.
20 *Ibid.*, copy, Malmesbury to Loftus, 12 January 1859.
21 *Ibid.*, copy, Malmesbury to Bloomfield, 12 January 1859.
22 *The Times*, 26 April 1859, Mansion House speech, 25 April 1859.
23 *Ibid.*, 15 June 1859.
24 Derby Papers, 920 DER (14) 145/6, Disraeli to Derby, 2 June 1859; *LQV*, vol. 3, p. 338, Derby to Queen Victoria, 2 June 1859.
25 Palmerston (Broadlands) Papers, GC/RU/560/1, Russell to Palmerston, 6 December 1859.
26 *Ibid.*, GC/RU/495, copy, Russell to Clarendon, 26 December 1858.
27 Granville Papers, PRO 30/29/18/6, fo. 26, Palmerston to Granville, 30 January 1859.
28 *Ibid.*
29 Palmerston (Broadlands) Papers, GC/CL/1184/2, Clarendon to Palmerston, 22 January 1859.

30 Nick Carter has illustrated this point in a series of articles, including, e.g., 'Hudson, Malmesbury and Cavour', *HJ* (1997), p. 391; 'Administering the Constitutional Pill', p. 62.
31 Lords, 3 February 1859, *Hansard*, 152, col. 43.
32 'Italy: Her Nationality or Dependence', *Blackwood's Edinburgh Magazine*, 255 (March 1859), p. 351.
33 'Lord Castlereagh', *Quarterly Review*, 111 (January 1862), pp. 229–30.
34 Cowley Papers, FO 519/196, fo. 642, Malmesbury to Cowley, 7 December 1858; see also fo. 647.
35 Palmerston (Broadlands) Papers, GC/CL/1184/2, Clarendon to Palmerston, 22 January 1859.
36 *The Times*, 2 May 1859, speech at Tiverton, 29 April 1859.
37 Derby Papers, 920 DER (14) 144/2, Malmesbury to Derby, 28 April 1859.
38 According to Clarendon, Derby had received a telegram from the Tsar, protesting that he 'had not thought of a Congress & had only proposed it at the request of the Empr. of the French': Palmerston (Broadlands) Papers, GC/CL/1190/2, Clarendon to Palmerston, 21 April 1859.
39 *LQV*, vol. 3, p. 326, Queen Victoria to Malmesbury, 22 March 1859. The feeling was mutual: the Tsar even used the same words. He believed that 'there had been some double dealing (*double jeu*) on the part of England': FO 65/536, no. 221, Crampton to Malmesbury, 9 May 1859.
40 John Charmley, 'Palmerston: "Artful Old Dodger" or "Babe of Grace"?', in Otte (ed.), *Makers of British Foreign Policy*, p. 91. His reference is to the Granville Papers, PRO 30/29/18/6, fo. 26, Palmerston to Granville, 30 January 1859; see above, p. 209.
41 Derby Papers, 920 DER (14) 144/2, Malmesbury to Derby, 11 May 1859.
42 Palmerston (Broadlands) Papers, D/19, diary, 10 January 1859.
43 For the definitive account of the reform proposals, the Government's deliberations and the political consequences, see Hawkins, *Parliament, Party*, chapters 9–12, pp. 177–265. Useful brief accounts may be found in: Bentley, *Politics Without Democracy*, pp. 112–14; Angus Hawkins, *British Party Politics, 1852–1886* (Basingstoke, 1998), pp. 69–73.
44 Malmesbury Papers, 9M73/447/15, Pakington to Malmesbury, 18 January 1859.
45 Derby Papers, 920 DER (14) 144/2, Malmesbury to Derby, 15 January 1859.
46 Malmesbury Papers, 9M73/20/48, Derby to Malmesbury, 5 January 1859.
47 *Ibid.*, 9M73/54, copy, Malmesbury to Loftus, 5 January 1859.
48 *Ibid.*, 9M73/52/114, copy, Malmesbury to Queen Victoria, copy, 3 May 1859.
49 *Ibid.*, 9M73/20/51, Derby to Malmesbury, 26 April 1859.
50 See, e.g., the account of the meeting in Newcastle, 10 May 1859, in *The Times*, 11 May 1859.

51 See below, pp. 237–8.
52 Clarendon Deposit, c. 561, Bedford to Clarendon, 20 June 1859.
53 Palmerston (Broadlands) Papers, GC/RU/517, Russell to Palmerston, 23 August 1859.

10

European war, Conservative struggle

> Malmesbury did not reassure me, & it was impossible that he could, because I perceive, that he was himself very imperfectly acquainted with the state of affairs. (Disraeli to Derby, 7 January 1859

> Disraeli never reads a word of my papers wh[ich] go round, & knows nothing but what the Jews at Paris & London tell him. (Malmesbury to Derby, 7 January 1859)

The last months of Derby's second administration witnessed the first serious clash between Disraelian and Derbyite ideas about foreign policy in government. Disraeli's interventions in 1859, foreshadowing those of 1876–8, were more serious manifestations of the tension that had been building since 1855. This phase of Conservative government requires a more significant place in the narrative of foreign policy.

The Paris mission

In 1858–59, Disraeli's private foreign policy network was as busy as ever. He had continued to cultivate his old friend Sir Henry Bulwer (promoted to Constantinople in 1858), from whom he requested updates.[1] He had for some time been receiving, via Ralph Earle, reports from the mysterious Georges de Klindworth, who sent regular bulletins about foreign policy during 1859.[2] Meanwhile, Earle was scurrying about at his master's bidding. Disraeli's first intervention in policy was preceded by a bizarre secret mission.

Unknown to his colleagues, in late December 1858 Disraeli sent Earle to meet with Napoleon.[3] Disraeli expressed his desire 'to see His Majesty [Napoleon III] fairly reconciled with the people of this Country'.[4] He went on to suggest that Napoleon stated publicly, among various expressions about peace, the pacific intentions of his navy: 'the effect would be so great that, if in the spring there was any movement towards Italy, the public opinion of England would prevent interference in the quarrel, and no one would be persuaded that ... Austria should be encouraged and supported'.[5] While there are many examples of prime ministers (Disraeli not least among them) conducting their own foreign policies, this was an extremely unusual initiative. It is difficult to find other examples in modern British history of a Cabinet member, without the knowledge of the prime minister or foreign secretary, taking it on himself to initiate contact with a foreign ruler.

Disraeli's instructions to Earle were significant. They revealed a rather different view of the European settlement from that held by Derby and Malmesbury. With regard to Napoleon's European schemes, Earle told Disraeli that he could see 'no danger in encouraging the visions, provided they be discarded for the present'.[6] Disraeli concurred and went further: 'I have no jealousy of the external movement of France ... I contemplate the possib[ilit]y of the eventual increase of his dominions. He is an Emperor & he must have an Empire'.[7] This was not the kind of language Derby or Malmesbury would have used. It displayed an almost Palmerstonian pragmatism. Indeed, it went further than Palmerston, whose views on Italy were determined by balance-of-power considerations and an antipathy towards Austrian rule.

Disraeli was contemplating French aggrandisement with equanimity, even romantic satisfaction. Blake has suggested that 'he analysed Napoleon with the acumen of one who half sympathised'.[8] This was a rather different proposition from the non-discriminatory approach to foreign governments advocated by Derby. Disraeli's vision of Europe was not liberal, but neither was it conservative in the sense that either Derby's or Malmesbury's was. Here was another hint of a different view of foreign policy, one based on pragmatism and power, not the settlement of 1815.

Disraeli's message to Napoleon was marked by strange leaps of logic almost as curious as the mission itself. However accurately Disraeli analysed Napoleon, his understanding of the interaction of diplomacy and politics was limited; his wish was often father to his thoughts. It seems mildly unlikely that one statement by Napoleon about the navy would have had 'so great' an effect on British opinion. Earle, though, reported the Emperor's positive response to the overture, and that he had 'contrasted your [Disraeli's] opinions with the declarations of L[or]d Malmesbury in a spirit decidedly unfriendly to his lordship'.[9]

Earle was no friend of Malmesbury, and he may have exaggerated, but it is unlikely he would have invented the exchange. The Emperor apparently agreed 'to make the declaration for which he [Disraeli] asks' at the opening of the French Chambers in February.[10] It is unclear whether he therefore agreed to make *all* the points suggested by Disraeli. It seems odd that Napoleon would have been prepared to announce, as Disraeli had proposed, that 'there w[oul]d be no jealousy in France, if the English Fleet were twice the strength of that of France'.[11] He certainly did nothing of the sort when he made his speech.[12] Nevertheless, Disraeli had apparently secured a victory. Given his surreptitious methods, however, he had a problem: how could he inform his colleagues of his *coup* without attracting censure? Therein lay the basis for the first of his dramatic but ultimately impotent interventions.

The marginality of Disraeli I

Diplomatic problems that prove not to be quite as critical as they first appear are often not accorded much importance by historians. This is especially the case when they are resolved away from popular attention. Such *near*-crises can, however, be as illuminating as any outbreak of war. The first week of January 1859, as European capitals considered the implications of Napoleon's hostile remarks to the Austrian Ambassador, saw one such crisis. It turned out to be a false alarm before the real crisis developed over the next two months, but it provided the opportunity for a Disraelian intervention. That intervention generated fourteen letters in less than a week.

The correspondence is worth examining in some detail; it presents in microcosm the problems and dynamics of the Malmesbury–Derby–Disraeli foreign-policy relationship, and reveals more about the different strands of Conservative opinion. While this episode has certainly attracted some attention from historians, none has analysed the full range of papers in a broader Conservative context. Derby's important letter to Malmesbury on 8 January seems to have escaped all previous analysis. Historians have glossed over the episode's threefold significance: it demonstrated Disraeli's lack of judgement (the more striking when examined with his other interventions in foreign affairs); it displayed his marginality in foreign policy-making; and it illuminated the central importance of Derby.

Disraeli had left himself with a problem. How could he inform his colleagues of his apparent *coup* – Napoleon's agreement to make a conciliatory gesture to Britain – without attracting censure for bypassing Malmesbury and Derby? Blake has observed that, in 'writing an account of Earle's mission to Derby, Disraeli said nothing about his own message to the Emperor'.[13] He certainly did not say anything about it; he could hardly have done so. In fact, Disraeli did not inform Derby about the mission at all; to have done so would have created a minor political crisis. The agitated correspondence in January 1859 arose in part from Disraeli's attempt to prepare the ground for a Napoleonic overture without revealing his sources. But the correspondence was more significant than that: it was also the product of his broader concern about Malmesbury.

That concern was initially registered in the context of Serbia, not Italy. On 2 January Disraeli wrote an agitated letter to Malmesbury: 'Are you in town? My accounts from Paris are bad – I must see you as soon as possible, particularly about Servia [sic] ... Derby ought to be in town to consult. If we make a false move now, we may get into a terrible mess'.[14] On 23 December, Prince Alexander of Serbia had been forced by nationalist politicians to abdicate. On 28 December, Malmesbury had warned Derby, partly in the context of Serbian developments, that there might be new international difficulties over the Balkans.[15] It was, however, the status of Moldavia and Wallachia – the formerly Ottoman 'Danubian principalities' – that was a greater source of great-power tension in the region. Exactly why Serbia should have been of such significance to the Chancellor is unclear. It is probable that events in Belgrade simply presented the most useful excuse available for an intervention. The subsequent exchanges were complex.

On receiving Disraeli's letter of 2 January, the Foreign Secretary had an interview with Disraeli in London, after which Malmesbury headed off to his Hampshire home, Heron Court, feeling that Disraeli was 'more tranquil'.[16] Displaying his customary disregard for Disraeli's moods and judgement, he warned Derby of the state of Disraeli's 'nervous system'.[17] Derby was nonplussed by the reference to Serbia: 'I do not exactly see what influence, for good or for evil, my being in town three days sooner or later could have'.[18] He expressed himself 'sorry for the state of Disraeli's nerves'.[19] Meanwhile, in London on 4 January, the Chancellor's 'nerves' were generating much activity. Disraeli buttonholed Hammond about foreign policy.[20] Evidently unsatisfied with the Permanent Secretary's response, he wrote to Derby to alert him. Disraeli expressed his regret that the Government were 'all scattered' at a 'very critical' moment.[21] He singled out Malmesbury 'who ought to be at [the] F.O. and nowhere else'.[22] He cautioned against 'appearance of negligence' and 'vagueness of language'.[23] He nevertheless felt that out 'of this nettle danger, we might extract a good result'.[24] His substantive policy proposal was that 'a calm & decisive carriage' would force Austria to end its occupation of the Papal States.[25] In his opinion that would 'conclude the business'.[26] He also wanted the Cabinet summoned.

After 4 January, the exchanges became more heated. On 5 January, Derby had dismissed Disraeli's concerns: 'you know ... how soon he is up and down again'.[27] Receipt of Disraeli's condemnation of the Foreign Secretary could not, however, be ignored. It prompted Derby to write to both of his lieutenants on 6 January. To Disraeli, he poured cold water on the idea of a British initiative with regard to the Papal States: 'nothing that I have heard or seen leads me to the conclusion that the existing state of things would be put an end to by the withdrawal of Austrian troops from the Legations'.[28] While dismissing the need for a Cabinet meeting, he agreed to come back to London earlier.[29] He afterwards wrote to Malmesbury informing him that, given Disraeli's 'excessive agitation', he had decided to return.[30] He requested a meeting and asked Malmesbury if he knew the identity of Disraeli's Paris informant.[31] Crossing over with this letter was one from the Foreign Secretary, also written on 6 January, noting that 'everything is quieting down', and passing on Thiers's rather optimistic opinion that war was not imminent '*this year*'.[32] The same day, a 'very uneasy' Disraeli again saw Hammond and reiterated his concerns about Napoleon resorting to a 'desperate measure' in Italy.[33]

The next two days saw the episode escalate acrimoniously. Malmesbury agreed to return to London, though he could see no 'cause for agitation wh[ich] only breeds more alarm'.[34] He indignantly observed: 'Disraeli *never reads a word of my papers* wh[ich] go round, & knows nothing but what the Jews at Paris & London tell him'.[35] In his opinion, there was little more he could do, even if war was imminent. Disraeli, in his reply, stopped Derby from returning early as he 'could not bear' the Prime Minister making such an effort.[36] Nevertheless, in a very long letter, he enlarged on his criticism of the Foreign Secretary, whom he condemned for not being active enough in seeking ways to avert war: 'Malmsy. did not reassure me – & it was impossible that he could, because I perceived that he was himself very imperfectly acquainted with the state of affairs'.[37]

Disraeli professed to detect in Malmesbury's conversation with him 'an incipient reserve & jealousy'.[38] Cowley fared no better: he was 'off the rails'.[39] Disraeli outlined his assessment of the way in which the Emperor's mind had worked 'since the Orsini business': 'he has been, more or less, fitful & moody, & brooding over Italy ... He is alarmed for his life ... He is resolved, therefore, "to do something for Italy". It is purely a personal impulse in its origin, but, indulged in, it, necessarily, mingles with political ideas'.[40] Disraeli pointed out that

Napoleon's mood occurred at a time when Cavour was 'always on the watch', but, he asserted, Napoleon's army was 'not in a condition to move with effect', while the Emperor was keen for reconciliation with Britain.[41] He slipped in his revelation of the *'profound secret'* that Napoleon was 'meditating a great rhetorical coup' to 'put himself right with England'.[42] This was of course Disraeli and Earle's own coup.

Disraeli's practical suggestion, however, was to impress on Austria that Britain would remain neutral in a Franco-Austrian war. He alleged that the British Court had led the German powers to doubt the likelihood of British neutrality: 'Austria is unwilling to believe this: the relations bet[wee]n the Prince Consort & Germany tend to convey a different impression. On this you may rely. Messages have been conveyed (I will not say from H.R.H.) wh[ich] neutralise the declarations of our Ministry'.[43] In Disraeli's view, all this could be resolved very simply. If Austria really was convinced of British neutrality all would be well: Austria would be 'conciliatory' and would agree to 'a revival of the Conferences at Paris'; this would 'enlist English opinion' on Austria's side; once 'opinion here' had 'sanctioned' this 'conciliatory movement' by Austria, Napoleon would agree to a conference.[44] He concluded triumphantly: 'All immediate danger of war will, certainly, then be averted'.[45]

Derby put a close to the correspondence with two letters on 8 January, to Malmesbury and Disraeli. The former has been overlooked by historians. It was written with the frankness habitually reserved for the Foreign Secretary. In it, Derby expressed his opinion that Disraeli was 'substantially correct' about the way in which Napoleon's mind worked.[46] He was, however, sceptical about the claim that the French Army was not ready. This scepticism may well have been directed at Malmesbury, too, given his similarly optimistic views about the pace of French preparations. Derby also thought Disraeli was too quick to dismiss the possibility of British public support for a war for Italian liberation. He considered that Malmesbury had 'fully impressed' on Apponyi the likelihood of English neutrality and noted that any British intervention on Austria's side would be 'most unpopular'.[47] He dismissed Disraeli's allegations of encouragement of Austria 'in high places' (i.e. the Court).[48]

Derby's analysis of Austrian policy was striking. He thought that Disraeli 'greatly underrates the stubbornness of Buol's nature'.[49] As far as an international conference was concerned, this 'stubbornness' would mean that 'he and his Emperor would prefer being dispossessed by force of their Milanese dominions, to making (I believe even to accepting) such a proposition'.[50] This was an uncannily accurate assessment of Vienna's intentions, and he judged the situation rather more shrewdly than did either his Foreign Secretary or Chancellor. On the substantive foreign-policy points, Disraeli in his turn received a courteous rebuttal. After having concurred in the analysis of Napoleon, Derby dismissed Disraeli's suggestions. To keep the peace, Derby played down any suggestion of Malmesbury's 'jealousy' in foreign affairs.[51] He noted, however, that the Foreign Secretary was 'inclined, when accounts differ, to place greater reliance, which is not unnatural, on his recognised official channels of information than on private, and, so far as he is concerned, anonymous intelligence which reaches you'.[52] His rebuke was gentle, but the message was clear.

This episode is at the root of the historiographical tendency to emphasise Disraeli's greater perceptiveness about the deteriorating continental situation. For example, in Buckle's unfavourable contrast with the Foreign Secretary, Disraeli's 'insight ... was far quicker and more penetrating'.[53] Malmesbury 'was soon driven from his optimism by the march of events, and forced to realise that Disraeli's information was correct'.[54] Blake was more sceptical: 'The wisdom of thus crossing lines with Malmesbury was extremely dubious'.[55] Nevertheless, he suggested that 'Disraeli may well have been more realistic than Malmesbury' about Napoleon, as 'Disraeli perceived the eventual necessity of the Emperor increasing his dominions'.[56] These and other accounts of this episode have unwittingly obscured a number of aspects of Conservative foreign policy.

Firstly, Derby was, once again, firmly in control. Disraeli had miscalculated in underestimating what Angus Hawkins has described as Derby's 'steadfast loyalty to his Foreign Secretary', for which Disraeli's long acquaintance with both colleagues should have prepared him.[57] Perhaps Disraeli never really understood, and quite probably he resented, the close relationship between the two men. In this, as in so much else, he was the outsider. But Derby's defence of Malmesbury was not just about loyalty. Disraeli had underestimated the extent to which Derby thoroughly approved of Malmesbury's conduct. Derby's own analysis led him to support Malmesbury's policy. Given that the Prime Minister monitored and sanctioned Malmesbury's policy, it was not surprising that Disraeli found Derby unsympathetic.

Secondly, Derby's analysis of foreign policy was shrewd. Hawkins has concluded that 'events ... forced Malmesbury and Derby to acknowledge that Disraeli's forebodings had greater weight than they initially granted them'.[58] The Prime Minister was, however, by no means complacent. He was much less certain than Disraeli or Malmesbury that Napoleon's military preparations were 'such that he could not, at a very short notice ... campaign in Italy'.[59] Derby had become concerned enough about Disraeli's warnings that he was prepared to go to London earlier than intended, and he wanted to see the Foreign Secretary 'as soon after as possible'.[60] While he did not share Disraeli's view of the imminence of the crisis, he was unequivocal in his statement: 'Matters abroad are critical, there is no doubt';[61] the second half of his sentence – 'and we have plenty to occupy our attention at home' – was a gloomy acknowledgement that events abroad *and* at home presented difficulties.[62] He was not brushing off foreign problems. Indeed, he believed Disraeli had underestimated them: 'I look on the state of the North of Italy as very critical; and the more so as I think you underrate the dogged obstinacy of the Austrian character'.[63]

This kind of close analysis matters, given that historians have accorded to Disraeli a prescience and to Malmesbury (and, to a certain extent, Derby) a kind of diplomatic myopia. Derby perceived exactly the mindset of the Austrian leaders, and correctly predicted the likelihood of Austria resorting to war to protect her 'Milanese dominions'.[64] Derek Beales has suggested that the Government 'failed to appreciate properly that Austria was prepared to fight for her rights in Italy, preferring as she did the possibility – even the probability – of defeat in war to the certainty of defeat at the conference-table'.[65] Neither Derby nor Malmesbury was that naive about Austria. What they and others (of both parties) failed to appreciate was not Vienna's preparedness to fight, but that it might seriously consider *starting* a war. Given that neither Austria nor any other great power (even in 1853) had deliberately provoked a war with another since the Napoleonic era, this was not surprising.

Thirdly, though they differed on details, Derby and Malmesbury did not disagree significantly with Disraeli's diagnosis of the European situation. They merely expressed their doubt that the crisis was as imminent as Disraeli believed. In this they were correct. Malmesbury has been criticised for his blindness to French intentions throughout the 1859 crisis.[66] The Foreign Secretary may have been unduly optimistic about Napoleon's willingness to avoid war, although the precedent of 1852 would certainly have suggested that peace could be maintained. More importantly, it was far from clear what more could have been done, as Malmesbury explained to Derby: 'If however he [Napoleon] does mean war I can do nothing more than what I have done, wh[ich] is to urge Buol to be *prudent*, to tell Napoleon that he risks his crown, & Sardinia that she is humbugged by him. To press on Prussia to be neutral if the war does break out, & to support the above advice & warnings to the various parties'.[67]

If (as it turned out) Buol was imprudent, if Napoleon perceived that Russian connivance, Prussian forbearance and British neutrality would preserve his crown, and if Sardinia did not feel 'humbugged' (or realised it could 'humbug' Napoleon in turn), all Malmesbury's efforts would come to nought. Or, as Derby put it: 'France and Austria both seem so much inclined to fly at each other's throats, that it will not be very easy to keep matters quiet'.[68] It is difficult to perceive what other practical options were available to a British minority Government wary of losing public support. Disraeli did not have a significantly different or viable alternative.

What did his suggestions amount to? There were so many 'ifs' and 'buts' in his proposal for a firmer assertion of British neutrality that it was certainly, as Beales has suggested, 'excessively optimistic'.[69] Assuming Disraeli's hypothesis about Austria's view of Britain to have been correct, what more could have been done to convince Vienna of British determination to remain neutral? Disraeli had, after all, conceded that Malmesbury had 'urged' the point 'upon Apponyi'.[70] Derby felt that 'we have done all in our power' to convince Austria.[71] Perhaps, though, an even more definitive statement could have been made. But there was no certainty that Austria was counting on British support against France. Steele has suggested that the Austrians moved against Piedmont in April on the expectation of British backing, but the evidence is inconclusive.[72] Malmesbury had explicitly warned Vienna time and again of his powerlessness if Austria initiated hostilities.

Disraeli's suspicions about the Court, and in particular the Prince Consort, certainly did not convince Derby: 'I can hardly think D is correct in his belief that Austria is encouraged, in high places, to expect a different result'.[73] The Prime Minister had experienced Court interference in 1852, and he was by no means an unquestioning admirer of royal diplomacy. Only a few days later, he would register his satisfaction that critical reports about the Belgian King had been sent on to Albert, who – he thought – should be made to appreciate 'that when crowned heads (or quasi-crowned ones) take upon themselves to meddle in la haute politique, they cannot do so with impunity, and that they may create complications which they cannot easily resolve'.[74] Derby's scepticism about the nature of royal communications with Austria was therefore significant. Albert himself was concerned that others might accuse him of dabbling in private diplomacy with his German relatives, and it seems most unlikely that he would have risked encouraging Austria to expect British support.

Whatever the nature of royal involvement, and even if the British had made further strenuous efforts to persuade Austria of the importance of peace, it was quite possible that the Austrians would have proceeded anyway, as indeed they did. Disraeli's views owed much to wishful thinking and an over-estimation of British influence on the Continent. In the course of drawing his conclusions about Austria being convinced about neutrality, and thus leading English opinion to support Austria in a conference, thereby resolving the matter, Disraeli had not been merely 'excessively optimistic': he had been building a diplomatic house of cards.

Even Disraeli's analysis of British politics was dubious. Derby was politely sceptical about the Chancellor's assumption that British opinion would be inimical to French policy in Italy: 'who shall say that if Lombardy should rise, and Piedmont support her, such a war, even if France took part in it, would not meet with much popular sympathy here?'[75] He recognised, and the spring and summer proved, that it was unlikely that British public opinion could be propelled into supporting illiberal Austria in Italy. Leading liberals would of course find much to applaud in the struggle for Italian liberation.

There was also little likelihood that, in response to British public opinion, Austria would unilaterally withdraw from the Papal States as Disraeli had first proposed on 4 January. When the Austrian evacuation of the Papal States *was* announced in February it was jointly with France in response to a papal request. A unilateral withdrawal would merely have encouraged Piedmontese ambitions. The existence of a Franco-Piedmontese alliance suggested there was rather more at stake than could be solved by such a demonstration of Austrian weakness. Although Disraeli could not have known the exact conclusions reached at Plombières in July 1858, he was well aware that Napoleon was in close communication with Cavour. Only a few days earlier, the marriage of Prince Napoleon to Victor Emmanuel's daughter had shown, as Malmesbury noted, 'a complete alliance between France[,] Russia and Sardinia'.[76]

It is unclear exactly what significance Disraeli really attached to specific suggestions or proposals. On 4 January, evacuation of the Papal States was of such significance that it would 'conclude matters'; three days later the subject merited not a single mention in his letter.[77] His overriding concern seems to have been to raise an alarm. He was searching for any ammunition with which to attack Malmesbury's foreign policy, in which – for whatever reason – he no longer had confidence. He may also have been concerned about the potential for more calls on defence spending, which in January 1859 he was attempting to curtail.[78] Exactly which type of ammunition he used against

Malmesbury may not have mattered greatly to him. His letters certainly suggest a worried man dashing off letters without too much care for details. On 7 January, for example, there were 'two things' that were 'urgent'.[79] His letter had, however, apparently been written in such haste that, as Derby pointed out, 'you have omitted to say what you consider the second'.[80]

It must have been difficult for Disraeli's colleagues to take such outpourings very seriously. His previous interventions, public and private, had rarely been helpful. It is therefore unsurprising that they took little account of his latest concerns. They had never ruled out the possibility of war, but they were sceptical about its imminence and Disraeli's proposals for averting it. The Disraeli–Earle *coup* meanwhile came to nothing, as its principal author acknowledged a few weeks later, after Napoleon spoke at the opening of the French Chambers: 'the Emperor's speech has relieved no one'.[81] This did not, however, deter the Chancellor in his quest to redirect foreign policy. He remained dissatisfied with Malmesbury's diplomacy, and would return with another initiative in February.[82]

The search for peace: internal and external challenges

The Foreign Secretary meanwhile persisted in his policy of attempting to prevent and localise any war. In many ways, it resembled his diplomacy in 1852. It required wholehearted engagement with what remained of the European concert. Concern about the danger from France and the desire to avoid British involvement in any war continued to overshadow relations with all the powers.

The one concrete continental military commitment Britain did have was bound up with the problem of Napoleonic ambitions as much as was the situation in northern Italy. In 1859, it briefly seemed as if there might once more be difficulties about Belgium. Reports reached the Government that King Leopold might be drawing closer to Napoleon, and Malmesbury and Derby were immediately concerned that Belgium should remain entirely neutral. Malmesbury warned that '"Our uncle" [Leopold – uncle to both the Queen and Prince Albert] is a sad burden upon us. If attacked we must defend him & his cowardly army, but ... it is not impossible that in a row he may go over to the French'.[83] Any French presence in Belgium concerned the Government on strategic grounds just as much as it had in 1852: 'it would not suit us to see them in the Scheldt & in Antwerp'.[84]

The last thing the Government needed was any muddying of the waters by minor powers, especially ones whose neutrality was guaranteed by Britain. The Prime Minister was determined to avoid any risk of war, as he noted with a disdain for the Saxe-Coburgs that only an ancient earldom could deploy: '"Our uncle" is beat in playing too fine a pawn; and he must be made to feel that he is not the dependant of France but that he is the occupier of a petty throne, whose neutrality is guaranteed only so long as it is real and actual'.[85] He accepted that Leopold 'may depend on us ... for the support we are bound to give him in the event of his being attacked', but pointed out that 'he must not expect to run at the same time with the hare and the hound'.[86]

As far as Belgium was concerned, Derby proposed a similar approach to that adopted in 1852: working with the conservative powers to restrain France. The Prime Minister suggested coming to 'an understanding with Prussia, Austria, *and Russia*' to preserve Belgian neutrality.[87] This was a government that was expecting French imperial ambitions to produce military complications sooner or later, and responding with tried and tested methods. Prince Albert was drafted in to help remind King Leopold of his loyalties. Malmesbury explained to the Prince that both he and Derby 'feel the urgent necessity that his M[ajesty] should not put himself under the special *protection* of France if he expects that support which both we and Prussia are bound to give him'.[88] Such was the Government's irritation that it even elicited a Belgian royal apology. The situation was not without relevance to Italian affairs, as Malmesbury noted, prophetically: 'We never can I hope be induced to join a protectorate of Italy – we have enough of the protectorate of Belgium which will probably be invaded by one of its protectors'.[89]

In his relations with Prussia, the power most likely to go Austria's aid, Malmesbury had to ensure that policy was sufficiently concerted to promote peace, but not to the extent of antagonising Napoleon. The Foreign Secretary had made it clear to Prussia that, in the event of French involvement in a war on Piedmont's side, if the latter was attacked by Austria, Britain 'would preserve as long as possible a strict neutrality'.[90] He had also urged Prussia to encourage German 'amity' in the hope that Napoleon might think twice about a war. He had proposed that if there was a war, Britain and Prussia should 'concert together the best means of resisting the storm which they failed to confine'.[91] Malmesbury feared, however, that Napoleon would think that Britain was planning a German league against France.

The path he trod was therefore a delicate one. When Malmesbury believed, erroneously, that Bloomfield had let Prussia have a copy of the secret despatch about British neutrality, he was greatly concerned: 'I am rather alarmed at y[ou]r letting Schlienitz have my *secret* paper because he is sure to *copy* it whatever he may have promised and there is a phrase in it respecting the restraint [by Germany] upon France ... that w[oul]d well nigh be a casus belli in Napoleon's state of mind if he saw it'.[92] The Prince Consort was again called in to use his influence, to prevent the news of Anglo-Prussian negotiations leaking out in Berlin.[93] Malmesbury's other concern was that Prussia might launch itself at France if there was an Austro-French conflict. When war did break out, he told Derby of his fear about the 'danger' from the German states 'wh[ich] I fear will break upon France ... & produce an inextinguishable conflagration'.[94] Bloomfield was convinced that it was only Britain that was restraining Prussia, 'who would go farther but for us'.[95]

Malmesbury's efforts to stop war did not end at Berlin. He channelled his energies into preserving the concert of Europe. This was no isolationist foreign policy; short of military intervention, it was as active a policy as could be pursued by a neutral government in unpropitious domestic circumstances. On 13 February, Russell told Palmerston that 'we shall be wanting in our duty if we allow the affairs of Italy to drift to war without urging upon our govt the necessity of endeavouring to prevent such a calamity while it is yet time'.[96] Malmesbury needed no such warnings. The very same day, he had instructed Cowley to go to Vienna. Cowley was instructed to seek a deal with Austria that might calm the unrest in Italy.[97] The four points that were intended to be the basis of such a deal were: a Franco-Austrian withdrawal from the Papal States; reform of the Papal States; a declaration of peaceful intentions (regarding Piedmont in particular); and the annulment or revision of Austria's treaties with Italian states, which permitted Austrian interference in the region.

The mission may have forestalled Whig criticism, but it did not please everyone. Although the Court could do little to block it, Prince Albert signalled royal displeasure:

> L[or]d Cowley's mission has taken us quite by surprise! It may do good but is not without some risk. If he were to propose to Austria, what he could not grant ... the Emp[eror] Napoleon [will] get the advantage of being able to say to us: 'You see I have put myself into your hands, Austria refuses what *you* proposed to her, you cannot object to my now taking the matter into my own hands.' We should then stand diplomatically before the world as adverse to Austria.[98]

The Prince's letter was symptomatic of the Court's efforts to give the German powers succour whenever and wherever it could. This was not merely a pro-Austrian response to Franco-Austrian conflict. It was a systematic effort to put German concerns at the heart of British policy-making, accompanied by virulent anti-Russian and anti-French sentiments. For the royal family, foreign policy revolved around the German powers, and British and German fortunes were inextricably linked.

Having been forced to accept Cowley's mission, the royal couple instead reported Berlin's irritation at not being included on the ambassadorial itinerary. Quite apart from being irrelevant to a Franco-Austrian dispute, such a visit, as Malmesbury explained to Bloomfield, was exactly the sort of complication that would enrage Napoleon: 'I hoped that both the Prince Regent [of Prussia] and yourself would see at once that such a step would be regarded by Napoleon as a mission not of *mediation* ... but as a *coalition* between England and Germany'.[99]

With fresh memories of the bitterness over the Orsini case, French naval might displayed at Cherbourg, British defensive worries and the potential vulnerability of the German states or Belgium, the Foreign Secretary had plenty of good reasons to avoid Anglo-French tension. The Queen and Prince Consort were not, however, the only ones with doubts about Malmesbury's strategy. The preparation for Cowley's mission provided the backdrop for another Disraelian assault on foreign policy. It was as unsuccessful as the previous one.

The marginality of Disraeli II

On 20 February, as Malmesbury, Derby and Cowley consulted on the details of the Vienna mission, Disraeli intervened once again. His latest letter to Derby was even more panicked and incoherent than those he had penned in January. It demonstrated a fundamental misunderstanding of the motivations driving Malmesbury's policy. Although his ostensible justification was the German states' concern about the European situation, he outlined a threat from *Russia*, and then described a plan for Anglo-Prussian co-operation to thwart Austria and France. In the context of what he described as 'a strange excitement' in Germany, he cautioned that the threat to the German powers 'is not from France, but Russia'.[100] He declared, dramatically, that 'within a few weeks of the declaration of [presumably Austro-French] war a Russian army is to be at the gates of Vienna'.[101] Though he suggested that a Berlin–London–Vienna axis would compel Napoleon to 'back out of the affair', he then went on to propose an Anglo-Prussian solution to 'the Italian question'.[102] This was the exposition of a novelist, not that of a diplomatist.

His plan had four elements: concerting policy with Prussia in order to force the Italian states to adopt reforms; using Anglo-Prussian 'good offices' to induce France and Austria to evacuate Rome; endeavouring to secure the abrogation of the 'special treaties' between Italian and foreign states which guaranteed the help of the latter in crushing revolts; agreeing to communicate with Prussia in the event of a European war over Italy and 'to guard the equilibrium of Europe against any dangers by wh[ich] it may be threatened'.[103] Disraeli clearly intended such an arrangement to be public, noting that it would be 'a significant demonstration' which would 'be popular in this country, proving that our policy is, at once, liberal & conservative. We take our stand, at once, against Austrian despotism, & French aggression'.[104] He went over the Foreign Secretary's head from the outset, adding a casual afterthought: 'I have had no opportunity of mentioning this to M[almesbur]y, to whom you can send this, if you like'.[105] Here was an arrangement that would combine the neutral powers, be bold, popular and decisive, and thwart Austria, France and, by implication, Russia.

Predictably, the Foreign Secretary was unimpressed when informed by Derby; it must have been galling to him, as he had worked carefully to concert policy with Prussia. He dismissed the letter contemptuously: 'Disraeli, as usual, has neglected to read a word of what has passed between the F.O.[,] Germany & France or he w[oul]d know that we & Prussia understand each other perfectly on the Italian questions'.[106] This rather avoided Disraeli's point, which was not the extent to which there was Anglo-Prussian understanding, but the use to which it might be put. Nevertheless, Malmesbury's principal concern remained Napoleon's suspicion about an Anglo-German alliance. The problem with taking the sort of stand that Disraeli proposed against France and Austria was that it would be antagonistic and could easily backfire: 'Any thing like the "demonstration["] he speaks of is in my opinion to be positively avoided. It w[oul]d drive Napoleon mad & bring us at once into the row'.[107] As far as the Russian threat was concerned, Malmesbury was dubious: 'I feel as sure as one has a right to feel on such subjects that the Emperor of Russia has no intention of going to war now or hereafter if he can help it – that it is entirely against his nature & that his whole mind is bent on internal improvements. His armies are reduced to the lowest scale'.[108]

He did not comment on the first three of Disraeli's points for Anglo-Prussian co-operation, and it is easy to see why. Apart from the focus on Prussia, the proposals were not particularly innovative. The evacuation of the troops in the Roman states and reforms of Roman government were already common currency in British diplomatic correspondence.[109] The modification of the Austro-Italian treaties had been specifically mentioned by Malmesbury in his letter to Cowley, outlining the mission objectives, a week earlier.[110] It was the proposal for the 'significant demonstration' by Britain and Prussia that was new.

It is difficult, however, to see what Malmesbury would have had to gain by going beyond his existing communications with Prussia. Public provocation of France and or Austria raised the spectre of at best a diplomatic morass and at worst war. What were the British and the Prussians to do by themselves to prevent a European war, short of threatening war themselves? Derby's Government had been born of Anglo-French antagonism, and Malmesbury and Derby had dedicated themselves to its reduction in order to survive. Neither was about to risk exacerbating Anglo-French tension by openly posturing with Prussia. If the risk from Russia was so great, would it be prudent to risk antagonising Austria and France without prior Anglo-Russian coordination? Would the Prussians so readily have agreed to being detached from Austria? As in January, Disraeli had got hold of an existing policy, twisted it in all kinds of impractical ways and presented it as an alternative.

C. T. McIntire has suggested that Disraeli's proposal represented 'his own four points which were partially reflected in the final version' of the four points Cowley took with him on his mission to Vienna.[111] One must be careful, however, of assuming that a proposal generated a policy merely because the former preceded the latter. While three of Disraeli's suggestions were indeed 'reflected' in Cowley's four points, there is little evidence to suggest that this was as a result of Disraeli's intervention. Malmesbury was already establishing a mediating position that had as its basis three of the points Disraeli was raising. Although it is possible that Disraeli was contributing to the ongoing discussions about Cowley's mission, the context in which he placed his plan was specifically the position of the German powers and the Russian threat. It seems highly unlikely that either Derby or Malmesbury would have solicited Disraeli's opinion, given their response to his earlier intervention. Instead, it bears all the hallmarks of a flash of Disraelian inspiration. Although the evidence is flimsy, at best one might speculate that Malmesbury found the format (i.e. the four points) a useful one to adopt.

The antagonism between Malmesbury and Disraeli simply increased. This was not just a personal difference; their disagreements had always been more about policy than personality. Disraeli's desire for activity for its own sake, and his readiness to take risks, clashed with Malmesbury's caution. By early May, Disraeli was constructing all sorts of schemes to preserve the Government. Malmesbury's removal from the FO featured prominently in them. On 3 May, when the Chancellor decided to invite Palmerston to join the Government, Disraeli's lack of concern about existing policy was clear: 'The foreign policy of every government, of wh[ich] you are a member, must be yours, even if you might think it expedient, that another shod [sic] undertake the duties of the F.O.'.[112] This was breathtaking disloyalty. He followed it with a proposal to install Lord Elgin at the Foreign Office, which Derby dismissed: 'the Col[onial] Office would have suited him better than the For. Office. I should, I confess, be very sorry to see any change made in that Department at the present moment. It is of great importance to have a man there who has at his fingers' ends the whole thread of the complicated negotiations in which we have been engaged ... I should much deprecate such a change'.[113]

While Malmesbury and Derby – despite disillusionment about first France and then Austria – meanwhile persevered in their pursuit of peace, they were frustrated by external and internal forces beyond their control. Although Cowley appeared to have made some limited gains when he returned from Vienna in March, he was upstaged by the Russian proposal for a congress to discuss Italy. This was in turn rendered irrelevant by the Austrian demand for Piedmont's disarmament, provoking a war in which Napoleon enthusiastically intervened on Piedmont's side. Napoleon's collusion with Cavour, Austria's aggressive attitude towards Piedmont and, finally, the Queen's determination to resist any Anglo-Russian co-operation all thwarted attempts to prevent or 'localise' the Franco-Piedmontese–Austrian war that ensued in April and May.

Malmesbury has been criticised for his focus on Vienna in this period, via initiatives such as Cowley's mission, rather than addressing Napoleon's readiness to risk a military conflict.[114] Malmesbury and Derby had certainly underestimated the extent to which Napoleon was prepared to collude with Cavour and sacrifice European peace. It remains, however, an open question whether Napoleon genuinely wanted or expected war, rather than simply a congress that would denude Austria of northern Italy in the same way that the Paris conference had weakened Russia.[115] Whatever Napoleon's intentions, Malmesbury had, in any case, become increasingly suspicious about his old friend. By late January, Malmesbury was convinced that Napoleon was hostile to the Conservatives and, what was more, was actively encouraging the pro-Palmerston *Morning Post* to publish reports that 'write me down'.[116] At the end of March, Malmesbury told Derby that it was 'now evident that the French Emperor is no longer the same man in mind or body that he was formerly'.[117] Neither was Malmesbury sure he was getting accurate information from Paris, warning Derby that Cowley was 'altogether French & ... like all men he imbibes the complexion of the Court at wh[ich] he resides'.[118]

But Malmesbury's room for manoeuvre was extremely limited. Only a credible threat of British military intervention, which the Government was in no position to make, might have dissuaded France from backing Piedmont. In the event that the Government had been prepared to sanction a British intervention, the public (and, perhaps, the Court) would have been unlikely to support it. Such a policy would have risked the Government's precarious position in Parliament. It would have relied on the French not calling the British bluff, despite the fact that British military preparations were clearly deficient. There would have had to be certainty that the Russians would not act to support the French; the details of their arrangement remained murky. Alternatively, British backing for the Italian states against the French, in order to preserve the balance of power if the Austrians were ousted (as was suggested by Sir James Hudson at Turin), carried all the same risks.[119]

The important misjudgement Derby and Malmesbury made was not about France, but Austria. Despite Derby's appreciation of Hapsburg pride, the Government and other British observers underestimated the desperation and frustration in Vienna. It seemed, as Derby observed to Pakington in early March, that, up to that point, Austria had appeared 'disposed to make every reasonable concession'.[120] Later the same month, he felt confident enough to tell Disraeli: 'Nothing can be better than the aspect of our foreign affairs. I look on peace as all but certain'.[121] Derby was not alone in his misjudgement. The day before the Austrians issued their ultimatum to Piedmont, even such a seasoned (and anti-Austrian) observer of foreign affairs as Palmerston told Granville that he would not believe 'that the Austrian Govt. can be so insane as to begin hostilities till I hear that powder has actually been burnt'.[122] Palmerston was, however, sanguine about the prospect of war: 'The result will be that they will be driven out of Italy; and though one must lament the means, one shall rejoice at the end'.[123]

In contrast, Malmesbury observed, once war had broken out, that 'there is not a pin to choose between the merits of the antagonists'.[124] His objective continued to be the localisation of the conflict and to prevent others – Russia, Prussia or, worst of all, Britain – becoming involved. When the Foreign Secretary gained the impression from Duke Ernest of Saxe-Coburg (Prince Albert's brother) that, after an

Austrian defeat, 'Germany would attack on the Rhine', he hastened to warn the Queen that 'Lord Derby agrees with him in thinking it would be impossible in such a case for England to defend Germany'.[125] Derby had already made the Government's stance on the war explicitly clear to the Queen, citing public opinion as evidence, on 1 May.[126] The Queen protested that 'she is extremely sorry to find ... that he [Malmesbury] is under the impression that the Duke of Coburg was eager for war', and that, had there been more time, 'she is certain that he w[oul]d not have been left with this impression'.[127] This cut little ice with Malmesbury, who pointedly noted that the Duke had 'distinctly expressed' his position.[128] The Foreign Secretary reminded her of Conservative policy: 'by every act of policy & patience to try to localise the war'.[129]

'Localising' the war, however, might require more than advice to the other powers, and in that event, the Queen could still obstruct foreign policy. The story of May 1859 was one of uneasy constitutional stalemate. The Court did its best to pursue a pro-German policy, and caused rather greater difficulties than Disraeli. Malmesbury and Derby had continually to reiterate and defend Conservative policy against a Court that could be every bit as awkward for them as it had once been (and would be again) for Palmerston and Russell. Bagehot would note, just over a decade later, that when it came to making treaties, 'the real power is not in the hands of the Sovereign, it is in the Prime Minister and in the Cabinet'.[130] The picture was not so clear when it came to the broader question of foreign policy.

Several historians have noted the way in which ministers, at the outbreak of war, had to resist the Queen's efforts to draft a stronger condemnation of French policy than they considered advisable.[131] Malmesbury felt able to challenge the Queen only up to a certain point, however, conceding a number of alterations in deference to her wishes.[132] This was a small tussle between ministers and the Court, but it was a prelude to a more significant one. The catalyst was a Russian initiative.

The historiographical focus on Franco-Italian manoeuvres has obscured Russia's place in British deliberations in 1859. The Government was suspicious of Russia, but it was aware of the limitations of Russian capabilities, and of its potential uses if relative peace and the balance of power were to be maintained. As early as December 1858, Derby had noted: 'I feel very confident that Russia will not be over anxious to engage in new hostilities'.[133] He nevertheless remained concerned about Russia's 'projects of aggrandisement' in the Near East.[134] He appreciated the danger posed by Russia, especially once it had become clear that there had been close Franco-Russian co-operation. In April, as war loomed, he warned Pakington to make extra naval preparations: 'if Germany joins with Austria; and in the event of the French & Russian fleets uniting, under circumstances in which we should be drawn into war (which God forbid!) we should be in a very unpleasant position in respect of our naval power'.[135]

Active Russian hostility, however, remained a distant possibility. In late May, once the Franco-Austrian war was underway, the British Minister in Russia, Crampton, was unequivocal: Russia 'does not desire and is not ready for war'.[136] He even felt that 'both the public and Government are a shade less French than they were'.[137] As in 1852, neither Derby nor his Foreign Secretary was about to be squeamish on the subject of co-operation with Russia when circumstances demanded. They had been prepared to co-operate over Belgium, and, as Malmesbury pointed out, Russia was 'the only Power who has any influence at present with France'.[138] The Court, though, was instinctively more suspicious.

In late May 1859, Gorchakov proposed a Russo-British effort to localise and 'arrest' any war.[139] This neatly accorded with Conservative policy. Exactly what the proposal meant is (and was at the time) unclear, but Malmesbury and Derby were minded to accept, and on 20 May, matters came to a head. Having seen a draft telegram accepting the offer, the Queen bombarded ministers with her views, sending three letters to Malmesbury in one day. Her pro-German sympathies were once more evident: 'The Queen can see no way ... [of working with Russia for *localisation*, other] than uniting to prevent Germany from saving Austria from being overpowered by France'.[140] This logic was dubious. A 'localisation' might indeed have meant threatening war if other powers became involved. It might equally have meant another congress, or an Anglo-Russian threat of war if Austria or France took military action outside a certain area, or Anglo-Russian guarantees to other states, or diplomatic pressure on France.

Malmesbury protested: 'the *only* chance we have of *arresting* the conflict, or of restraining it within the peninsula is to come to an understanding with the neutral Powers *to be ready to do so,* & to act with us whenever the phases of the war gives [sic] us hopes of interfering with effect'.[141] The Queen, while not explicitly forbidding a positive British response, hoped, however, that 'L[or]d Malmesbury will stop the communication of this message to Gortchakoff'.[142] The hope was interpreted as an expectation, and the Government acquiesced. Malmesbury was unusually explicit in his diary, noting his suspicion that the Queen and the Prince were 'evidently anxious not to stop the war but to let Germany go at the French'.[143] Nevertheless, neither he nor Derby seems to have felt able to do anything about it.

This incident represented not merely a minor royal victory: it was effectively a royal removal of a plank of the Government's foreign policy. It was a logical culmination of the Court's pro-German efforts. When the Palmerston ministry was being constructed, John Bright was sure Stanley was alluding 'to the tendencies of the Court', when he told Bright: '"If you become a Minister, you will discover that there are high people whose wishes are not like yours and mine, and it is not easy to withstand them."'[144] The Court had succeeded in obstructing the Government's will, and did not even need Cabinet allies as the Queen did when she later frustrated Palmerston and Russell over Schleswig–Holstein.[145] This may have been because the Government was vulnerable and reluctant to make a stand on a controversial matter; its political power, and perhaps inclination, was on the wane. It was, however, a risk for the Queen. It must be doubted that she would have got her way if the Government had stood firm, but she clearly felt able to press the point. Mosse has suggested that, over Schleswig–Holstein, the Queen, by intervening, was 'exceeding the bounds of constitutional propriety'.[146] Constitutional propriety may not have appeared as clear-cut to the Queen or her ministers.

The Queen certainly did not stop trying to influence policy. A few days later the Queen supported her daughter's informal request for British 'help' for Germany, though exactly what kind of 'help' was unspecified.[147] The Government did manage a final riposte, stopping the Queen from inserting a more ambiguous description of British neutrality than ministers wanted in her speech to Parliament after the general election.[148] This was a minor victory in the wake of the more serious disagreement about Anglo-Russian co-operation. The dispute about the wording of the speech demonstrated Derby's continuing role at the centre of Conservative strategy. It was he who rejected Victoria's amendment of the description of neutrality, in another letter previously overlooked. While Disraeli concurred, the Prime Minister made his opinion clear from the outset: 'My own impression is to accept her amendment on the subject of the increase of the navy, but strongly to urge upon her the reconsideration of the other paragraph [on the Franco-Austrian war]. We *must* avoid any thing which throws a doubt upon our neutrality'.[149]

Disraeli himself had little further part to play in foreign policy in 1859. One final clash came in the last days of the ministry, when Malmesbury's 'blue books' setting out the Government's course in foreign policy were not published and tabled in the Commons by Disraeli. This was despite Malmesbury's repeated calls for their presentation.[150] He maintained that their publication could have saved the Government in the close vote on the Address. In the Introduction to his *Memoirs*, he noted how, in 1859, 'we were beaten on a false issue'.[151] He reverted to Disraeli's decision against presenting the 'blue books', in a much-quoted passage: 'Why he chose not to do so I never knew, nor did he ever explain it to me'.[152]

Historians have speculated as to why Disraeli did not produce the books. Given the impossibility of knowing whether their publication would or would not have affected the vote, however, the dispute was of no greater political significance. Hawkins has aptly called it 'a final footnote to the personal resentment between Disraeli and Malmesbury'.[153] Just before the Conservative defeat, Clarendon met the Foreign Secretary and noted the depth to which his relationship with Disraeli had sunk: 'I have seen Malmesbury who told me that they expected to win but admitted that his only ground for thinking so was the assurance of Dizzy who *always lied*. He ... said that he had no party feelings, that he was dead sick of his office wh[ich] he only retained out of deference to Derby ... 2/3ds. of the party, M said, hate Dizzy intensely'.[154]

What had marked Disraeli's foreign-policy interventions? Boldness, taking the initiative, cutting through the diplomatic niceties; yet on closer inspection, his contributions resemble those of a well-informed newspaper reader who, periodically alarmed at developments, writes to the editor with bold plans on the assumption that those charged with responding to them have missed a cunning and decisive solution. The insubstantial and impracticable nature of the proposals on closer inspection became evident. Although Malmesbury and Derby were hardly infallible, and would certainly not have been the first premier and foreign minister to have missed opportunities, close analysis of Disraeli's plans reveals little to justify the perceptiveness that historians have hitherto accorded them or the prominent part accorded to him in analyses. Whatever Disraeli represented in foreign policy, it was clearly different from Malmesbury and Derby, initially in presentation, but increasingly in substance. Although 'Conservative' foreign policy was ultimately to become Disraeli's, in the 1850s it was determinedly directed by Conservatives of a different ilk.

Notes

1 See e.g. Norfolk Record Office, Bulwer Papers, BUL 1/212/39, Bulwer to Disraeli, draft, 3 August 1858: 'You wished now & then to hear from me'. The letter does not survive in Disraeli's papers.
2 See, e.g., the surviving reports, Hughenden Papers, Dep. Hughenden 75/1.
3 See Monypenny and Buckle, *Disraeli*, vol. 4, pp. 217–20; Henderson, 'Ralph Anstruther Earle', pp. 181–2; Blake, *Disraeli*, pp. 403–4; Hawkins, *Parliament, Party*, p. 193.
4 *DL*, vol. 7, ed. M. G. Wiebe, Mary S. Millar, Ann P. Robson and Ellen L. Hawman (2004), 3253, Disraeli to Earle, 20 December 1858.
5 *Ibid.*
6 Henderson, 'Ralph Anstruther Earle', p. 181, Earle to Disraeli, 20 December 1858.
7 *DL*, vol. 7, 3253, Disraeli to Earle, 20 December 1858.
8 Blake, *Disraeli*, p. 404.
9 Earle to Disraeli, 24 December 1858, in Monypenny and Buckle, *Disraeli*, vol. 4, p. 219.
10 *Ibid.*
11 *DL*, vol. 7, 3253, Disraeli to Earle, 20 December 1858.
12 *The Times*, 8 February 1859, speech of 7 February 1859.
13 Blake, *Disraeli*, p. 404.
14 Malmesbury Papers, 9M73/22/179, copy, Disraeli to Malmesbury, 2 January 1859.
15 Derby Papers, 920 DER (14) 144/2, Malmesbury to Derby, 28 December 1858.
16 *Ibid.*, Malmesbury to Derby, 4 January 1859.
17 *Ibid.*
18 Malmesbury Papers, 9M73/20/48, Derby to Malmesbury, 5 January 1859.
19 *Ibid.*
20 *Ibid.*, 9M73/20/66, Hammond to Malmesbury, 4 January 1859.
21 Derby Papers, 920 DER (14) 145/6, Disraeli to Derby, 4 January 1859; Derby apparently did not receive this on 5 January until after writing to Malmesbury.
22 *Ibid.*
23 *Ibid.*
24 *Ibid.*
25 *Ibid.*
26 *Ibid.*
27 Malmesbury Papers, 9M73/20/48, Derby to Malmesbury, 5 January 1859.
28 Hughenden Papers, Dep. Hughenden 110/1, Derby to Disraeli, 6 January 1859; the Legations were the divisions of the Papal States in the Romagna, ruled over by papal legates.

29 *Ibid.*
30 Malmesbury Papers, 9M73/20/49, Derby to Malmesbury, 6 January 1859.
31 *Ibid.*
32 Derby Papers, 920 DER (14) 144/2, Malmesbury to Derby, 6 January 1859.
33 Malmesbury Papers, 9M73/20/68, Hammond to Malmesbury, 6 January 1859.
34 Derby Papers, 920 DER (14) 144/2, Malmesbury to Derby, 7 January 1859.
35 *Ibid.*
36 *Ibid.*, 920 DER (14) 145/6, Disraeli to Derby, 7 January 1859.
37 *Ibid.*
38 *Ibid.*
39 *Ibid.*
40 *Ibid.*
41 *Ibid.*
42 *Ibid.*
43 *Ibid.*
44 *Ibid.*
45 *Ibid.*
46 Malmesbury Papers, 9M73/450/6, Derby to Malmesbury, 8 January 1859.
47 *Ibid.*
48 *Ibid.*
49 *Ibid.*
50 *Ibid.*
51 Hughenden Papers, Dep. Hughenden 110/1, Derby to Disraeli, 8 January 1859.
52 *Ibid.*
53 Monypenny and Buckle, *Disraeli*, vol. 4, p. 229.
54 *Ibid.*, p. 225.
55 Blake, *Disraeli*, p. 403.
56 *Ibid.*, p. 404.
57 Hawkins, *Parliament, Party*, p. 195.
58 *Ibid.*
59 Malmesbury Papers, 9M73/450/6, Derby to Malmesbury, 8 January 1859.
60 *Ibid.*, 9M73/20/49, Derby to Malmesbury, 6 January 1859.
61 *Ibid.*
62 *Ibid.*
63 Hughenden Papers, Dep. Hughenden 110/1, Derby to Disraeli, 8 January 1859.
64 Malmesbury Papers, 9M73/450/6, Derby to Malmesbury, 8 January 1859.
65 Beales, *England and Italy*, p. 44.

66 See, e.g., Carter, 'Hudson, Malmesbury and Cavour', pp. 392–4.
67 Derby Papers, 920 DER (14) 144/2, Malmesbury to Derby, 7 January 1859.
68 Malmesbury Papers, 9M73/20/47, Derby to Malmesbury, 4 January 1859.
69 Beales, *England and Italy*, p. 49.
70 Derby Papers, 920 DER (14) 145/6, Disraeli to Derby, 7 January 1859.
71 Hughenden Papers, Dep. Hughenden 110/1, Derby to Disraeli, 8 January 1859.
72 Steele quotes from a letter from Franz Josef in March 1859 in which the Emperor suggested that 'we may yet count upon England in the event of a big war': *Palmerston and Liberalism*, p. 257. The hope that Britain *might* support Austria if there was a *big* war did not, however, necessarily translate into the expectation of support in a pre-emptive war.
73 Malmesbury Papers, 9M73/450/6, Derby to Malmesbury, 8 January 1859.
74 *Ibid.*, 9M73/450/7, Derby to Malmesbury, undated; Derby's copy (Derby Papers, 920 DER (14) 187/1) is dated 17 January.
75 Malmesbury Papers, 9M73/450/6, Derby to Malmesbury, 8 January 1859.
76 Derby Papers, 920 DER (14) 144/2, Malmesbury to Derby, 1 January 1859.
77 *Ibid.*, 920 DER (14) 145/6, Disraeli to Derby, 4 January 1859.
78 See, e.g., Malmesbury Papers, 9M73/447/15, Pakington to Malmesbury, 18 January 1859.
79 Derby Papers, 920 DER (14) 145/6, Disraeli to Derby, 7 January 1859.
80 Hughenden Papers, Dep. Hughenden 110/1, Derby to Disraeli, 8 January 1859; this section was edited out by Buckle: *Disraeli*, vol. 4, p. 224.
81 Derby Papers, 920 DER (14) 145/6, Disraeli to Derby, 9 February 1859.
82 See below, pp. 230–2.
83 Derby Papers, 920 DER (14) 144/2, Malmesbury to Derby, 15 January 1859.
84 *Ibid.*
85 Malmesbury Papers, 9M73/450/7, Derby to Malmesbury, undated; Derby's copy (Derby Papers, 920 DER (14) 187/1) is dated 17 January 1859.
86 *Ibid.*
87 *Ibid.*
88 *Ibid.*, 9M73/60/4, copy, Malmesbury to Prince Albert, 16 January 1859.
89 Hughenden Papers, Dep. Hughenden 99/2, fo. 100, Malmesbury to Disraeli, undated.
90 Bourne, *Foreign Policy*, p. 337, Malmesbury to Bloomfield, 7 January 1859 (draft in Royal Archive); original not preserved in Prussian despatches, FO 64/470.
91 *Ibid.*, p. 339.

92 Bloomfield Papers, FO 356/32, Malmesbury to Bloomfield, 26 January 1859.
93 *Letters of the Prince Consort*, p. 320, Prince Albert to Prince Regent of Prussia, 26 January 1859.
94 Derby Papers, 920 DER (14) 144/2, Malmesbury to Derby, 11 May 1859.
95 Bodleian Library, Oxford, Crampton Papers (viewed on microfilm), 47, fo. 129, Bloomfield to Crampton, 4 February 1859.
96 Palmerston (Broadlands) Papers, GC/RU/496, Russell to Palmerston, 13 February 1859.
97 Cowley Papers, FO 519/196, fos 771–4, Malmesbury to Cowley, 13 February 1859; a detailed account may be found in C. T. McIntire, *England Against the Papacy, 1858–1861* (Cambridge, 1983), pp. 88–93.
98 Malmesbury Papers, 9M73/449/27, Prince Consort to Malmesbury, 17 February 1859.
99 Bloomfield Papers, FO 356/32, Malmesbury to Bloomfield, 1 March 1859.
100 Derby Papers, 920 DER (14) 145/6, Disraeli to Derby, 20 February 1859.
101 *Ibid.*
102 *Ibid.*
103 *Ibid.*
104 *Ibid.*
105 *Ibid.*
106 *Ibid.*, 920 DER (14) 144/2, Malmesbury to Derby, 21 February 1859.
107 *Ibid.*
108 *Ibid.*
109 See e.g. Lord Augustus Loftus, *The Diplomatic Reminiscences of Lord Augustus Loftus*, 2 vols (1892), vol. 1, p. 383, Malmesbury to Loftus, 12 January 1859.
110 Cowley Papers, FO 519/596, fo. 773, Malmesbury to Cowley, 13 February 1859.
111 McIntire, *England Against the Papacy*, p. 89.
112 Palmerston (Broadlands) Papers, GC/DI/140/1, Disraeli to Palmerston, 3 May 1859.
113 Derby Papers, 920 DER (14) 186/2, fo. 108, copy, Derby to Disraeli, 8 May 1859.
114 See, e.g., Carter, 'Hudson, Malmesbury and Cavour', pp. 393–4.
115 This is certainly Keith Wilson's hypothesis in *Problems & Possibilities: Exercises in Statesmanship 1814–1918* (Stroud, 2003), pp. 75–7.
116 Derby Papers, 920 DER (14) 144/2, Malmesbury to Derby, 27 January 1859; see also Cowley Papers, FO 519/196, fos 742–3, Malmesbury to Cowley, 26 January 1859; and Malmesbury, *Memoirs*, vol. 2, pp. 150–2.
117 Derby Papers, 920 DER (14) 144/2, Malmesbury to Derby, 25 March 1859.
118 *Ibid.*, Malmesbury to Derby, 6 January 1859.
119 This was Sir James Hudson's suggestion: Carter, 'Hudson, Malmesbury

and Cavour', pp. 405–10.
120 Hampton (Pakington) MSS, 705:349/3835/1/iii/52, Derby to Pakington, 4 March 1859.
121 Derby Papers, 920 DER (14) 186/2, fo. 58, copy, Derby to Disraeli, 20 March 1859.
122 Granville Papers, PRO 30/29/19/24, fo. 1., Palmerston to Granville, 22 April 1859.
123 *Ibid.*, fo. 2.
124 Derby Papers, 920 DER (14) 144/2, Malmesbury to Derby, 27 April 1859.
125 Malmesbury Papers, 9M73/52/112, copy, Malmesbury to Queen Victoria, 2 May 1859.
126 *LQV*, vol. 3, p. 330, Derby to Queen Victoria, 1 May 1859.
127 Malmesbury Papers, 9M73/448, Queen Victoria to Malmesbury, 3 May 1859.
128 *Ibid.*, 9M73/52/118, copy, Malmesbury to Queen Victoria, 4 May 1859.
129 *Ibid.*, 9M73/52/119.
130 From the Introduction to second edition (1872) of Walter Bagehot, *The English Constitution*, reprinted in *ibid*. (London, 1993), p. 290.
131 See, e.g., H. Hearder, 'Queen Victoria and Foreign Policy: Royal Intervention in the Italian Question, 1859–60', in K. Bourne and D. C. Watt (eds), *Studies in International History* (Hamden, 1967), pp. 176–7; Beales, *England and Italy*, p. 71.
132 Malmesbury Papers, 9M73/52/119, copy, Malmesbury to Queen Victoria, 4 May 1859.
133 *Ibid.*, 9M73/20/46, Derby to Malmesbury, 30 December 1858.
134 *LQV*, vol. 3, p. 330, Derby to Queen Victoria, 1 May 1859.
135 Hampton (Pakington) MSS, 705:349/3835/11/iii/56b, Derby to Pakington, 26 April 1859.
136 FO 65/536, no. 247, Crampton to Malmesbury, 24 May 1859.
137 *Ibid.*
138 Malmesbury Papers, 9M73/52/127, copy, Malmesbury to Queen Victoria, 20 May 1859.
139 *Ibid.*; see also *Letters of the Prince Consort*, pp. 333–5, Prince Albert to Prince William of Prussia, 25 May 1859; Hearder, 'Queen Victoria and Foreign Policy', p. 177.
140 Malmesbury Papers, 9M73/448, Queen Victoria to Malmesbury, 20 May 1859.
141 *Ibid.*, 9M73/52/128, copy, Malmesbury to Queen Victoria, 20 May 1859.
142 *Ibid.*, 9M73/448, Queen Victoria to Malmesbury, 20 May 1859; this letter was subsequently published in *LQV*, vol. 3, p. 334.
143 Malmesbury Papers, 9M73/79, unpublished political diary, 20 May 1859.
144 *Diaries of John Bright*, 12 June 1859, p. 240.
145 See W. E. Mosse, 'Queen Victoria and Her Ministers in the

Schleswig–Holstein Crisis 1863–1864', *EHR*, 78 (1963), pp. 263–83.
146 *Ibid.*, p. 282.
147 Malmesbury Papers, 9M73/79, unpublished political diary, 28 May 1859; Steele has suggested that it was 'active British participation': *Palmerston and Liberalism*, p. 257.
148 *LQV*, vol. 3, pp. 335–40: Queen Victoria to Derby, 1 June 1859; Derby to Queen Victoria, 2 June 1859; Queen Victoria to Derby, 3 June 1859; see also Hawkins, *Parliament, Party*, p. 252.
149 Hughenden Papers, Dep. Hughenden 57/2, fo. 11, Derby to Disraeli, 2 June 1859.
150 *Ibid.*, 99/2, fo. 78, Malmesbury to Disraeli, 2 June 1859; fo. 80, Malmesbury to Disraeli, 7 June 1859.
151 Malmesbury, *Memoirs*, vol. 1, p. 41.
152 *Ibid.*, vol. 2, pp. 188–9.
153 Hawkins, *Parliament, Party*, p. 257.
154 Palmerston (Broadlands) Papers, GC/CL/1195, Clarendon to Palmerston, 5 June 1859.

11

The politics of Conservative foreign policy

Foreign policy needs to be relocated in our analyses of the mid-Victorian era. Indeed, it is easier to perceive the dimensions of nineteenth-century politics if debate about foreign policy is integrated into domestic political history, as it too rarely is.

Foreign policy played a significant part in the Conservatives' calculations. Before they returned to government in 1852, every policy area formed a front in their war against the perceived radicalism of the Whigs. Economic policy represented the most prominent iniquity, but, for Conservatives, Whig–Peelite domestic changes were tangled up with Palmerston's disruptive foreign policy: the power of the landed classes was being chipped away at home; the wider European order was being disturbed overseas. Nevertheless, Conservative unease with Palmerstonian foreign policy also offered a possible basis for party reunion. Even after hopes for that reunion had faded, events abroad enabled domestic opponents to unite, providing parliamentary opportunities for the Conservatives throughout the mid-Victorian period.

In government prior to the 1852 election, all of the party's strategic calculations were made in the knowledge that nothing could be done to rock the boat while an election was imminent: an election on which depended the future of Conservative government and British economic policy. All areas of ministerial responsibility needed to avoid controversy. At the same time, the opposition was determined to protect the post-1846 economic orthodoxy by savaging the Government it perceived as a threat to it. Any means would do. Foreign policy, partly because of its unpredictability, was particularly vulnerable to attack; but it was also vulnerable because Derby and Malmesbury were consciously pursuing a conciliatory policy, differing from Palmerston's in a number of respects. After the election, when the Conservatives failed to secure enough parliamentary troops, there were consequences, too, for foreign policy: relations with Rome were exploited for domestic purposes, while there was an extra incentive to establish the Anglo-French *entente* Malmesbury favoured.

What was the Conservative *raison d'être* after protection was defeated? Arguably, the party leadership never found one during the 1850s, but it cast around for the largest rocks to hurl at the Government. Russell's obsession, electoral reform, certainly gave the Conservatives persistent cause for concern. But, after 1855, Palmerston, a well-known enemy of reform, was Prime Minister. That Conservative gun was, if not spiked, certainly much quieter, at least until Russell was back in Downing Street after Palmerston's death. In the interim, foreign affairs provided powerful political ammunition. It was no accident that, in early 1857, Malmesbury proposed the iniquity of Palmerston's foreign policy as a Conservative cause, and Derby took up the idea; no accident, either, that foreign policy provided the grounds for Palmerston's parliamentary defeats in 1857 and 1858. Economic consensus closed one route to power; foreign policy offered an alternative, though by no means the only one. Events overseas thus offered domestic advantages for the Conservatives in two ways: Palmerston's controversial policies provoked debate and they united disparate factions against him.

This was no less the case after 1859. During the seven years in opposition after the collapse of the second Derby Government, the Conservatives for the most part reverted to 'masterly inactivity', consciously avoiding opposition to Palmerston's conservative domestic agenda. They calculated that he was much less of a threat than his radical hangers-on. Until Russell and Gladstone re-opened the reform question, foreign policy offered some of the best opportunities for liberal disagreements and Conservative advantage. In the imbroglio over Schleswig–Holstein in 1863–64, as Bismarck manipulated affairs to isolate the Danes, Palmerston's ineffectual sabre-rattling once more opened his flank to his domestic opponents. In July 1864, the Government was defeated in the Lords on the Danish question, as it had been over Don Pacifico, and only just survived in the Commons. Just as in 1850 and over China in 1857, Derby attacked Palmerston for departing from the principle of non-intervention, and in February 1864 he famously attached the tag of 'meddle and muddle' to Palmerstonian foreign policy.[1]

But espousing non-intervention did not equate to a lack of concern about continental events, and it never had. During the Schleswig–Holstein crisis, one rising Conservative star, Northcote, noted that 'there is a mean between fussy interference and absolute indifference, and ... England's policy ought to be directed to that mean'.[2] Derby or Malmesbury could not have summarised their approach better. There continued to be a clear and profound difference between Palmerstonian liberal and Conservative conceptions of foreign policy, but the Conservatives were not indifferent to European developments. Throughout the mid-Victorian period, they actively sought to maintain European stability, but to avoid over-commitment. The 'mutual protection and Security of different Powers' via 'a general System of Public Law in Europe' was every bit as much Derby's and Malmesbury's aim as it had been Pitt's.[3] Jones's Derby, the isolationist, is unconvincing. But Steele's Tories, who 'did not think isolationism either feasible or desirable', are equally problematical.[4]

The Conservatives did not contemplate isolation at all; it was simply not on their 'mental map'. They perceived, as Castlereagh had done, the necessity for a British continental involvement in some respect; Britain was a part of the European concert, and they took their responsibilities in that direction very seriously. It was not that they wanted to avoid being 'too closely' involved: close diplomatic involvement was a hallmark of Conservative diplomacy.[5] Rather, they wanted to avoid hefty commitments of men or money, or to be involved in a way that would threaten either British bargaining power or the European balance. As Stanley told Bloomfield during the Franco-Prussian wrangle that almost led to war over Luxembourg in 1867, his position was clear: 'to avoid committing ourselves so far as to get involved in the dispute; but to do what we can to keep the peace'.[6] It was exactly the strategy that Malmesbury had adopted. That policy had failed to prevent war in 1859, but it had poured oil on troubled waters over the Empire in 1852.

It was a fine line to tread. In 1867, Stanley was very reluctant to enter into any agreement to maintain Luxembourg's neutrality.[7] In his reluctance, he was acting on exactly the same principles that had motivated Malmesbury: the implications of Palmerston's Belgian guarantee had long concerned Conservatives, and they were in no hurry to consent to another. Their fears about the relative weakness of Britain's position were not new in 1867, and account for the way in which Derby and Stanley attempted to limit the commitment they finally made in 1867. But that agreement was a necessary expedient if the greater threat – war in the strategically vital Low Countries – was to be averted. The Conservatives were willing to engage actively in policies that would limit change or render it unnecessary. They were far less ready than liberals such as Russell or Palmerston to accept the necessity for alterations to the status quo.

That stance did not, however, translate into an intention to prop up despotism or, for the most part, actively to oppose liberalism or nationalism. Stability was more important than who provided it. Just as Wellington had recommended the recognition of Louis Philippe in 1830, so the Conservatives appreciated the value of Louis Napoleon's firm control over France. His disruptive foreign policy was another matter. They worked hard to dissuade France and other powers from precipitous or provocative policies. Malmesbury's beloved Anglo-French *entente* was not blindly pursued to the exclusion of all else. Much energy was expended in the pursuit of good relations with Russia and Austria. Carter has suggested that, in 1859, Malmesbury's friendship with Napoleon affected his judgement during the crisis over Italy.[8] While that may well have been the case, Malmesbury's judgement about Napoleon was by no means the only determinant of policy. Derby and Malmesbury were also deeply suspicious of Napoleon's grandiose designs. Moreover, in 1859 they wanted to maintain Austria in Italy in the interests of broader stability. The Conservative and liberal leaders had fundamentally different conceptions of the balance of power.

Malmesbury and Derby underestimated Napoleon's readiness to resort to war in 1859, but they were not completely naive about his intentions. Neither had they many viable alternative policies from which to choose. Their failure to prevent war had more to do with the realities of minority government than blindness to Napoleonic designs. Generally, though, they thought it dangerous to interfere in overseas events, unless absolutely necessary. They pointedly pursued a policy of non-interference, to the extent that they created domestic difficulties for themselves by doing so.

Foreign policy was not, however, defined simply by differences between parties. It was increasingly clear by 1859 that Derby and Malmesbury also differed from Disraeli. In 1866, when it looked likely that Derby would be asked to form another administration, Malmesbury ruled himself out of the FO, citing ill-health.[9] Privately, he was more candid about his decision: 'I had another reason for this determination[,] namely the hostile feeling of Disraeli who has always coveted & asked for that Dept.'.[10] Malmesbury feared that, with his old deputy Seymour Fitzgerald out of Parliament, he would have been 'left entirely at the mercy of … Disraeli who was always too lazy or too sulky to go into foreign affairs & then blamed me for not keeping him informed'.[11] This might simply have been a way for Malmesbury to justify to himself a decision he had been forced to make; nevertheless, there is no doubt that Disraeli's interventions in foreign policy had produced significant tension. This was not merely a difference over style; Disraeli was proposing policies about which his colleagues were deeply sceptical.

Stanley, Malmesbury's successor in 1866–68, would again be at the helm of foreign policy when the Conservatives obtained an absolute majority in 1874, but there is no doubt that the political plates were shifting, and profoundly so. Palmerston predicted, not long before he died, that Gladstone would 'soon have it all his own way', and that, then, 'we shall have strange doings'.[12] Disraeli, too, would eventually have it all his own way, and then there would be 'strange doings' indeed.

Notes

1 Lords, 4 February 1864, *Hansard*, 173, col. 28.
2 BL, Iddesleigh Papers, Add. MS 50015, fo. 119, copy, Northcote to Disraeli, 6 July 1864.
3 Pitt's Memorandum on the Deliverance and Security of Europe, 19 January 1805, in Harold Temperley and Lillian M. Penson, *Foundations of British Foreign Policy (1792–1902)* (Cambridge, 1938), p. 11.
4 Steele, *Palmerston and Liberalism*, p. 150.
5 *Ibid.*
6 Bloomfield Papers, FO 356/33, Stanley to Bloomfield, 23 April 1867. For a useful account of the Luxemburg crisis, see Christopher Howard, *Britain and the Casus Belli, 1822–1902* (London, 1974), pp. 64–85.
7 See, e.g., *DDCP*, 7 May 1867, p. 307.
8 Carter, 'Administering the Constitutional Pill', pp. 56–8.
9 Derby Papers, 920 DER (14) 144/2B, Malmesbury to Derby, 20 April 1866; *ibid.*, 190/2, fos 87–90, copy, Derby to Malmesbury, 22 April 1866. Only after this exchange did Derby offer Stanley the FO, for which, see Stanley's unpublished diary, Derby Papers, 920 DER (15), 24 April 1866. A typographical error in *DDCP*, p. 248, dates this offer to 24 *March* 1866.
10 Malmesbury Papers, 9M73/79, unpublished political diary, '1866'.
11 *Ibid.*
12 Shannon, *Gladstone: Peel's Inheritor*, p. 556.

Bibliography

Primary sources

Manuscripts
Bodleian Library, Oxford
Clarendon Deposit
Hughenden Deposit

British Library, London
Aberdeen Papers
Gladstone Papers
Greville Papers
Herries Papers
Iddesleigh Papers
Lansdowne Papers
Peel Papers
Seymour Papers

Hampshire Record Office, Winchester
Malmesbury Papers

Hatfield House, Hertfordshire
Salisbury Papers

Liverpool Record Office
Derby Papers

National Archives, Kew
Bloomfield Papers
Cardwell Papers
Cowley Papers

Ellenborough Papers
Foreign Office correspondence
Granville Papers
Russell Papers

Norfolk Record Office, Norwich
Bulwer Papers

Somerset Record Office, Taunton
Hylton MSS

University of Southampton Library
Palmerston (Broadlands) Papers

West Sussex Record Office, Chichester
Goodwood MSS

Worcestershire Record Office, Worcester
Hampton (Pakington) MSS

Official publications
Dod's Parliamentary Companion
Hansard's Parliamentary Debates, Third Series

Parliamentary papers
'Further correspondence respecting the foreign refugees in London' (1852), 54
'Correspondence respecting the Assault committed on Mr. Erskine Mather at Florence' (1852), 55
'Correspondence relating to the Affairs of Naples' (1857), Session 1, 18
'Correspondence respecting relations with Persia', 1857 Session 2, 43
'Paper relative to the Imprisonment of the Engineers, Watt and Park, at Salerno' (1857–58), 59
'Correspondence respecting the "Cagliari"' (1857–58), 59
'Further Correspondence respecting the "Cagliari"', (1857–58), 59
'Paper respecting Foreign Refugees in England' (1857–58), 60
'Correspondence respecting Foreign Refugees in England' (1857–58), 60
'Report of a Committee appointed by the Treasury to inquire into the navy estimates, from 1852 to 1858 and into the comparative state of the navies of England and France' (1859), Session 1, 14

Newspapers and periodicals
Blackwood's Edinburgh Magazine
Edinburgh Review
Fraser's Magazine
Illustrated London News
Macmillan's Magazine
National Review
Punch
Quarterly Review
Saturday Review
The Times

Pamphlets
'A nobleman' (Lord Fitzharris), A reply to the pamphlet entitled 'The policy of England towards Spain' (1837)

Published journals, letters, speeches and works
Bagehot, W., *The English Constitution* (London, 1993 [1867])
Bright, John, *The Diaries of John Bright*, ed. R. A. J. Walling (New York, 1931)
British Documents on the Origins of the War, 1898–1914, ed. G. P. Gooch and H. Temperley, vol. 2 (London, 1927)
Burke, E., *Reflections on the Revolution in France* (London, 1790, 1968)
Cavendish, F. H. W., *Society, Politics and Diplomacy 1820–1864: Passages from the Journal of Francis W. H. Cavendish* (London, 1913)
Croker, J. W., *The Croker Papers*, ed. L. J. Jennings, 3 vols (London, 1884)
Dallas, G. M., *The Diaries of G. M. Dallas*, ed. S. Dallas (Philadelphia, PA, 1892)
Dearest Child: Letters between Queen Victoria and the Princess Royal 1858–1861, ed. R. Fulford (London, 1964)
Disraeli, Benjamin, *Selected Speeches of the Earl of Beaconsfield*, ed. T. E. Kebbel, 2 vols (London, 1882)
Disraeli, Benjamin, *Disraeli's Reminiscences*, ed. H. M. Swartz and M. Swartz (London, 1975)
Disraeli, Benjamin, *Benjamin Disraeli Letters*, vol. 5, ed. M. G. Wiebe, J. B. Conacher, J. Matthews and M. S. Millar (Toronto, 1993); vol. 6, ed. M. G. Wiebe, M. S. Millar and A. P. Robson (Toronto, 1997); vol. 7, ed. M. G. Wiebe, M. S. Millar, A. P. Robson and E. L. Hawman (Toronto, 2004)

Disraeli, Derby and the Conservative Party: Journals and Memoirs of Edward Henry, Lord Stanley, 1849–1869, ed. J. R. Vincent (Hassocks, Sussex, 1978)

Gladstone, W. E., *The Gladstone Diaries*, ed. M. R. D. Foot and H. C. G. Matthew, 14 vols (Oxford, 1968–94), vol. 4 (1974)

Harris, James, *Diaries and Correspondence of James Harris, First Earl of Malmesbury*, ed. Lord Malmesbury, 4 vols (London, 1844)

Hertslet, Sir E., *Recollections of the Old Foreign Office* (London, 1901)

Hurst, M. (ed.), *Key Treaties for the Great Powers, 1814–1914*, 2 vols (Newton Abbot, 1972)

Letters of the Prince Consort 1831–1861, trans. E. T. S. Dugdale, ed. K. Jagow (London, 1938)

Lytton, Edward, *Speeches of Edward Lord Lytton*, ed. R. Lytton, 2 vols (Edinburgh and London, 1874)

Malmesbury, Lord, *Memoirs of an Ex-Minister: An Autobiography*, 2 vols (London, 1884)

Royal Archive, 'Changes of Government, Cabinet Reconstructions and Political Crises, 1837–1901' (Brighton, 1980)

Stanley, E. H., *The Diaries of Edward Henry Stanley, 15th Earl of Derby (1826–93) between 1878 and 1893*, ed. J. R. Vincent (Oxford, 2003)

The Letters of Queen Victoria: A Selection from Her Majesty's Correspondence between the Years 1837 and 1861, ed. A. C. Benson and Viscount Esher, 3 vols (London, 1907)

The Prince Consort and His Brother: Two Hundred New Letters, ed. H. Bolitho (London, 1933)

Trelawny, J., *The Parliamentary Diaries of Sir John Trelawny, 1858–1865*, ed. T. A. Jenkins (London, 1990)

Secondary sources

Books and articles

Anderson, M. S., *The Eastern Question* (London, 1966)

Appleman, P., W. A. Madden and M. Wolff (eds), *1859: Entering an Age of Crisis* (Bloomington, IN, 1959)

Beales, D., *England and Italy, 1859–60* (London, 1961)

Beasley, W. G., 'Lord Malmesbury's Foreign Office Circular of 8 March 1858', *Bulletin of the Institute of Historical Research*, 23 (1950)

Bebbington, D. W., *The Mind of Gladstone: Religion, Homer and Politics* (Oxford, 2004)

Bell, H. C. F., *Lord Palmerston*, 2 vols (London 1936)
Bentley, M., *Politics Without Democracy 1815–1914* (London, 1984)
Bentley, M., *Lord Salisbury's World: Conservative Environments in Late-Victorian Britain* (Cambridge, 2001)
Biagini, E. F., *Liberty, Retrenchment and Reform: Popular Liberalism in the Age of Gladstone, 1860–1880* (Cambridge, 1992)
Billy, G. J., *Palmerston's Foreign Policy: 1848* (New York, 1993)
Blake, R., *The Conservative Party from Peel to Major* (London, 1997)
Blake, R., *Disraeli* (London, 1966)
Bourne, K., *The Foreign Policy of Victorian England, 1830–1902* (Oxford, 1970)
Bourne, K., *Palmerston: The Early Years, 1784–1841* (London, 1982)
Brown, D., 'The Power of Public Opinion: Palmerston and the Crisis of December 1851', *Parliamentary History*, 20 (2001)
Brown, D., *Palmerston and the Politics of Foreign Policy, 1846–55* (Manchester, 2002)
Bullen, R., *Palmerston, Guizot and the Collapse of the Entente Cordiale* (London, 1974)
Bullen, R., 'Party Politics and Foreign Policy: Whigs, Tories and Iberian Affairs, 1830–6', *Bulletin of the Institute of Historical Research*, 51 (1978)
Bullen, R., 'The Great Powers and the Iberian Peninsula, 1815–48', in Alan Sked (ed.), *Europe's Balance of Power 1815–1848* (London, 1979)
Burn, W. L., *The Age of Equipoise: A Study of the Mid-Victorian Generation* (London, 1964)
Carter, N., 'England and the Building of the Italian Nation, 1848–61', in P. Cooke, D. Sadler and N. Zurbrugg (eds), *Locating Identity: Essays on Nation, Community and the Self* (Leicester, 1996)
Carter, N., 'Hudson, Malmesbury and Cavour: British Diplomacy and the Italian Question, February 1858 to June 1859', *Historical Journal*, 40 (1997)
Carter, N., 'Administering the Constitutional Pill: Britain, Italy and the Italian Policy of Lord Malmesbury', in R. Stradling, S. Newton and D. Bates (eds), *Conflict and Coexistence: Nationalism and Democracy in Modern Europe: Essays in Honour of Harry Hearder* (Cardiff, 1997)
Cecil, A., *Queen Victoria and Her Prime Ministers* (London, 1953)
Chamberlain, M. E., *Lord Aberdeen: A Political Biography* (Harlow, 1983)
Chamberlain, M. E., *Lord Palmerston* (Cardiff, 1987)
Chamberlain, M. E., *'Pax Britannica?' British Foreign Policy*

1789–1914 (Harlow, 1988)
Chambers, J., *Palmerston: 'The People's Darling'* (London, 2004)
Charmley, J., *Splendid Isolation? Britain and the Balance of Power 1874–1914* (London, 1999)
Conacher, J. B., *The Aberdeen Coalition 1852–55* (Cambridge, 1968)
Connell, B., *Regina v. Palmerston, 1837–1865* (London, 1962)
Costin, W. C., *Great Britain and China 1833–1860* (Oxford, 1937)
Crosby, T. L., *The Two Mr. Gladstones: A Study in Psychology and History* (London, 1997)
Dalling, Lord, *The Life of Viscount Palmerston*, 3 vols (London, 1871–74)
De Groot, E., 'The Florentine Tragedy of Mr Mather of South Shields', *Durham University Journal*, 45 (1952)
Feuchtwanger, E., *Disraeli* (London, 2000)
Fitzmaurice, Lord E., *The Life of Lord Granville, 1815–1891*, 2 vols (London, 1905)
Francis, P. (ed.), *The Gladstone Umbrella* (Hawarden, 2001)
Gambles, A., *Protection and Politics: Conservative Economic Discourse, 1815–1852* (Woodbridge, Suffolk, 1999)
Gardiner, A. G., *The Life of William Harcourt*, vol. 1 (London, 1923)
Ghosh, P. R., 'Disraelian Conservatism: A Financial Approach', *English Historical Review*, 99 (1984)
Goldfrank, D. M., *The Origins of the Crimean War* (Harlow, 1994)
Green, E. H. H., *The Crisis of Conservatism: The Politics, Economics and Ideology of the Conservative Party, 1880–1914* (London, 1995)
Guedalla, P., *Palmerston* (London, 1926)
Gurowich, P. M., 'The Continuation of War by Other Means: Party and Politics, 1855–1865', *Historical Journal*, 27 (1984)
Halévy, E., *Victorian Years: 1841–1895* (London, 1946)
Hamilton, C. I., *Anglo-French Naval Rivalry, 1840–1870* (Oxford, 1993)
Hannell, D., 'Lord Palmerston and the "Don Pacifico Affair" of 1850: The Ionian Connection', *European History Quarterly*, 19 (1989)
Hawkins, A., 'British Parliamentary Party Alignment and the Indian Issue, 1857–1858', *Journal of British Studies*, 23 (1984)
Hawkins, A., *Parliament, Party and the Art of Politics in Britain, 1855–59* (Stanford, CA, 1987)
Hawkins, A., 'Lord Derby and Victorian Conservatism: a Reappraisal', *Parliamentary History*, 6 (1987)
Hawkins, A., '"Parliamentary Government" and Victorian Political Parties, c.1830–c.1880', *English Historical Review*, 104 (1989)
Hawkins, A., 'Lord Derby', in R. W. Davis (ed.), *Lords of Parliament:*

Studies, 1714–1914 (Stanford, CA, 1995)

Hawkins, A., *British Party Politics, 1852–1886* (Basingstoke, 1998)

Hawkins, A., '"A Host in Himself": Lord Derby and Aristocratic Leadership', *Parliamentary History*, 22 (2003)

Hayes, P., *Modern British Foreign Policy: The Nineteenth Century 1814–80* (London, 1975)

Hearder, H., 'Napoleon III's Threat to Break Off Diplomatic Relations with England during the Crisis over the Orsini Attempt in 1858', *English Historical Review*, 1972 (1957)

Hearder, H., 'Queen Victoria and Foreign Policy. Royal intervention in the Italian Question, 1859–1860', in K. Bourne and D. C. Watt (eds), *Studies in International History* (London, 1967)

Hearder, H., *Italy in the Age of the Risorgimento 1790–1870* (London, 1983)

Henderson, G. B., 'Ralph Anstruther Earle', *English Historical Review*, 58 (1943)

Henderson, G. B., *Crimean War Diplomacy and Other Historical Essays* (Glasgow, 1947)

Hicks, G., 'Don Pacifico, Democracy, and Danger: The Protectionist Party Critique of British Foreign Policy, 1850–1852', *International History Review*, 26 (2004)

Hogan, J., 'Party Management in the House of Lords 1846–1865', *Parliamentary History*, 10 (1991)

Hoppen, K. T., 'Tories, Catholics, and the General Election of 1859', *Historical Journal*, 13 (1970)

Hoppen, K. T., *Elections, Politics, and Society in Ireland, 1832–1885* (Oxford, 1984)

Hoppen, K. T., *The Mid-Victorian Generation, 1846–1886* (Oxford, 1998)

Howard, C., *Britain and the Casus Belli, 1822–1902* (London, 1974)

Howe, A., *Free Trade and Liberal England 1846–1946* (Oxford, 1997)

Jagger, P. J. (ed.), *Gladstone* (London, 1998)

Jones, R., *The Nineteenth-Century Foreign Office: An Administrative History* (London, 1971)

Jones, R. A., *The British Diplomatic Service 1815–1914* (Ontario, 1983)

Jones, W. D., *Lord Derby and Victorian Conservatism* (Oxford, 1956)

Jones, W. D., and A. B. Erickson, *The Peelites, 1846–1857* (Ohio, 1972)

Kebbel, T. E., *The Earl of Derby* (London, 1890)

Kennedy, P., *The Realities Behind Diplomacy: Background Influences*

on *British External Policy, 1865–1980* (London, 1981)
Kitson Clark, G., *The Making of Victorian England* (London, 1962)
Knox Stevens, J., 'The Franco-Russian Treaty of 1859: New Lights and New Thoughts', *Historian*, 28 (1966)
Lambert, A. D., *The Crimean War: British Grand Strategy Against Russia, 1853–56* (Manchester, 1990)
Lewis, C. J., 'Theory and Expediency in the Policy of Disraeli', *Victorian Studies*, 5 (1961)
Loftus, Lord A., *The Diplomatic Reminiscences of Lord Augustus Loftus*, 2 vols (London, 1892)
Lorne, Marquess of, *Viscount Palmerston K.G.* (London, 1892)
Macdonagh, O., *States of Mind: A Study of Anglo-Irish Conflict 1780–1980* (London, 1983)
McIntire, C. T., *England Against the Papacy, 1858–1861* (Cambridge, 1983)
Mack Smith, D., *Victor Emmanuel, Cavour and the Risorgimento* (Oxford, 1971)
Mandler, P., *Aristocratic Government in the Age of Reform: Whigs and Liberals, 1830–1852* (Oxford, 1990)
Martin, T., *The Life of the Prince Consort*, vol. 4 (London, 1879)
Matsumoto-Best, S., *Britain and the Papacy in the Age of Revolution, 1846–1851* (Woodbridge, Suffolk, 2003)
Matthew, H. C. G., 'Disraeli, Gladstone and the Politics of Mid-Victorian Budgets', *Historical Journal*, 22 (1979)
Matthew, H. C. G., *Gladstone* (Oxford, 1986)
Mitchell, L., *Bulwer Lytton: The Rise and Fall of a Victorian Man of Letters* (Hambledon, 2003)
Monypenny, W. F. and G. E. Buckle, *The Life of Benjamin Disraeli, Earl of Beaconsfield*, 6 vols (London, 1910–20)
Morley, J., *The Life of William Ewart Gladstone*, 3 vols (London, 1903)
Mosse, W. E., *The European Powers and the German Question, 1848–71* (Cambridge, 1958)
Mosse, W. E., 'Queen Victoria and Her Ministers in the Schleswig–Holstein Crisis 1863–1864', *English Historical Review*, 78 (1963)
Newton, Lord, *Lord Lyons: A Record of British Diplomacy*, 2 vols (London, 1913)
Otte, T. G. (ed.), *The Makers of British Foreign Policy from Pitt to Thatcher* (Basingstoke, 2002)
Parker, C. S., *The Life and Letters of Sir James Graham*, vol. 2 (London, 1907)

Parry, J. P., *Democracy and Religion: Gladstone and the Liberal Party, 1867–1875* (Cambridge, 1986)

Parry, J. P., *The Rise and Fall of Liberal Government in Victorian Britain* (New Haven, CT, and London, 1993)

Parry, J. P., 'Disraeli and England', *Historical Journal*, 43 (2000)

Parry, J. P., 'The Impact of Napoleon III on British Politics, 1851–1880', *Transactions of the Royal Historical Society*, 6th series, 11 (2001)

Pemberton, W. B., *Lord Palmerston* (London, 1954)

Pinnington, J. E., 'The Consular Chaplancies and the Foreign Office Under Palmerston, Aberdeen and Malmesbury: Two Case Histories – Rome and Funchal', *Journal of Ecclesiastical History*, 27 (1976)

Pinto-Duschinsky, M., *The Political Thought of Lord Salisbury, 1854–1868* (London, 1967)

Platt, D. C. M., *Finance, Trade and Politics in British Foreign Policy, 1815–1914* (Oxford, 1968)

Porter, B., *The Refugee Question in Mid-Victorian Politics* (Cambridge, 1979)

Porter, B., *Britain, Europe and the World 1850–1982: Delusions of Grandeur* (London, 1983)

Pottinger Saab, A., 'Foreign Affairs and New Tories: Disraeli, *The Press*, and the Crimean War', *International History Review*, 19 (1997)

Prest, J., *Lord John Russell* (London, 1972)

Price, R., *The French Second Empire: An Anatomy of Political Power* (Cambridge, 2001)

Pugh, M., *The Tories and the People, 1880–1935* (Oxford, 1985)

Riall, L., *The Italian Risorgimento: State, Society and National Unification* (London, 1994)

Ridley, J., *Lord Palmerston* (London, 1970)

Roberts, A., *Salisbury: Victorian Titan* (London, 1999)

Saintsbury, G., *The Earl of Derby* (London, 1892)

Salevouris, M. J., *'Riflemen Form': The War Scare of 1859–1860 in England* (New York, 1982)

Sandiford, K. A. P., *Great Britain and the Schleswig–Holstein Question 1848–64: A Study in Diplomacy, Politics, and Public Opinion* (Toronto, 1975)

Schroeder, P. W., *Austria, Great Britain and the Crimean War: The Destruction of the European Concert* (New York, 1972)

Schroeder, P. W., *The Transformation of European Politics* (Oxford, 1994)

Shannon, R., *Gladstone: Peel's Inheritor, 1809–1865* (London, 1982)

Smith, P., 'Disraeli's Politics', *Transactions of the Royal Historical Society*, 5th series, 38 (1987)
Smith, P., *Disraeli* (Cambridge, 1996)
Southgate, D., *The Most English Minister: The Policies and Politics of Palmerston* (London, 1966)
Stanmore, Lord, *Sidney Herbert, Lord Herbert of Lea: A Memoir*, 2 vols (London, 1906)
Steele, E. D., *Palmerston and Liberalism, 1855–1865* (Cambridge, 1991)
Steele, E. D., *Lord Salisbury: A Political Biography* (London, 1999)
Stenton, M. (ed.), *Who's Who of British Members of Parliament*, vol. 1 (Hassocks, Sussex, 1976)
Stenton, M. and S. Lees (eds), *Who's Who of British Members of Parliament*, vol. 2 (Hassocks, Sussex, 1978)
Stewart, R., *The Politics of Protection: Lord Derby and the Protectionist Party, 1841–1852* (Cambridge, 1971)
Stewart, R., *The Foundation of the Conservative Party, 1830–67* (London, 1978)
Stuart, C. H., 'The Formation of the Coalition Cabinet of 1852', *Transactions of the Royal Historical Society*, 5th series, 4 (1954)
Stuart, C. H., 'The Prince Consort and Ministerial Politics, 1856–59', in H. R. Trevor-Roper (ed.), *Essays in British History Presented to Sir Keith Feiling* (London, 1964)
Sumner, B. H., 'The Secret Franco-Russian Treaty of 3 March 1859', *English Historical Review*, 48 (1933)
Taylor, A. J. P., *The Struggle for Mastery in Europe, 1848–1914* (Oxford, 1954)
Taylor, A. J. P., *The Trouble Makers: Dissent Over Foreign Policy* (London, 1957)
Taylor, A. J. P., *Essays in English History* (Harmondsworth, Middlesex, 1976)
Taylor, M., *The Decline of British Radicalism, 1847–1860* (Oxford, 1995)
Taylor, M. and M. Wolff (eds), *The Victorians Since 1901: Histories, Representations and Revisions* (Manchester, 2004)
Temperley, H. and L. M. Penson (eds), *Foundations of British Foreign Policy (1792–1902)* (Cambridge, 1938)
Thompson, J. M., *Louis Napoleon and the Second Empire* (Oxford, 1954)
Vincent, J. R., *The Formation of the Liberal Party, 1857–1868* (London, 1966)
Vincent, J. R., 'The Parliamentary Dimension of the Crimean War',

Transactions of the Royal Historical Society, 5th series, 31 (1980)
Vincent, J. R., *Disraeli* (London, 1990)
Ward, A. W. and G. P. Gooch (eds), *The Cambridge History of British Foreign Policy 1783–1919*, vol. 2 (Cambridge, 1923)
Whibley, C., *Lord John Manners and His Friends*, 2 vols (London, 1925)
Whyte, J. H., *The Independent Irish Party, 1850–9* (Oxford, 1958)
Wilson, K. M. (ed.), *British Foreign Policy and Foreign Secretaries: From Crimean War to First World War* (Beckenham, 1987)
Wilson, K. M., *Problems and Possibilities: Exercises in Statesmanship 1814–1918* (Stroud, 2003)
Woodall, R., 'Orsini and the Fall of Palmerston', *History Today*, 26 (1976)
Woodward, E. L., *The Age of Reform 1815–1870* (Oxford, 1938)
Young, G. M., *Victorian England: Portrait of an Age* (London, 1936)

Unpublished PhD theses
Anderson, M. A., 'Edmund Hammond, Permanent Under-Secretary of State for Foreign Affairs, 1854–1873' (University of London, 1956)
Carter, N., 'Sir James Hudson, British Diplomacy and the Italian Question, February 1858 to June 1861' (University of Wales, College of Cardiff, 1994)
Gurowich, P. M., 'Party and Independence in the Early- and Mid-Victorian House of Commons: Aspects of Political Theory and Practice, 1832–68, Considered with Special Reference to the Period 1852–68' (Cambridge University, 1986)
Hearder, H., 'The Foreign Policy of Lord Malmesbury, 1858–9' (University of London, 1954)
McCracken, D. E., 'The Conservatives in Power: The Minority Governments of 1852, 1858–9, and 1866–8' (University of Virginia, 1981)
Major, W. E., 'The Public Life of the Third Earl of Malmesbury' (University of Georgia, 1981)

Index

Aberdeen, 4th Earl of 1, 3, 4, 12, 16, 25, 28, 30, 31, 32, 33, 41, 46, 48, 50, 53, 54, 70, 72, 73, 75, 81, 84, 92, 94, 97, 116, 120, 124, 130, 133, 139–53 *passim*, 175, 206
Addington, Henry Unwin 87, 124
Albert, Prince (Prince Consort) 54, 59, 129, 132, 199, 222, 225, 227, 228, 229, 230, 237
    see also Court (British)
Alexander, Prince (of Serbia) 220
Alexander II, Tsar 161, 231
America 43, 188
Anstey, Thomas Chisholm 49
Antonelli, Cardinal Giacomo 98, 99, 102, 104, 105, 106
Apponyi, Count Rudolf 208, 222, 225
Austria 2, 6, 7, 8, 11, 13, 19, 39, 43, 45, 47, 48, 54, 59, 69, 72, 74, 75, 76, 77, 78–80, 82, 84, 86, 90, 91, 92, 94, 96, 101, 117, 124, 128, 129, 144, 145, 159, 165, 167, 168, 169, 187, 205, 206, 207, 208, 209, 210, 211, 212, 218, 221, 222, 224, 225, 226, 228, 229, 230, 231, 232, 233, 234, 236, 248

Bagehot, Walter 235

Baillie, H. J. 54
Baillie Cochrane, Alexander 43
Barron, Henry 86
Beales, Derek 7, 224
Beasley, W. G. 7
Bedford, 7th Duke of 213
Belgian guarantee (1839) 71, 80–1, 83, 228, 247
Belgium 7, 47, 55, 71, 75, 80–3, 84, 85, 124, 125, 144, 209, 227, 228, 230, 236
Bentinck, George William Pierrepoint 160
Bentinck, Lord George 25, 60
Bentley, Michael 5, 8, 69
Bernal Osborne, Ralph 90, 92–3
Biagini, Eugenio 9
Bismarck, Otto von 19, 129, 246
Blackwood's Edinburgh Magazine 209
'Black Sea clauses' (Treaty of Paris, 1856) 164, 194
Blake, Robert 4, 8, 49, 59, 218, 219, 223
Bloomfield, 2nd Baron 79, 84, 208, 228, 230, 247
'blue books' 18, 85, 87, 89, 147, 213, 237–8
Bonaparte, Prince Jerome 121
Bourne, Kenneth 5, 8
Bowring, Sir John 166, 170, 171,

172, 174
Bright, John 71, 131, 159, 237
Brougham, 1st Baron 119
Brown, David 10, 29, 41, 48, 173
Brunnow, Baron Ernst Philipp von 49, 54, 81, 82, 84, 85, 128, 141
Buckle, G. E. 5–6, 8, 98, 223
budget
   (1852) 14, 130–1, 133, 175
   (1858) 192–3
   (1859) 212, 226
Bulwer, Sir Henry 86, 87, 92, 95, 96, 98–102, 104–6, 217
Bulwer Lytton, Edward 150, 159, 160, 161, 170, 175
Bunsen, Baron Christian von 128
Buol, Count Karl Ferdinand von 50, 75–6, 77, 78, 79, 83, 85, 86, 91, 206, 208, 212, 222, 225
Burke, Edmund 14
Burn, W. L. 7

Cagliari 191, 192, 193, 196
Cairns, 1st Earl 70
Canning, Stratford 17, 48, 59, 60, 122, 132, 133
Canning, Viscount (Charles) 34, 48, 132
Cardwell, Edward 70, 193
Carter, Nick 11, 207, 209, 248
Castlereagh, Viscount 13, 34, 210, 247
Catholics (and Catholicism) *see* Roman Catholics (and Catholicism)
Cavour, Count Camillo 205, 209, 222, 226, 233
Cecil, Algernon 6
Cecil, Robert *see* Salisbury, 3rd Marquess of
Chamberlain, Muriel 28
Chamberlain, Neville 7, 10, 122
Channel Islands 118
Charles Albert, King (of Piedmont-Sardinia) 31, 44, 75
Charles et Georges 199–200
Charmley, John 9–10, 211
Cherbourg naval base 187, 199, 230
China 15, 166, 170, 172, 174, 178, 187, 246
   debate (1857) 170–1
Civis Romanus sum 40, 41, 90
Clarendon, 4th Earl of 1, 16, 58, 96, 100, 103, 119, 120, 143, 146, 148, 153, 158, 159, 161, 167, 169, 174, 177, 186, 187, 191, 195, 197, 200, 209, 210, 238
Cobden, Richard (and Cobdenites) 3, 45, 47, 71, 159, 170, 172
commercial treaty, Anglo-French (proposed, 1852) 119
Conacher, J. B. 142
Conspiracy to Murder Bill 176, 177, 187, 188, 189, 190, 194, 195
Cornewall Lewis, George 195
Corn Laws, repeal of (1846) 1, 6, 12, 14, 25, 30, 52
country gentlemen 26, 58, 142, 148, 150, 151
Court (British) 31, 225, 229, 234, 235, 237
Cowley, 1st Earl 17, 79, 84, 120, 121, 126, 127, 128, 167, 168, 169, 190, 205, 210, 221, 229, 230, 232, 233, 234
   Vienna mission (1859) 205, 206, 229, 230 232, 233
Crampton, John Fiennes 236
Crimean war 10, 11, 15, 84, 139, 141, 149–64 *passim*, 167, 173, 210
   see also Danubian Principalities; Eastern question; Near East; Ottoman Empire
Croker, John Wilson 26, 132, 133

Dallas, George 207

Danubian Principalities 166, 192, 220
De Groot, E. 7
Delane, J. T. 193
Denmark 19, 94, 246
diplomatic correspondence (published) *see* 'blue books'
Diplomatic Relations (Court of Rome) Act 51
Disraeli Letters 11, 28, 98
Dom Miguel 30
Don Carlos 30
Donoughmore, 4th Earl of 119
Don Pacifico 15, 29, 38, 39, 48, 61, 71, 72, 86, 89, 90, 246
Drummond, Henry 159
Drummond Wolff, Sir Henry 199

Earle, Ralph 7, 166, 167, 198, 217, 218, 219, 222, 227
Eastern question 140, 142
    see also Crimean war; Near East; Ottoman Empire
Ecclesiastical Titles Bill 50, 51
Eglinton, 13th Earl of 51, 105, 106, 151, 175
'Eglinton Clause', 51, 101
election
    (1847) 30
    (1852) 12, 88, 100, 245
    (1857) 17–18, 173–4
    (1859) 12, 212, 213
Elgin, 8th Earl of 233
Ellenborough, 1st Earl of 73, 130, 152, 157, 170, 171, 193
Ernest, Duke (of Saxe-Coburg) 234–5

Far East 166
    see also China
Ferdinand II, King (of Naples) 13, 31, 44, 166, 191
Feuchtwanger, Edgar 11
Finlay, George 39

Fitzgerald, Sir William Vesey 192, 248
Fitzwilliam, 5th Earl 87
France 2, 6, 7, 15, 31, 32, 33, 34, 38, 39, 40, 43, 44, 47, 53, 54, 55, 56, 57, 75, 80, 83, 116–33 *passim*, 139, 140, 144, 145, 163, 165, 166, 167, 168, 169, 176, 177, 187, 188, 190, 191, 195, 205, 206, 208, 209, 210, 211, 212, 218, 219, 226, 229, 230, 231, 232, 233, 234, 236, 248
Franco-Russian alliance (1859) 206, 210–11
Fraser's Magazine 89, 133

Gambles, Anna 10
Genoa, Duke of 44
Gladstone, William 3, 9, 16, 19, 46, 48, 50, 70, 90, 92, 103, 124, 159, 160, 173, 246, 249
Gorchakov, Prince Alexander 236
Graham, Sir James 46, 50, 70, 97, 144, 176
Granby, Marquess of (later 6th Duke of Rutland) 27, 43, 45, 52, 67, 89, 147, 149, 159
Granville, 2nd Earl 16, 41, 55, 69, 73, 74, 75, 76, 80, 93, 94, 141, 153, 172, 196, 209, 234
    memorandum on principles of foreign policy (1852) 73–4
Greece 35, 39–50 *passim*, 71, 76, 170, 172, 209
    treaty regarding (1832) 39, 44
Green, E. H. H. 9
Gregory XVI, Pope 97, 105
Greville, Charles 68, 122, 164, 167, 195
Grey, 2nd Earl 1, 25, 96
Grey, 3rd Earl 152, 158
Guiccioli, Countess 29
Guizot, Francois 28, 33

Gurowich, P. M. 9, 11, 12

Halévy, E. 6
Hamilton, Lord Claud 147, 148, 159
Hammond, Edmund 195, 220, 221
Hapsburgs 46, 211
Hardinge, 1st Viscount 131
Hardwicke, 4th Earl of 143, 147, 175
Harris, George 118
Hawkins, Angus 2, 4, 9, 11, 12, 165, 172, 223, 238
Hayes, Paul 8
Haynau, Marshal 72, 92, 101
Hearder, Harry 7, 192
Henderson, G. B. 7
Herbert, Sidney 16, 45, 46, 68, 70, 120
Herries, J. C. 70
Holy Alliance (1815) 83, 119, 207, 210
Hortense, Queen 29
Howe, Anthony 9, 119
Hudson, Sir James 234
Hungarians 39, 48, 49, 52, 53, 72, 101

Iberian peninsula 46, 74
  see also Portugal; Spain
Illustrated London News 117
income tax 165, 171, 197
India 210
Indian Mutiny 174, 187, 193, 194, 195, 197
Inglis, Sir Robert 42, 44
Ionian Islands 39, 44
Ireland 95–106 *passim*, 187, 210
Irish MPs 100
Italy (and Italian states) 2, 7, 8, 14, 30, 31, 42, 44, 45, 46, 49, 74, 76, 167, 168, 205–13 *passim*, 217–38 *passim*, 248
  see also Lombardy; Modena; Naples; Papal States; Piedmont-Sardinia; Sicily; Tuscany; Vatican; Venetia

Jolliffe, Sir William 151, 160, 161
Jones, W. D. 4, 7, 97, 247

Kennedy, Paul 17
Ker Seymer, Henry 159, 160
Kitson Clark, George 19–20
Klindworth, Georges de 217
Kossuth, Louis 52, 53

Lambert, Andrew 158
Lansdowne, 3rd Marquess of 55, 120
Lennox, Lord Henry 102, 198
Leopold I, King (of Belgium) 80, 225, 227, 228
Lloyd Davies, John 159
Loftus, Lord Augustus 208, 212
Lombardy 43, 205, 210, 212, 226
Londonderry, Lady 28, 151
Lonsdale, 2nd Earl of 70, 122, 178
Louis Philippe, King (of the French) 29, 80, 130, 248
Luxembourg 247
Lyons, Richard 191

Macchiavelli, Niccolo 160
McCracken, D. E. 9
McIntire, C. T. 232
Madiai, Francisco and Rosa 93, 102
Mahé, Father 106
Major, W. E. 9
Mandler, Peter 9
Manners, Lord John (afterwards 7th Duke of Rutland) 41, 43, 44, 45, 175, 188, 192
Mansion House speech
  (1852) 68
  (1858) 198

(1859) 208, 213
Mather, Erskine 7, 76
Mather case 69, 79, 86–92, 96, 101, 118, 191
Matsumoto-Best, Saho 10, 50
Mellish, Richard 124
Metternich, Prince Clemens von 28
Militia Bill (1852) 58
Milner Gibson, Thomas 159, 176, 178, 179
Modena 75–6, 78
Molesworth, Sir William 47
Monckton Milnes, Richard 86
Moniteur, Le 176
Monypenny, W. F. 5–6, 8, 98
Morning Post 233
Mosse, W. E. 237
Murray, Edward 95, 98, 101

Naples 13, 50, 90, 92, 166, 172, 191, 193, 196
 see also Ferdinand II
Napoleon III (Louis Napoleon Bonaparte) 2, 6, 7, 8, 11, 13, 15, 16, 29, 31, 32, 33, 34, 38, 44, 50, 53, 54, 55, 56, 57, 59, 60, 71, 81, 82, 116–33 *passim*, 139, 143, 144, 148, 150, 161, 163, 164, 169, 176, 177, 187, 189, 190, 199, 200, 205, 206, 210, 211, 217, 218, 219, 221, 222, 223, 224, 225, 226, 227, 228, 229, 230, 233, 248
 coup (1851) 13, 34, 38, 53, 54, 71, 117
naval defences 10, 187–8, 212, 236
Neapolitan prisoners 50, 92
Near East 45, 139, 142, 143, 145, 151, 235
 see also Crimean war; Danubian Principalities; Eastern question; Ottoman Empire
Nesselrode, Count Karl 81, 82

memorandum (1844) 81, 145, 146
Neufchâtel 94, 102
Newcastle, 4th Duke of 27
Newcastle, 5th Duke of 16, 69, 70, 141
Newton case 91, 92, 93
Nicholas I, Tsar 81, 139, 145, 146, 147, 148
Normanby, 1st Marquess of 54
Northcote, Sir Stafford 162, 246
Northumberland, 4th Duke of 129–30

Orsini, Felice 176, 193, 205, 221, 230
Otho, King (of Greece) 39
Otte, Thomas 11
Ottoman Empire, 39, 48, 53, 60, 81, 139, 140, 145, 146, 147, 151, 160
 see also Crimean war; Danubian Principalities; Eastern question; Near East

Pakington, Sir John 142, 147, 171, 175, 212, 234, 236
Palmerston, Viscount 1–2, 5, 6, 8, 9, 10, 11, 12, 16, 19, 27, 28, 29, 30, 31, 35, 38–61 *passim*, 68, 70, 71, 72, 73, 74, 75, 76, 82, 83, 86, 90, 92, 93, 120, 123, 130, 141, 142, 143, 144, 145, 148, 149, 151, 152, 153, 157–79 *passim*, 189, 191, 193, 194, 195, 196, 197, 200, 206, 207, 209, 210, 211, 218, 229, 233, 234, 235, 237, 246, 247, 249
Palmerstonian policy 41, 50, 82, 247
papal aggression 50–1, 96, 100
Papal States 75–6, 78, 95, 96, 205, 207, 221, 226, 229, 231
Parry, Jonathan 9, 11, 129, 207

Peel, General Jonathan 188
Peel, Sir Robert 1, 4, 12, 25, 26, 31, 61, 67, 97, 145, 168
Peel Government 1, 46, 96
Peelites 3, 12, 15, 25, 26, 27, 28, 29, 30, 40, 41, 42, 43, 45, 46, 52, 57, 68, 88, 89, 119, 133, 140, 141, 148, 170, 245
Persia 166
Persigny, Count Jean de 118, 177, 190
Petre, William 95, 97
Phipps, Colonel Charles 54
Piedmont-Sardinia 2, 31, 43, 44, 187, 205, 206, 208, 209, 210, 211, 224, 225, 226, 228, 229, 234
Pitt, William (the younger) 247
Pius IX, Pope 10, 51, 69, 96, 97, 99, 102–5, 207
Plombières, pact of (1858) 205, 226
Poland (and Poles) 49, 145
Portugal 30, 42, 199
  see also Iberian peninsula
Pottinger Saab, Ann 11, 160
Press, The 11, 150, 161, 163, 165
Prest, John 8
Protectionists 12, 25, 26, 27, 28, 29, 30, 33, 38–61 *passim*
Prussia 7, 19, 69, 82, 84, 117, 124, 128, 129, 144, 208, 211, 224, 225, 228, 229, 230, 231, 232, 234
Pugh, Martin 9
Punch 89, 90

Quadruple Alliance 117
Quarterly Review 26, 77, 132, 133, 210

radicals 12, 31, 42, 45, 47, 119, 131, 170, 172, 176
reform 13, 52–3, 143, 144, 212, 246
Reform Act
  (1832) 72
  (1867) 6, 18, 19, 119
refugees 39, 48, 49, 53, 60, 77–8, 85, 101, 118
revolutions (1848) 25, 28, 31, 42, 44, 45, 210
Ridley, Jasper 8
Roebuck, John Arthur 40, 43, 152
Roman Catholics (and Catholicism) 51, 96–7, 103, 104, 207
Russell, Lord John 1, 2, 8, 12, 13, 16, 45, 51, 52, 53, 54, 55, 56, 57, 60, 70, 89, 90, 92, 95, 96, 103, 141, 143, 144, 145, 148, 153, 170, 173, 175, 176, 190, 193, 195, 207, 209, 213, 229, 235, 237, 246, 247
Russell Government 25, 26, 35, 38, 46, 47, 51, 72, 97, 140
resignation
  (1851) 48, 51
  (1852) 58, 70
Russia 7, 13, 15, 33, 39, 40, 43, 44, 45, 46, 47, 48, 54, 59, 60, 69, 75, 80–5, 94, 117, 124, 128, 129, 139, 140, 143, 144, 145, 146, 147, 150, 151, 159, 160, 161, 162, 165, 187, 188, 206, 208, 210, 211, 225, 226, 228, 230, 231, 232, 233, 234, 235, 236, 237, 248

St Leonards, 1st Baron 122
Salisbury, 2nd Marquess of 186, 193
Salisbury, 3rd Marquess of 4, 9, 168, 171, 191, 210
Saturday Review 168
Scarlett, Hon. Peter Campbell 86, 87, 91, 92, 94
Schleswig-Holstein 14, 48, 94, 237, 246
Schroeder, Paul 128
Schwarzenberg, Prince 78–9, 92

Sebastopol 160
Serbia 220
Seymour, George Hamilton 81, 82, 147
Shaftesbury, 7th Earl of 101, 193
Shannon, Richard 46
Sicily 31, 44, 45
Slough, Disraeli's speech at 6, 193–7, 198
Smith, Paul 11, 192
Sotheron Estcourt, Thomas 189
Southgate, D. 8
Spain 30
   see also Iberian peninsula
Stanley, Edward Henry (afterwards 15th Earl of Derby) 4, 9, 10, 13, 16, 19, 29, 49, 50, 69, 83, 99, 103, 117, 121, 122, 123, 129, 132, 133, 143, 147, 148, 149, 150, 151, 153, 158–9, 160, 162, 163, 164, 178, 188, 189, 191, 199, 237, 247, 249
Steele, E. D. 2, 10, 13, 225, 247
Stewart, Robert 8, 10, 41, 179
Stratford de Redcliffe, Viscount see Canning, Stratford

Taylor, A. J. P. 7, 8, 54
Taylor, Miles 4, 9
Thesiger, Sir Frederick 42, 43, 44
Thiers, Louis Adolphe 221
Times, The 88, 102, 143, 146, 174, 193, 195, 199, 208
treaty of London (1839, regarding Belgium) see Belgian guarantee
treaty of London (1852, regarding Schleswig-Holstein) 94
treaty of Paris (1856) 15, 164, 167
treaty of Vienna (1815) see Vienna settlement
Trelawny, Sir John 196
Turgot, Marquis de 54
Turkey see Ottoman Empire

Tuscany 7, 73, 76–7, 79, 80, 86, 87, 91, 92, 172
Two Sicilies, Kingdom of see Naples; Sicily

Vasa, Princess Caroline Stephanie de 118
Vatican 14, 50, 51, 95–106, 245
Venetia 205, 209
Victor Emmanuel II, King (of Piedmont-Sardinia) 205, 226
Victoria, Queen 12, 53, 54, 56, 59, 60, 73, 123, 126, 129, 130, 131, 152, 153, 157, 176, 177, 190, 199, 208, 209, 211, 212, 213, 227, 230, 233, 235, 236, 237
   see also Court (British)
Vienna mission (1859) see Cowley, 1st Earl
Vienna peace negotiations (1855) 159
Vienna settlement (1814–15) 13, 32, 34, 46, 71, 94, 121, 125, 126, 128, 207, 209, 218
Villiers, Charles 58
Vincent, John 8, 9, 11, 28, 158

Walewski, Count Alexandre 54, 117, 118, 121, 144, 167, 169, 176, 177, 189, 190, 200, 206
Walpole, Spencer Horatio 41, 42, 43, 86, 149, 159, 177, 179
Walsh, Sir John 43, 44, 77
Ward, J. T. 8
Warren, Samuel 170
war scares 15, 71, 130
Wellington, 1st Duke of 9, 48, 94, 101, 104, 248
Westmorland, 11th Earl of 77, 78, 79
Whiggish historiography 74
Whigs 1, 2, 12, 26, 27, 30, 38, 45, 46, 52, 53, 55, 56, 57, 72, 75,

78, 84, 88, 89, 96, 133, 140, 194, 197, 245
Whiteside, James 159, 171
Wilson, Keith 11
Wiseman, Cardinal Nicholas 50

Wood, Sir Charles 144, 188
Woodward, E. L. 6
Wyse, Thomas 39–40

Young, G. M. 6